AUSTRALIANS ON T

POZIEKLS
1916
PETER CHARLTON

AUSTRALIANS ON THE SOMME

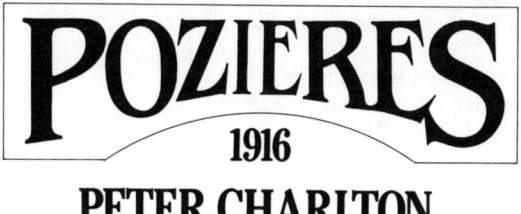

POZIERES

1916

PETER CHARLTON

With a Foreword by John Terraine

Leo Cooper
in association with
Secker & Warburg

First published in 1986 by
Methuen Haynes
(an imprint of Methuen Australia Pty Ltd)

First published in Great Britain in 1986 by Leo
Cooper in association with Secker & Warburg Ltd,
54 Poland Street, London WIV 3DF

ISBN: 0-436-09580-7

Printed and bound in Singapore

Contents

List of maps

List of illustrations

Mouquet Farm, before the war and after the Canadian
and British assaults.
German shells bursting near the Windmill.
A British shell bursting on the OG lines near the Windmill.
German shells bursting on the Australian lines.
Centre Way trench system.
A 6 inch 26 cwt howitzer in the mud near Pozières.
Unveiling of the memorial to the 1st Australian Division.

Foreword

It is an ancient cliché that Australia and New Zealand 'came of age' at Gallipoli in 1915. I began to doubt it quite a long time ago. That the two Pacific Dominions began to acquire a new degree of national self-consciousness in 1915 is a perfectly reasonable proposition; but when one compares the levels of experience of that year with what happened when their soldiers reached the Western Front in 1916, 'came of age' seems to belong without challenge to the later date. Peter Charlton's book endorses this view and, indeed, carries it some distance further. The reader must decide how far to go along with him.

It is also a long-standing belief of mine that, certainly in 1918, but probably even by 1917, the ten Dominion divisions in the British Expeditionary Force had become its spearhead — and that is to say, in 1918, the spearhead of the whole final victorious Allied offensive. There is no point in even attempting any 'pecking order', as between the five Australian, four Canadian and the New Zealand Divisions. The whole lot constituted an élite, and the words used by General Monash in describing the Australian Corps can well be applied to all: 'an outstanding feature was the uniformity of standard achieved by all the five divisions, as well as the wonderful comradeship which they displayed towards each other.'

Even the best of élites, however, are human. It is a condition not inherited, but acquired *per ardua*. Battle skills in war are born of battle experience — they come the hard way. In 1916 the Canadians, whose performances during the next two years were so distinguished, had some bad beginnings — a depressing apprenticeship. The New Zealand Division's début in September cost it nearly 7,000 casualties. Peter Charlton here describes with a wealth of moving detail what the first lessons in éliteship cost the Australians in the dust of what had been Pozières, and around the site of the Windmill where the Australian dead lay thicker than on any other battlefield of the war.

'The Australian soldier,' said General Monash, 'had the political sense highly developed, and was always a keen critic of the way in which his battalion or battery was "run", and of the policies which guided his destinies from day to day.' He was indeed. No Second Lieutenant, no Lance-Corporal of the Australian Imperial Force entertained the slightest hesitation in pronouncing judgment on his brigade, divisional or corps commander (and their staffs), on the general commanding the Army to which they all belonged, or the field-marshal commanding-in-chief and the whole of GHQ. Such judgment, it is to be understood, would be forthrightly expressed. The powerful feelings that inspired the contemptuous anger of the frontline troops in the shambles that passed for battles at that stage of the war did not always fade with time; among many Returned Servicemen the bitterness never died. Peter Charlton says that those battles 'damaged forever the regard in which (the Australian soldier) held the British ... Australia was never the same again'. It is a point of view; the AIF performance in 1917 and 1918 (and, indeed, 1940-5) does not seem to bear it out.

I cannot agree (he would not expect me to) with the virtually unrelieved anti-High Command and anti-Staff tone of Charlton's book, though I accept that it does very clearly reflect the mood of the most articulate 'grousers' in a formation whose reputation for 'grousing' was second only to its reputation for fighting. I think the author should have been a bit more severe with such material; one should judge men by their acts, not their words. The words were the words of mutineers; the deeds were the deeds of very fine soldiers.

What the soldiers themselves cannot offer — cannot be expected to offer — is understanding of what was happening on the other side of the hill they were attacking, and which often so obstinately refused to permit itself to be captured. The blemish in most British accounts of the First World War (Second, too!) is the virtual absence of the enemy. Peter Charlton deserves credit for making some effort to express the German contribution to the Somme battle — he is quick to notice the constant deadly counter-attacks which were the feature of their defence. But no description of action is complete unless it speaks for both sides — not always an easy matter. When Charlton says 'There were no victories — at least, none worth trumpeting', he is not being fair to the men who died in such heart-wringing numbers at Pozières. They — like so many others whose immediate achievements seemed so slight in relation to their sufferings and loss — had made their contribution to the ultimate result of the Battle of the Somme, succinctly expressed by General Ludendorff: 'The Army had been fought to a standstill and was utterly worn out.' That amazing army of amateurs which was all the British Empire had in 1916 had produced this result against Germany's last professionals, the last of the peace-trained troops and their magnificent NCOs. As Field-Marshal von Hindenburg said: '1916 spoke a language that made itself heard.' It was the language of Germany's defeat — which is another pronunciation of Pozières.

JOHN TERRAINE

Introduction

Pozières today is an unlovely village of undistinguished buildings astride the ancient Roman road that runs, as straight as a javelin, from Albert to Bapaume. In July and August, high summer in the northern hemisphere, this part of France is serene and undisturbed. Far enough from the tourist attractions to be immune from day tripper and camper, it is agricultural land, dull and prosperous. The little traffic attracted here moves swiftly across the modern motorways intersecting the peaceful countryside. Local vehicles stick to the subsidiary roads and tend to be agricultural machinery moving unhurriedly from farm to farm.

The sub-soil is chalky, soft white limestone below a layer of prime rich dirt. Because of the sub-soil no drainage ditches are needed here; no hedgerows delineate the fields; few woods break the landscape. In this prudent part of France, the land is cultivated up to the road edge. Yet the Australian visitor feels curiously at home here for, on a clear day, the distances have an antipodean perspective, the light a southern clarity. The countryside is similar to parts of the Darling Downs in Queensland or the plains around Bathurst in New South Wales; fields of wheat and the straight Roman road complete the illusion.

These chalk downlands take their name from the river which flows to the south as lethargically as the agricultural traffic, through beech wood and dank marshland; a river and a name which has passed into western consciousness as a stark symbol for the mass slaughter of the First World War: the River Somme. In this famous passage, Winston Churchill supplies what John Terraine calls the 'central mythology' of the Somme.

> If two lives or ten lives were required by their commanders to kill one German, no word of complaint ever rose from the fighting troops. No attack, however, fatal, found them without ardour. No slaughter however desolating prevented them from returning to the charge. No physical conditions however severe deprived their commanders of their obedience and loyalty. Martyrs not less than soldiers, they fulfilled the high purpose of duty with which they were imbued. The battlefields of the Somme were the graveyards of Kitchener's army.

Another war later, the 'battlefields of the Somme' were still haunting Churchill. 'I was not convinced that [the invasion of Europe] was the only way of winning the war, and I knew that it would be a very heavy and hazardous adventure. Memories of the Somme and Passchendaele and many lesser frontal attacks upon the Germans were not blotted out by time and reflection.' Churchill's concern, the very real concern of a politician subject to electoral support and approval, was reflected among the planners for OVERLORD, the invasion of Europe. In March 1944, his chief of staff, General Sir Hastings Ismay, wrote to Wavell, then viceroy of India: '. . . a lot of people who ought to know better are taking it for granted that OVERLORD is going to be a bloodbath on the scale of the Somme or Passchendaele'. Today, if the Somme is considered at all, it is the first day of the battle — 1 July 1916 — which commands attention. On that day, Britain's casualties were 60,000; mostly Kitchener's army volunteers with only the hardy Newfoundlanders as representatives of Britain's empire. The later participation of the other Imperial troops is oddly overlooked as successive historians* have followed the lead set by General (as he then was) Sir Douglas Haig who dismissed the Australian participation in the Somme battle under the heading of 'Minor Operations'.

Minor Operations? About 1,000 metres north-east of the village is a simple memorial, a grassy mound of earth dotted with wildflowers in summer and neatly fenced from the surrounding fields. Near the road in the fence is a weathered wooden gate carved with the Rising Sun badge of the Australian Imperial Force. A concrete block path leads to a stone tablet, inscribed with the following words: 'The ruin of Pozières Windmill which lies here was the centre of the struggle in this part of the Somme battlefield in July and August 1916. It was captured on August 4th by Australian troops who fell more thickly on this ridge than on any other battlefield of the war.'

A modest tribute — modest tributes, if you include Haig's 'minor operations' — to such sacrifice. Away to the north-west but still on the high ground of the Pozières' Ridge, Sir Edwin Lutyen's awesome arched memorial pin-points Thiepval, one of the strongest positions in the German line. About a thousand kilometres south-west of the Pozières village, almost hidden from the Roman road by a cluster of trees, is a gaunt stone obelisk. Adorned with the Rising Sun badge and a simple dedication to the 'Officers, NCOs and Men', this is the memorial to the 1st Australian Division. It lacks the rugged splendour of the memorial to the 2nd Australian Division at Mont St Quentin, a stone soldier

---

*Anthony Farrar-Hockley's book *The Somme* (London, 1964) gives scant mention of Australian participation, although John Terraine's study of Haig is much fairer.

with slung rifle and bowed head. It lacks the quiet dignity of the memorial outside the church at Bullecourt, a slouch hat commemorated in bronze. Despite its unmistakable insignia, the 1st Division memorial is oddly anonymous, but none the less moving for that.

Apart from the memorials and the beautifully kept cemeteries with the Rising Sun badge sadly common on the headstones, few traces of the Somme fighting remain around Pozières. If the assiduous visitor turns over this rich earth with an inquiring foot, it is easy to retrieve jagged, rusting chunks of metal. Still menacing and ghastly, these are shrapnel remnants of the hundreds of thousands of artillery shells that exploded during the fighting. Of the unexploded shells — nearly one in three fired by the British artillery — the visitor will see little dumps by the side of the road, awaiting collection and detonation by soldiers of today's French army.

At Vimy, to the north and scene of the great Canadian victories of April 1917, the shell holes, the craters and the trenches have been preserved, if slightly obscured by the plantings of trees. Near Beaumont Hamel, a few kilometres north of Pozières where the first battalion of the Newfoundland Regiment was literally annihilated on 1 July 1916, one can still see the trench systems, the wire, the obstacles and the superb reverse-slope defensive position occupied by the German defenders. Between Mametz and Carnoy is Mansel Copse* in which the remnants of a trench system can still be detected. Except for the untidy mound of the Windmill, nothing remains around Pozières for this is good agricultural land, too good to be devoted to any morbidly sentimental celebration of a war nearly seven decades ago. Besides, this region of France has known wars and rumours of wars for decades.

David Campbell, the Australian poet and decorated veteran of the later war, wrote:

> The skylark goes up
> Like a flare over Pozières
> Where peasant women
>
> In bright colored skirts
> Are hoeing our men in.

Today, the 'peasant women/In bright colored skirts' have been replaced by the latest in agricultural machinery but the indifference to foreigners, in or out of uniform, dead or alive, remains. Identify yourself as an

---

*Above the copse is the Devonshire Regiment cemetery which contains the grave of the poet W. N. Hodgson, a contemporary of Rupert Brooke, who was killed on 1 July 1916.

Australian in the village estaminet over a glass of the excellent local beer and you are likely to be met with a typically Gallic shrug of the shoulders. The remark 'So what?' needs neither articulation nor translation.

For the locals, the fighting here of 1916 was between two foreign armies, the British (including the Australians) and the Germans. Their French army was involved further to the south. Nearly 70 years have passed; it is ancient history for them, without meaning or compulsion. After the war, the village was rebuilt and indeed, is now showing signs of deterioration; there are no feelings of sympathy for the Australians, such as that which exists in the nearby village of Villers–Bretonneaux.

Even if you have read widely — immersed yourself in the literature of the First World War — it is almost impossible today to imagine the desolation of Pozières in 1916. Standing on the Windmill mound, with the trench maps in my hand, I found it perplexingly difficult to make the leap of the imagination to the landscape described by C.E.W. Bean:

> Imagine a gigantic ash heap, a place where dust and rubbish have been cast for years outside some dry, derelict God-forsaken up-country township. Imagine some broken-down creek bed in the driest of our dry central Australian districts, abandoned for a generation to the goats in which the hens have been scratching for as long as man can remember. Then take away the hens and the goats and all traces of any living or moving thing. You must not even leave a spider. Put here, in evidence of some old tumbled roof, a few roof beams and tiles sticking edgeways from the ground, and the low faded ochre stump over the top of the hill, and there you have Pozières.

'. . . and there you have Pozières.' The problem was, of course, that the Germans had Pozières. It had been an objective for the British 8th Division on 1 July; it formed part of the vital ground for the British assault, the highest point on the Somme; it was, in the words of the commander of the Fourth Army, General Sir Henry Rawlinson, 'the key to the area'. This key was turned by the Australians, but only after they had suffered the most appalling casualties. The aftermath of the battle for Pozières — proportionately more casualties than at Gallipoli the previous year — affected the Australian Imperial Force, and Australia itself, deeply and drastically. It soured feelings between the Australian troops and their British commanders; it influenced relations between the British and Australian Governments and directly affected the conscription debates of 1916 which led to the split of the Australian Labor Party. Not all the casualties of Pozières fell in those chalky Picardy fields.

1

The Wearing-out Battle: Origins

Decisive results will only be obtained if the offensives of the Armies of the Coalition are made simultaneously, or at least at dates so near together that the enemy will not be able to transport reserves from one front to another.

Unanimous resolution of the Inter-Allied Military Conference, Chantilly, 6–8 December, 1915.

The year 1915 was a year of failure for the Allied powers of the war. The French called it *L'Année Sterile*, aptly enough, for the campaigns embarked upon in that year had ended in little tangible strategic or even tactical results. Gallipoli, audacious in concept, breathtakingly close to success in its early stages, had failed with disgrace for its proponents and death for all too many of its participants. In the east, the numerically mighty but pathetically equipped Russian Army had been pushed back across Poland, losing nearly three quarters of a million men as prisoners alone.

Yet, almost imperceptibly, the balance was beginning to tip in favour of the Allies. Despite her huge losses, Russia was not yet defeated. Britain was gathering in the debts of an empire as, all over the world, anxious young colonials voted with their enlistment forms to fight for the country their parents still called Home. Italy was building her capacity to wage modern war almost with impunity; France, despite her grievous losses, had arguably the most effective army on the European continent. But how were these resources to be used — how were they to be concentrated — in that most difficult of undertakings, a coalition war?

On a bright, cold, clear day in December 1915, the Allied commanders met at the French General Headquarters, the *Grand Quartiers-General* at Chantilly in northern France. Long associated with the manufacture of fine lace, Chantilly was a popular resort for Parisians, celebrated for both its château and park and as the scene of the races of the French Jockey Club. It was in the château that General Joseph Jacques Cesaire Joffre had made his headquarters, indeed had installed his court, and it was to this château that the Allied commanders came to solve the problems of coalition war.

Although ostensibly a conference of equals, 'Papa' Joffre was very much *prime inter pares* among the Allied commanders. The French politicians had decamped from Paris in 1914 as the sound of the German guns were heard clearly in the French capital. They set up government, of a sort, in Bordeaux and remained there for the rest of the war; the conduct of the war shifted to Joffre and his *GQG*. Joffre was elderly, portly, unmistakably bourgeois, politically powerful and immensely popular. Since the battle of the Marne, his popularity had grown, bringing with it daily gifts of cigars, chocolates and an avalanche of fan mail which he managed to read with evident pleasure.

Joffre was a sapper, an engineer officer who had made himself an expert on trains. This knowledge had proved invaluable for the rapid mobilisation of the French army in 1914. He had been born in 1852, the son of a cooper and one of a family of 11 children. As a student in 1870 he found himself commanding an artillery battery during the siege of Paris, after his commander collapsed with a nervous breakdown.

After graduating as an engineer from the Polytechnic, he was sent to French Indo-China where he developed an expertise in what today would be called logistics. His organisation of a supply column in Timbuktu in 1894 further enhanced his reputation and at 33, Joffre was the youngest engineer lieutenant-colonel in the French army. By 1904 he was director of engineers and professional head of his corps. But his experience in handling infantry soldiers was limited; he commanded a division and then a corps for brief periods only between 1906 and 1910. Joffre was an excellent administrator and first-rate logistician, but an indifferent trainer of troops and an extremely limited tactician. His appointment as Chief of the General Staff in 1911 was largely because of his loyalties to the republic. It was both safely and correctly assumed that he knew little of tactics and even less of strategy.

Alistair Horne describes Joffre as a

> ... true viscerotonic ... he thought from his belly rather than with his mind, with the intuitive shrewdness of a peasant. Even one of his most loyal associates, and biographer, General Desmazes, comments on his extraordinary lack of intellectualism. Before the war he read little on military theory; afterwards he read not one of the books on the war in which he had played so large a role. He was totally lacking in curiosity and imagination.

For all his limitations as a military commander, however, Joffre had two attributes sorely needed in time of war. One was an imperturbable confidence; the other was a swift ruthlessness in dealing with inadequate subordinates. Yet this second quality was little in evidence around *GQG*, as his staff officers reflected Joffre's evident *sang froid* with their own brand of obsequious sycophancy. An atmosphere of Byzantine intrigue prevailed at *GOQ*; the separate operations and intelligence branches rarely spoke to each other.

As Alistair Horne put it:

> The rare sally of Asquith's about the war office keeping three sets of figures, 'one to mislead the public, another to mislead the Cabinet and the third to mislead itself' applied with even greater force to *GQG* . . . Partially discredited and reduced in power, after 1914, the Government found it practically impossible to intervene in the mightily sealed brotherhood that was the *GQG*.

Selection and maintenance of the aim is an excellent and necessary principle of war at all levels, both strategic and tactical. Joffre had no doubts about his aim. After the war, he wrote:

> The best and largest portion of the German army was on our soil, with its line of battle jutting out a mere five days' march from the heart of France. The situation made it clear to every Frenchman that our task consisted in defeating this enemy, and driving him out of our country.

In the previous year, Joffre had tried just that against a German army that was, after its attack at Ypres in April, largely on the defensive in the west.

Imbued with fine martial spirit and still largely influenced by the military eccentric ideas of Colonel de Grandmaison — *l'attaque à outrance*, with its emphasis on regaining lost ground however unimportant that ground might be — throughout 1915 Joffre and *GQG* pursued a policy of attempting to force a breakthrough and to defeat the German army in open warfare. During September, in both Artois and in Champagne, the French tried to do so supported by the British at Loos. Each attack failed, not because of any lack of martial spirit on the part of the attackers — *l'élan vital* in de Grandmaison's mystical nonsense — but because in each case the attackers lacked sufficient artillery support. Artillery conquers; infantry occupies. Time after time in these melancholy offensives, artillery failed to conquer. Machine gun positions, skilfully sited by the most professional army of the war, remained untouched by the inadequate bombardments. When the French and British infantry began their assaults they were easy targets. One French officer described a typical scene during the Artois offensive in the northern autumn: 'Three hundred men of our regiment lay there in sublime order. At the first whistling of bullets, the officers had cried "Line-up" and all went to their death as in a parade'.

By the end of 1915 France had lost half her pre-war regular officers, either killed or invalided out of the army. Its total casualties were beginning to approach the total for Britain during the entire war, but it still possessed some 95 divisions in the Western Front, compared with less than 50 British divisions, 38 infantry and five cavalry. Britain still had responsibility for a relatively small portion of the Western Front, some 140 kilometres in length.

By comparison, the French front line was about 500 kilometres long while the Belgians held about 25 kilometres of their own territory north of the British from the Ypres salient. Strict geographical comparisons are misleading, however, for much of the French front was quiet and indeed, in the south, just north of the Swiss-German-French conjunctions, the French lines were actually dug in German soil and remained virtually undisturbed by conflict through the war. The British sector included much of industrial France, from north of Ypres in Belgium, across the border and through the mining area around Lens, across Vimy Ridge and over the River Scarpe near Arras, and then down through Picardy to meet the French just south of the River Somme.

Douglas Haig was not at Chantilly, but took command of the British forces after this 'vital date in the history of the conduct of the War'. Few British generals have answered such passion and controversy; few have been so reviled, so subjected to such continuous emotional and frequently unfair criticism. Haig, whose taciturnity matched that of Joffre, was in many ways an unfortunate scapegoat for an ill-informed population that only after the war understood the full extent of the killing.

John Terraine's sympathetic and controversial study of Haig is sub-titled *The Educated Soldier*. 'Educated', as Terraine points out, has a definite but subtle meaning in the military context:

> ... it means an officer who takes his work seriously, who studies it from all aspects, who (above all) has the mind, as well as the aspiration, to think an issue through for himself, from first to last; the reading, the battlefield experience, the staff courses and other qualifications are taken for granted. 'Educated' means a man who has learned and will put into practice *all* [Terraine's emphasis] those lessons and many more.

In the two decades since *Douglas Haig — The Educated Soldier* was published Terraine has been an assiduous defender of the British Commander-in-Chief and an enthusiastic debunker of some of the more absurd myths that have grown up about Haig's generalship in particular and the First World War in general.

Haig's personality — shy, taciturn, diffident — make him an unlikely commander compared with the generals of the Second World War and their penchants for personal publicity. Haig hated the Press and shied away from reporters although he warmed to newspaper publishers. He was a dour, careful lowland Scot, a fervent Christian, a friend of the King, a favourite at Court and, when so inclined, an enthusiastic military politician. He was also a prize winner at Sandhurst, a graduate of the Staff College, a wise and thoughtful trainer of troops, a painstaking and careful staff officer and, even as a general, aware of his limitations and the gaps in his knowledge. Anthony Farrar-Hockley, himself a general in the British army, has described Haig thus: 'Talented, self-effacing, handsome, orthodox, he was the very model of a British Major-General'. That description, with its (deliberate?) Gilbertian echoes is almost too glib: certainly Haig took command in 1915 'with every confidence'; certainly he had made mistakes and not admitted them in the privacy of his diary; certainly he had deplored the efforts of his predecessor, Sir John French, and the manner in which French had attempted to disguise those mistakes.

But Haig also took command of the British forces at an extremely difficult, almost perilous, time, when the future direction of the war was still unclear, when Britain was still a junior partner to France in their Western Front endeavours and when the Kitchener thousands were still largely untrained. Charles Carrington, a young British officer, thought his comrades were 'enthusiastic amateurs when the fighting began, the British were soldiers at the end'. Haig himself remarked that 'I have not got an Army in France, really, but a collection of divisions untrained for the field. The actual fighting Army will be evolved from them'. Haig's comments were made in March 1916, well after the initial great response to Kitchener's famous appeal translated itself into crowded depots and parade grounds all over England.

The material of 1916 however, was that with which Haig had to make the major British contribution to coalition war. In 1915 the introverted Haig noted modestly his accession to command of the British Army:

> Sunday, December 19, I took over command of the Army in France and Flanders today at noon. I sent a telegram to War Office announcing the fact, and asking who was to take command of 1st Army. Up to 11 p.m.

no reply reached me. Then Sir Wm. Robertson arrived from England and telephoned from St. Omer that the Prime Minister and Lord K. (Kitchener) had gone out of London for the weekend, and nothing could be settled until Monday! And this is war-time!

On one aspect of his command — relations with the French — Haig had no illusions. Although he had total responsibility for the British army, he was still under operational control, if not under command, of Joffre. Less than a fortnight after becoming C-in-C in December 1915, he interviewed the Head of the French Mission at British GHQ. 'I pointed out that I am *not under* [emphasis in the original] General Joffre's orders, but that would make no difference, as my intention was to do my utmost to carry out General Joffre's wishes on strategical matters, as if they were orders.'

In this, Haig was simply following Kitchener's instructions. On 28 December 1915, the Minister for War had written to Haig thus: 'The defeat of the enemy by the combined Allied Armies must always be regarded as the primary object for which British troops were originally sent to France, and to achieve that end, the closest co-operation of French and British as a united Army must be the governing policy . . . '. Compare this with Kitchener's instructions to Sir John French in 1913: 'every effort must be made to coincide most sympathetically with the plans and wishes of our Ally'. Kitchener, much more a military politician than Haig, had added a qualification to his instructions to the new C-in-C: 'But I wish you distinctly to understand that your command is an independent one, and that you will in no case come under the orders of any Allied General further than the necessary co-operation with our allies'. It was left to Haig to decide how far 'necessary co-operation' extended; given the relative size of the two armies, Haig could have adopted virtually no other course other than place his forces under Joffre's operational control.

At the time, there were 51 infantry divisions in training in the United Kingdom and in secondary theatres, but only 38 in France. These divisions were themselves about 75,000 below establishment strengths. By comparison, France had 95 divisions employed on the Western Front. France had, however, begun to reach the limits of its manpower resources; it was time for Britain to share a greater responsibility in the war.

The Chantilly conference produced agreement among the representatives of France, Russia, Italy, Belgium, Serbia and Britain. The agreement is simply stated, and central to understanding the events of the following months:

> ... that the decision of the war can only be obtained in the principal theatres, that is to say in those in which the enemy has maintained the greater part of his forces (Russian front, Franco-British front, Italian front). The decision should be obtained by co-ordinated offensives on those fronts. All the efforts of the Coalition should therefore be directed at giving these offensives their maximum force from the point of view of both men and material. Decisive results will only be obtained if the offensives of the Armies of the Coalition are made simultaneously, or at least at dates so near each other that the enemy will not be able to transport reserves from one front to another. The general action should be launched as soon as possible ... The wearing down 'usure' of the enemy will henceforward be pursued intensively by means of local and partial offensives, particularly by those powers which still have abundant reserves of men. The Conference are unanimous in recognising that only the minimum forces should be employed in the secondary theatres, and that the troops now in the Orient seem, as a whole, sufficient to meet requirements.

It is not necessary to examine in detail the arguments between the 'easterners' and the 'westerners', but a brief recapitulation might be useful. By mid-November 1914, the mobile war in the west had halted. The protagonists faced each other across No Man's Land of varying width and from trenches that extended from the North Sea to the Swiss border. As Kitchener exclaimed: 'I don't know what is to be done — this isn't war'. No flanks existed to assault or 'roll-up' or 'turn'; no mechanical means yet existed of crossing the trench lines and the terrain in between with relative impunity. This war of the Industrial Revolution required technological solutions that were still beyond the wit and resources of inventive men. In 1915, and indeed in 1916 (as we shall see later), the commanders at all levels were faced with this seemingly insoluble problem. So long as the defensive positions were well sited; so long as the technical characteristics of the existing weapons were understood and the weapons properly employed; so long as the defensive positions were held by stout-hearted, well led troops; so long as those troops were kept supplied by a flexible and competent administrative system, then there was no apparent solution. This did not stop politicians from seeking easier methods. As J.F.C. Fuller wrote:

> Exasperated by these unprofitable assaults, and ignorant of tactical considerations, the allied statesmen accused the soldiers of lack of imagina-

tion and set out to recapture mobility by a change of front, as if the locality itself was to blame for the stalemate. What they were unable to appreciate was, that should another locality be found in which the enemy's resistance was less formidable than on the Western Front, it would only be a matter of time before the same tactical considerations prevailed. It was the bullet, spade and wire which were the enemy on every front, and their geographical locations were purely incidental.

Overwhelmingly military opinion supported the westerners. Orthodox military minds saw the necessity for defeating Germany in the west; all else was peripheral. Moreover, any diversion of Allied effort from the west to other theatres might allow the German army that necessary superiority, that concentration of force, needed to break through. Which argument was right remains one of those imponderables of historical debate. The easterners certainly had the advantage of rhetoric and prose; their arguments were best expressed by David Lloyd George in his six volumes of *War Memoirs* and by Winston Churchill in his volumes of *World Crisis*. In most cases, however, the easterners' arguments were a combination of political expedience and wishful thinking. Politicians were never quite prepared to accept that the efforts to find a 'penetrable front' were, in Fuller's words, 'the strategy of evasion'. The generals, less sanguine and more realistic, were led by training, experience and inclination to accept the unpalatable truth.*

Real or apparent advantages of campaigns other than in France and Flanders continued to attract members of the British Government's War Committee through the early months of 1916. On 28 December 1915, the newly-appointed Chief of the Imperial General Staff, Field Marshal Sir William Robertson, told Haig that the committee had agreed France and Flanders were to be the main theatre and that every action would be placed behind a spring offensive. Even gaining such a limited agreement taxed the considerable powers of Robertson in dealing with politicians. A week later he wrote to Haig: 'It is deplorable the way these politicians fight and intrigue against each other. They are

---

*The soldiers realised the truth with even greater clarity. Consider this description by a private soldier of the new warfare during the first battle of Ypres in October 1915. 'The enemy rose up and started to advance. They were stopped at once: with the parapet as a rest for our rifles it was impossible to miss. The attack was over before it had hardly commenced . . . ten men holding a trench could easily stop fifty who were trying to take it.'

my great difficulty here. They have no idea how war must be conducted in order to be given a reasonable chance of success, and they will not allow professionals a free hand'.

The difficulties experienced by both Robertson and Haig are succinctly set out in a letter from the CIGS to the C-in-C on 13 January 1916. Robertson wrote:

> There is a fairly strong party in the Cabinet opposed to offensive operations on your front in the Spring or indeed at any time. One wants to go to the Balkans, another to Baghdad, and another to allow the Germans to 'attack us'. I have used all the arguments you or any other soldier would use, but not with complete success. In the War Committee decision I sent you a few days ago you will see that we are to make every effort 'to prepare' for offensive operations in the Spring.
>
> By a decision made today (which I will send you later) it has now been watered down to the effect that we are to 'prepare' for offensive operations in the Spring 'but without committing ourselves definitely to them'. In general there is a deal of wobbling, and it is bound up with the question of the size of our army, a matter which is not yet settled. There is an influential party which is urging the scrapping of some of our present T.F. [Territorial Force] divisions which we wish to get ready and send out. The fact is they are not showing the necessary grit and determination to see the thing through, now that the shoe is beginning to pinch a little. As a matter of fact, it pinches exceedingly little in this country yet. It is scarcely noticeable.

Asquith's Liberal Government had failed the previous May; Britain was being governed by an uneasy coalition of Liberals and Conservatives under his leadership. It was hardly an ideal way of achieving unanimity of purpose, a problem exacerbated by the lack of a streamlined War Cabinet until December 1916. Instead, Robertson had to deal with the cumbersome War Committee, a large and ad hoc organisation of political egos and muddled aims. It was not until 7 April 1916 that Robertson was able to obtain a direct and unambiguous statement of support in favour of the joint Allied offensive in the west; a week later, on 14 April, that commitment was passed to Haig in France.

The difficulties faced by the politicians, however, should not be underestimated. They were charged with prosecuting war on a scale for which they had no experience and no precedent. Giant armies, hundreds of thousands of men, were being recruited and trained with only the most rudimentary material |support. Weapons of all calibres and kinds were in short supply; so were uniforms and hut accommodation; so were experienced officers and NCOs to train the Kitchener volunteers. Importantly too, Britain lacked much of the industrial infrastructure for prosecuting a mass war in a technical age. It lacked the kind of chemical industry needed to make artillery shells; in peacetime it had depended upon the German chemical industry. It lacked too, the semi-automatic equipment necessary for making artillery shells and it lacked the capacity to make that equipment. The politicians who, in peacetime, had so severely criticised proposed military spending were quick in wartime to deplore the shortages evident in all aspects of military equipment.

2

'A Victory for Me'

General Joffre began the discussion by giving away on the question of the wearing-out fight. He admitted . . . that attacks were necessary to prepare the way for the decisive attack to attract the enemy's reserves were necessary, but only for some 10 or 15 days before the main battle, certainly not in April for a July attack. This seemed quite a victory for me.

Sir Douglas Haig, 14 February 1916.

On 14 January Haig received a report from a liaison officer at the British Mission at Chantilly. For a commander contemplating a joint offensive, the report was disquieting. In the French view, the Russians would not be ready to attack until the end of July. Because of this lack of men, the French could only make one more big offensive so they were anxious to wait until the Russians could attack. The French were now looking to England and Italy to carry on a wearing out fight until they and the Russians were ready.

These attacks begin early in Spring, they think — say April or May. They can give seven divisions for one attack. The rest of the wearing–out attacks will be left to British and Italians. Then, according to French *GHQ* there should come an interval of about a month before the big attack is launched. For the latter the French can put in 50 Divisions. I think that the French man-power situation is serious as they are not likely to stand another winter's war. There is no doubt to my mind but that the war must be won by the Forces of the British Empire.

Haig noted the possible course of action for his command:

1 'Winter sports' or raids continued into the spring, i.e. capturing lengths of the enemy's trenches at favourable points.
2 *Wearing–out fights* similar to 1 but on a larger scale at many points along the whole front. Will last about three weeks *to draw in the enemy's reserves.*

3 *Decisive attacks* at several points, object to break through. The amount of ammunition for 2 and 3 will be *very large indeed*. [Emphases in the original.]

Little wonder then that Haig, although loyally and carefully subordinate to Joffre, was beginning to examine critically the French plan. There was no doubt that the awesome burden of the 'wearing-out fight' would fall to the British, leaving the French army to participate in the decisive battles which were to follow. Haig noted on 14 January that 'The possibilities [of the wearing-out fight] must be limited by the quantity of munitions we can spare and by the need to assure ourselves that the enemy is likely to suffer at least as heavily as we do'. And on 1 February he wrote to Joffre questioning the proposed conduct of the 'wearing-out fight'. Haig saw these falling into two categories: those immediately before the main battle with the aim of forcing the enemy prematurely to commit its reserves, and those without such an intention but merely the aim of attrition. Of the latter, Haig wrote:

The '*batailles d'usure*' which you ask me to undertake in April, and again (in certain circumstances) in May, would not have the same result, as the Germans would have time to replace losses from their depots and to reorganise and refit the Reserves before the commencement of our general offensive two months later.

For these reasons I feel that we should reap little, if any, advantage from such '*batailles d'usure*' carried out a long time before the commencement of the general offensive. They would undoubtedly entail considerable loss on us with little to show for it; while the results on the morale of the troops, and more especially on public opinion in England, Germany and elsewhere might be unfortunate. The enemy would claim that he had defeated an attempt to 'break through' and, as our real object would not be generally understood, his claim would probably be accepted. We cannot ignore the possible effect of this on public opinion and on the financial credit of the Allies — a serious consideration. For these reasons I submit that it is most desirable that once fighting begins this year on a large scale it should be carried through as quickly as possible to a decisive issue.

At the vital conference on 14 February 1916 to settle the offensive, Joffre accepted Haig's views. The latter noted in his diary:

General Joffre began the discussion by giving away on the question of the wearing-out fight. He admitted (no doubt on Castelnau's advice) that attacks were necessary to prepare the way for the decisive attack to attract the enemy's reserves were necessary, but only for some 10 to 15 days before the main battle, certainly not in April for a July attack. This seemed quite a victory for me.

Each victory has its cost. Haig was pressed to relieve the French Tenth Army, oddly located holding the line between the British First and Third Armies. He agreed, in principle. 'When?' asked Joffre. 'Next winter', replied Haig.

> The old man laughed and I remarked we could not do impossibilities; besides, he was short of men in the depots and it was much more costly to attack than to hold the line so the British must now attack and not be detailed to hold passive fronts. I added I had no doubt that under proper arrangements the attack will be a success. General Joffre argued no more. I agreed to the French left being pushed to the north side of the Somme for the attack and that the main French and British attacks are to be 'jointives' that is, side by side . . . Today was a most important conference. Indeed the whole position of the British Army in the operations of this year depended on my not giving way on:
> 1 The nature and moment of carrying out the wearing–out fight and
> 2 Not using up divisions in relieving the 10th Army.
> By straightforward dealing I gained both these points. But I had an anxious and difficult struggle. I had to be firm without being rude to gain my points.

Certainly Haig had not given way over the wearing–out fights, a point that was to save countless British lives; certainly he had prevailed over relieving the Tenth Army. But the price was the location for the offensive.

On 29 December 1915, Haig attended a conference with Joffre at Chantilly, presided over by the French President, Poincaré. That conference was also attended by the Prime Minister, Briand, the Minister for War, General Gallieni and three French Army Group commanders, Generals Dubail, de Langle de Cary, and Marshal Foch. After that conference, Joffre wrote to Haig seeking the relief of the French Tenth Army and proposing a combined French–British assault on a 96 kilometre front athwart the Somme. Joffre's letter is worth quoting in detail:

> I have directed the General Commanding the Group of the Armies of the North (Foch) to make a study of a powerful offensive south of the Somme in the region comprised between the river and Lassigny. This study is part of a general plan drawn up for the French Armies as a whole, and will permit me to determine the points against which our

principal effort will be made in the coming spring. It is part of a scheme of preparation of a great number of different areas of intended sectors of attack, some to be utilised in the general offensive, others designed for the purpose of holding the enemy in uncertainty as to the points of attack, which will be selected later. Without prejudice to the area where our principal attack will be made, the French offensive would be greatly aided by a simultaneous offensive of the British forces between the Somme and Arras. Besides the interest which this last area presents on account of its close proximity to that where the effort of the French Armies will be made, I think that it will be a considerable advantage to attack the enemy on a front where for long months the reciprocal activity of the troops opposed to each other has been less than elsewhere. The ground is, besides, in many places favourable to the development of a powerful offensive. I request, therefore, that you will kindly let me know your views on the subject of an attack by the British forces on a large front in the area of your Third Army.

Haig, however, thought differently to Joffre. In February, he ordered General Sir Henry Rawlinson, who was to command the new Fourth Army, to study possible operations on the Somme and at Ypres.

Almost at the same time, General Sir Herbert Plumer, commanding the Second Army in the north, was told to prepare a plan for the capture of the Messines-Wytschaete Ridge. Haig had no great expectations of an attack here, however, for he noted that it would be 'more of a subsidiary nature and unlikely to promise any far reaching results'. More attractive propositions in Plumer's sector were the Forêt d'Houthoulst and the railway junction at Roulers and an attack on Lille. Brig.-Gen. Charteris, Haig's Chief Intelligence Officer noted on 8 February: 'I am sure Flanders is the right place to hit. I think D. H. agrees, but the Operations Section (or some of them) are all for the Somme, on account of it being easier ground to attack over'.

Although planning for these possible attacks went ahead during the latter weeks of January and into February, the planning was bedevilled by a lack of direction from both the French and the British governments. As we have seen, support for the great offensives was noticeably lacking among some members of the War Committee. Haig's difficulties were exacerbated by a lack of support from his Government and by Joffre's limitations as a strategic commander. Joffre, despite his reference to a decisive victory, was thinking more in terms of a wearing–down battle, 'a war of attrition which must be chiefly carried on by our [i.e. France's] Allies, England, Russia and even Italy'.

This is the plan that Joffre had in mind at the conference of 14 February: a plan that, if the archives are any guide, had the benefit of neither appreciation nor logical thought. The Somme was not selected because it offered strategic or tactical advantages; there were no railway terminals or weaknesses in the German defences. It was selected because it was the location where the two armies, French and British, met. According to the British official historian, Sir James Edmonds: 'The decision of the French Commander-in-Chief to make the main offensive of 1916 astride the Somme seems to have been arrived at solely because the British would be bound to take part in it'.

Farrar-Hockley agrees, pointing out that Joffre had been seeking relief of the French Tenth Army by the British and for the British to take over more of the line:

> ... nowhere was he more anxious to see this done than at Arras. If a joint summer offensive should be mounted in that region, Tenth Army's relief would be indefinitely postponed — as unsatisfactory from the logistical as from the operational aspects — while the command of the overall offensive might logically have demanded for Haig by the British Government in view of the preponderance of their troops. Joffre looked forward to a rising British share in the responsibilities on the western front in 1916 but he did not want it on those terms. Though there were no immediate strategic objectives on the Somme — such as the railway complex at Verdun — the British and French were side by side. Here Joffre could be sure of maintaining overall control of effort and extent, direction and date.

Even allowing for the benefit of hindsight, the reasons advanced by Joffre at the end of December 1915 did not justify an offensive in the Somme sector. Certainly the sector had been quiet for nearly two years but the lack of activity had enabled the Germans to prepare their defences. Joffre's assertion that the 'ground is ... in many places favourable to the development of a powerful offensive' is open to argument. The open rolling downlands of Picardy, broken only by the occasional wood, sloping upwards towards the Pozières-Thiepval Ridge, might well present some advantages to attackers: control would be easier; so would observation. But these advantages hardly outweighed the greater benefits conferred upon the German defenders by the terrain. Given the limited mobility of the attacking forces, the chalky nature of the soil which enabled the Germans to dig deeply below the surface, the large number of small villages that could be fortified, the Somme sector provided formidable problems.

Still, in mid–February 1916, the offensive was still more than four months away. Few battle plans survive contact with the enemy, especially plans made months before an offensive. Within a week of Haig's most 'important conference' the Germans launched their offensive at Verdun. Now the problems facing both Joffre and Haig became even more urgent.

Attrition had its adherents on the other side of No Man's Land; none greater than General Erich von Falkenhayn, Chief of Staff of the German army, second only to the Kaiser himself in command and, until January 1915, Minister of War. Although the Emperor, Kaiser Wilhelm II, could theoretically interfere at any moment, the running of Germany's huge war effort was left largely to this enigmatic Prussian. Enigmatic, because little is known of his personal life. He was described by one of his German biographers as the 'Lonely Warlord', an apt tag for this cold, impersonal, secretive man who shunned publicity, contact with most of his fellows and whose autobiography — more than usually self-serving even for a defeated commander — was written in an odd, remote third person.

Falkenhayn was a Junker, born in 1861 to a family that could trace its military service back to the twelfth century. The family farmed near Thorn, now Polish territory. It is bleak, miserable country, fit only for eking out a living. Little wonder then that the sons of such areas were attracted elsewhere; little wonder too that they adapted with ease to the spartan, austere life of the Prussian army. Falkenhayn's military career was hardly spectacular; promotion to captain came at 32 and at 41, still a major, he was commanding a line battalion of infantry. His chance came in 1906 when, as chief of staff to the incompetent von Prittwitz, he impressed his superiors with his abilities and caught the eye of the Kaiser.

In this all-important matter of royal patronage, significant similarities exist in the careers of Haig and von Falkenhayn. By 1911 Falkenhayn was a colonel commanding a Guards Regiment, a remarkable achievement for a line officer. Like Joffre, Falkenhayn possessed considerable talents as an administrator; unlike Joffre, however, he possessed considerable abilities as a strategist. His limitations, odd for a man of such background and ambition, were indecisiveness and secretiveness; characteristics which, according to Alistair Horne, were to bring 'heartbreaking tragedy to both France and Germany at Verdun and eventually to play a vital part in losing the war for the central powers'.

Falkenyhayn was, in the manner of orthodox military thinkers, a dedicated westerner. Germany also maintained a considerable advantage over the Allies in that it had, since the very beginning of the war, retained the strategic initiative. As well, on the Western Front it possessed the ability to move its reserves quickly to meet real or perceived threats. Falkenhayn, this cold, hard man — 'casualty lists moved him even less than either Haig or Joffre', Horne tells us — appreciated with chilling clarity the role of the British forces. He understood well enough the inherent risks to Germany of prosecuting war simultaneously on two fronts; from the beginning he had feared that Britain's intervention might eventually prove fatal to Germany's chances of success.

He advocated a submarine blockade of the British Isles, a course rejected by the German government for fear of bringing the United States into the war. On land, however, Falkenhayn perceived just one method of bringing the giant armies of the Allies to their collective knees. He wrote in his appreciation of December 1915:

> For England the campaign on the Continent of Europe is at bottom a side-show. Her real weapons are the French, Russian, and Italian armies. If we put those armies out of the war England is left to face us alone, and it is difficult to believe that in such circumstances her lust for our destruction would not fail her. It is true there would be no certainty that she would give up, but there is a strong probability. More than that can seldom be asked in war.

Falkenhayn resiled from a direct attack on the British forces in France, although he advocated an increase in the submarine campaign — 'our most effective weapon'. Instead, the objective for 1916 was to knock England's best sword from her hand; the best sword being, of course, the French army. A section of Falkenhayn's appreciation, addressed to his Emperor, is worth repeating in detail because it was the first time that a military commander had advocated defeat of an army by a gradual process and not by a swift, decisive, telling blow.

> To achieve that object (the object of breaking the French Army) the uncertain method of a mass break-through in any case beyond our means, is unnecessary. We can probably do enough for our purposes with limited resources. Within our reach behind the French sector of the Western Front there are objectives for the retention of which the French General Staff would be compelled to throw every man they have. If they do so the forces of France will bleed to death — as there can be no question of a voluntary withdrawal — whether we reach our goal or not. If they do not do so, and we reach our objectives, the moral effect on France will be enormous. For an operation limited on a narrow front Germany will not be compelled to spend herself so completely that all other fronts are practically drained. She can face with confidence the relief attacks to be expected on these fronts, and indeed hope to have sufficient troops in

hand to reply to them for counter-attacks. For she is perfectly free to accelerate or draw out her offensive, to intensify it or break it off from time to time, as suits her purpose.

The objectives of which I am speaking now are Belfort and Verdun.

Falkenhayn preferred to attack at Verdun, left as the extremity of a salient after the battle of the Marne. It has often been suggested that Verdun appealed to both Falkenhayn and the Kaiser because the former could use the German Fifth Army, commanded by the heir to the throne, the Crown Prince. Evidence to support these suggestions is difficult to find, although excellent strategic reasons exist for supporting Falkenhayn's selection. The tip of the Verdun salient was just 240 kilometres east of Paris; it had deep historical and military significance for the French people dating back to its days as a fortified camp for the Romans when it was known as *Virondunum*.

So began the planning for operation *Gericht*, a word capable of several meanings: a tribunal, a judgement or occasionally, an execution place. Falkenhayn concealed — if indeed, he made clear anywhere — his true intention of the Verdun offensive. His subordinate commanders, when they received their orders, were left with doubts that Falkenhayn's intention in launching his offensive was to capture the ancient French fortress in the salient. For example, in his directive to the Fifth Army, Falkenhayn spoke only of 'an offensive in the Meuse area in the direction of Verdun'. This, however became translated in the Crown Prince's orders to his army of an objective thus 'to capture the fortress of Verdun by precipitate methods'.

According to Falkenhayn's Chief of Staff, von Tappen, 'the seizure of Verdun was never represented as the real aim of the offensive, but it was the destruction of the French forces that we had to find there. If in the process Verdun fell into our hands, so much the better'. Tappen's comments accord with his commander's memorandum which, it must be pointed out, was not seen either by the Crown Prince or by his Chief of Staff, Schmidt von Knobelsdorf. It is a sobering indication of Falkenhayn's character and his approach to war that he approved the plans submitted by his subordinate commander although the aim varied so distinctly from that which he had proposed. If there is an explanation, it must be that of morale. The German troops would fight better if they believed they were intended to capture a fortress, rather than simply batter away at the walls in the hope that those within might literally and metaphorically bleed to death.

On 18 February 1916, General de Castelnau dined with Haig at the latter's headquarters. After dinner, the two generals had, in Haig's words, 'a long talk on the military situation'. Once again Castelnau pressed

Haig for relief of the French Tenth Army. His persistence annoyed the British Commander-in-Chief, although Haig was careful not to show it. But de Castelnau was insistent; the French were expecting an immediate attack on Verdun and needed to be able to concentrate there all the available French divisions. In a letter to Robertson the following day, Haig set out his reaction to these demands and expectations.

> I, of course, said that if the Germans did attack, the British Army would support the French to the utmost of its power, and in the best possible manner. That is either by taking over more of the line, or by counter-attacking. I preferred the latter as being the soundest method of defence. I also pointed out that so far only some nine divisions were located opposite the Verdun Salient, which with eight holding the line only makes 17 Divns — not enough for a decisive result. I therefore ventured to think that a blow will be dealt against the British, and that it might even be found to be the main effort . . .
>
> General de Castelnau gave many reasons why he expected an early attack on this front, and not against Russia. With many of them I agreed: they were, as he said, 'très logiques' — but I asked him what had happened since our Conference at Chantilly three days before when Gen Joffre was as equally positive as he (Castelnau) was now, that the attack would be on the Russian front! All he would say was that his own views were 'très logiques'! These French are funny fellows are they not! In any case, while preparing for the offensive action, of which you know, I am also acting as if the main German attack is likely to fall against the British front fairly soon.

In that letter to 'Wully' Robertson, we see so many of Haig's characteristics: his caution; his incipient Francophobia; his Anglocentricity, for there was no real reason to believe that, as Haig put it, 'a blow will be dealt against the British'. In the Flanders sector, the weather (the same consideration which Haig overlooked the following year) precluded any major offensive until the summer; both Arras and the Somme posed considerable problems for any German commander who intended to attack on a narrow front and, given Falkenhayn's limitation on manpower because of the two-front war, any German offensive would have to be mounted on a narrow front. Verdun, allowing for the distinction between a 'bleeding to death' offensive and an offensive intended to capture the fort, should have commended itself to Haig as a likely objective.

Two days after Haig wrote to Robertson, the German offensive at Verdun began. What followed was a ten month battle; a battle planned by Falkenhayn to bleed France to death; a battle which almost certainly ended Germany's chances of victory. Cyril Falls, in his book *The First World War,* has pointed out that in Falkenhayn's thinking there was a remarkable tendency towards compromise. Alone among the superior commanders, it was the enigmatic Falkenhayn who entertained the doctrine that a 'good peace' was the goal, rather than decisive and overwhelming victory.

It is necessary to consider only briefly the battle of Verdun. The planning of the German offensive bore all the curious hallmarks of reticence so characteristic of Falkenhayn. The initial assault was confined only to one side of the Meuse, although the Fifth Army planners had wanted simultaneous assaults on both sides of the river. In artillery support however, there was little of the 'imbecile moderation'. The attacking divisions were supported by the heaviest artillery concentration ever produced: 1,400 guns, howitzers and mortars, deployed along a front of 12,000 metres. Falkenhayn's confidence in the power of his artillery was such that he believed there would be no need to launch massed infantry attacks. All opposition would be ended from the ghastly ferocity of the artillery concentration; that same artillery would then be available to prevent the French reinforcing the fortress itself.

Again, a commander's plan did not survive contact with the enemy. Despite the devastation of their defensive positions, the French troops hung on grimly, helped in small measure by the weather and by Falkenhayn's reluctance to supply the Fifth Army with crucial reserves. For the Germans, the battle for Verdun was lost in the first week, and lost by Falkenhayn's habitual indecisiveness. By the end of February, General Henri Philippe Pétain, now in command of the entire Verdun sector, had steadied the defenders and the advantage had switched from the attackers, although the fighting and the dying was to continue for months.

The casualty figures are important for they give an indication of the extent of the fighting, and also of the enormous demands that fighting was making on both the French and German armies. By the end of February, Pétain's French defenders had suffered 30,000 casualties, and the Germans, 25,000. A month later, those figures had risen to 90,000 and 82,000 respectively. By the beginning of May, the French casualties were 133,000 while the German casualties were 120,000. Falkenhayn's policy of bleeding the French army to death might have been working, but it was doing so with enormous cost to his own forces.

In June, Falkenhayn was faced with another problem in the east. General Brusilov, arguably the best Russian commander, launched a 40 division attack against the Austrians at Galicia. For Brusilov, it was a masterly stroke; the Austrians had thinned out their line at that point to prepare for an assault against the Italians. Here, Falkenhayn's innate secretiveness and his dislike for his Austrian allies contributed largely.* He had not warned the Austrians of his intentions at Verdun, typical of the poor relations which prevailed between the German and Austrian general staffs. For the British, however, the German assault at Verdun had one important consequence: it made an assault on the Somme all the more urgent.

---

*He had once shouted at the Austrian Archduke Karl, heir to the Hapsburgs: 'What is your Imperial Highness thinking of? Whom do you think you have in front of you? I am an experienced Prussian general'.

3

The 'Difficult Allies'

To encourage France, to encourage doubters at home, to persuade amateur strategists of the right course to adopt, and to confirm in practice the confidence of the British troops, the urgency of obtaining at least sufficient success to show that the enemy was not invincible on the Western Front and that greater success could be gained with greater forces, was very great.

Reasons for the Somme Offensive, according to the Memorandum on Operations on the Western Front, 1916–18.

The memorandum from which the above extract is taken was drafted by Haig's Chief of Staff, Lt.-Gen. Sir Lancelot Kiggell, substantially revised by Haig himself and deposited in the British Museum in 1920 with strict instructions that it not be released until 1940. It is illuminating to consider the priority given by the author of that particular passage, whether Haig or Kiggell, to the reasons for embarking on the Somme offensive: 'To encourage France'. Considering Haig's Francophobia it is odd how often this reasoning appears in the documents and records. In his own despatches, first published in December 1916, Haig listed three reasons for the Somme offensive:

(i)   to relieve the pressure on Verdun,
(ii) to assist our Allies in the other theatres of war by stopping any further transfer of German troops from the Western Front,
(iii) to wear down the strength of the forces opposed to us.

The German onslaught at Verdun immediately caused Haig to change his mind about relieving the French Tenth Army. Joffre, in spite of contrary advice from his own intelligence staff, considered the Verdun offensive was merely a preparatory attack, and that the main blow would fall elsewhere. For this, he needed a considerable reserve; the Tenth Army must be relieved. Haig agreed, although he did not share Joffre's opinion about the weight of the German offensive at Verdun.

During the first, frantic weeks of the Verdun fighting, relations between the two allies were showing distinct signs of strain. On 6 March Robertson wrote to Haig from the War Office:

> Joffre has apparently no idea of ever taking the offensive if he can get other people to take it for him. So far as I can make out, he no longer has any confidence in himself. In every way we possibly can, we must take the lead, or at any rate refuse to be led against our own judgment. I hope I am getting a little more manliness and courage into some of those in higher places. I have not much use for Castelnau.

Haig noted the details of Robertson's letter in his diary and added, 'This rather agrees with my opinion too. My difficulties are to know who is the real Commander-in-Chief of the French Army. There seem to be so many advisers behind Joffre, and they frequently change'.

Haig's diary for this period gives us some idea of the tension between the allies. On 28 March, Haig's headquarters received a demand from the French *GQG*, signed by Joffre, asking *'per voie de reciprocite'* for a detachment of 2,000 men in lieu of the 68 heavy guns left on the Tenth Front which the British had recently taken over. 'They also want "compensation" for the ammunition in shape of 1,000 workmen, i.e. a total of 3,000.' Haig had no intention of bargaining with Joffre, and said so to the latter's senior liaison officer at the British headquarters.

> . . . I had already taken over the front of the 10th Army with 150,000 men, and if the situation required it, I was ready to go to the greatest extremes in supporting the French. But I had no 'labourers' to bargain with against so many 'cannons'. . . . The truth is that there are not many officers in the French Staff with gentlemanly ideas. They are out to get as much from the British as they possibly can.

Unlike Sir Henry Wilson who was an ardent Francophile,* spoke the language fluently and who spent long periods in France, Haig regarded his allies with a mixture of disdain and infuriation. Much of this derived from his own singular, almost-aristocratic outlook; much was fueled by his friends and acquaintances. Take, for example, the note in Haig's diary for 14 April. He had just met the banker Leo Rothschild who told him 'about the demands on the French Government for a loan as

---

*It was Wilson who, in 1910, discussed the problems of the French-British alliance with General Foch. 'What is the smallest British military force that would be any use to you?' Wilson asked Foch. 'A single British soldier — and we will see that he is killed,' replied Foch.

they were afraid to tax their people. It appears also that the French people would rather make peace with the Germans than submit to a War Tax!'

Still, it was an anxious time. Joffre could see his plans for the joint offensive disappearing in the face of the onslaught at Verdun; Haig had to balance the competing demands of the French and the limitations placed on his own forces by their standard of training and by the politicians' misgivings about an expensive offensive. On 7 April Haig noted of Joffre: 'The old man . . . is really past his work . . '. It was an observation he was to make again later in that year.

The Fourth Army was created on 1 March 1916, under the command of General Sir Henry Rawlinson. Its birth was neat and relatively painless. In relieving the French Tenth Army, Haig passed half its sector to General Monro's First Army on the north side and the other half to Allenby's Third Army in the south. In simple terms, the Third Army took a series of paces to the left, leaving the three corps on the right of the line under command of the newly created Fourth Army. Its responsibility for the line extended for 32 kilometres, from slightly north of the River Somme to Fonquevillers.

Three years younger than Haig, Rawlinson was the same rank as his Commander-in-Chief and a marked contrast in personality. Where Haig was taciturn, Rawlinson was a brilliant speaker; whereas Haig was shy, Rawlinson was gregarious. He was also an infantry officer, serving in both the King's Royal Rifle Corps and the Guards, a former commandant of the Staff College and, according to Duff Cooper, 'full of ambition and suspected to be not incapable of intrigue'. Evidence of this intrigue is difficult to find — Rawlinson's biography gives us few indications — although Haig nurtured his suspicions of his subordinate general, remarking much later in the war that Rawlinson's fidelity to him would remain 'as long as my star was in the ascendant'.

Even before the Fourth Army had officially come into existence, Rawlinson had begun his reconnaissance for the planned offensive. 'Time spent in reconnaissance is seldom wasted', runs the old military adage; Rawlinson carried out a detailed and careful inspection of the terrain and the enemy positions to his front.

It will be recalled that Joffre, in his selection of the area between the Somme and Arras for the British simultaneous offensive, thought that it would be 'a considerable advantage to attack the enemy on a front where for long months the reciprocal activity of the troops opposed to each other has been less than elsewhere. The ground is, besides, in many places favourable to the development of a detailed offensive'. For a detailed description of the enemy's position, we need look no further than Haig's own despatches. First, the terrain itself:

> The enemy's position to be attacked was of a very formidable character, situated on a high, undulating tract of ground, which rises to more than 500 feet above sea level, and forms the watershed between the Somme on the one side and the rivers of south-western Belgium on the other. On the southern face of this watershed, the general trend of which is from east-south-east to west-north-west, the ground falls in a series of long irregular spurs and deep depressions to the valley of the Somme.

In the north of the Fourth Army sector, on the British left as they faced the Germans, the British trenches had the advantage of height and position. They were sited on the forward slopes, able to keep the German positions below under some observation. South of the village of Hamel, however, the advantages were reversed. Here, the high ground — south-east from Thiepval village through Pozières to Guillemont — was held by the Germans. The trench lines zigzagged, cleverly using the spurs and re-entrants, to provide the best fields of fire for their inhabitants. As well, in this artillery war, the Germans had excellent observation from the high ground. They could easily make out the basilica of Albert and any traffic approaching that town from Amiens. They could see the length of the Ancre valley, west of Albert, where the tributary of the Somme flowed through the town to Corbie.

On the high ground between the Somme and the Ancre, the Germans had taken the advantage of 'the long months [when] the reciprocal activity . . . [had] been less than elsewhere' to contract a second line of defences covering the vital ground. In military terminology today, 'vital ground' has a specific, agreed meaning: 'ground, the possession of which by the enemy will seriously interfere with the successful defence of the position'. The Germans appreciated that the high ground Thiepval-Pozières-Guillemont was the key to the successful defence of this sector. How they prepared their defences is a reflection of the professionalism and skill of their army. Again, Haig's own despatches give us the best description.

> The first and second systems each consisted of several lines of deep trenches, well provided with bomb-proof shelters and with numerous communication trenches connecting them. The front of the trenches in each system was protected by wire entanglements, many of them in two belts forty yards broad, built of iron stakes interlaced with barbed wire, often almost as thick as a man's finger.
>
> The numerous woods and villages in and between these systems of defence had been turned into veritable fortresses. The deep cellars usually to be found in the villages, and the numerous pits and quarries common to a chalky country, were used to provide cover for machine guns and

trench mortars. The existing cellars were supplemented by elaborate dug-outs, sometimes in two storeys, and these were connected up by passages as much as thirty feet below the surface of the ground. The salients in the enemy's lines, from which he could bring enfilade fire across his front, were made into self-contained forts, and often protected by mine-fields; while strong redoubts and concrete machine gun emplacements had been constructed in positions from which he could sweep his own trenches should these be taken. The ground lent itself to good artillery observation on the enemy's part, and he had skilfully arranged for cross fire by his guns.

These various systems of defence, with the fortified localities and other supporting points between them, were cunningly sited to afford each other mutual assistance and to admit of the utmost possible development of enfilade and flanking fire by machine guns and artillery. They formed, in short, not merely a series of successive lines, but one composite system of enormous strength and depth.

Admittedly that description was written in December 1916 with the benefit of hindsight and experience, but in detailing the difficulties by the assaulting troops, it is admirably succinct. How much of that knowl-edge was available to Rawlinson and his staff before the operation began is, of course, open to question. It should be remembered, however, that the British had achieved a measure of air superiority; that activities along the front included patrolling to gain prisoners and information and, of course, the locations of fixed, prepared defensive positions in chalk soil are easily determined.

Locations, certainly. Extent ... that is quite another matter. John Terraine has argued that GHQ simply did not know what it was up against. 'This is not a criticism of the Intelligence. Until the German line was captured, and could be studied, it is hard to see how this information could be obtained.' Terraine is probably too charitable to the staffs of GHQ and Fourth Army in general and to Haig and Raw-linson in particular. To be fair to the latter, however, the early plan he submitted to GHQ covered in some detail the 'hostile defences'.*

The German defences consist of a front system and a second line. The latter is at a distance varying from 2000 to 5000 yards behind the front system. Parts of it, though not actually out of range of our guns, will be difficult to deal with, as they are only observable from the air.

---

*Similar defences, in a nearby sector had been captured earlier. As well, prisoners taken during trench raids also gave details of the defensive positions. These positions were underestimated, not unknown.

> There are a number of strongly fortified villages both in the front system and between it and the second line of the German defences.

Tactically, the planning of the Somme offensive was influenced by the simple lack of experience of commanders at all levels, from Haig down, in operations of this size. It was also influenced, as we shall see, by a sanguine optimism in the effectiveness of the artillery preparation. And it was influenced too, by the abundant enthusiasm of troops and regimental officers for this, their first major offensive — their first 'big push' of the war.

Again, the enormous benefits of hindsight allow us to be critical of the planning. Rawlinson, upon whose shoulders fell most of the responsibility for planning the battle, was charged with the task of capturing the high ground running south-east from the River Ancre above Albert to the River Somme, about 11 kilometres in length. To do so, Rawlinson's army had to capture both the German's first and second lines of defences. Here, the third lines of defences were still under construction; capturing the first two lines would have meant that the defences were breached, that a hole had been punched in the long line from the Belgian coast to the Swiss border. But merely punching a hole in the defences was not enough. The initial successes had to be followed up, exploited, and the only arm available for exploitation in 1916 was the cavalry.

Here Haig's concept was bold enough. It was based on what might have been achieved the previous year at Loos when Haig fretted for a mobile reserve force that he could commit to exploit the initial successes achieved by his infantry. No such force was forthcoming. Sir John French, cautious about the possibilities of success and lacking confidence in the plan, had kept reserves under his own command. The opportunities, hard won by the infantry, went begging for hours. In 1916, however, the German defences on the Somme were much stronger than they had been at Loos the previous year.

Still, the exploitation plan might have worked — had the breakthrough been made.

The Commander-in-Chief planned to capture Bapaume, behind the partially completed German third line. He realised that to burden Rawlinson with such a task was unreasonable; sufficient for his army to make the initial rupture in the lines. This was clearly an opportunity for the cavalry, then cooling its heels, hooves and opportunities behind the lines. Haig created the 'Reserve Army' on 23 May and placed General Sir Hubert Gough in command. It had, or was to have, three cavalry and two infantry divisions. All during the planning phase of the battle, Haig was pushing Rawlinson to think beyond the mere capture of a few kilometres of front. His determination, as Commander-in-Chief and as a cavalry general, was that the enemy should be fought in the open, away from the almost incalculable advantages presented by their formidable defensive positions. It was his experience at Loos, too, that convinced Haig the opportunities came in the earliest stages of the battle, when the enemy disarray was at its greatest and before there was time to move up reinforcements. But for Haig, the mechanics of the battle were only the means to an end.

Terraine believes it is:

> easy to understand Haig's mind, if one is disposed to do so. He was acting in the spirit of the resolution made by the Allied Powers at Chantilly in December, 1915, to seek a resolution in the following year. The weakened condition of Russia was palpable; Joffre and Poincaré had told him France had only one more large effort in her; this was confirmed by Clemenceau, and by every other source of information at Haig's disposal; now he observed the remaining strength of France being sucked remorsely down the vortex of Verdun. The conclusion was obvious: the British effort must be made with the maximum strength, aiming at the maximum result — the defeat of the German Army in the field.

Yet Haig can and has been criticised frequently, at both the strategic and tactical levels. Strategically, because of the selection — or his easy agreement with Joffre's selection — of the Somme as a location for the offensive; because the offensive was then selected for the most power-fully defended area of that sector, the apex of the salient instead of the more vulnerable flanks; because, as we have seen, the locality offered no immediate military or non-military objectives.

Moreover, the British commanders must accept responsibility for the way in which the battle was tactically planned. Basically two alternatives were available to Rawlinson and his Fourth Army planning staff. The first method was the 'assaut brutal', along the length of the front se-lected, a sustained attack with the objective of keeping the enemy unbalanced. 'The trouble is', remarked Rawlinson, 'that this method frequently exhausts the attacker first'. If he needed evidence for that observation, it was being provided by the German army south at Ver-dun.

The other alternative was to strike for the enemy's vital ground and to capture this feature in separate distinct phases: the first phase to assault, capture and occupy the enemy's first line of trenches, then, using these as a firm base, repeat the process on his second line, and so on, as many times as necessary. Rawlinson set out the courses open with admirable clarity:

The first, and the most alluring one, was to attempt to capture the whole of the enemy's lines of defence ... in one attack. The second, less ambitious, but in my opinion more certain to divide the attack into two phases, the first of which would give us possession of the enemy's front system, and the all important tactical points between the front system and the second line. The second phase to follow as soon as possible after the first, so as to give the enemy as little time as possible to construct new defences and to bring up guns and reserves. The first alternative I considered, was a gamble which involved considerable risks.

That assessment was written after the war. When Rawlinson's first outline plan was delivered to Haig he argued that the attempt to rush the whole of the enemy's defences would 'involve very serious risk and will be in the nature of a gamble'. Added Rawlinson:

It does not appear to me that the gain of 2 or 3 kilometres of ground is much consequence, or that the existing situation is so urgent that we should incur very heavy losses in order to draw a large number of German reserves against this portion of our front. Our object rather seems to be to kill as many Germans as possible with the least loss to ourselves, and the best way to do this appears to me to be to seize points of tactical importance which will provide us with good observation and which we may feel quite certain the Germans will counter-attack. These points to be, not only ones of special tactical importance with a view to a further advance, but to be such that the Germans will be compelled to counter-attack them under disadvantages likely to conduce to heavy losses, which we can only ensure if these tactical points are not too far distant from our guns positions.

On the basis of that argument, Rawlinson told Haig that he proposed to adopt a phased attack plan. Haig disagreed. In his diary he noted:

I studied Sir Henry Rawlinson's proposals for attack. His intention is merely to take the enemy's first and second system of trenches and 'kill Germans'. He looks upon the gaining of three or four kilometres more or less of ground as immaterial. I think we can do better than this by aiming at getting as large a combined force of French and British as possible across the Somme and fighting the enemy in the open.

But was Rawlinson arguing in the narrow manner Haig maintained? His original outline, submitted to Haig's headquarters on 3 April 1916, seems to be a criticism of the general push along the line approach, and to argue strongly for assaults on key features.

Whichever method were adopted — the phased, feature-by-feature attack or the general push forward — success would be heavily dependent upon the artillery preparation. Here, the problems faced by Haig and Rawlinson were considerable. Quite simply, the British had insufficient guns, particularly of heavy calibres, and insufficient ammunition for such an offensive; shortages that were to handicap commanders throughout 1916 and into 1917. As well, the inexperience of the munitions manufacturers contributed to the high percentage of 'dud' rounds — blinds, in army parlance — fired during the battle. Some estimates have placed this as high as one in three rounds.

The commanders were faced with a choice of basic fire plans: A short, sharp bombardment or a long, continuous period of preparation fire. Consider these quotes, each by prominent military historians and former serving officers. First, General Sir Anthony Farrar-Hockley:

> Haig was known to favour the short bombardment because it offered surprise. Rawlinson proposed the lengthy preparation. He did not believe they could cut the enemy wire or sufficiently soften the enemy with less, a view in which he had the support of Brich, the chief gunner.

Now, General Sir James Marshall-Cornwall:

> Rawlinson was in favour of a short, intense bombardment, in order to effect surprise, and of launching the infantry assault before dawn, so as to cross No Man's Land under cover of darkness. The French however, being more liberally endowed with ammunition, insisted on the bombardment being prolonged over several days, followed by a daylight attack. Haig felt that he must conform to Joffre's wishes in both matters.

It is necessary to turn to Rawlinson's original appreciation, forwarded to Haig's headquarters on 3 April 1916, for an explanation of this apparent discrepancy. In that appreciation, Rawlinson outlined two possibilities for the artillery bombardment: 'an intense bombardment of some 5-6 hours duration with every available gun and howitzer immediately prior to the assault. (b) a longer, more methodical, but less intense bombardment of 48-72 hours duration'.

Rawlinson explained both the advantages and disadvantages for each course, but favoured the longer bombardment, as it would 'fit in best with the general plan selected, and I would therefore propose to have 50-60 hours bombardment previous to the assault'.

Haig disagreed, and his headquarters criticised Rawlinson's artillery plan thus:

> ... the possibility of surprising the enemy and the effect on his 'morale' both seem likely to be greater as a result of the comparatively short intensive bombardment immediately preceding the assault than if the bombardment is spread over a longer period. Your further consideration to this question is therefore desirable.

Rawlinson gave the matter his 'further consideration', and replied that the French were contemplating a long bombardment, as well they could, given their supplies of both guns and ammunition: '... it seems to me that our action ... must be to a certain extent, dependent upon theirs'. But Rawlinson was also worried about the inability of a short bombardment to cut the German wire.

> Effective wire-cutting cannot be carried out in five or six hours, nor can we carry it out at the same time as the bombardment of heavy howitzers, or the destruction of the enemy's trenches and strong points, on account of the dust and smoke, which will prevent any possibility of accurate observation.

Even so, Rawlinson was not convinced at this stage. The length of the bombardment would depend on several factors: the action of the French; the amount of ammunition available when offensive operations began; the length of time that the gun detachments could work without breaking down.

Haig's interest in the detail of Rawlinson's plan might seem odd today, nearly seven decades and another world war later. But it must be remembered that the techniques of staff work, the detail of commanding such huge armies and the responsibilities of commanders at each level was by no means clearly defined in 1916. Finally, the nature of the artillery bombardment was settled in a letter from Haig's headquarters on 16 May 1916, by Rawlinson. 'As regards artillery bombardment, it should be of the nature of a methodical bombardment and be continued until the officers commanding the attacking units are satisfied that the obstacles to their advance have been adequately destroyed.'

What is 'adequate' destruction? The ambiguity of such an order was to have important consequences later. But before we leave this particular document it is important to look at what it says about Rawlinson's objectives: '... the Commander-in-Chief desires that the Serre-Miramont spur; Pozières, Contalmaison, and Montauban be the objectives to be attained during the first day's operations. . .'

'. . . objectives to be attained during the first day's operations.' These words still have a ring of sad futility.

Rawlinson has been criticised: Farrar-Hockley considered he was 'an expert at laying bets on and off any project for which he was responsible — in covering himself against failure'; Martin Middlebrook, in his analysis of the Somme commanders, thought him rigid and slow to react to changing circumstances. Yet an analysis of his plans reveals Rawlinson in a more reasonable light. His concern about the artillery shortages and inability to cut the German wire proved well-founded.* When Haig criticised Rawlinson's original plan as lacking strategic purpose, the British Commander-in-Chief was scarcely being fair to his subordinate army commander. It was not Rawlinson's task to produce a plan of strategic purpose; as the army commander he was concerned with the tactics of planning and fighting the battles. By the end of April, however, Rawlinson had been persuaded to his commander's view and noted in his diary:

> I am quite clear in my mind now, about the plan. The bombardment is to be deliberate, four or five days, according to ammunition supply. The attack is to go for the big thing. I still think we would do better to proceed by shorter steps; but I have told DH I will carry out his plan with as much enthusiasm as if it were my own.

But was it, in fact, D.H.'s plan? It must be remembered that the Somme offensive was a joint operation, with the French on the right, largely south of the River Somme itself, and the British on the left. Joffre's original plans were to use 39 French divisions in the assault, but the constant demands of Verdun meant that this figure had to be reduced. By 24 May Haig was noting:

> General des Varrières brought me a letter from General Joffre in which the latter stated that owing to the hard fighting at Verdun he had not the number of divisions available for a combined attack which he had hoped. The minimum number would be 22, or possibly 26, depending on the fighting at Verdun. Des Vallières also stated that owing to the great losses of the French at Verdun, which would soon reach 200,000 General Joffre was of opinion that the offensive cannot be delayed beyond the beginning of July.

Two days later, Joffre arrived at Haig's headquarters to explain the general situation and reinforce the concern about French casualties at

---

*It was not until later in the war, with the invention of the instantaneous graze fuse, that wire could be cut effectively with high explosive shells. The results of the uncut wire will be described later.

Verdun. Joffre told Haig that his army had supported the entire weight of the German attacks for three months. If this went on, the French army would be ruined. Joffre wanted the British offensive to begin on 1 July. Haig replied that he would like to indicate the state of preparedness of the British army on certain dates and compare its condition.

> I took 1st and 15th July, and 1st and 15th August. The moment I mentioned August 15th, Joffre at once got very excited and shouted that 'The French Army would cease to exist if we did nothing till then'. The rest of us looked on at this burst of excitement, and then I pointed out that, in spite of the 15th August being the most favourable date for the British army to take action, yet, in view of what he had said about the unfortunate condition of the French army, I was prepared to commence operations on 1st July or thereabouts. This calmed the old man.

With that agreement, the party trooped into lunch. Later Haig noted that:

> ... Joffre had enjoyed himself so much that it was 2.20 p.m. before he went. So the meeting was a great success and the French all went away thoroughly delighted at the way I had met their proposals, and also with my entertainment of them. They are, indeed, difficult Allies to deal with! But there is no doubt that the nearest way to the hearts of many of them, including that of the 'Generalissimo', is down their throats, and some 1840 brandy had a surprisingly soothing effect on both him and Castelnau!

The old brandy might have done the trick, but if Haig was looking at methods to sooth his French allies, his agreement to their proposals probably worked better than his postprandial liquor. First Haig had agreed to the Somme area for the joint offensive; now, he was agreeing to the French proposals for the date, despite his own misgivings about the state of training of his armies: 'a collection of divisions untrained for the field', in his words.

And yet Haig had serious reservations about Joffre's abilities as a tactician. On 7 April, Joffre had visited Haig's headquarters to discuss the plans in preparation. Haig thought there were three main points to settle: the objective, the dividing line between the two forces and the timing of the attacks.

> I explained my views but Joffre did not seem capable of seeing beyond the left of the French army (which the French propose should be at Maricourt), or, indeed, of realising the effect of the shape of the ground

on the operations proposed. He said that I must attack northwards to take Montauban Ridge, while the French troops attacked eastwards from Maricourt. I at once pointed to the heights away to the north-east of Maricourt, and showed that his proposed movement was impossible until the aforesaid heights were either in our possession or closely attacked from the west.

The old man saw, I think, that he was talking about details which he did not really understand, whereas I had been studying this particular problem since last January and both knew the map and had reconnoitred the ground. The conclusion I arrived at was that Joffre was talking about a tactical operation which he did not understand, and that it was a waste of my time to continue with him. So I took him off to tea. I gather now that he signs everything which is put in front of him now and is really past his work, if, indeed, he ever knew anything practical about tactics as distinct from strategy. Joffre was an engineer.

Haig's dismissive remarks about Joffre's tactical abilities and experience cannot be interpreted in terms solely of his apparent dislike for the French or his sense of superiority as a cavalry officer over an officer of engineers. Within his own army, also, Joffre had his critics, most prominently Ferdinand Foch.

A deep thinker and the French Army's leading intellectual, Foch also has claims to being an 'educated soldier'. His approach to war, a curious yet effective combination of tactics and metaphysics, derived from both his long periods as an instructor at the French war college or *Ecole Superieure de la Guerre* and his early education by the Jesuits. Foch broke his studies to serve briefly as an infantry private in late 1870, but the following year returned to his books. In October 1873, Foch was commissioned as an artillery officer* but quickly won notice as an instructor and a member of the general staff.

Foch was an instructor at the war college between 1885 and 1901 and its commandant between 1908 and 1912. He commanded the French Ninth Army at the battle of the Marne and the Northern Army Group in Flanders and Artois from October 1914 to the end of the Somme fighting in November 1916. But it was during his periods at the war college that Foch's influence on the French Army was greatest. His education by the Jesuits had developed an admirable flexibility which Foch brought to his military studies. He had little faith with the post-Clausewitz views of the German Army theorists who maintained

---

*It seems curious that, in this overwhelmingly infantry war, the leading generals were from other corps — Haig was a cavalry officer, Joffre an engineer, Foch a gunner. Only Rawlinson had the experience of an infantry soldier and his ability to apply that experience was limited by his personality and his intellect.

that war could be reduced to timetables and planning. Foch argued the need to improvise, to adapt and to seize the initiative without waiting for orders from above.

The Jesuits had given him an appreciation of metaphysics, which he brought to his teaching of tactics. But there was always a solid tactical frame behind the abstract metaphysical facade. Grandmaison, a devoted pupil of Foch, had adopted the metaphysics but ignored the tactics; the result was faith without foundation.

Foch had come to believe that massed assaults on well prepared German defensive positions was military madness. He realised the deficiencies in training and experience in the British army and was opposed to the Somme offensives in 1916. He was fiercely criticised when he raised that opposition at a conference on 31 May. Noted Haig: 'Foch came in for a reprimand from M. Briand because he had stated to the politicians that he was against the offensive this year. His excuses seemed very lame, he ate humble pie and I thought he looked untrustworthy and a schemer'. Foch's experiences earlier in the war, particularly his attacks on Vimy Ridge and the continued fighting at Verdun, made him wary of the *assaut brutal*. As well, the Somme offensive proposed to attack the German lines at the very apex of the salient — its strongest point — rather than on the more vulnerable flanks. Like Rawlinson, Foch believed that the better approach was the phased, step-by-step methodical attack, moving the artillery up after each phase to support the next. Joffre disagreed with Foch; Haig agreed with Joffre.

Planning for the offensive was beset by political as well as military difficulties. Even after the extent of the German offensive at Verdun was apparent, Haig had difficulty in extracting wholehearted support from his government for the British offensive in support. As we have seen, it was mid-April before Haig was able to obtain from both Kitchener and Robertson an unequivocal approval to undertake the Somme offensive. As well, the grave manpower shortages which had reduced the British strength in France continued well into 1916. While thousands of untrained Kitchener volunteers waited anxiously in Britain for their posting orders across the channel, battalions, brigades and whole divisions in France were under strength. In mid-June 1916, for example, the British army in France was more than 40,000 men below its war establishment figure, the equivalent to two divisions.

Over the months of May and June the plans for the attack crystallised amid political and military crises afflicting the French. In brief, the French were to attack on a front of 20 kilometres, from Maricourt (about 2,000 metres north of the Somme) to Chaulnes. The original 39 divisions dwindled to 11, with 6 divisions in the initial assault and 5 in reserve.

The main burden of the attack would fall to the British, and to Rawlinson's Fourth Army. On a front of 24 kilometres, from Maricourt in the south to Hebuterne in the north, 11 divisions would begin the assault with 5 in reserve. To the north, General Allenby's Third Army would launch a subsidiary attack with 2 divisions on a front of 6 kilometres. The objective was a salient in the German line at Gommecourt. Thus the British would be attacking a front of 30 kilometres with 18 divisions while the French were attacking on a front of 20 kilometres with 11 divisions. In terms of frontages and troops to task, the proportions were roughly equivalent. The French, however, were handsomely equipped with supporting artillery: 787 field and 617 heavy guns, compared with the British 1,010 field and 483 heavies. But would the artillery conquer, allowing the infantry to occupy?

4

'All the Way to Pozières'

> When you go over the top, you can slope arms, light up your pipes and
> cigarettes, and march all the way to Pozières before meeting any live
> Germans.
> *Brig.-Gen. H. Gordon to troops of the Eighth Battalion, the King's Own*
> *Yorkshire Light Infantry, shortly before the 1 July offensive.*

U p and down the line, Brig.-Gen. Gordon's jaunty optimism was
being repeated: by other brigade commanders to their battalion
commanders; by battalion commanders to their company and
platoon commanders; by platoon commanders to their corporals and
soldiers. Those officers with misgivings about their attack plans were
in a minority, and they kept their doubts to themselves. This was to be
'the big push'; this was why the Kitchener Hundred Thousands had
joined. And, as John Keegan has pointed out, Rawlinson's Fourth Army
in those closing days of June was a trusting army.

> It believed in the reassurances proffered by the staff who, to be fair,
> believed them also. It believed in the superiority of its own equipment
> over the Germans. It believed in their dedication and fearlessness of its
> battalion officers — and was right to believe so. But it believed above all
> in itself.

Such self-assurance is evident from the surviving letters and diaries,
and from the survivors' accounts. And Rawlinson's Fourth Army also
derived no small measure of its confidence from its commander. Despite
the misgivings he confided to his diary, it was overwhelmingly Rawlinson's plan. He had resisted Haig's suggestion to shorten the artillery
bombardment and thus achieve greater surprise; he had resisted Haig's
suggestion that the advance of the infantry should be by small detachments. 'The advance of isolated detachments', declared some now anonymous staff officer at Rawlinson's headquarters, 'should be avoided.
They lead to the loss of the boldest and the best without result. The

enemy can concentrate upon these detachments. Advance should be uniform'.

It was thought that these tactics — advance in small detachments, or what was familiar in the later war as 'fire and movement' — would be too complex for the new soldiers of Kitchener's armies. Instead, the divisions were to attack with a precision that, more properly, belonged on a parade ground. In the army parlance, each division would have usually 'two brigades up', that is, two brigades in the leading waves and one in reserve. In turn, each brigade would, depending on the ground to its front, have two battalions up, one in reserve and one in support. For the soldiers, it meant that in every battalion, about one thousand men, each carrying about 22 kilograms on their backs, would climb out of their trenches, extend in four lines, a company in each line, about two or three metres between lines and advance across No Man's Land to the German trenches. To do so they would have to pass through gaps in their own barbed wire and through gaps created — so they hoped — by the British artillery in the German wire. Once across No Man's Land, the leading waves were expected to jump into the German trenches and kill any surviving German defenders. These, in essence, were the tasks facing the private soldiers of the infantry. If they failed, all the careful planning, all the confident predictions, all the brave ideas for exploitation would come to nought.

What were the obstacles to the British infantry? We have already noted, from Haig's own observations, the extent of the German strong-points, both reinforced villages and constructed redoubts. As well, we have Haig's words to describe the siting of the machine guns in those redoubts. The Germans had also constructed vast banks of barbed wire, 40 and 50 metres deep in parts, a seemingly impenetrable barrier to infantry soldiers. No wire entanglement, however stoutly constructed, is absolutely impenetrable to infantry. It does, however, slow down an infantry assault, channel the assaulting troops into the killing grounds of the machine guns and allow the defenders time to select targets on the ground of their own choice.

In mid-1916 the British relied upon light artillery to cut lanes through the German wire. Gunners would sweep the banks of barbed wire with shrapnel shell from 18-pounder field guns. If, however, the fuse in the shrapnel shell was set too short, the shell would burst in the air, doing little or no damage to the wire. If it was set too long, the shell would penetrate the wire, bury itself in the earth and explode harmlessly. To cut wire with such methods required skill and precision on the part of the gunners and reliable ammunition for the guns. Sadly, all qualities were in relatively short supply in June 1916.

Not that the artillery plan was scanty or ill prepared; on the contrary, it was detailed and elaborate. First, the German trenches were to be subjected to a week-long bombardment, concentrating not only on the forward positions, but also the communication trenches to prevent food, water and ammunition being brought forward.

Then, to follow was the barrage: literally a curtain of fire behind which the advancing infantry could shelter until, at the precise moment in time and space, the barrage would lift and the assaulting troops would be on the defenders before the latter could appear. At least, that was the theory. The lack of communications between infantry and artillery meant that such planning had necessarily to be rigid; the artillery fire could not be delayed or advanced to conform with the progress of the artillery.

As well, the barrage presented other problems. Certainly the range of the British weapons was sufficient to reach the forward German trenches. After allowing for safety factors, the frequent inability of the artillery observation officers to see where their shots were falling and the need for them not to become involved with the leading assault waves, the range of the British field artillery was very much reduced. Effectively, it was not much more than about 4,000 metres. And, on much of the Somme front, this distance was less than the distance to the German second lines.

Thus the barrage was effectively limited to the first lines; the second lines would have to have been taken out by the preliminary bombardment of the heavier guns.

Haig, the 'educated soldier', objected to aspects of Rawlinson's planning but in matters of infantry tactics the cavalry general deferred to the infantry general. Both had serious reservations about the standards of training in the Fourth Army; both had unquestioning confidence in the ability of the British artillery to devastate the German defences so that 'nothing could exist at the conclusion of the bombardment in the areas covered by it'. And throughout the planning Haig stressed the importance of the British attack maintaining its momentum: 'the assaulting columns must go right through above ground to "the objective" in successive waves or lines . . . From the moment when the first line of assaulting troops leaves our front trenches, a continuous forward flow must be maintained . . .' These factors — the confidence in the artillery, the obsession with maintaining momentum along the line — offer some explanation for Rawlinson's confidence and Haig's sanguinity.

Yet a tragic inevitability surrounds the first day of the Somme offensive. It has drawn the attention of military and social historians almost to the point of obsession. Accounts of the Somme fighting invariably concentrate on the first day, and often treat cursorily the months which followed. Claims that 'The Battle of the Somme was lost by three minutes' have passed into military folklore, without much attempt at either explanation or elucidation. The obsession is however, understandable: the casualties, the scale of the fighting, the small gains are at once fascinating and horrifying, seductive and repulsive.

The story has been told many times before;* its detail need not be repeated here, except to give a brief outline of what happened and look rather more closely at the sector of the front which was to become later that month the responsibility of the Australians.

1 July was a bright, cloudless, almost perfect summer's day. At 7.30 that morning, the artillery lifted from the German forward trenches and, after slight pauses by the perspiring, deafened gunners, switched to second and support lines. At that moment, the synchronised watches of the platoon commanders along the front were checked, the signals were given and the infantry assault began. Some have seen this part of the battle as a race — a contest between the British infantry to get out of their trenches, across No Man's Land and into the German trenches before the defenders could come up from their dugouts deep in the Picardy soil. If so, it was a race with fatal handicaps. In some sectors, the two trench lines were as close as 50 metres apart. In other sectors as much as 750 metres separated the two lines. But the success of the infantry attack depended not only on the resourcefulness, the dash, the skill and the bravery of the assaulting troops; it depended also on how well the gunners had done their job.

We have already seen Haig's thoughts on Rawlinson's artillery plan: 'a methodical bombardment . . . continued until the officers commanding the attacking units are satisfied that the obstacles to their advance have been adequately destroyed'. Yet among the troops in the trenches during those last days of June, considerable doubts existed as to whether the wire had been 'adequately destroyed'. For the infantry, it was relatively simple, although dangerous, to check the extent of the destruction. Each night fighting patrols would push out into No Man's Land, checking the wire in their front, estimating the damage caused by that day's bombardment. The reports of those patrols disconcerted some commanding officers: uncut wire, singing and laughing Germans deep in the dugouts. Yet while the many individual regimental officers had doubts about the attack, few expressed them. They were mindful of Rawlinson's orders in May: 'It must be remembered that all criticism by subordinates of their superiors, and of orders received from superior authority, will in the end recoil on the heads of the critics and undermine their authority with those below them'. This reluctance of regi-

---

*Easily the best account of this day's fighting is Martin Middlebrook's masterly reconstruction, *The First Day of the Somme* (London, 1971).

mental officers to pass on information about uncut wire to their higher formations must form part of the explanation for the sanguine confidence of both Haig and Rawlinson before the attack.

Haig noted in his diary on 30 June: 'The wire has never been so well cut, nor the artillery preparation so thorough'. On that same night, Rawlinson made some notes — 'noteworthy facts' as he termed them — about his coming attack. 'The artillery work during the bombardment, and the wire-cutting, has been well done except in the VIII Corps, which is somewhat behindhand'. VIII Corps was commanded by Lt.-Gen. Sir Aylmer Hunter-Weston (Hunter-Bunter to his soldiers) about whom Haig also had doubts. 'The only doubt I have is regarding VIII Corps (Hunter-Weston) which has had no experience in fighting in France and has not carried out one successful raid.' Haig's first reason, 'no experience for fighting in France' is simply more evidence of his prejudice against any unit or formation which had taken part in the fighting at Gallipoli.* His second reservation, 'not carried out one successful raid' is rather more pertinent. As Farrar-Hockley remarked with some acerbity: 'It must be regretted that the Commander-in-Chief had not made searching enquiries into the reason for the failure of "Hunter-Bunter's" command'.

Typical of the Rawlinson confidence was his optimistic listing of the objectives for the first day of the battle. 'To seize and consolidate a position on the Pozières Ridge extending from the vicinity of the River Ancre, so as to secure good observation over the ground to the eastward of that ridge.' It made military sense; Pozières Ridge was vital to the successful offensive; whoever held the ridge dominated the Somme uplands. Its capture was entrusted to III Corps, under the command of Lt.-Gen. Sir William Pulteney. Three divisions comprised this Corps, the 34th, the 8th and the 19th, each consisting of battalions of some of the oldest county regiments in the British army. The industrial north of England contributed heavily to these battalions, as did the Midlands and the Border districts. There were no smart guards or rifle regiments; many typified the jibe still current in the British army that the smartness of a regiment diminishes with the distance of its headquarters from London. Pulteney had one old regular division and two formed from Kitchener's New Army volunteers. But many of the soldiers serving in the regular division were still recent additions to the British army which had virtually ceased to exist, at least in its pre-war form, by the end of 1914.

---

*VIII Corps was indeed, a veteran of the Gallipoli fighting but Hunter-Bunter had few of the veterans under his command. His corps had been reconstituted and was comprised of very inexperienced troops with no experience of fighting anywhere.

Pulteney had probably the most difficult task of all the British Corps commanders. In simple terms, III Corps was to assault the German trenches straight up the Roman Road, a division on each side of the road. On the right, the 34th Division was ordered to capture the German defences on the Fricourt spur and astride Sausage Valley as far as La Boiselle.

Then it was to advance to a line drawn between the villages of Contalmaison and Pozières, halting about 800 metres short of the German second position. To its left, the 8th Division was to capture the defences north of the road, including the entire Ovillers spur and the village of that name. Then, it was to advance to a line between Pozières village and Mouquet Farm. As the British official historian remarked: 'The two assaulting divisions had thus to capture two fortified villages and six lines of trenches, and to advance into the German position to a depth of roughly two miles on a frontage of four thousand yards — a formidable task'. Formidable seems to be an understatement.

The Germans had used the ground cleverly. Pozières Ridge itself ran roughly north-west south-east, and from this ridge ran three spurs roughly south-west north-east. The centre spur, named La Boiselle from the village, was bisected along its length by the Albert-Bapaume Road. To the north, on the British left of the road, was the Ovillers spur; to the south, on the British right of the road, was the long Fricourt spur. Between these spurs were two re-entrants or depressions, known locally as Sausage and Mash. The soldiers believed that the Sausage re-entrant, south of the road, derived its name from an observation balloon tethered in the valley floor; the similar depression north of the road was inevitably Mash as a result. Neither re-entrant — valley is too grand a noun — was more than 1,000 metres wide. They were bare, and open, and the topsoil had almost disappeared to reveal the chalk below. From their positions on the ridge above, the Germans could see clearly into the depressions and just to aid this observation, movement of troops, vehicles and horses left a chalky, dusty signature in the air.

The Germans had sited their trenches and machine guns down the spurs to cover any movement up the depression. Indeed, the depressions would naturally channel assaulting troops into a narrow funnel, in which the German machine guns and riflemen could select targets almost at their leisure. As well, the attackers had to contend with the Thiepval spur, to the north, which posed an almost insurmountable threat to the left flank.

Let us follow the misfortunes of the 70th Brigade, whose commander, Brig.-Gen. Gordon, so confidently predicted that the assault would be a gentle stroll with rifles sloped and pipes lit. Gordon's 70th Brigade was on the left of the left hand division. It had to advance up the southern slope of Nab Valley, which ran roughly parallel to Mash, and immediately to the north. From Nab Valley, the brigade had to attack that part of the Ovillers spur north of the fortified village and then across almost level upland to the German position north of Pozières with the left of the brigade on Mouquet Farm itself. Then, a brigade consisted of four battalions. Gordon had two battalions of the York and Lancaster Regiment, which, despite its name, recruited only in south Yorkshire, a battalion of the Sherwood Foresters (as the Derbyshire Regiment was universally known), and a battalion of the KOYLIs or King's Own Yorkshire Light Infantry.

The task of the initial assault fell to the KOYLIs and the 8th Battalion of the York and Lancaster Regiment. At first, the assault went well; the German defenders on their left flank being diverted by an attack further north.

The first waves managed to get across the German first line and trenches and into the second line, but these successes, limited as they were, could not be exploited. By the time the British third and fourth waves were crossing No Man's Land, the attention of the German defenders turned to them; machine guns sited on the Thiepval spur took them from a flank. For the attackers, there was nowhere to go and nowhere to hide.

J.F.C. Fuller described the machine gun as the 'concentrated essence of infantry'. The memorial to the British Machine Gun Corps at Hyde Park Corner in London invokes the Book of Samuel to describe the killing power of this weapon: 'Saul hath slain thousands, but David his tens of thousands'. Because of the varying trajectory of the rounds fired from a machine gun, the bullets do not strike the ground at an identical point. Some fall short, others long. The elliptical area covered by this fall of shot is called the gun's 'beaten zone'. It is precisely this characteristic that requires the gun to be sited to a flank or, to use the military expression, in 'enfilade'. Thus sited, a machine gun can pick up a line of assaulting troops and knock the entire line over like so many skittles, or like a scythe cutting wheat.

The official historian described what happened to the 9th Battalion of the York and Lancaster Regiment, in support of the leading battalions.

> The 9/York & Lancaster, following the leading battalions, tried to get forward to support them; but the machine gun fire from the Thiepval spur, which enfiladed the advance at a range of six hundred to eight hundred yards, now greatly increased. The battalion lost 50 per cent of its strength almost at once, and very few men reached the German front trench.

Faced with such intense fire from a flank, there was simply nothing that the York and Lancaster junior officers could do. They had no means of communicating with their artillery to suppress the fire; no weapons with which to engage the German machine gunners or at least to keep their heads down; no troops to spare to take out the machine positions.

Still, Gordon pressed on with his attack. The reserve battalion, the 11/Sherwood Foresters, was moving up automatically. Should it, too, be committed to what seemed certain destruction? Gordon pondered the decision briefly. On his flanks, the neighbouring brigades seemed to be doing well. The brigade commander did not order the Sherwood Foresters to halt. As they moved up, these troops stepped over the bodies of the Yorks and Lancasters who had preceded them. They formed up and jumped across the trench, only to be immediately shot down by the same machine gunners. Few of the Sherwood Foresters even reached the German wire. By late morning on 1 July, the handful of survivors of the early waves were completely cut off from support or relief. So fierce was the machine gun fire sweeping the spur that it was impossible for runners to make their way forward or back.

The 70th Brigade lost more than any of the other three brigades in the division and was among the heaviest losses for the day. Two of the battalion commanders were killed and the other two wounded. Although an assault late in the afternoon of the first day was considered, it was quickly abandoned. There were simply no troops left.

South of the Albert-Bapaume road, the 34th Division under the command of Maj.-Gen. E.C. Ingouville-Williams — Inky Bill to his soldiers — could not attack its objectives frontally. The German trenches at La Boiselle jutted towards the British lines in a salient; the difficulty of attacking a salient at its strongest point, its apex, was appreciated at corps and divisional level, if not always at army and national command level. Ingouville-Williams planned to assault with his 12 infantry battalions in the first assault, leaving nothing in reserve. The assault troops were to pass either side of the German trenches, dealing with the remaining defenders by sending in a platoon-sized bombing party. Serious doubts were raised by the regimental and staff officers of the 34th Division. If the trenches forming the German salient had not been destroyed, then the remaining defenders could well hold up the entire divisional advance. But again, the optimism in the effect of the artillery bombardment prevailed.

The day before the attack, the 34th Division put out working parties to clear a passage for the assaulting troops through the wire in front of the German positions. German defenders, so confidently expected by the army staff to be dead, fired on these working parties. Hurriedly, the division staff rewrote fire plans so that once the massive bombardment lifted the next morning, trench mortars would continue to fire on the village of La Boiselle.

On 1 July 1916, the 34th Division had been in existence for only slightly more than a year; its soldiers had been in the British army for slightly less than a year. They were drawn overwhelmingly from the north of England, raised (in the official historian's words) by 'local effort'. Nothing in the Australian experience of war is quite so poignant, quite so tragic, as the 'local efforts' in raising battalions for Kitchener's New Army. In the days of poor transport and rudimentary communications, whole villages would volunteer their young men who often ended up in the same platoon of the same company. In the industrial cities of the north, clerks and artisans volunteered, forming units such as the Manchester Pals, the Barnsley Pals or the Grimsby Chums, serving as the 10th Lincolns in Inky-Bill's 101st Brigade. Other battalions drew heavily from the Scottish and Irish populations in northern England. The Northumberland Fusiliers, for example had eight infantry battalions and one pioneer battalion in the 34th Division. Half of the infantry battalions were proud to proclaim themselves as Tyneside Scottish; the other half equally proud to proclaim themselves Tyneside Irish. No Irish or Scots regiment ever surpassed the feelings of national pride these transplanted Celts assumed for themselves.

At precisely 7.30 in the morning of 1 July, virtually the entire infantry strength of the 34th Division climbed out of their trenches and saps and went, in the phrase of the day, 'over the top'.

The two lines of battalions had as their objective the German first line of four trenches. The last trench, some 2,000 metres from the British jumping off points, was timed to take a precise 48 minutes. The second objective was the German intermediate line, or *KaiserGraben*, between the villages of Contalmaison and Pozières. This line was timed to be taken 40 minutes later, at 8.58 a.m. Then, the third line of battalions was to pass through the two assaulting brigades, capture the village of Contalmaison and advance to the third and last objective. This was to be a line between Contalmaison and Pozières. Once here, the troops were to dig in and prepare to assault the German second position, another 800 metres beyond.

So much for the plans — plans which were no more or less optimistic than any other division plan produced for that day. Within ten minutes of leaving their trenches, about 80 per cent of the troops in the forward battalions were dead or wounded. As the British artillery barrage lifted, the German machine gunners appeared from their safe dugouts. Many of the machine guns were behind the German front lines, extremely well sited and well hidden. In the words of the British official historian:

There was no surprise. The Germans were ready. Warned by the order which had been overheard,* and well drilled at manning the parapet, they came up out of their deep dugouts as if by magic directly the barrage moved, and established a rough firing line before the British had got across No Man's Land.

The 34th Division attack failed, with losses of more than 6,000. The reinforced villages of Ovillers and La Boiselle, objectives for the assault even before the British troops reached anywhere near Pozières, were still in German hands.

From the German positions, the British attacks seemed like terrible folly. One account reveals how the defenders waited for the bombardment to lift, knowing all too well that it signalled an infantry attack. It was vital, they knew, not to waste a second taking up their positions to meet the infantry in the open.

At 7.30 a.m. the hurricane of shells ceased as suddenly as it had begun. Our men at once clambered up the steep shafts leading from the dugouts to daylight or ran singly or in groups to the nearest shell craters. The machine guns were pulled out of the dugouts and hurriedly placed in position, their crews dragging the heavy ammunition boxes up the steps and out to the guns. A rough firing line was thus rapidly established. As soon as the men were in position, a series of extended lines of infantry were seen moving forward from the British trenches. The first line appeared to continue without end to right and left. It was quickly followed by a second line, then a third and fourth. They came on at a steady pace as if expecting to find nothing alive in our front trenches.

'nothing alive in our front trenches'. Those words echo the sanguinity of Haig and Rawlinson; they reinforce the fears of some British battalion commanders. Artillery conquers; infantry occupies. On the Somme uplands, however, the artillery did not conquer. Deep in their dugouts and tunnels the Germans endured the bombardments virtually unscathed. The attack of the 70th Brigade was so typical of so many attacks on that first day. Given the strength of the German defences, the Germans' ability to withstand the bombardment, their superb use of ground and employment of their weapons, the attacking British hardly stood a chance. Yet the plight of the attackers only moved many of the German defenders to remark and marvel at the courage of the British Tommy.

---

*At 2.45 a.m. on the day of the assault the Germans overheard a British order which left no doubts as to the day's activities.

One German eye-witness wrote:

> The British soldier has no lack of courage, and once his hand is set to the plough he is not easily turned from his purpose. The extended lines, though badly shaken and with many gaps, now came on all the faster. Instead of a leisurely walk they covered the ground in short rushes at the double ... The shouting of orders and the shrill cheers as the British charged forward could be heard above the violent and intense fusillade of machine guns and rifles and the bursting bombs, and above the deep thunderings of the artillery and shell explosions. With all this were mingled the moans and groans of the wounded, the cries for help and the last screams of death. Again and again the extended lines of British infantry broke against the German defence like waves against a cliff, only to be beaten back. It was an amazing spectacle of unexampled gallantry, courage and bull-dog determination on both sides.

Although the German defenders admired the courage of the British, they had no illusions about the standard of training reached by Haig's army. The German official history notes:

> The training of the infantry was clearly behind that of German; the superficially trained British were particularly clumsy in movements of large masses. On the other hand, small bodies, such as machine gun crews, bombers, and trench-blockers and special patrols, thanks to their native independence of character, fought very well. The strong, usually young, and well armed British soldier followed his officers blindly, and the officers, active and personally brave, went ahead of their men in battle with great courage. But, owing to insufficient training, they were not skilful in action. They often failed to grasp the necessity for rapid, independent decision. They were in many cases unequal to dealing with sudden unexpected changes in the situation. Great attacks were carried out in thick, often irregular lines and with small columns following close behind them. To this must be mainly attributed the heavy losses of the British in their attacks, although they were certainly made with the most conspicuous courage.

For the British, for Rawlinson's proud Fourth Army, the first day of the battle of the Somme was an almost unmitigated disaster. The only British success was on the right of the line, next to the French where the XIII Corps gained and held both its objectives, admittedly at a cost of 6,000 casualties in two divisions. Elsewhere, the melancholy stories of Gordon's 70th Brigade were repeated, with only minor variations on a sad theme.

Nearly 60,000 British officers and men fell, dead or wounded, on that first day. And, as the British official historian remarked in this famous passage:

> For this disastrous loss of the finest manhood of the United Kingdom and Ireland there was only a small gain of ground to show, although certainly the greatest gain yet made by the British Expeditionary Force: an advance into the enemy's position some 3½ miles wide and averaging a mile in depth; beyond this, merely a few minor holdings; the total number of unwounded prisoners who reached the cages on 1st July, only amounted to 25 officers and 1,958 other ranks.

How could it have happened? How could the British army have suffered nearly 60,000 casualties on one day alone?* And, once the commanders realised the extent of the casualties, why did they not call a halt to the whole ghastly business?

Perhaps the last question is easiest to answer. We must begin with the Commander-in-Chief. Haig could not have simply stopped the offensive: Day 1 of the Somme was Day 132 of Verdun. Given the constraints imposed upon Haig by the burden of coalition war, the almost daily demands by Joffre, it is almost inconceivable that he could have halted the offensive after just one day. As well, it is clear from the war diaries and other records that Haig's GHQ had, at first, little idea just how disastrously the first day had gone. At all levels, up and down the scales of military hierarchy, the enormity of the first day's losses were obscured. Battalions were launched into offensives across ground where others had been annihilated only minutes before; commanders produced orders for subordinates that were incapable of being obeyed, because the subordinates and their troops had simply failed to exist. As we have seen, Brig.-Gen. Gordon had lost his entire brigade by noon of that first day. Late that afternoon he was pressed by his divisional commander to continue his attack. 'You seem to forget, sir, that there is now no 70th Brigade.'

This was a war fought with only the most rudimentary communications; once an assault had been launched; once some young lieutenant had blown his whistle, waved his revolver and clambered out of his trench at the head of his platoon, his commanders had virtually no methods of communicating with him, no way of telling him to push

---

*The totals were:

	Killed/Died of Wounds	Wounded	Missing	POW	Total
Officers	993	1,337	96	12	2,438
Other Ranks	18,247	23,156	2,056	573	55,032

on, to watch the gun on his flank, to halt, to cover someone else's movements. 'This is a platoon commander's war', Haig remarked.

It was not a remarkably original observation: all wars are platoon commanders' wars or even section commanders' wars; junior leaders are expected to command their men and, if necessary, show them how to die. In subsequent wars, platoon commanders have had the benefit of wireless communications. They have been able to call for assistance; to pass on information; to move their platoons covered by another's fire; even to extract their casualties. Once into No Man's Land, no such communications equipment existed in 1916. Units experimented with semaphore flags and signalling mirrors (which worked well enough on the North-West Front or in some other corner of the empire); others carried carrier pigeons; even, in some battalions of the Tyneside Irish, small pieces of paper that were to be scattered across the battlefield behind the advancing troops so the signallers could follow up and lay their wire. But for communications, units depended on runners: brave, resourceful soldiers who were to scurry across the battlefield like so many crabs, from shell hole to shell hole, clutching urgent messages scribbled out on the pages of the Field Message Notebook. The communications of the Fourth Army — indeed, all the armies of all the combatant nations — depended on the luck and the courage of these men.

Admittedly, communications in the rear, from No Man's Land back to Haig's château de Val-Vion, were better: telephone and telegraph, in parallel and through an elaborate network, linked GHQ to Army HQ, to the corps headquarters and down to divisional headquarters and so on. But all this was useless once the troops had begun the assault.

Haig noted in his diary on the night of 1 July the details of the first day's fighting, as he then knew them. His entries give no indication of the horrendous losses; in fact, apart from reservations about VII Corps, the entry is remarkably complacent. The following day he noted that 'casualties are estimated at over 40,000 to date. This cannot be considered severe in view of the numbers engaged, and the length of the front attacked. By nightfall, the situation is much more favourable than we started today'. Little wonder that, with observations such as that Haig has attracted criticism over the years.*

Still, we are left with the question: why did it happen? Here, the answers have been easily found. The criticism of the tactical plan has

---

*One recent and fascinating examination of Haig's personality, and its impact on him as a military commander is by Dr Norman Dixon in *On The Psychology of Military Incompetence* (London, 1976). It is not necessary to go into Dr Dixon's arguments, but his views provide a useful counterpoint to John Terraine's spirited defences.

been comprehensive over the intervening years, but it is useful here to recapitulate some of the arguments, as they will impinge on the discussion of tactics adopted by the Australian divisions later in the battle.

As we have already noted, the level of training of the British army was far from high. The British official historian remarked that 'what the officers and men of these (New) Armies had learnt at home was of the most elementary nature, much time being devoted to physical training and the cult of the "bomb and bayonet" '. Even in 1916 there were no training branches of the general staff to issue manuals of instruction, pamphlets or other publications. Moreover, there was no branch of the general staff concerned with producing doctrine for fighting this new and perplexing form of warfare. The commanders, the regimental and the staff officers were aware of these deficiencies. In May 1916 Rawlinson's headquarters issued its *Fourth Army Tactical Notes,* distributed down to captains and, in the words of the British official historian, 'accepted as the last word on the subject'. Implicit in these tactical notes is the assumption that the training of the Fourth Army left much to be desired.

> We must remember that owing to the large expansion of our Army and heavy casualties in experienced officers, the officers and troops generally do not now possess that military knowledge arising from a long and high state of training which enables them to act instinctively and promptly on sound lines in unexpected situations. They have become accustomed to deliberate action based on precise and detailed orders.

So, the tactics were designed to be as simple as possible. While the tactics adopted by Rawlinson's subordinate commanders on 1 July led, in very many cases, to the catastrophe, it was not the fault of the authors of the tactical notes.

These tactical notes represented one of the earlier attempts at reaching a doctrine for the use of massed infantry. So much of the early training had been devoted to subjects such as 'the spirit of the bayonet' or the inevitable drill and weapons lessons. Read today, the tactical notes still have a relevance. But, as the British army discovered to its cost on 1 July 1916, there is a world of difference between formulating and publishing doctrine and training the soldiers in terms of that doctrine.

Observers of the French battalions which attacked that day noted how the advance was carried out in small rushes, as one group of men moved it was covered by the sustained fire of another group. Here we have the essence of 'fire and movement', which was to become the standard infantry minor tactic of the later world war and to remain so today. 'Fire and movement' was thought to be too difficult for the Kitchener armies. Besides, it requires an allocation of light machine guns — in that time, the Lewis gun — so that a section of men is able to produce a burst of sustained fire to enable movement. These authors of the tactical notes had foreseen this requirement:

> Many instances have been brought to notice in which our infantry assault has been arrested by the fire of hostile machine guns, which have escaped the previous bombardment. Even if accurately located, it has been found very difficult to bring sufficiently accurate artillery fire to bear on them, and so knock them out.

In that passage, the authors unwittingly predicted the cause of so many failures on that first day. The artillery had failed to conquer either the defender's spirit or their machine guns. Once the assault was launched, the difficulties lay in co-ordinating the British artillery fire so that the assaulting troops could walk almost immediately behind a moving curtain of shells. So, the assaulting troops were left with large open spaces to cross, all the time being fired upon the flanks by carefully sited and cleverly concealed machine guns.

Those guns were capable of killing troops in the open, however quickly they might be moving. If the movement forward of those troops was temporarily halted for any reason, such as uncut and insufficiently cut wire, then the German machine gunners had an even easier task.

The attackers also had to contend with the German artillery which burst, with precise accuracy, in the open gap of No Man's Land. Artillery too, added to the confusion between commanders in the field and the staff officers; it prevented the adoption of previously made plans to meet new circumstances; it prevented the reinforcement of the few successes along the line.

The Wearing-out Battle: Continued

I was . . . anxious to know whether the French would attack Guillemont. At this, General Joffre exploded in a fit of rage. '*He* could not approve of it.' He '*ordered* me to attack Thiepval and Pozières'. . . I waited calmly till he had finished. His breast heaved and his face flushed! The truth is the poor man cannot argue, nor can he easily read a map.
Sir Douglas Haig, 3 July 1916.

Haig spent the night before the offensive, the Friday night, at his own headquarters where he received the first reports of the fighting on the Saturday morning. After lunch, he motored to Rawlinson's headquarters at Querrieu. That night, he noted in his diary the successes on the right of the line: 'we hold the Montauban-Mametz spur and the villages of those names'. West of Mametz, the enemy were still in Fricourt, a fact dutifully recorded by the Commander-in-Chief. Of the strong points in the centre of the assault, he wrote: 'Ovillers and Thiepval villages have held our troops up, but our men are in the Schwaben Redoubt which crowns the ridge north of the last named village'.

Haig reserved his most bitter remarks for Hunter-Weston's VIII Corps:

> North of the Ancre, the 8th Corps (Hunter-Weston) said they began well, but as the day progressed, their troops were forced back into the German front line, except two battalions which occupied Serre village, and were, it is said, cut off. I am inclined to believe from further reports, that few of the 8th Corps left their trenches.

The last remark indicates some of the animosity Haig had for Hunter-Weston, dating back a year when the latter commanded the 29th Division at Gallipoli. Haig had always opposed the Dardanelles operation, believing that it had deprived his command in France of much needed men and material. That opposition translated itself (as we shall see in a later chapter) to a fierce dislike for those who had participated in the Dardanelles campaign and who had, worse still, derived some measure of public acclaim for their participation. Certainly his remark that 'few of the 8th Corps left their trenches' was totally unjustified. Hunter-Weston's VIII Corps had attempted to attack probably the strongest sector of the German line, between the villages of Beaumont-Hamel and Serre. In doing so, it suffered more than 14,000 casualties including the almost complete destruction of the Newfoundland battalion. Farrar-Hockley remarked that it was extraordinary this 'mean comment was not subsequently excised by the author when the facts of the fighting on Redan and Hawthorn ridges, for Y Ravine and Beaumont Hamel became known. If "few of the 8th Corps left their trenches", how did they suffer 14,000 casualties?' Precisely.

Either Haig did not understand what had happened to Hunter-Weston's Corps or was not particularly inclined to find out. Two or three lines later, he remarked that the '8th Corps had achieved very little'. It achieved little because it met ferocious enfilade fire from German defenders who were not under attack themselves.

Yet, despite the horrendous losses, Haig had some slight opportunity to break through the German lines and exploit this success. The high ground of Montauban-Mametz belonged to the British, but nowhere, either in Haig's own diaries or the official war diaries for his head-quarters, is there any suggestion that this success might be exploited. Haig had at his disposal such a force that might well have managed this task: the Reserve Army under the command of Lt.-Gen. Sir Hubert Gough, whose orders were simple enough:

> [They] were to the effect that in the event of a decided success by the Fourth Army and a break of the German front I was to raid Bapaume, to prevent the arrival of reinforcements and the escape of the retreating enemy, to secure the high ground south of Bapaume, and to cover the deployment of the Fourth Army northwards on Arras.

Haig had planned for this eventuality with his usual meticulous attention to detail, as seen in an OAD 17, issued on 21 June. This detailed the supposed British numerical advantage and added:

> . . . prompt action taken to develop a success gained in the assault on the first objective assigned may give great results. If the first attack goes well every effort must be made to develop the success to the utmost by first opening a way for our cavalry and then as quickly as possible pushing the cavalry through to Bapaume and establish itself in good positions in that neighbourhood. The cavalry in GHQ Reserve (1st and 3rd Cavalry Divisions) under Lt.-Gen. Sir H. Gough, is placed at the disposal of the GOC Fourth Army for the above purpose, and should be disposed in

positions of readiness to take immediate advantage of a favourable situation.

These orders, clear in intent, specific in content, conflicted with Rawlinson's own concept of the operation. Rawlinson believed that he had been ordered to do too much. Despite his apparent loyalty to Haig he was convinced the orders for exploiting a breakthrough were overly optimistic; in his own orders to his equally (if not more) cautious corps commanders, Rawlinson stressed the importance of consolidating objectives already gained. In the Fourth Army Operation Order issued 14 June 1916, Rawlinson's thinking is clear:

> The Army commander wishes to impress on all commanders that the success of the operations as a whole largely depends on the consolidation of the definite objectives which have been allotted to each corps. Beyond these objectives, no serious advance is to be made until preparations have been completed for entering the next phase of the operation.

In effect, Rawlinson ignored Haig's orders for a quick exploitation. In Congreve's area of command, the opportunity existed for exploitation alongside the French, but the careful corps commander resisted and indeed, restrained his subordinate commanders. Rawlinson also ignored the eyewitness reports of the Royal Flying Corps which gave an accurate indication of how the battle was progressing and the relative successes achieved on the right compared with the failures on the left. The opportunities for capturing the German second line on the right passed, as did the opportunities for exploitation behind the fixed, prepared defences, opportunities that had been planned for; opportunities that needed to be taken quickly by a decisive commander with accurate, up-to-date information. In many ways, Haig had set the stage by making his own intentions clear.

Sadly, there existed a giant gap between intentions and realisations. Haig had planned for the breakthrough; indeed, he had gambled on it. Yet the means for achieving that breakthrough were simply not available to him. All along the front the British lacked the preponderance of heavy artillery necessary to obliterate the German defences. He forced upon Rawlinson a plan designed to take the German defences in one big bite, rather than in the series of phased, controlled, planned nibbles the Fourth Army commander had in mind. He agreed to the longer bombardment, partially as a necessary compromise because of the lack of artillery. But with the longer bombardment, Haig forfeited any possibility of surprise. Without this surprise, the breakthrough was unlikely.

Haig should have been aware that surprise would be lost by a long bombardment. The year before, during the battle of Neuve Chapelle, Sir John French was forced to use a short bombardment because of the shortage of shells. The Germans were surprised and their line was broken. Still, the British troops could not exploit; they hesitated, tentative about moving through the breach they had made in the defences. Quickly the Germans reinforced troops on the flanks of the gap, closed the breach and the opportunity was lost. That lesson also appeared to be lost on Haig; despite his initial reluctance, he agreed to Rawlinson's plans for the longer bombardment. But surprise can also be achieved by attacking at a time when the enemy leasts expects it. As we shall see, Haig persisted with the dawn attack during the first phase of the Somme battle — persisted with disastrous results.

Gough's Reserve Army was formed on 23 May 1916. Initially, it consisted only of a very small staff given the task of planning the attack. Hubert Gough, then only 44, was always considered by his contemporaries to be destined for the highest ranks. Like Haig, Gough was a cavalryman, an intelligent and charming Irishman who provoked extremes of reactions. Some thought him indifferent to the safety of his troops, even callous — in Farrar-Hockley's phrase: 'a butcher among generals'. Others considered him to be careful and considerate. He was one of the few British generals who ever deigned to visit frequently his troops in the trenches and thus, he was one of the few who ever had any real notion of the conditions endured by the soldiers under his command. Gough possessed a singularly confident view of his own abilities. Allied to this was a marked degree of moral courage. Before the war he took a leading part in the officers' mutiny at the Curragh, a mutiny which challenged the concept of duty held by many Irish-born officers of the British army. Had it not been for the war, Gough's career might well have ended in military oblivion.

In quickly preparing his Reserve Army for its task, Gough created many enemies. Sackings were commonplace as the young general ruthlessly culled out subordinate commanders he thought inadequate for the tasks ahead. 'Now that Gough has become an army commander, he seems quite drunk with power', wrote one officer. 'There have been more sackings this past week which the people here consider a disgrace. Yet the chief (Haig) can see no wrong in him.'

The fleeting opportunities to break through on the right of the line were quickly lost after 1 July. The slow moving and cautious Rawlinson cannot be blamed entirely. His two corps commanders in that sector,

Horne and Congreve, resisted the chances offered to them and indeed, at times, ordered their infantry to halt rather than push ahead. After the first day of the assault, Rawlinson concentrated on continual attacks in the sectors where the enemy had proved strongest and the line most impenetrable. Instead of exploiting the successes, he reinforced the failures.

Here again, we see the enormous problems posed by prosecuting a coalition war. Those problems, and the demands they made on Haig, are evident in the Commander-in-Chief's diary. 'The enemy has undoubtedly been severely shaken . . . Our correct course, therefore is to press him hard with the least possible delay . . . in any case, pressure must be maintained both to relieve Verdun and to assist the French on our right.' But how was this pressure to be maintained? The advance up the main axis of the attack, the Albert-Bapaume road, had been almost non-existent; the resulting losses had been huge. South of the road, the reinforced strong point that was formerly the village Fricourt, threatened the left flank of the successes already achieved.

On the Sunday after attending church, Haig had impressed upon Rawlinson the need to capture 'Fricourt and neighbouring villages, so as to reduce the numbers of our flanks, and then advance on the enemy's second line. I questioned him as to his views on an advance from Montauban and his right'. Then, noted Haig blandly, 'He did not seem to favour the scheme'. Haig insisted. Rawlinson was made to comply. The following day, 3 July, with the extent of the casualties on 1 July still not apparent at GHQ, Joffre and Foch arrived at Haig's headquarters. They had come, wrote Haig, 'to discuss future arrangements'. Haig's diaries are normally pedantic, almost detached. They betray little emotion — at least in their edited form — and give little indication of the Commander-in-Chief's own feelings. The diary entry for this date, is, however, quite different.

Joffre began by pointing out the importance of the British capturing Thiepval Hill. Haig demurred. Rawlinson's successes had been on the right near Montauban. In view of the 'demoralised nature of the enemy's troops in that area', Haig was considering pressing an attack on Longueval. But to do so successfully would require the co-operation of the French. Would the French attack the village of Guillemont?

'At this', wrote Haig, 'General Joffre exploded in a fit of rage. "*He could not approve of it*". He *ordered* me to attack Thiepval and Pozières. If I attacked Longueval, I would be beaten etc, etc.

'His breast heaved and his face flushed! The truth is that the poor man cannot argue, nor can he easily read a map.'* Patiently, calmly,

---

*The emphases are in the original.

carefully, Haig waited until Joffre had finished. On a specially prepared raised model of the ground, Haig pointed out the features and the difficulties inherent in Joffre's plans.

> I quietly explained what my position is relative to him as the 'generalissimo'. *I am solely responsible to the British Government for the action of the British Army*; and I had approved the plan, and must modify it to suit the changing situation as the fight progresses. I was most polite.

According to Haig, Joffre saw then he had made a mistake. The Frenchman tried cajolery. This was 'the English battle'; 'France expected great things from me'. Haig thanked him. 'I have only one object', the British general said: 'To beat Germany'. With that, Joffre seemed much mollified. The party went into the garden, where Joffre presented awards and kissed the recipients twice, 'a resounding smack on each cheek'. Joffre, thought Haig smugly, seemed ashamed of his outburst. 'Still, Joffre has his merits. I admire the old man's pluck under difficulties and am very fond of him. However, I have gained an advantage through keeping calm.'

Of all the recorded conferences in all modern wars, this must have been one of the strangest: Haig the patrician, taciturn and imperturbable Border Scot; Joffre the petit bourgeois, taciturn yet excitable provincial Frenchman; Haig, dubious about the Frenchman's most elementary military skill, patiently pointing out the features on a raised model; Joffre exploding and fuming; their respective staffs no doubt looking on with a kind of wry amusement. Considering the fighting and dying by the ordinary soldiers, however, this encounter was bizarre and sad.

Still, it achieved an important purpose. Haig's control over the British army was unquestioned from this point on. Although the senior commanders, French and British, often disagreed in the future, never again was there such a scene, never again did Joffre attempt to order Haig to follow a certain course of action.

It was, according to John Terraine, the British army's coming of age.

Haig's published diaries jump from 3 July to 22 July. The intervening days, however, saw more heavy fighting. More importantly, if the aim of the Somme assault was merely an attempt to diminish the pressure being experienced by the French at Verdun, those intervening days saw some success.

On 3 July, the same day that Haig and Joffre had their altercation at GHQ, the commander of the German *II Army*, General Fritz von Below, issued an order of the day. It contained no illusions about the importance of the fighting on the Somme to the German army: the decisive issue of the war depended upon the victory of the *II Army*.

> We must win this battle in spite of the enemy's temporary superiority in artillery and infantry. The important ground lost in certain places will be recaptured by our attack after the arrival of reinforcements. For the present, the important thing is to hold on to our present positions at any cost and to improve them by local counter-attack.

Von Below's determination had been reinforced the previous day from a visit by Falkenhayn and Tappen. Falkenhayn had told his subordinate that 'the first principle in position warfare must be to yield not one foot of ground; and if it be lost to retake it by immediate counter-attack, even to the use of the last man'. Apart from the failure of the offensive on the first day, this attitude of the Germans makes the Somme fighting very important. Conventional wisdom sees the Somme fighting only in terms of the Allied offensive. Equally, the determination of the Germans to launch costly counter-attacks, to force the British soldier 'to carve his way forward over heaps of corpses' in von Below's uncompromising terms, makes the Somme significant. This was indeed, the wearing-out fight; this was one reason why the German High Command ceased to publish casualty statistics in December 1916; this was what gave — and for the Australians was soon to give — the battle its horrible qualities.

Despite Haig's disparaging remarks about Joffre's inability to read a map, the Scot agreed with the Frenchman on one significant point: the importance of Thiepval and its supporting position at Pozières. Rightly, Haig rejected the idea of a frontal assault on the two objectives. Although the complete extent of the casualties was still unclear at the time of Haig and Joffre's unpleasant meeting, it was clear that continued assaults from the same direction were bound to fail.

On the evening of 1 July, Lt.-Gen. Sir Hubert Gough had taken command of the two left flanks corps, north of the Albert-Bapaume road. Whether it was Rawlinson's idea, or whether it derived from Gough himself, is not clear; the change of command however, was to have important consequences. Instructed by Rawlinson to 'push' the two northern corps along, Gough immediately set off to see both Hunter-Weston and Morland, commanders of the VIII and X Corps respectively. Gough quickly realised that neither corps had sufficient men left for an attack. He cancelled the offensive planned for the next morning,

POZIERES MILL. (RUINS)

Above
Panorama shot of the Somme battlefield, on the high ground of the Pozières-Thiepval ridge. The absence of cover and significant undulations in the terrain are clearly visible. These shots were taken in the summer of 1916. (Q48148 IWM)

Below
Australian troops of the 24th Battalion marching past the Australian Prime Minister, William Morris Hughes. This photograph was taken on 1 June 1916, near Croix du Bac, south of Armentières. The Australians were employed in this quiet sector when they first arrived in France. (Q614 IWM)

Above
Field Marshal Sir Douglas Haig (left, with walking stick) with General Sir Henry Rawlinson at 4th Army Headquarters at Querrieu in July 1916. (Q817 IWM)
Below
The King and Field Marshal Sir Douglas Haig at Beauquesne, 12 August 1916. (Q994 IWM)

The battlefield at Fromelles, showing No Man's Land from the Sugar-loaf salient. This photograph was taken two years after the battle, from the German viewpoint. It was across this open ground that 'Pompey' Elliott's brigade was virtually annihilated. (E4029 AWM)

Above
Part of the German front line at Fromelles, taken on the morning of 20 July 1916 after the attack had failed and the Germans had reoccupied their positions. In the foreground can be seen a number of bodies, mainly German, covered with greatcoats and blankets. (A1560 AWM)

Below
Germans reoccupying their second line at Fromelles after the Australians withdrew. This portion of the line was on the left of the Australian assault. In the centre foreground can be seen the body of one Australian who fell in this ill-fated and ill-planned attack. (A1562 AWM)

Bombardment of the German trenches at the battle of Fromelles. This photograph was taken from the Australian front line ten minutes before the attack
was due to begin. (H2107 AWM)

Above
A barn in the village of Pozières before the Somme battle. Two German officers take time out to pose for a photograph. (J216 AWM)
Below
The 12th Battalion on the way to the Somme. This photograph was taken at Naours on 12 July 1916 before the Australians had swapped their 'hats, khaki fur-felt' for the steel helmets. (EZ163 AWM)

The tower of Albert Cathedral and 'Fanny Durack'. Virtually every soldier remarked about the leaning village in his letters home. The headquarters of the 1st and 2nd Divisions were located not far from the buildings in the foreground. (E167 AWM)

The main street of Pozières, looking towards the Windmill-Bapaume, before the war (above) and on 28 August 1916 from the trench known as Centre Way (below). (G1534i EZ95 AWM)

a cancellation that was greeted with relief by the officers and men. 'These new orders', wrote one officer, 'released us from a nightmare. In spite of everything we had reported about our casualties and the chaos in the trenches, we had been told to go over [that is, to attack] again in exactly the same way next morning. Just as all hope of sanity had gone, someone had the sense to say "no" '.

Gough pondered the possibilities for offensives available to his depleted command. He appreciated the folly of assaulting well prepared positions, protected by belts of wire and fortified with steel and concrete. On 3 July Gough was not dismayed to find that his command had been detached from Rawlinson's Fourth Army.

From then on, Gough's Reserve Army, originally intended as a cavalry force designed to exploit gaps made by Rawlinson's infantry, was now merely another assault force. From the moment Gough took over planning for the infantry assaults, he rejected the wasteful and useless frontal attacks adopted by Rawlinson. These had failed on 1 July; they would clearly fail again, particularly as the German defences had scarcely been affected. Gough and Rawlinson were now faced with the problem of co-ordinating their operations so as to take advantage of the others successes or, more likely, not to be jeopardised by the others failures.

Clearly Gough could not contemplate operations north of the River Ancre, in the area where Hunter-Weston's Corps had suffered so heavily on the opening day. South of the Ancre, between the river and the Albert-Bapaume road, the German positions were strongest on the Thiepval ridge. In turn these defences were protected by fortified posts, not merely to the west and the south, but also to the east, so that any attack on Thiepval from the rear would first have to contend with these posts of substantial strength. North of Thiepval was the Schwaben redoubt; to the east were Stuff and Goat redoubts; to the south the fortified village of Ovillers, which had caused so many problems on the first day; to the south-east was the village of Mouquet Farm. All these positions were linked by a complex of well dug, well revetted strong trenches, bristling with machine gun positions. At intervals along the trenches were intermediate positions of great strength. The entire defensive positions presented daunting problems to an attacker, irrespective of the direction from which the attack was launched.

Attacks launched by Rawlinson's Fourth Army and supporting attacks by Gough's Army on 3 July to capture the village of Ovillers failed, largely because the problems of co-operation proved insurmountable. The attacks were launched separately; the artillery bombardment was an ineffective compromise; failure was inevitable. Gough, who had watched his attacks from an observation post, remarked that if he had 'any sense at all I should have told the chief [Haig] that we were just wasting lives here'.

On 4 July the boundary of Gough's Reserve Army* was shifted to include the Albert-Bapaume road. This move, which seems pedestrian and unremarkable now, greatly assisted the planners in Gough's headquarters. The bombardments, the seemingly incessant fighting, had so churned up the ground as to make the few landmarks almost unrecognisable. At least the direction of the road could still be dimly discerned. Gough went further. South of the road, the village of la Boiselle had been captured. Gough sought the inclusion of this village in his area which would give him a possible entry point into the German positions south-west of Pozières.

During the next week, Gough attempted to move north from La Boiselle in a series of small, ferocious actions. The defenders were obstinate; the progress was limited; battalion after battalion fought a series of almost unrelated actions with machine guns, bayonets and bombs. Here in this maze of defences and ruins, the attackers and defenders were so close much of the time that artillery was of limited value. Not until 16 July was the village of Ovillers — a day one objective — taken.

By then, however, Rawlinson had revised his tactics; successes started to appear.

After the reallocation of forces and boundaries which gave Gough responsibility north of the Albert-Bapaume road, Rawlinson was faced with several problems. The first was to organise his attacks so as to co-operate not only with Gough, but with the French forces on the Somme itself and to the south. The second was to instil into his slow moving, slow thinking, slow acting corps commanders a sense of urgency and a need to adopt different approaches. With the second problem, Rawlinson had only limited success. Between 4 July and 12 July, Rawlinson's corps commanders launched a series of attacks that showed the planners had learned nothing and forgotten nothing about the setbacks of 1 July. Little skill or initiative was used in planning these attacks; little thought was given to the reasons for the failure on the first day. The division and brigade commanders protested, but to no avail. As Farrar-Hockley remarks, 'the methods used were those of the battering ram'.

But, in spite of the idiocy of the tactics, in spite of the sheer arrogant wastefulness of the planners, the attacks succeeded. Contalmaison was taken, thus securing the British left flank against the village of Pozières. To the east, the battered, splintered remains of the trees in Mametz Wood provided some limited cover for further assaults. Further to the

---

*Which became the Fifth Army on 18 October.

east, Trônes Wood, still heavily defended, needed to be taken before an advance of sufficient size could be mounted. On 12 July the British 18th Division was ordered, simply and bluntly, to take Trônes Wood 'at all costs'.

Somewhere in the still remote and dignified headquarters of the Fourth Army, some staff officer had the inspired idea that the assault should take place at dawn. Today, that idea seems unremarkable, even commonplace. But then, the complexities of mounting a dawn attack were considered to be beyond the abilities of Kitchener's armies. It is unclear who first thought of the idea of the dawn attack. The official historian leaves us none the wiser: 'After discussion with his corps commanders and their senior artillery officers, General Rawlinson decided, in agreement with the main body of infantry opinion, that the main attack should be made at dawn, before there was sufficient light for the enemy machine gunners to see very far'.

Rawlinson had wanted to form up in the dark before the assault on 1 July, but had been overruled by Haig and in effect, by the French, who considered movement by night to be impractical. Again, Rawlinson had to face Haig's resistance, particularly as the Fourth Army commander proposed only a five minute bombardment before the attack, instead of the days-long bombardments which had preceded earlier assaults. Movement by night, Haig thought was a manoeuvre 'which one cannot do successfully against flags in times of peace'!

When Haig learned of the Fourth Army plan, he went to Rawlinson's headquarters, taking with him Kiggell, his Chief of Staff. 'I gave him my opinion that it was unsound. He, at once, in the most broad minded way, said he would change it . . . Gen. Montgomery* was most anxious to adhere to the original plan, but I declined to discuss the matter further.' Not surprisingly, Rawlinson and his staff decided to press the point. Already in the Somme offensives, ample evidence existed of the stupidity of attacks in full daylight (remembering, of course, that in a northern hemisphere summer it is bright daylight at 7.30 a.m., the time of the 1 July offensive). That afternoon, Rawlinson spoke to Kiggell on the telephone, but again Haig refused to agree to a dawn assault. 'I considered that the experience of war, as well as the teachings of peace, are against the use of *large masses* in night operations, especially with inexperienced staff officers and young troops. . .' Again, Rawlinson pressed the point with Kiggell, telephoning the Chief of Staff after dinner. Haig relented slightly, agreeing to think the matter over. The next morning, Haig agreed to Rawlinson's plans provided that certain supporting points had been constructed and the assault held secure

---

*Maj.-Gen. A.A. Montgomery, Rawlinson's Chief of Staff.

flanks. Terraine believes that this incident reveals Haig's flexibility. Others believe it shows the Commander-in-Chief's rigidity of mind and purpose, his blind insistence upon failed methods, and his reluctance to agree to innovation or initiative.

The results of Rawlinson's plannings and preparation were surprising. More than 22,000 infantry soldiers, now more lightly burdened than they had been on 1 July, assembled in jumping off trenches within 500 metres of the German lines. At 3.20 a.m., the bombardment began, in the words of the British official historian, 'the whole sky behind the waiting infantry of the four attacking divisions seemed to open with a great roar of flame'. Five minutes later, the artillery lifted; the men of the New Army battalions rose from their waiting trenches and advanced in just sufficient light to distinguish their comrades from the enemy. The Germans were surprised by the shortness of the bombardment; the leading waves of the assault troops were in the wire before a shot was fired. By the time the enemy counter-barrage was fired, the rounds fell harmlessly behind the assaulting troops.

Considering the contrast with the tragic events on 1 July, this assault was more than remarkable. The same standard of troops prevailed; the same training; the same experience of staff officers. The differences were ones of surprise and momentum. How successful the 1 July assault might have been had Rawlinson not managed to convince Haig of his methods is one of the great unanswerable questions.

Rawlinson managed to convince more than Haig, however, by his methods. The French allies were similarly pessimistic and dubious about a night attack. On 13 July the British liaison officer with the French Sixth Army, Captain E.L. Spears, visited Rawlinson's headquarters. Spears carried a message from the French, General Balfourier: Rawlinson should abandon the night approach, for it would not work. Montgomery would have none of it. 'Tell General Balfourier', he told Spears, 'that if we're not on Longueval ridge by 8 o'clock tomorrow morning, I'll eat my hat'. Soon after 7 a.m. on the morning of 14 July, the French liaison officer at Rawlinson's headquarters, Captain Serôt, telephoned Balfourier, commander of the French XX on the right. The junior officer's message was suitably terse. '*Ils ont osé; ils ont réussi*'. The reply had a measure of Gallic resignation: '*Alors, le général Montgomery ne mange pas son chapeau*'.

Again, the breakthrough had been achieved by the infantry; again the opportunity to exploit this breakthrough by the cavalry was lost. The British attack, costing 9,000 men, was halted by strong defences based on three woods, Bazentin-le-Petit, High and Delville. Rawlinson suffered from the lack of assistance on his flanks, both from the French and Gough's weak Reserve Army.

He suffered also from the odd reluctance of Haig to ensure that assistance was forthcoming, both by reinforcing the Reserve Army or by insisting that the French play a greater part in the operation. Still Rawlinson's assault had breached the German second line to a width of more than 3 kilometres. Attempts by III Corps to extend it were defeated by the continued stubborn defence around Pozières.

However, the fighting made a tremendous impact upon the Germans. General Sixt von Arnim, who had command of the front from Longueval to the Ancre found there were no rear positions and no communications trenches. Von Arnim ordered his troops to hold, until reinforcements could be brought forward. These reinforcements were coming from as far away as Lille. Haig, realising the effect the fighting was having, had been pressing Rawlinson from the beginning. On 2 July for example, he told Rawlinson 'The enemy has undoubtedly been severely shaken and he has few reserves in hand. Our correct course, therefore, is to press him hard with the least possible delay. . .'

While the British were pressing hard during July, the Germans were responding with their own counter-attacks, of more or less intensity. 'The important thing', von Below had ordered on 3 July, 'is to hold our present positions at any cost and to improve them by local counter-attack. . . The enemy should have to carve his way over heaps of corpses'.

The first phase of the Somme battle is generally thought to have ended after the offensives of 14 July. Despite his initial reluctance to support Rawlinson's plans, Haig wrote in his despatches:

> The decision to attempt a night operation of this magnitude with an Army, the bulk of which has been raised since the beginning of the war, was perhaps the highest tribute that could be paid to the quality of our troops. . . I cannot speak too highly of the skill, daring, endurance and determination by which these results had been achieved.

Now Haig was faced with what he later called the second phase — the struggle for the ridge.

> West of Bazentin-le-Petit the villages of Pozières and Thiepval, together with the whole elaborate system of the trenches around, had still to be carried. An advance further east would, however, eventually turn these defences, and all that was for the present required on the left flank of our attack was a steady, methodical, step by step advance as already ordered.

Among the fresh troops he had available for this 'steady, methodical, step by step advance' were what John Terraine has generously described as a 'potent new weapon', the Australians. Before they were to take part in that 'steady, methodical, step by step advance' there was a diversionary attack for them in the north, in the Sugar-loaf salient, or what has become known as the battle of Fromelles. Few new troops could ever have experienced such a tragic and bungled introduction to battle.

6

'Kings in Old Poems'

We are the Anzac Army,
The A.N.Z.A.C.
We cannot shoot, we don't salute,
What bloody good are we.
And when we get to *Ber*-lin
The Kaiser he will say,
'Hoch, Hoch! Mein Gott, what a bloody odd lot
To get six bob a day'!
A song, popular with Australian soldiers of the First World War, sung to the tune of the hymn 'The Church's One Foundation'.

The Anzacs left Gallipoli, not as they had come with optimism and fervour and pride and the other mixed emotions of soldiers facing war for the first time, but with despair and relief and not a little shame. They had failed, despite their efforts, although that odd British fashion of celebrating defeat as victory was still a year away. The Australians and the New Zealanders, the proud Anzacs, had turned and slunk away from Gallipoli.

It was a difficult manoeuvre, an opposed withdrawal carried out by night and a 'famous victory'. It succeeded mightily and in the Australian War Memorial in Canberra today the tourist can gaze with bemusement and pride upon the devices that enabled this massive subterfuge to succeed. But it had failed, nevertheless. With winter had come the realisation that the campaign could not succeed: better to cut and run; better to bring back the troops and fight another day. So the diggers* and the Kiwis and the Tommies and the marines and the *poilus* left the peninsula, leaving behind their dead mates — about 46,000 allied soldiers were killed or died of wounds — and the political ambitions, for the time being, at least, of Winston Churchill, former First Lord of the Admiralty, former professional soldier and amateur strategist.

---

*Although the name 'digger' wasn't generally used until 1917 in France.

The Australian official historian, C.E.W. Bean, whose pride in the Australian soldier knew few bounds, noted that the Australians and the New Zealanders who returned from Gallipoli to Egypt were a different force from the adventurous body that had left only eight months before.

> They were a military body with strongly established, definite traditions. Not for anything, if he could avoid it, would an Australian now change his loose faded tunic or battered hat for the smartest cloth or headgear of any other army. Men clung to their Australian uniforms till they were tattered to the limit of decency.

The sartorial appearance of the Australians was important to others as well. John Masefield, whose praise of the original Anzacs was also elaborate, thought the Australian uniform was based on sense, not on nonsense.

> Instead of an idiotic cap, that provided no shade for the eyes, nor screen for the back of the neck, that would not stay on in a wind, nor help to disguise the wearer from air observation, these men wore comfortable soft felt slouch hats, that protected in all weathers and at all times looked well. Instead of bright buttons and badges, 'without which', as a general once said to me, 'no discipline could be maintained', these men carried in their equipment nothing that could be added to the worries of war.

At first, Masefield added, nobody knew who these strange fellows were, these 'very friendly people, easy to get on with, most helpful, kindly and hospitable'. When they arrived in England they had been preceded by the reputation that they were 'difficult' and they had to be camped out in the desert to keep them, as Masefield put it, 'from throwing Cairo down the Nile'. They were also preceded by stories of their prowess in battle, stories which 'not even the vigilance of all the censors could keep down'.

In fact, the Australians were the beneficiaries of an astute and cynical propaganda exercise which had the effect of blurring in the public mind the extent of the military catastrophe at Gallipoli. The Australians were fêted and honoured; the Australian High Commission in London used the arrival of the first body of troops in April 1916 to celebrate what it called 'ANZAC Day'. However, the occasion was not excessively militaristic; the troops carried no weapons in their great march through London to Westminster Abbey, where the service was attended by the King, the Queen and the Australian Prime Minister, William Morris Hughes. Later, after lunch at the Hotel Cecil, Hughes addressed the assembled soldiers from the stage of Her Majesty's Theatre. This wizened, gnarled little man with protruding ears and a high pitched nasal, whining voice told the soldiers their deeds had won them a place in the 'Temple of the Immortals'.

> The world has hailed you as heroes. On the shining wings of your glorious valour you have inspired us to a newer and better and nobler concept of life; and the deathless deeds of the valiant dead would yet be sung in sagas to generations of Australians until the end of time. The story of the Gallipoli campaign has shown that through self-sacrifice alone could men or a nation be saved. And since it has evoked this fire and spirit, who should say that this dreadful war was wholly evil now in a world saturated with a lust of material things came the sweet purifying breath of self sacrifice.

Londoners, fed a steady selection of 'brave Aussie soldier' stories and tales of how these bronzed heroes communicated with each other by cries of 'coo-ee', imitated the bushman's cry with variable success. *London Opinion* carried the report of a young soldier from the western districts of Victoria who, when told his leg had been amputated, simply said, 'Ah well, only one leg to be pulled now'. Whose leg, one wonders, was being pulled?

The first Australians to arrive in the United Kingdom were indeed splendid physical specimens. They had passed the most rigorous of medical examinations which, although slightly relaxed for later volunteers, still insisted upon artificially high standards. The official historian, Ernest Scott, noted that it was not wonderful that comments were made in Australia, in Egypt, and afterwards in England, upon the superb physique of the early volunteers. '. . . the doctors who passed them seemed to judge them as though they were selecting models for a Rodin or a Bertram McKennal rather than troops for war.' In two well-known descriptions, Masefield and the novelist Compton McKenzie set down their reactions to these soldiers at Gallipoli. For Masefield,

> They were . . . the finest body of young men ever brought together in modern times. For physical beauty and nobility of bearing they surpassed any men I have ever seen; they walked and looked like kings in old poems . . .As the officers put it, 'they were in the pink of condition and didn't care a damn for anybody'.

McKenzie thought their 'heroic beauty' should have been celebrated 'in hexameters not headlines'.

Their almost complete nudity, their tallness and majestic simplicity of line, their rose-brown flesh burnt by the sun and purged of all grossness by the ordeal through which they were passing, all these united to create something as near to absolute beauty as I shall hope ever to see in this world.

Compare these descriptions to John Terraine's assessment of the recruits who offered themselves to the British army following Kitchener's call. For the first time, Terraine argues, the British army met the British people.

The shock was considerable; the image of a sturdy, strapping population (by comparison with weedy foreigners) was rudely dispelled when the results of callous nineteenth century industrial expansion flocked into view. Robust enough in spirit, the men of the narrow streets of the industrial towns, offspring of long working hours, low wages, persistent poverty and persistent malnutrition, simply did not meet the physical standards laid down by a small professional army that which could normally pick and choose its recruits.

Compare also the Anzacs, these 'models for Rodin', with recruits being inducted into British Bantam battalions because they were unable to meet the army's minimum height requirement of five feet three inches. This was not late in the war, when the reserves of British manpower had been sorely and sadly depleted; the first Bantam battalion was formed in December 1914. Sir Philip Gibbs, the noted and knighted war correspondent, called them 'the dwarfed children of industrial England and its mid-Victorian cruelties'.

In 1918, Charles Carrington, a young officer who had served his time in the trenches, was training conscripts. Carrington noted that the 'skinny, sallow, shambling, frightened victims of our industrial system . . . were unrecognisable after six months of good food, fresh air and physical training'. These recruits added an inch in height and a stone in weight on average; they developed into:

. . . ruddy, handsome clear-eyed young men with square shoulders who stood up straight and were afraid of no one, not even the sergeant major. The effect on me is to make me a violent socialist when I see how underdeveloped industrialism has kept them and a Prussian militarist when I see what soldiering makes of them.

By comparison to their own soldiers, the Australians must have indeed seemed like bronzed gods to the British. Barely a century of white settlement had seen remarkable changes in the sons of the original settlers. Even for the high proportion of Australian soldiers born in the United Kingdom — as many as one in four — life in the dominions had been demonstrably better and demonstrably more healthy. Their accents had changed to take on that distinctive, nasal Australian twang; their singular ideas of democracy and equality accorded ill with the rigid British system of caste, class and military discipline. Not surprisingly the Australians loved the glory and the attention. Battery Sgt.-Maj. Nigel Ellsworth, a former Mint official from South Yarra in Victoria, wrote that the Australians were given

> the most magnificent reception from the population of London, who turned up in one vast crowd, and threw flowers and cigarettes and all that sort of thing at us and cheered themselves hoarse at us, and in fact, we felt rather swelled headed at the way we were treated, and the way people shook us by the hand and women embraced us and all that rot, and attempted to cry 'coo-ee' and some very wonderful noises these attempts developed into.

The 'most magnificent reception' was not, however, universal. For many Britons, the march organised by the High Commission was more colonial boasting. Others thought that the British 29th Division, commanded by Maj.-Gen. Hunter-Weston, should also have been represented in the march. Protesting letters were written to *The Times*, even before the march, pointing out that British casualties in the campaign had been three times those of the Australians. Bean noted in his diary that the enthusiasm shown by the British people for the Australians was not shared by the British officers. 'British staff here [in the United Kingdom] hate the Australians pretty badly — it is the English common people who like us; with the exception of those British officers who have fought with us, the British officer generally does not like us.' These feelings were not confined merely to lower ranks among the British officers. Gen. Sir Archibald Murray, formerly Chief of the Imperial General Staff who, in late 1915, was appointed to command all troops in the Middle East, detested the Australians. Bean had little sympathy for the austere and remote Murray who had come, in the official historian's words, 'from the hushed corridors of the War Office'. Murray, wrote Bean:

> was constantly shocked by the lack of discipline to which he was naturally, and rightly, accustomed. He was not, like his predecessor, sufficiently a man of the world to be able to judge these defects for what they were — mainly slackness or a lack of training to be remedied by vigorous human leadership.

Murray drafted a letter to his successor, the wise and sensible 'Wully' Robertson, condemning what he regarded as 'the extreme indiscipline and inordinate vanity of the Australian forces'. But Murray also showed a copy to Lt.-Gen. Sir William Birdwood, who had commanded the Anzacs at Gallipoli and was now commanding them in the Middle East. 'Birdie' was not without faults; his vanity was legion, as was his ambition. Bean described him as 'one of Lord Kitchener's most trusted assistants in South Africa', which is a typically charitable remark by the official historian and another way of saying Birdwood was a Kitchener man. Small, pugnacious and determined, 'Birdie' nurtured ambitions of becoming Governor-General of Australia after the war. But for all his ambition, Birdwood both loved and admired his difficult-to-command troops.

A short, lean man who neither drank nor smoked, 'Birdie' was a popular commander among the Australians who responded to his concern for their welfare. One historian of the campaign has described this popularity as something of a newspaper myth, quoting an anonymous observer as saying: 'He bored the men and they bored him'. Bean does not confirm this view, nor indeed does Birdwood's commander, Gen. Sir Ian Hamilton, who described him as 'the soul of Anzac'.

Lt.-Gen. Sir Frederick Morgan, later one of the planners for the OVERLORD invasion in 1944, but then a young gunner officer with the 4th Australian Division, wrote later that he derived great inspiration from being part of Birdwood's Anzac Corps.

> Rarely can there have been a more brilliant example of the exercise of personal command. It really did seem as though the General knew personally every man in the whole army corps. And they knew him, and, so far as such a thing was possible to a back-blocks digger, they loved him. They spoke to him, they spoke of him as 'Mr Birdwood', which, as anyone who knew the Australian Army of 1916 will recognise, was indicative of a very considerable respect.

Birdwood was worried about Murray's letter. His position was still unclear. Perplexed by Murray's unfriendly opinion and worried about his responsibilities as a national commander, Birdwood showed the draft to his Chief of Staff, Brig.-Gen. Cyril Brudenell White, whose reaction was immediate. If that was Murray's opinion of Australian soldiers, then Birdwood must bring it to the notice of the Australian Government. And if this represented the official view of soldiers destined for drafts to France, then the Australian Government had a right to know and Birdwood, as commander of the Australian force, had an obligation to pass on that knowledge. Bean was unable to discover whether Murray's draft of the letter to Robertson was ever sent. But Murray, on inspections of troops in Egypt training for service in France, hinted that he would be unable to recommend their transfer to the Western Front unless their saluting and their discipline improved.

Complaints about diggers not saluting officers, particularly British officers, were legion; the Australian digger took a perverse delight in being unfavourably compared with his Canadian counterparts already in France who were, according to Lt.-Gen. Alexander Godley commanding the II Australian Corps, 'second to none in discipline, smartness and efficiency'. For the Australian soldier, saluting implied respect for the officer being saluted. And not every officer deserved that respect. 'We came here to fight for freedom, not to be slaves to our superiors — we haven't got any. If I salute an officer I like to feel that we are exchanging man to man compliments, and I reckon the officers worth saluting feel the same way.'

The Australians too, despite Masefield's remarks, were not exactly reticent about their qualities or their record as fighting troops. Masefield noted that they sang, to the tune of 'The Church's One Foundation':

> We are the Anzac Army,
> The A.N.Z.A.C.
> We cannot shoot, we don't salute,
> What bloody good are we.
> And when we get to *Ber*-lin
> The Kaiser he will say,
> 'Hoch, Hoch! Mein Gott, what a bloody odd lot
> To get six bob a day'!

They might very well have been an 'odd lot to get six bob a day', but they also had no doubts about their abilities. The old soldiers, the veterans of Gallipoli, had realised that the Australian lacked nothing in martial qualities. They were imbued with that strange, almost mystical self-assurance, of the original volunteer.* For the newer soldiers, the reinforcements, volunteers who had flocked to the recruiting offices around the country on the first news from Gallipoli, there was the overwhelming desire to do as well as the originals. One 35 year old lieutenant, F.W. Appleton, wrote home in June 1916, 'I am in the best of health and spirits and not at all nervous about the ordeal we have to

---

*Recently, I attended a meeting of the 9th Battalions' Association which includes among its members veterans of the 9th Bn, AIF. I was talking to one First World War veteran about another. He remarked, 'But you realise he's only a reinforcement?' 'Reinforcement?' I asked. 'Yes, he wasn't with us at Gallipoli. Didn't join us until France.'

face and hope we all keep up the great reputation the Australians had for bravery'.

Mid-1915 saw a frenzy of recruiting activity in Australia, the first such organised campaign of the war. The landings at Gallipoli; the sinking of the *Lusitania* in May; the gradual but perceptible realisation that the war was not going as well as the official communiqués were making out — each factor contributed to an enthusiastic response to the Australian Government's call. It had asked the British Government in June 1915 whether it could accept every soldier enlisted in Australia. Within three days the reply came from Whitehall. It could and it would. Despite some initial reluctance in Victoria, recruiting stepped up sharply. Enlistments rose from 6,250 in April to 10,526 in May and 12,505 in June, a gradual but important increase. After June, and the campaigning, the figures started to climb sharply: 36,575 in July; 25,714 in August and 16,571 in September. Training camps in Australia bulged with the new soldiers.

These new soldiers, the tangible results of this remarkable response to patriotic fervour and national pride, had to be trained and transformed into battalions, brigades and divisions. In November, the Australian Government said it would send 50,000 new troops, organised as nine infantry brigades with attendant brigade troops but without artillery. Although the War Office in London said it would prefer those nine brigades to be organised into three divisions, the Australian Government replied that it could not provide the necessary artillery pieces, nor indeed the trained gunners and officers to man them.

Australian casualties at Gallipoli had been 7,600 killed and 19,000 wounded. Even during the campaign, Birdwood had asked that the high scale of Gallipoli reinforcements, then about 5,300 a month, be increased to 9,331. Now, with the withdrawal from the peninsula, the staff officers and commanders of the Australian Imperial Force faced a massive task of organising a force that had doubled. As well, the expanded AIF was being concentrated in Egypt and tasked also with the defence of that country. But not all of the reinforcements sent to Egypt were being usefully employed. More than 40,000 Australian and New Zealand soldiers had not been allotted to units; the prospect of 30,000 partly-trained Australians roaming the streets of Cairo was not one that encouraged equanimity among the British officers.

Originally General Godley, who was administering command of the AIF in Egypt, proposed that the reinforcements could be used to expand the AIF from two to four divisions and that the additional New Zealanders arriving in the Middle East could be added to the existing brigade to form a New Zealand Division. Together, the Australian and New Zealand divisions could be expanded to form two corps. Godley suggested Birdwood should administer the entire Australian and New Zealand Forces, with Brudenell White as his Chief of Staff. The success of this plan, however, depended greatly upon the ability of the Australians and the New Zealanders to train the new reinforcements in the depots and holding battalions.

The War Office agreed to a proposal to form a fifth Australian division. Thus, within the space of a very few months, the AIF had gone from two infantry divisions to, on paper at least, five infantry divisions. As well, there was the New Zealand infantry division and the Anzac mounted division which need not concern this narrative.

Most of the responsibility for the new organisation fell on Brudenell White who, as Brigadier-General, General Staff, of the Anzac Corps in the previous December, had planned the evacuation of the Australian sector of the peninsula. White's plan, a 'model of precision and clear thinking' was largely responsible for the successful evacuation, particularly on the final two days when 20,000 troops slipped away without being noticed. Curiously enough, a recent assessment of White pays no attention to his role in planning the expansion of the AIF;* Bean's assessment of White as a staff officer is, perhaps understandably, coloured by a strong admiration for his close friend. But there is little doubt that once Birdwood made the original decisions about the method of the expansion, White carried those decisions through with painstaking care and meticulous attention to detail.

Birdwood decided that, whatever happened on the expansion of the new force, the original character should be maintained. Rather than simply creating new units as such, and staffing them with officers and NCOs promoted from the ranks, Birdwood ordered that the original units be split in two, and that the reinforcements be used to expand each half to a whole. Two 'wings' were to be formed, a headquarters wing and a reinforcement wing. The division then being formed in Australia was to be known as the 3rd Division, the 4th and 5th Divisions would be formed in Egypt.

As important as creating the new units was the task of finding suitable commanders. Young officers who had proved themselves on Gallipoli suddenly found themselves commanding brigades and battalions. At least four of the battalion commanders were only 24 and one was 25

---

*Guy Verney in D.M. Horner (ed.), *The Commanders, Australian Military Leadership in the Twentieth Century*, (Sydney, 1984).

years old. But inevitably some units were commanded by officers who lacked either the right temperament, or the ability to select and inspire subordinates. In many cases, the new battalions derived their morale and their discipline from what Bean called 'some spirited and high-minded subordinate, usually a company commander'.

The effect on discipline and morale of splitting the original 16 battalions, particularly on the veterans of Anzac, cannot be over-estimated. The split itself was done quickly; rolls were perused and the manpower divided evenly, if competitively, between commanders of the old and new. In some battalions, the allocation of troops was made before the commanders were appointed; the eventual selection being made in the officers' mess by the toss of a coin. But to watch their old comrades disappear into a new unit was for many a distressing sight. One officer wrote: 'I felt as though I was having a limb amputated without any anaesthetic'. Another battalion simply handed over 'two splendid companies'.

In the 4th Battalion, recruited from the south-western areas of New South Wales, the parting was scrupulously fair. Everything, including regimental funds was split evenly with the new battalion, the 56th. Everything, that is, except the regimental goat 'Buller'; it remained with the 4th.

With the expansion and the split, however, some of the old links were retained. The identifying colour patches, although of different shapes for the new divisions, retained the same colour scheme; indeed, one of the best ways of tracing battalion growth in the First AIF is by the charts of the colour patches. The new battalion and company commanders took the opportunity of pressing the importance of discipline upon the reinforcements, many of whom had an exaggerated idea of what was expected of a soldier on leave. The inevitable laxness of some of the more irksome forms of discipline which had crept in at Gallipoli were rapidly stopped; saluting drill was carried out, sometimes for hours; blanket rolls and other seemingly minor military rituals were rigorously enforced; shorts were banned. The 'kings in old poems' started to look like soldiers once more.

That these undoubted restrictions upon what the Australian soldier regarded as his 'rights' were implemented without great difficulties or problems in a significant tribute to the great commonsense of the soldiers, and particularly that of the officers and NCOs.

Bean, whose notions of Australian nationalism and of antipodean democracy were never far from the surface of his writings, thought this a tribute to the lack of sharp social distinctions between officers and men. But the distinctions existed, although they were not as pronounced as in the British army. The Australian system of commissioning officers who merited such promotion had as much to do with their singular qualities as any real or apparent lack of social distinction.

General Sir John Monash, about whom a lively degree of military mythology has arisen, wrote after the war that Australian society singularly fitted its members for command.

> There was no officer caste, no social distinction in the whole force. In not a few instances, men of humble origin and belonging to the artisan class rose, during the war, from privates to the command of battalions ... the whole Australian army became automatically graded into leaders and followers according to the individual merits of every man, and there grew a wonderful understanding between them.

As a civilian soldier, a colonial and a Jew, Monash experienced the discrimination of the British officer caste.

Yet there are other reasons for the attitude of the Australian soldier of the First World War towards his officers. Before the war, the Australian army virtually did not exist, except for the enthusiastic amateurs of the militia. There was no great tradition of a standing army; no regimental custom to preserve and cherish; no great enthusiasm for 'going for a soldier'. Indeed, the colony's origins had made its inhabitants sceptical and watchful of authority and the antics of the Rum Corps hardly accorded with the concepts of disinterested service to the Crown.

The attitude of the Australian soldier towards rank, saluting and the other petty aspects of military discipline is worth examining in some detail because it affected so greatly the perceptions of senior British officers, particularly those who had not served with Australian troops. It affected the attitude of Haig; it affected the attitude of Murray; it was significant in causing severe stress between Australian and British staffs. The decision by the Australian Government on the command of the AIF was either imperfectly understood or deliberately ignored by the British High Command. From the beginning of the war, the Australian Government had appointed a general officer commanding the AIF and had vested in him powers as a national commander, as distinct from those of a merely military commander. It was the clash of those powers, inevitable in war, that led often to official disagreements; it was the Australians' overwhelming sense of superiority which to the British was colonial arrogance, that led to the personal tensions.

As well, the continuing tensions over Australia wanting a national army in the context of a force comprised of two or more corps, commanded by an Australian or, at least, a sympathetic British officer, bedevilled relationships. The great commonsense of Birdwood who, as an Indian Army officer was relatively free of the prejudices that afflicted both Haig and Murray, has been under-estimated over the years.

The impact of Falkenhayn's offensive on 21 February was felt in Egypt. Five days after the attack began, Murray received a telegram from Robertson, warning of the possible need to despatch troops from the Middle East. 'We find it necessary that we should give the French early proof of our intention to support them in every possible way.' Murray promised three British divisions, the 31st, the 29th and the 11th. Robertson replied that three would not be enough.

> Things at Verdun are going none too well . . . We must accordingly be prepared to risk something in Egypt. . . Originally it was intended by you and by us that the Australians should come to France first, but they have gradually taken fourth place. Do not allow ideas of forming an Australian army to influence matters as that cannot materialise in any case for months, and you should generally work on the principle that three Australian divisions in France in April may be worth six at a later date.

Robertson had little sympathy for the idea of an Australian army. When he turned down the proposal Bean noted: 'He didn't see it served a useful purpose — and the fact that we were a nation and wanted to fight and carve our history as a nation didn't go for anything with him. To the British, of course, the Australians were part and parcel of the British army' — a phrase used by Lord Derby, the War Minister, in a letter to Haig as late as November 1917.

William Morris Hughes had been in England since early March 1916, during the expansion of the AIF and the discussions over the possible formation of an Australian army. On 11 March Hughes saw Robertson and discussed the situation in France and the need for Australians to be committed to the Western Front. Robertson had been receiving regular cables from Murray in Egypt, explaining the level of training reached by the difficult Dominion troops. 'I have no wish,' Murray cabled Robertson in mid-February, 'to keep back the Australians or to form them into an army. I have latterly placed them in order of departure behind the British divisions because they are most backward in training and discipline, and I am trying to wheel them into line'. No doubt the Australians' level of training was much below the equivalent British divisions in the Middle East. Many recruits had left Australia with only rudimentary training; some had received virtually no instructions in musketry, that most elementary of military skills; others had been promised training in Egypt that did not eventuate when they first arrived. Murray's remarks about discipline, however, simply echo earlier complaints and show an understandable British confusion between the forms and the substance of military order.

After his meeting with Robertson, Hughes cabled Senator George Pearce, the Minister for Defence.

> Two Australian divisions now being formed for France, first leaving almost immediately, the others as soon as transport available. Two other divisions follow. Birdwood to remain in Egypt to organise until these last two divisions are ready. Idea then is to have Australian army with probably Birdwood in command. Meanwhile Godley to command divisions first despatched. What is your opinion Godley's fitness for this position?

Hughes also added in his cable that he was still 'hammering away at machine guns' trying to get an allocation of 16 to the battalion. (This was the Lewis Gun, which was allocated in those numbers by mid-year.) Although Pearce replied that Godley was suitable for command, Hughes went back to see Robertson and insisted that Birdwood should command the Australian Corps coming to France. After that meeting Robertson's ADC noted that the CIGS 'had had a bad morning with Hughes'. Robertson referred Hughes' request to Murray who favoured Godley, because the latter was thought to be a stronger disciplinarian. 'Godley has done splendidly with the A & N Z Army Corps, and his alleged unpopularity may be due to the fact that he has very strict ideas of discipline, which [is] much needed.' Finally, however, Hughes won his point. Robertson cabled Murray: 'It is essential that the Corps should be given every chance to make a good beginning in France, and therefore the Secretary of State and I have decided that Birdwood must go'. It was only after the question was referred to Kitchener, Birdwood's old friend and patron, that the issue was decided.

On the second question, that of a national army for Australia, Hughes lost badly. Birdwood, whose ambitions for an army command were clearly apparent, set off for London in the hope of seeing Kitchener and personally arguing the case. However, at Marseille *en route* to London, Birdwood and Brudenell White were ordered to Haig's head-quarters where they were told they could proceed to London only if General Plumer, under whose command the Australians would come, could spare them.

'It was clear', writes Bean, 'that the Commander-in-Chief did not recognise the right and need of self-government in the administration of the Australian force, and White was therefore of opinion that a full and frank, though courteous, statement of the Australian view should be drawn up and laid with him'. Birdwood objected and this opportunity for clearing the relationship from the beginning was lost. On seeing Plumer, Birdwood and White were told they could both not be spared and so Birdwood was forced to make the journey to London without the invaluable services of his Chief of Staff.

Armed with the proposals drafted for him by Brudenell White, Birdwood was able to persuade the War Office that he should have the administrative, if not the tactical, command of all Australians and that the administrative and training headquarters of the AIF should be shifted from Egypt to London. It was left to Hughes to convince Haig that Birdwood would be able to combine both the administrative and field commands of the AIF. Hughes did so, but only after some difficulties. Even suggesting the possibility of a sixth Australian division did not persuade Haig about the need for a national army. According to the Commander-in-Chief, the strength of the Australian and New Zealand Force was not sufficient for an army; as it was, he could not even promise the Australian divisions would all be placed under Birdwood's tactical control. But, Haig conceded, Birdwood could have full administrative command and 'if at any future time I can see my way to employing all the Australian forces together under his command for some special operation, I will gladly do so'. Hughes, astute politician that he was, set out precisely those conditions in a letter to Haig a fortnight later.

And so ended, for the time being at least, any possibility of Birdwood commanding an Australian army. Bean is charitable to the Commander-in-Chief: 'It is probably true that the forming of an actual army was impracticable — the combining of the Anzac divisions in a solid block might, in 1916, have encountered difficulties too great to be prudently encountered; certainly such a policy would have interfered with the plan of that year's fighting'. Bean's charity is more than reasonable, but it ignores the facts of military life in 1916. Corps were reallocated within armies during the Somme fighting, as we have already seen; Gough's Reserve Army was reinforced with the Australian divisions after the offensives began and in the most *ad hoc* manner. As Bean admits: 'To the British staff as a whole, there seemed no more reason for combining Australian divisions than for combining those from London or Lancashire'. At the time of writing, Bean could not have had the advantage of seeing Derby's letter to Haig in November 1917:

> What I do want to write to you about is the Colonial Forces. I am having a great deal of trouble with them at the present moment, especially with regard to the Australian Corps, and I am afraid, for various reasons, we

must look on them in the light in which they wish to be looked on rather than the light in which we should wish to do so. They look on themselves, not as part and parcel of the English army* but as Allies beside us and I see they are beginning to take the analogy of the Portuguese, not from the point of view of fighting but from the point of view of administration and self-control. The Australians have an implicit belief in Birdwood, and are quite determined that he shall be their Chief in the field. I do not know what your feelings are with regard to his military capacity but I am afraid in this respect we shall have to humour them.

Haig had no respect for Birdwood's military qualities and allowed the latter's close relationship with Kitchener to affect his judgment. On 7 November 1915, when Birdwood had been promoted over Rawlinson, Pulteney and other major-generals, Haig noted: 'Birdwood will be a tool in K.'s hands'. His opinion of Birdwood was not to change after Kitchener's death. In February 1918, Haig wrote to his wife that he had spent some time with the Canadians.

They are really fine disciplined soldiers now and smart and clean. I am sorry to say the Australians are not nearly so efficient. I put this down to Birdwood, who, instead of facing the problem, has gone in for the easier way of saying everything is perfect and making himself as popular as possible.

Whatever his faults, no one could ever accuse the Commander-in-Chief of excessive striving for popularity among his troops.

But the organisation of the Australian force was settled: two Anzac Corps, one commanded by Birdwood and the other by Godley, with the staffs of those corps still drawn heavily from the British army. The divisional commands were split, with Maj.-Gen. H.B. 'Hooky' Walker, a Dublin-born British professional soldier and former Chief of Staff on the division headquarters, commanding the 1st Australian Division and Maj.-Gen. J.G. Legge, an Australian gunner and later commandant of the Royal Military College, Duntroon, commanding the 2nd Australian Division. Maj.-Gen. John Monash was to command the 3rd Australian Division, then forming and training on Salisbury Plain in England. Of the other divisions, the 4th was to be commanded by a veteran of the Indian Army, Maj.-Gen. Sir Herbert Cox and the 5th Australian Division by Maj.-Gen. The Honourable James Whiteside M'Cay, an

---

*English? Derby's insensitivity to 'Colonials' extended to the Welsh, Scots and the Irish.

Australian politician, former Minister for Defence, lawyer, journalist and enthusiastic militia officer.

On 29 February 1916, Murray warned Birdwood that the Anzac Corps would have to start moving to France within two weeks. At the same time, Birdwood was also told that the War Office required the Australian and New Zealand artillery be brought up to the scale of the 'New Army divisions' then moving in France. It will be recalled that when the Australian Government offered to expand the AIF, it warned that it could not provide sufficient artillery pieces or trained artillery-men. Now, the problem facing the Australians was acute. In February the total Australian artillery component in the AIF comprised just 18 batteries. By doubling the AIF, this had been increased to 36 batteries, but this was still well below the artillery strength, on a divisional basis, of the New Army divisions in France. By the end of March 1916, the Australian artillery was to expand once again, this time to 60 batteries.

Clearly the divisions moving to France had to have their full complement of artillery. This could be done only by transferring the partly-trained artillery batteries from the other two divisions to the 1st and 2nd Australian Divisions; the laborious process of re-raising, re-equipping and training new gunners began again. Although undoubtedly the right decision at the time, taking the 5th Division's artillery was to have important consequences at the battle of Fromelles.

7

'A Bloody Holocaust'

'If you put it to me like that, sir, I must answer you in the same way as man to man. It is going to be a bloody holocaust.'
Major H.C.L. Howard, a British staff officer to Brig.-Gen. H.E. 'Pompey' Elliott before the Battle of Fromelles.

The older Australian divisions began arriving in France from mid-March 1916, disembarking at Marseille, to the fears of the British military authorities who were apprehensive about these wild colonial boys. The fears proved groundless. Four Australian divisions — some 60,000 men — were to pass through the port and the British transport control with not one single instance of misbehaviour, something of a record according to the British port commandant.

From Marseille they took the first of many train journeys, into northern France and the British zone, then some 200 kilometres north of Paris. For the veterans of Gallipoli and the reinforcements alike, the train journey had a wondrous, magical quality. Bean wrote that it was 'like a plunge into Fairyland'. Sergeant E.J. Rule, of the 14th Battalion had, with many of his comrades of the 4th Division, fretted and worried about when they were going to follow the 1st and 2nd Divisions. When his unit finally made the crossing of the Mediterranean, the trip through France 'left an impression on our men's minds which was never erased — a memory which men fondled to themselves, certain that no greater joy was awaited them in the years to come'. Added Rule:

It was the month of June and everything was radiant. Perhaps we were suffering from the reaction of our experiences in the desert. For sixty hours we forgot that we were on a deadly mission, and in imagination lived within the pages of Grimm's fairy-tales.

Mansions nestling into the folds of hills, and old castles perched on crags, overlooked the verdant valleys, while the beautiful River Rhône was never out of the picture in the early stages of the journey. The farms were the envy of us all. Everything was so peaceful that the existence of a state of war was almost incredible.

The I Anzac Corps, consisting of the 1st and 2nd Divisions, was sent first to the 'nursery sector' in the northern third of the British zone, near the comfortable French town of Armentières, then with a population of about 30,000 people. To the south-east was the larger town of Lille, a strong manufacturing area, about 5 kilometres behind the German lines. In this sector, the British and the Germans had reached a kind of unofficial truce; the British did not want to shell Lille; the Germans responded by only occasionally shelling Armentières. And, as if to avoid the temptation of either side launching an offensive in the area, the River Lys running diagonally through the region, was a considerable obstacle to any attacker.

For the Australians, newly arrived from the desert, the experience of war on the Western Front in this relatively placid sector was almost pleasant. Food was plentiful, and brought up to troops in the trenches each night by work parties. Water, which at Gallipoli had to be laboriously carted ashore across shingled beaches and then up into the forward positions, here was piped and on tap. There were farms and civilians close to the lines; there were villages and shops and the inevitable *estaminet*.

These particularly French establishments, a cross between a café and a pub, sold thin beer and cheap wine. One was less than a kilometre from the Australian lines and the soldiers were quick to cross the fields and slake their thirsts. But although this was a quiet sector, the rumble of the guns was ever present. 'As night fell,' wrote Bean, 'trees, hedges and houses to eastward were constantly outlined against the swift flicker of gun flashes and the pale quivering halo of the white flares by which each side illuminated the No Man's Land between the lines. For two and a half years to come those sights and sounds were never to be absent'.

At first the Australians were confined to patrolling and sniping; short, sharp sudden actions carried out in the confusion of the 200 metre or so stretch of No Man's Land that separated the two lines. They experienced also the suddenness of artillery fire falling on their positions, dropping without warning. And soon too, they experienced the ferocity of the Western Front. On 6 May, troops of the 20th Battalion, a 2nd Division unit drawn largely from New South Wales, were occupying the Bridoux salient, a prominent bend in the line. During the day, the Australians had been shelled, but in a desultory, almost haphazard fashion. They responded with their own medium trench mortars and the new, still secret Stokes mortar. By midday, the firing had stopped and the afternoon passed in a quiet peace.

Just on dusk, as the company which had spent the day in the front trenches was being relieved, four rounds from the German field guns straddled the Australian position. In an instant, it seemed, that fire was followed by an intense concentration of artillery and mortar. The commander of the company being relieved, a former University of Sydney student, Captain A.G. Ferguson, tried to dash the 10 metres from his headquarters to the SOS rockets outside, but was thrice blown over by shell blasts. Officers at the battalion headquarters, about 500 metres to the rear, could only peer into the gloom at the maelstrom of fire. It was frightful, quite unlike anything within the experience of the Gallipoli veterans. The area covered by the bombardment extended across the 20th Battalion's front, more than 200 metres. All communications from the front trenches to the headquarters had been cut by the artillery fire; communication trenches had been blocked and collapsed. Both the troops in the heat of the bombardment and those in the rear feared a German offensive.

The bombardment lasted from 7.40 p.m. until 9.30 p.m. One officer from the headquarters made his way forward and reported that, although casualties had been heavy in the forward company and damage to the breastworks severe, the line was being held by the survivors. The next morning, as the relieving company searched among the damage for further casualties, a few German hand grenades were discovered and from the survivors was pieced together a patchy account of Germans entering the trench lines during the latter stages of the bombardment.

That information was passed up from the battalion headquarters to brigade, and then on to the 2nd Division headquarters. That night, the communiqué from Haig's GHQ devoted two lines to the action on the 20th Battalion position. 'The enemy made a raid on and entered our trenches south-east of Armentières, after bombarding them. He was at once driven out.' In the headquarters of General Plumer's Second British Army, the German daily communiqués were monitored and translated. That night, also the Germans gave their version of the action. 'To the south-east and south of Armentières some operations carried out by our patrols were successful. Some prisoners were captured and two machine guns and two mine-throwers were captured.'

Plumer reacted angrily, demanding from Birdwood the truth of the incident. The 'mine-throwers' or Stokes mortars were highly secret, one of the few technical advantages the British then possessed. Their use was governed by the strictest conditions and orders issued from the GHQ itself; they were not to be left in the line overnight. To make the matter worse, although both the battalion and the brigade staffs had known that the mortars had probably been captured, and had passed that suspicion on to the staff of the division headquarters, that was as far as the information had gone. At Maj.-Gen. Legge's 2nd Divison headquarters, the staff officers were waiting for confirmation that the mortars had been captured before informing Birdwood's corps headquarters. It was not until that afternoon, when two of Birdwood's intelligence officers interviewed the 20th Battalion survivors, that their capture was confirmed.

The incident, seemingly so minor in the history of the war, was to have important repercussions for the Australians. Plumer demanded a court of inquiry, and the courts martial of the officers in charge of the mortars. Birdwood reported in the most effusive terms to his commander. 'I much regret', he wrote personally to Plumer, 'what I cannot help considering to be the unsatisfactory results of this attack by the Germans, and I cannot sufficiently express regret for the loss of the two Stokes mortars, which is inexcusable'.

Ironically, the Germans never realised the value of the weapons they had captured. The Stokes mortar, invented in 1914 by Wilfred Stokes, was the forerunner of the most familiar forms of modern mortars, the only important survival of muzzle loaded artillery. Unlike the German *minenwerfer*, the Stokes mortar could be drop-fired; that is, loaded and fired by the simple action of dropping the bomb down the barrel. This meant that the mortar could be fired extremely quickly, the only limit to the rate of fire being the ability of the loader to drop the bombs down the barrel. Bean made an extensive search of the German archives, but could find no indication that anyone in the German army recognised what they had captured or attempted to imitate such a device.

The courts martial proved inconclusive. Blame could never be sheeted home to any one officer. The senior commanders seemed to be more worried that the 20th Battalion troops had failed to keep the enemy out of their section of the line — a failure that was regarded with less sanguinity then than later. Bean said the loss of the two Stokes mortars rapidly became known throughout the army, a cause of much embarrassment at a time when the British newspapers were lauding the bronzed Anzac heroes. It is more than possible, however, that Bean overreacted to the incident, regarding it as a slight upon the proud record of his heroes. By comparison, the British official historian makes no mention of the raid nor of the loss of the weapons, though admittedly his is a much less detailed account. The real blow was to Australian pride.

The 4th Australian Division, as we have seen from Rule's account, began arriving in France in June, soon to be followed by the 5th

Australian Division. By the end of that month, they were entering the line, supported by the divisional artillery, whose gunners only three months before had been lighthorsemen and infantrymen. By 5 July, the comparative veterans of the 1st and 2nd Division in Birdwood's I Anzac Corps had been relieved by the newcomers of the 4th and 5th Divisions under Godley and the II Anzac Corps. Monash, who had served under Godley as a brigade commander, had mixed feelings about his superior.

> Godley always gave me a square deal . . . yet I am bound to say that he was cordially hated by all New Zealanders, and is now hated by all the Army Corps Staff. The truth is that he belongs to the Army Clique which holds all militia officers in contempt as 'mere amateurs'. Yet he has done my brigade very well, and for that I am grateful to him.

Monash also thought that he had prior claim to command of the 4th Division ahead of Cox and thought, largely because both were professional soldiers, that Birdwood and Godley were prejudiced against him.

As Godley's Corps took over the 'nursery sector', Birdwood's troops moved south, first to the area opposite Messines for participation in a proposed offensive there and later to Amiens, to take their part in the Somme offensive. Through the first two weeks of July from that ghastly first day, the armies of Rawlinson and Gough continued to battle over mere metres of bitterly contested ground. Haig was determined that, although the great brunt of the fighting was being borne by those two armies, commanders elsewhere should continue to apply pressure on their fronts. To do so, however, was not easy. Ammunition was in short supply, and the armies fighting above the Somme had first priority.

The trickle of prisoners being captured by the British on the Somme convinced Haig that the pressure should be maintained. On 3 July it was discovered that the 13th *Jäger* Battalion had been sent from the 'nursery sector' opposite Godley's Corps; on 13 July British intelligence officers identified troops fighting on the Somme that had previously been at Lille. Now, the British command looked for a plan that would increase the pressure in the quieter northern sectors and prevent the enemy reinforcing his armies to the south. The commander of the British XI Corps, Lt.-Gen. Sir Richard Haking, had been formulating just such a plan.

At a conference on 8 July General Sir Charles Monro, commanding the First British Army, explained to his corps commanders the need to carry out offensive operations to prevent the Germans withdrawing troops and using them to reinforce the Somme. Monro had discussed the situation with Sir Herbert Plumer, commanding the flanking Second Army, and they had decided that the operations should probably be carried out in the vicinity of the junction of the First and Second Army fronts. As a result of this conference, Monro ordered Haking to prepare for an attack, on the basis that he would be given an additional division and extra artillery from Plumer's Second Army.

Three days earlier, on 5 July, the prospect of a breakthrough by Rawlinson's army on the Somme appeared so good that Haig ordered the other armies under his command to prepare to take advantage of the situation. Although in Haig's planning, the main burden of these attacks would fall on the Third Army, the Commander-in-Chief also ordered the First and Second Armies to be ready. 'The First and Second Armies should each select a front to attempt to make a break in the enemy's lines, and to widen it subsequently.' In reply, Plumer ruled out offensives at Messines and Ypres, where the Germans had been strengthening their defences. The best prospect, Plumer thought, was the Sugar-loaf salient near Fromelles where it was thought the German defences were less strong and less well developed. Plumer knew of Haking's plans for the area; he also saw an opportunity to employ the Australians. 'The only place', he wrote to Monro, 'I can attempt to make a break would be somewhere on my right — in conjunction with your left. If it should happen that your left was the place you chose, we might make a joint arrangement. . .'

Haking had first suggested the plan in the middle of June. Much more ambitious than the raids then proposed for troops not involved in the Somme offensive, Haking's plan was to capture and hold a salient known as the Boar's Head, then about 7 kilometres south-west of the Anzac Corps flank. As well, Haking planned a larger but basically similar operation against the Sugar-loaf salient, which jutted towards the junction of the British and Anzac lines. Haking had sent a copy of his proposed plan to Birdwood, whose corps was then holding the line, for his plan included a small attack by the Australians. Nothing came of Haking's plans* — one of many being produced by similar head-quarters up and down the line — while Birdwood's Corps held the line, but with the offensive on the Somme needing support, it was exhumed and examined.

When planning the attack, Haking had assumed that he would be required to capture the Fromelles-Aubers ridge, one and a half kilo-metres behind the enemy's front lines and just south of Lille. Monro could see little point to such an attack, particularly if the aim of any offensive in his area was merely to help the pressure on the Somme.

---

*Neither Birdwood nor White showed any enthusiasm for the plan, which they considered to be foolish, ill-considered and unnecessary.

On 12 July Haking was told that he would not be required to carry out his more ambitious project. Now the attention switched south once more, to the great offensives mounted on 14 July (see chapter 5). On 13 July the 5th Australian Division was warned that it could be involved in an attack; much of the information passed to Maj.-Gen. M'Cay being similar to, and not updated from, the information passed by Monro to his Corps commanders nearly a week before. On the same day, however, Haking was told by Monro that some nine enemy battalions had been withdrawn from Lille and he was to expedite his attack. The on-off, on-again, off-again operation was on once more.

The attack Haking was planning, and the concept of the operations held by Haig's headquarters, however, were vastly different. Haig's staff thought that operations at the junction of the First and Second Armies should be an 'artillery demonstration' which would form 'a useful diversion and help the southern operations'. On 13 July Maj.-Gen. R.H.K. Butler, Deputy Chief of the General Staff, visited Plumer and told him that Haig required offensive operations at the junction of the First and Second Armies. According to Edmonds, the British official historian, Butler thought that two diversions might be employed, with the bombardment beginning the following day and culminating in an assault three days later.

It is one thing to issue orders; quite another to issue orders that are capable of being obeyed. These orders were plainly absurd, for they took no account of the planning and preparation necessary for them to be carried out. In a word, they were silly. And by ordering such a bombardment Butler and the GHQ officers were being remarkably foolish. It would have been impossible to move all the artillery batteries that were supposed to be participating in the attack into place overnight, which was the time frame laid down by Butler to Plumer. Bean is positive that the operation was ordered merely as an 'artillery demonstration' but that view is not born out by Edmonds' account of Butler's orders to Plumer. The GHQ war diary for the period shows that on 14 July, OAD 66, an operation order for the offensive operations by the First and Second Army was issued. This operation order is not specific however, and we must rely on the British official historian's account that the operation was intended to be a local attack intended to hold the enemy to his ground and teach him that he could not, with impunity, reinforce the main battle by thinning out his line on this front. Importantly, the British historian continued: 'At 6.30 p.m. on the 13th General Haking received verbal orders from the First Army commander, who desired that the preliminary bombardment should 'give the impression of an impending offensive operation on a large scale and limited the infantry objective to the German front-line system'.

Haking issued his orders accordingly. The aim was 'to prevent the enemy from moving troops southwards to take part in the main battle'. For this purpose, Haking's orders added, 'the preliminary operations, so far as is possible, will give the impression of an impending offensive operation on a large scale, and the bombardment which will be commenced on the morning of the 14th inst will be continued with increasing intensity up till the moment of the assault'.

Brig.-Gen. H.E. 'Pompey' Elliott, who commanded a brigade in the attack, later described the planning which had produced these orders as a 'tactical abortion'. The demonstration had suddenly become much larger; instead of the minor raids, now Haking was to attack and capture a sector of the German front line system. In this hybrid attack, the worst features of both plans were incorporated. First, because the lone bombardment would precede the infantry attack, any hope of surprise would be lost. Secondly, Haking had made his plans without knowing that the artillery, upon which he predicated such an important aspect, would be in short supply. Haking thought that he would have artillery from three divisions. Instead, he was to have only two divisional artillery, the 4th and 5th Australian, and they were inexperienced and still largely untrained. Thirdly, Haking planned his attack on one of the strongest areas held by the Germans, but the attack was to be carried out by two divisions of very limited experience. The Australian 5th Division had only just arrived in France, and had no experience of fighting on the Western Front. It had been denuded of its artillery earlier in the year; it had suffered from the lack of experienced officers and NCOs during the training in Egypt. The British division which Haking proposed to use, the 61st, was in an even worse state. It was a Territorial army division, had been milked of its best men to provide reinforcements for the Somme fighting and had only just arrived from England.

When Haking discovered that he was short of both artillery and infantry, he was forced to adjust his original plans. Another British division, the 31st, had been allocated to Haking but it also had recently withdrawn from the Somme fighting where it had formed part of Hunter-Weston's VIII Corps on the first day and had suffered hugely. Faced with such difficulties, Haking shortened the front by 1,822 metres and limited his attack to two divisions. The 'tactical abortion' was becoming worse.

Haking had learned little from an operation he mounted against the Boar's Head salient on 29 June. This operation, similar in so many respects, had failed disastrously. One participant later wrote, 'The Divisional general was ungummed,* but it seemed to us that there were

---

*That is, dismissed.

others who were responsible, and, if they had lost their commands after this failure, possibly greater disasters might have been avoided . . .'

On 13 July when M'Cay was first informed of the possible operation, he was told merely that his division, the artillery from the 4th Australian Division and some other heavy batteries would be placed under Haking's command for the attack. That night at 11 p.m., a hurried conference at II Anzac Corps headquarters explained further details of the plan. M'Cay was told that the attack, provisionally fixed for 17 July, would be made by three divisions, including his own.

M'Cay was gratified to discover that his division, the last to be formed and the last to arrive in France, was to be first into action on a major scale. Importantly, Godley did not raise any objections, either to Plumer or to Birdwood who had administrative command of the AIF. Godley's reluctance to raise any objections about the plan might be compared to the opposition expressed both by Birdwood and Brudenell White when Haking's proposals were put forward originally. Nor, so far as it is possible to tell from the remaining records, was any objection raised by any member of Godley's headquarters staff, which was overwhelmingly comprised of British army officers, although the divisions under his command were Australian.

It would be almost impossible to overestimate the difficulties faced by M'Cay and his staff. Here was a brand new division, just into the line, that had been removed from its parent corps and handed over to a new corps on just a few days' notice. Here was a plan, that had been subjected to revision after revision as the tactical situation both in the area of operations and on the Somme battlefields changed. Here was a British Corps commander planning a three division attack on a 5.5 kilometre front being forced almost overnight to alter his plans because one of the divisions he had planned to use had been severely battered in fighting two weeks before. Here was a plan being based on the availability of artillery that proved to be heroically optimistic, and the most charitable explanation of that optimism is that Haking had been misled accidentally. Here too was a plan for a corps attack being cobbled together, with all the revisions and the second thoughts, in just three days, and while the artillery preparation was being fired.

Still M'Cay was enthusiastic about the attack but his feelings were not shared by Harold Edward 'Pompey' Elliott, his most outstanding brigade commander. For any general, even one as easy going and tolerant as M'Cay, Elliott would have been a handful as a subordinate commander. He was a prominent Melbourne lawyer and had been a distinguished sportsman as a student at the University of Melbourne. He was also, in that rather hackneyed phrase, a born soldier. During the South African war, Elliott had left his studies and enlisted as a private soldier, fighting with distinction and being awarded the Distinguished Conduct Medal, the highest award (apart from the Victoria Cross) which was available to other ranks. Returning to complete arts and law degrees, in the intervening 14 years, Elliott combined part time soldiering with the practice of law and on the outbreak of war he was commanding the Essendon Rifles.

He left Australia as the commanding officer of the 7th Battalion and led it with great distinction and personal courage throughout the Gallipoli campaign. According to the historian of the 5th Division he was:

> A big man with big generous impulses, he was known and loved by every member of his command, and his appointment to the 15th Brigade was hailed by all ranks as a matter for sincere rejoicing. He commanded the 15th Brigade from its earliest days till its latest, and throughout the whole war he directed every moment of his time, and every ounce of his energy, to promoting and maintaining its efficiency.

Within a fortnight of taking command of the 15th Brigade, Elliott attempted to sack three of his four battalion commanders and replace them with younger men with whom he had served and whom he trusted. These attempts brought him into direct conflict with both Birdwood and White and he was forced to accept the officers he had been allocated. Eventually, however, Elliott prevailed and his efforts were largely responsible for building a 'brigade marked for its fighting spirit and *esprit de corps*.'

'Pompey' Elliott was altogether typical of the best kind of citizen soldier this country has produced: successful in both his professional and military life, although his success at the latter was achieved at huge cost to the former; gregarious and a natural leader of men; totally devoted to his troops and their welfare; openly contemptuous of the more ponderous methods and procedures adopted by Staff Corps officers noted more for their rigidity of mind than their flexibility of purpose.

Elliott had the greatest misgivings about the attack. He wrote later:

> When I moved into the line I had carefully reconnoitred it from every point of view. It had been the scene of an attack early in the war (May 9th, 1915) by some 30,000 (three divisions) of Regular British Troops with another 25,000 in Reserve, supported by 500 guns who fired 80,000 rounds of ammunition. They suffered 10,000 casualties, and did not gain a single yard, and the attack was abandoned at nightfall on the grounds that a continuance of the attack would mean a useless waste of life.

> Moreover, General Haking had a little farther south on the 29th June, 1916, carried out a similar attack, which was repulsed with heavy loss.

Because of his doubts about the attack, Elliott persuaded one of Butler's assistants at Haig's GHQ, Major H.C.L. Howard, to accompany him forward from brigade headquarters to the front line. The fighting brigadier and the English staff officer went forward to No Man's Land. Elliott showed Howard his orders.

> I pointed out the difficulties. I explained why I had placed machine guns in the space between my right and the British left so as to cover my flank in the event of the British failing to take the Sugar-loaf and to cover our advance until they had done so, a measure of which he warmly approved.

Elliott then asked Howard if he could give him any suggestion to better his orders. Howard replied he could not. Elliott turned on him and said: 'Now you know all I do. You have been on this front nearly two years; I've been here 10 days. I give you my fixed opinion that we have not an earthly chance of success. I want you to tell me what you think of it all?' Howard replied bluntly. 'If you put it to me like that, sir, I must answer you in the same way as man to man. It is going to be a bloody holocaust.' Elliott, for whom the proprieties of the chain of command never held much attraction, then made a simple request of Howard. 'Well then, if that is your real opinion, will you promise me that you will go tonight on your return to General Haig, tell him that is your opinion and that it is mine also?' Now the civilian soldier was at his disrespectful best: ignoring his own divisional commander and headquarters; ignoring the British corps commander who was planning the attack; using as emissary a member of Haig's staff to go directly to the Commander-in-Chief.

Elliott did not discover whether Howard had taken this apparently impertinent request to Haig until 1929 when the third volume of Bean's history was published. In July that year, shortly after its publication, Elliott addressed the United Service Institution on the battle. He remarked then that Howard was 'much moved by this appeal' and promised faithfully to take the matter to Haig. Howard did take the matter up with Haig, but the British staff officer had more to do than simply investigate the reasons for the doubts shown by one Australian brigadier-general. Howard had the responsibility of collecting a summary of the plans made for the attack by the Chiefs of Staff of both the First and Second Armies and by Butler, Haig's deputy Chief of Staff. Howard's remarks about Elliott's reservations formed only a minor part of that report, because all the Chiefs of Staff agreed on the plans. His report to Haig, however, included Elliott's reservations and Haig noted, 'Approved, except that infantry should not be sent in unless adequate supply of guns and ammunition for counter-battery work is provided. This depends partly on what guns enemy shows'. The day after that report was submitted and noted by Haig, Butler saw both Plumer and Monro and pointed out that the Commander-in-Chief did not want the infantry to attack unless the commanders were satisfied that they had sufficient artillery and ammunition, not only to capture, but to hold and consolidate the enemy's trenches. As well, Butler brought the latest intelligence information. No longer was there an urgent need to attack on 17 July; the information in possession of GHQ concerning the transfer of German reserves 'did not impose the necessity for the attack to take place tomorrow, 17th, as originally arranged'.

Haking was adamant that his attack should go ahead. He 'was most emphatic that he was quite satisfied with the resources at his disposal; he was quite confident of the success of the operation, and considered that the ammunition at his disposal was ample to put the infantry in and keep them there'. Again, the conference notes record Haking's view: 'The troops are worked up to it, were ready and anxious to do it, and he considered that any change of plan would have a bad effect on the troops now'.

Both Monro and Plumer had their doubts about the operation: unless it could be of direct advantage to the main battle on the Somme, it should not go ahead. But they were swayed by the possible advantages on the Somme; in the meantime, the plan should stand. Haking, perhaps sensing that the conference was backing his scheme, chanced his arm further. In the event of a great success, might he be allowed to press on and take Aubers Ridge? The answer from Haig's staff officers was an emphatic 'No'; the objective was to be strictly limited and Haig did not intend allowing it to go further, 'however inviting' the prospects.

That afternoon, heavy rain caused Butler to think again about Haking's plan of attack. He returned to the headquarters of the First Army and although he did not see Monro, impressed upon his staff that 'if the weather or any other cause, rendered a postponement desirable, it was to be clearly understood that it was in the power of the Army commander to postpone or cancel the operation at his discretion'. On being informed of Butler's actions, however, Haig approved.

The rain that afternoon also prevented the heavy artillery from registering its targets. At 4 a.m. on 17 July when the final seven hours' bombardment should have begun, the countryside was blanketed by a thick mist which made observation, and thus registration, impossible. Five hours later, Haking reluctantly postponed the operation. 'The infantry and the field artillery are not fully trained', he wrote to Monro, 'and GHQ, from what was said at your conference yesterday, do not appear to be very anxious for the attack to be delivered . . . I should be glad to know if you wish me to carry it out tomorrow on the same programme. It is important, with these new troops, that this information should be given to me as early as possible, so that I can issue such instructions as will minimise any loss of morale owing to postponement'.

So, within a day, Haking had changed his opinion about the morale of the troops under his command. In fact, the Australians welcomed the opportunity to rest. Preparations for the attack had been frantic since M'Cay had received his first orders a bare five days before. In fact, the 5th Division had never been in the front line before, even in a quiet 'nursery' sector; now it was to be flung into a major attack.

As the heavy rain fell on into the afternoon, Haking also discovered to his chagrin that some of his heavy artillery had never fired before. This was not unusual in either the British or Australian armies at this stage of the war. Many staff officers, including gunners who should have known better, held the singularly optimistic view that such training could be carried out in action. So, with the weather and the more complete knowledge of the forces at his disposal combining to increase Haking's doubts, the British corps commander was beginning to admit that his initial optimism might have been unjustified.

On receiving Haking's request for the postponement, Monro also decided that the operation should be cancelled. He informed Haig, asking also for leave to tell Plumer of his decision. Haig's headquarters replied:

> The Commander-in-Chief wishes the special operation . . . to be carried out as soon as possible, weather permitting, provided always that General Sir Charles Monro is satisfied that the conditions are favourable, and that the resources at his disposal, including ammunition, are adequate both for the preparation and execution of the enterprise.

After the war, the lawyer Elliott was particularly acerbic about this reply from Haig's headquarters. 'The word "adequate" should, in my opinion, be forbidden in all military instructions. It leaves too much to the imagination.'

So, despite all the doubts about the Sugar-loaf salient attack, and the seemingly endless revisions, it would still go ahead. Not one commander or senior staff officer was prepared to counter Haking's excessive enthusiasm for this ill conceived, ill planned and ill prepared plan. Neither Haig nor Monro possessed the necessary moral courage to say to Haking: 'Your plan is nonsense. It will result only in unnecessary loss of life without any appreciable gain'. And Butler, who as Haig's deputy

Chief of Staff exercised considerable powers on both his own behalf and on behalf of his commander, also lacked the necessary moral courage to stand up to his chief and say: 'This is simply not on'. Bean is charitable to Haig: 'It is known that Haig was then apprehensive of a German counter-attack on the Somme — it actually fell next day. The form of his telegram was obviously determined by his principle of standing to a decision already given'. But as Monro had already said the resources made available for the attack were adequate, Haig's telegram gave no possible alternative for the army commander or his enthusiastic corps commander. In this passage, Bean brilliantly summarised the background to this wretched operation:

> Suggested first by Haking as a feint-attack; then by Plumer as part of a victorious advance; rejected by Monro in favour of attack elsewhere; put forward again by GHQ as a 'purely artillery' demonstration; ordered as a demonstration but with an infantry operation added, according to Haking's plan and through his emphatic advocacy; almost cancelled through weather and the doubts of GHQ — and finally reinstated by Haig, apparently as an urgent demonstration — such were the changes of form through which the plans of this ill-fated operation had successively passed.

The final bombardment, of seven hours duration, was ordered by Haking to begin at 11 a.m. on 19 July. The infantry attack, originally planned to take place at noon, was now to be made at 6 p.m., three hours before dusk. Clearly Haking was not persuaded by the victories of Rawlinson's army five days before which had followed their night attacks.

The Fromelles battlefield was one of the lowest areas of the Western Front. A flat, dank, marshy area, only 15 metres above sea level and torn, like so much of the front line, by shell holes which cratered the surface so that it resembled a heaving swelling sea. The rain and the naturally high water table combined to fill the bottoms of these shell holes with putrid water and thick, glutinous mud. Through the area trickled a tiny stream, the River Laies; a course unjustly dignified with the description 'river'. Little more than a couple of metres at its widest, this stream was some small impediment to infantry. Shells which had exploded in the stream bed had left craters that increased the obstacles. Aubers Ridge, the high ground which Haking was so enthusiastic about capturing, was about 3,000 metres to the south. The Germans had sited their defences with typical skill and precision between the high ground

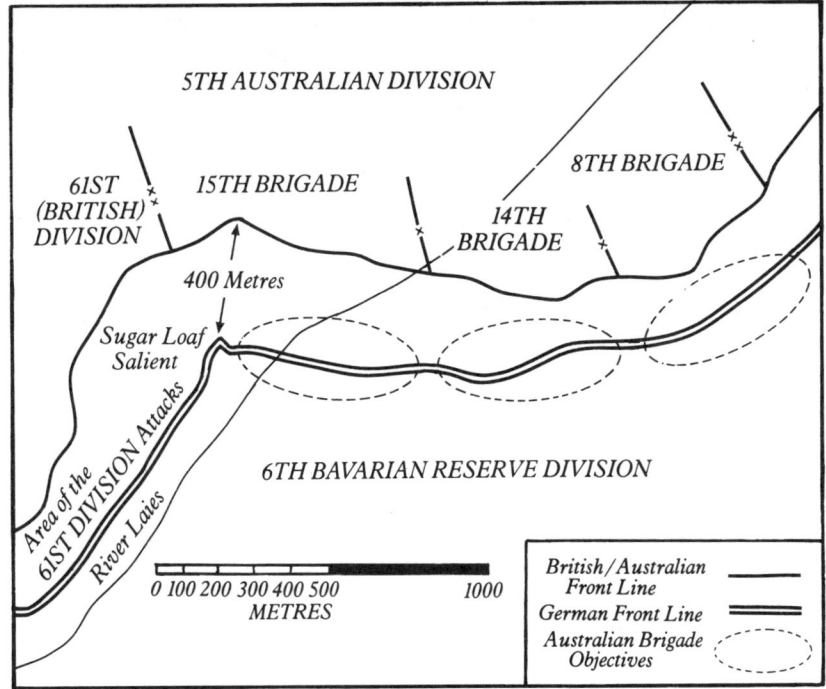

Fromelles area, showing British and Australian objectives before 5th Division attack.

and the front line. This was an expanse of generally low-lying ground, with trenches, wire and mutually supporting strong points, gradually rising to commanding heights. Thus, the Germans had the advantage of ground, for any assaulting infantry would have to cross considerable obstacles. They also had the advantage of height, and the inestimable value of observing all the preparations for the attack.

In front of the British 61st Division, the Laies ran behind the German front lines. Opposite the junction point between the two divisions, the stream crossed No Man's Land and entered the Australian lines at the junction of the 14th and 15th brigade fronts. The front lines themselves were not parallel. Although they ran in the 5th Division sector, almost due east-west, on the right of the Australian lines the German line suddenly deviated south-west. The effect of this deviation, cleverly planned by the Germans to take advantage of a slight rise, was to create a salient towards the British and Australian lines; this was the Sugar-loaf. This position had been reinforced with concrete protection and machine gunners could, with impunity from all but the heaviest artillery fire, bring flanking fire to bear on any assault.

On the right of the Australian sector, the lines were about 500 metres apart; on the left, a bare 100 metres or so separated the Australians and the Germans. But the Sugar-loaf salient was the key to the position for, from here, the Germans could fire upon assaults from both the British and the Australian lines. It was this salient that had worried Elliott when he took Howard forward. What would happen to the Australian assault if the British failed to take the Sugar-loaf as planned? Tragically, Elliott was to discover that his fears were well justified.

Both the British and the Australian troops were condemned to an advance of varying distances across open, water-logged ground under the direct observation of the enemy on Aubers Ridge and in Fromelles. They were committed to attacking across the same ground, and using a similar plan, that had failed so demonstrably the year before. The latest plan depended upon the artillery successfully cutting the German wire and the infantry being able to get across No Man's Land quickly under cover of the guns. As well, the troops were committed to a plan that, even if successful, could bestow no great tactical advantage. So long as the Germans held the high ground of Aubers Ridge, they would have this sector of the front. Had it succeeded, Haking's plan would have simply meant that his forces would be holding a salient going nowhere; then they would have been faced with horrendous problems in its retention.

The artillery plan was simple enough: wire cutting, and destruction of the strong points. For the final bombardment, the gunners planned a succession of lifts or breaks, in the hope that the Germans would leave their dugouts and man their defences. During each such lift, the men in the front line were instructed to show their naked bayonets and dummy figures over the parapet so as to encourage the enemy to think the assault was about to begin.

The infantry plan matched that of the artillery in simplicity. The British and Australian divisions were to attack on converging axes, meeting on the Sugar-loaf. Haking had ordered that all brigades in the two divisions should be committed to the initial assault; his only reserve being a battalion from each brigade. Thus to commit any kind of fresh troops to the battle, either to reinforce a momentary success or to prevent a failure, was unnecessarily complicated because of the passage of the orders through an additional headquarters. His reserve force also lost the essential control measure of being commanded by its own brigade headquarters. As well, the bulk of the assaulting force was required to be in the front trenches or at the jumping off points at the same time. All this in clear observation by an enemy that had been guided to expect an offensive by the bombardment of the previous days and could now watch its final preparations.

After the opening day of the Somme battle, when GHQ realised that the artillery preparation had not annihilated the defenders and the lifting of the fire gave the Germans time to man machine guns, various training memoranda were issued covering these discoveries. Haking read these carefully and his planning directed that the infantry should deploy as closely as possible to the enemy positions. In this sector, however, the problem was exacerbated by the varying distances between the two lines, from 400 metres opposite the Sugar-loaf itself, to about 200 metres between the British and German positions, and about 100 metres at the narrow point between the Australian and German positions.

M'Cay's Australians were faced with a frontage of less than 2,000 metres. The three brigades were to attack on a two battalion frontage, with the third battalion carrying stores for the assaulting troops and the fourth battalion in reserve. The assaulting troops would cross No Man's Land in four waves, each of about 200 men about 100 metres apart. Worried about keeping to the carefully timed programme, M'Cay ordered his first and second wave troops to be ready in their own front trenches three hours before the assault. The troops of the third and fourth waves were to assemble in trenches about 300 metres behind the front and were to be ready to occupy the front trenches as the first and second waves left.

M'Cay stressed that the first wave should capture the first line of German trenches, with the second wave passing through and taking the second line. The subsequent waves had to deal with the German third line which was supposed to be about 150 metres further back. But there were no orders about the first wave holding the first line.

The Australians were still smarting over the loss of the Stokes mortars. M'Cay ordered that the mortars and the Vickers machine guns be brought forward only when it was clear the Australians had captured and were holding the enemy positions. The battalions' Lewis guns could be brought forward after the last waves of each battalion had passed. The concentrated firepower available from the Lewis guns would have been invaluable to assaulting troops; leaving them behind was a mistake of inexperience.

In the Australian division, six battalions had not even seen the front trenches before the attack; the other six had been there only for two days and two nights. About a quarter of the 14th and 15th Brigades were experienced veterans but the 8th Brigade had virtually no old soldiers. Brig.-Gen. E. Tivey, commanding the 8th Brigade, selected his assault battalions carefully; they were the 32nd and the 31st, the former comprised largely of West Australian and South Australian miners and farmers, the latter of Queensland miners and bushworkers.

On 18 July Haking published an order which was read to the troops. Its tone was decidedly casual and chatty.

> As you know we were going to have a fight on Monday, but the weather was so thick that our artillery could not see well enough to produce the very accurate shooting we require for the success of our plan. So it had to be put off and GHQ said do it as soon as you can. I have fixed Zero for Wednesday and I know you will do your best for the sake of our lads who are fighting down south.

8

'Minor Offensive' or Raid?

OAD 78. C-in-C's appreciation of the gallant efforts made by troops of the First Army in the minor offensive at Fauquissart* on 19th July 1916. *Entry in the War Diary of Haig's GHQ.*

Zero day, 19 July 1916, dawned fine with a mist hanging in wisps over the sodden marshlands. In the Australian Division, the troops made their final preparations, curious about the action they were about to face, determined that they would uphold the standards established at Gallipoli the previous year. In the 54th Battalion, Lieutenant Jacques d'Alpuget, a 30 year old accountant from Woollahra in Sydney and a former Australian rugby international, wrote:

> We . . . are preparing for something big . . . the biggest move any Australians have done in France . . . long before this letter reaches you you will know the result which I feel certain will be to the credit of Australia. If I happen to be one of the unlucky ones you will know I have done my best and lead a straight life up to the finish.

According to Captain A. D. Ellis, the 5th Division historian, the troops received only five hours' warning of the attack. At 11 a.m., the artillery began promptly, a fascinating tumult for these anxious diggers who had yet to experience action. Even the veterans of Gallipoli had never before been through anything like a Western Front artillery barrage. They could only marvel at the noise and the smells and the constant detonations on the German lines, only a few hundred metres to their front.

In 'Jack' d'Alpuget's brigade, H.R. Williams, then a sergeant in the 56th Brigade, stood with his comrades and watched the final bombardment. 'The forward area was shrouded in a pall of dust and smoke and shell-bursts, and we believed that no man could live in an inferno.'

---

*Fauquissart, the nearest major village to the Fromelles battlefield on the British side of the lines.

Brig.-Gen. 'Pompey' Elliott who, as Bean noted characteristically had been among his men in the front line genuinely relishing the danger, was also impressed by the extent of the bombardment. 'Boys, you won't find a German in the trenches when you get there.' Shades of Gordon at Pozières just 19 days before.

Captain Ellis wrote that the morning was quiet, 'with little enemy retaliation to the fire of our guns and trench mortars. It almost seemed that he knew our forward lines were not yet packed with the infantry assembling for the attack'.

At 2.15 p.m., however, the enemy fire began to intensify and by 3 p.m.:

> a heavy and continuous volume of fire was falling over the front and support line and the saps leading to them, now filled with the assembling infantry. *Minenwerfer* were reaching our lines on the left and centre sectors, while Pinney's Ave [a communications trench in the centre of the Australian line] was already badly damaged and the 15 Brigade area was being raked with shrapnel. In these circumstances, casualties commenced to mount steadily but reports from the front line stated that the enemy wire and parapets were suffering severely and were likely to prove of little protection to him.

The excited soldiers watched the bombardment and cheered every time a German position appeared to be hit but cooler heads noted that the strongest defences, at the apex of the Sugar-loaf salient, had not been affected and the wire here remained uncut. In mid-afternoon, the British artillery increased its fire on to this position.

Before the parade for the attack, Sergeant Williams had time to stroll back to an *estaminet* and found the place full to overflowing. 'Madame and her assistants were hard pressed to cope with the rush. The men were in the best of spirits and looked forward to the attack as if it were a football match. All talk was of "stunt" and the women of the *estaminet* knew the details as well as we did.' The fear of 'spies' was never very far from the Australians in these early days in France; carrier pigeons were observed crossing No Man's Land heading in the directions of the Germans; suspicious movements of civilians were reported, often suspicions unreasonably entertained.

In fact, the Germans had an excellent idea of the British plans from their observations of the preparations. 'Pompey' Elliott visited the area after the Armistice.

> In the village of Fromelles the church ... had been turned into a solid cube of concrete, except for a stair so narrow that only with difficulty

could a normally built man ascend it. At its head near the ridge pole it terminated in a loophole for an observer who, with a telescope could, with perfect safety to himself, count every sentry in our lines. He had also an extensive view across our back areas, and could at once detect any preparation for attack.

On 17 July the increased bombardment by the Australian artillery must have aroused German suspicions of an impending attack; on 18 July the observer in the Fromelles tower would have been able to see carrying parties bringing forward ammunition, grenades and rolls of mats for crossing wire obstacles. Those observations were quickly acted upon. Three German reserve battalions were warned out, either for carrying duties or to reinforce part of the German line. Despite the impressive artillery fire falling on the German positions, the defenders were hardly affected, and early afternoon on 19 July, the Germans were beginning to reply to the artillery bombardment with their own fire. This was to increase in intensity throughout the afternoon, with the heaviest fire directed on to the left of the Australian line, held by troops of the 8th Brigade. Here, where barely 200 metres separated the two positions, the Germans were most perturbed about the possibility of attack. The Australians might well have been able to cross No Man's Land under the cover of artillery fire and be on the German positions before the defenders had time to recover and man their weapons.

The Australians in these positions were also suffering casualties from their own artillery fire falling short. Although faults in the ammunition certainly contributed to these casualties, inexperience of the gunners was also a major factor. And, each time the British and Australian artillery lifted or paused as part of Haking's plan to deceive the enemy, the German fire increased in intensity. Haking's ruse was proving expensive to his own troops.

Right along the Australian line, the infantry suffered casualties from the German artillery. Packed shoulder-to-shoulder in crowded trenches and huddled behind ineffective breastworks, they could only wait for the signal to start moving in the assault. The stretcher bearers, who had the unenviable job of collecting the casualties and carrying them back to the rudimentary treatment available from the doctors at the regimental aid post, were at even greater risk. Private W.J.A. Allsop of the 8th Field Ambulance wrote:

We crept along, seeking first of all the serious cases of wounded. Backwards and forwards we travelled between the firing line and the RAP with knuckles torn and bleeding due to the narrow passage ways. 'Cold

> Sweat' not perspiration, dripped from our faces and our breath came out only in gasps . . . By the time we had completed 2 trips . . . we were . . . completely exhausted.

All through the afternoon, the Australians continued to assemble for the attack. Fortified with what Ellis called 'good breakfasts and dinners' (and, no doubt, with *estaminet* wine and beer), the Australians were in good spirits despite the artillery fire which raked up and down their lines.

In the 56th Battalion, the reserve battalion of 14th Brigade, Sergeant Williams had returned from the *estaminet* with his mates.

> We had issued to us an extra bandolier each of cartridges, done up into khaki-cloth formed into pouches, with a loop to slip over the shoulder, iron rations and some extras that a thoughtful Captain Fanning had secured for us. NCOs had wire-cutters fitted to their rifles. Each man carried a pick or a shovel and several sandbags. We fell-in in the school yard, children gazing at us with a look of awe on their small old-fashioned faces.

At 5.45 p.m. Williams was sitting on the roadway in front of the 60-pounder battery.

> One of the guns had suffered a premature explosion of its breech, which had made a mess of its crew. We saw the stretcher-party hurry over and collect the wounded. The fire of the other guns was maintained; we could see their shells skimming the treetops on their journey. Many eyes had been watching the time; at zero hour our platoon sergeant remarked — 'They are over!' Floating back from the front line came the sound of heavy machine gun fire to tell us that the attack had been launched.

On the extreme right of the Australian attack, the men of the 59th Battalion got halfway across No Man's Land with only small losses, mainly from rifle fire. About 10 minutes after the first Australians had crossed the parapet, a machine gun was heard firing from the Sugar-loaf despite the artillery fire still falling on the enemy position. When the artillery stopped, the enemy machine gun fire increased in intensity.

As we have noted, the Sugar-loaf itself was a British objective. In the 61st Division, the method of leaving trenches or breastworks for an attack was through a sally-port, a method which, as the British official historian remarked, 'did not facilitate a rapid deployment beyond the British wire, and on those parts of the front where the German machine gunners were ready and waiting to open fire each sally-port became a death trap'. One commanding officer, seeing the casualties as his men left through these 'death traps', leapt on to the parapet and urged his troops across. Within minutes, he was killed by accurate machine gun fire.

As well casualties in the battalions nearest the Australian flank had been heavy from the German artillery fire; more than 140 men were killed and the assaulting forces were hurriedly reorganised to give some kind of cohesion to the attack.

Even as the British troops managed to get across the parapets, they were quickly seen and fired upon from the Sugar-loaf machine gunners who had hardly suffered from the artillery bombardment. On the right of the British attack, some limited successes were achieved, but on the vital left, the strong defences of the Sugar-loaf proved impossible to counter.* Here, the British attack had failed completely; the wire had not even been cut by the artillery fire; the defenders had withstood the bombardment with impunity. Even as the attack faltered and halted, the British artillery could not fire on to the strongest German defensive positions because the guns being used were the oldest on the front and the gunners could not guarantee their aim. According to Elliott, 'They were really afraid, as we learnt later on, of aiming at the Sugar-loaf at all for fear of hitting our own lines'.

But the Sugar-loaf was the key. So long as the Germans held this small rise, jutting defiantly towards the British and Australian lines, they could bring fire from a flank on to both the British and the Australian assault.

Elliott had moved his brigade headquarters forward, and was only a couple of hundred metres behind the lines. There he waited anxiously for news of the assault. As the sound of firing rose and died, Elliott hoped that the assault had succeeded and that his battalions were in the German forward trenches on this, the strongest part of the lines. He sent runners forward to discover what had happened to his battalions, as all communications with the assaulting troops were lost from the moment they crossed the parapet. One young officer, Lieutenant D.B. Doyle, sent to find the 60th Battalion, found he could not get across to the left of the brigade front. Contacting the second in command of the 59th Battalion who had been sent back to say the battalion's progress was blocked, Doyle returned to Elliott's headquarters with the gloomy news. At 7.18 p.m., Elliott told M'Cay that the trenches were still full of the enemy. 'Every man who rises is being shot down. Reports

---

*One small group actually reached the German wire before they were killed; their skeletons were found draped over the rusty entanglements in November 1918.

from the wounded indicate that the attack is failing from want of support.'

The wounded were indeed telling the story. The assaulting troops crossed the parapets and moved quickly across the broken ground down toward the Laies; here, they were sheltered from the Sugar-loaf fire. But once they crossed this muddy ditch and moved up the other side, they came under increasingly intense machine gun fire. The 59th had stopped first, being nearest the enemy; the 60th managed to get almost to the enemy lines.

> The records of the 16th Bavarian *RIR*, which faced (the Australians) attributed the repulse of the Australians and of the neighbouring British to the determination of that regiment to sustain, in spite of the fire playing on it, continuous observation from its front-line trenches. As soon as one of its men, killed or wounded, fell from the parapet, another took his place. Thus rifle and machine gun fire was kept up, and officers had a good grasp of the situation. 'Riflemen of the 16th Bavarian *RIR*, lying at and west of Rouges Blanc,' says the official historian, 'cooly, eagerly awaited the approach of the enemy and shot him down with heavy loss. Officers were marked leading their men, and were quickly picked off.

In the Australian 60th Battalion, next to the 59th, the casualties were severe. Captain Ellis wrote:

> To halt in No Man's Land . . . was to court certain death and Major G.G. McRae* led his troops right on towards the enemy parapet. It was his last act of defiant leadership. Just at the enemy wire the enfilade fire from the Sugar-loaf became intense and there, almost at his goal, he fell. His adjutant fell beside him, and there, too, the greater part of the 60th Battalion melted away.

Gradually, it became clear to Elliott that the British had also failed on the other side of the Sugar-loaf and that their failure was ruining the 15th Brigade attack. 'Thus', wrote Ellis, 'on the entire front of the 15th Brigade, within half an hour from the time of assault, it was apparent that the 61st Division had failed to take the Sugar-loaf, and it was beyond human power to cross so wide a No Man's Land in the face of the machine gun fire that streamed continuously from it'.

The battalion in the centre of the Australian assault suffered similarly. In the reserve battalion of the centre brigade, Sergeant Williams noted

---

*McRae, a 26 year old architecture student and a member of the literary family, was commanding the battalion. He had been one of Elliott's protégés.

that the communication trench from the support to the front line had ceased to exist as defined work.

> ... the bodies of dead men lay thickly along its length. Here the supporting battalion, moving up, had suffered severely in the passage. The German shells still searched this sap and blew great craters along its length as we struggled along, trampling underfoot the dead that cluttered it. All the while we were losing men. Some of the wounded lay in pools staining the water with their blood. Dead men, broken trench material, shattered duckboards that tripped us as we passed; the smell of the fumes of high explosives, and the unforgettable odour of death made this trench a place of horror.

To the left of Elliott's 15th Brigade, where No Man's Land was only 100 to 200 metres wide, the Australians had more success. Here, however, the German artillery fire was heavy, even before the Australians left their assembly trenches. In one battalion area a bomb and ammunition dump exploded and the battalion headquarters group nearby was severely wounded. On the extreme left of the Australian line, the assaulting troops took casualties from Germans further north who were not being shelled.

Despite the casualties from the artillery and the German defenders, the Australians in the centre and on the left achieved their objectives. In doing so, however, many young officers were killed and some troops who reached the German trenches found themselves leaderless. But the Australians had not had to contend with the accurate and deadly fire from the Sugar-loaf. As the barrage lifted, they dashed across the broken ground of No Man's Land and were on the German parapets before the defenders had time to recover.

Ellis' account of this fighting is understandably proud, although the Australians did achieve a reputation for combat at close quarters. 'The enemy was caught in the act of manning his parapets and some bitter hand-to-hand fighting followed. It terminated, as all such hand-to-hand fighting terminated throughout the war, in the absolute triumph of the Australians and the extinction or termination of the Germans.' The assaulting troops had been ordered to leave their Lewis guns behind until the positions had been secured. Thus, armed with only rifles, bayonets and hand grenades the Australians were forced to resort to savage fighting.

The forward positions secured, the last stubborn German defender silenced, these Australians went looking for the third line. Off in the distance, through the haze of smoke covering the battlefield, they could dimly discern small parties of Germans fleeing from the higher ground.

The Australians 'strolled on through the grass', wrote Bean, 'like sportsmen after quail, occasionally shooting at Germans who had settled in shell holes and who now started up to run further'.

But apart from the small parties of Germans, broken and demoralised by this fierce onslaught, nothing could be found: no organised defensive positions; no third line; nothing but some old fragmentary trenches and a muddy, watery ditch.

So, instead of regrouping and reorganising, these troops, without leaders and without new orders, went looking for the definite and well constructed third line. By now, night was falling and the few officers who were left frantically attempted to bring some order to the apparent chaos, worried about the possibility of a German counter-attack. Gradually the position was consolidated, and rudimentary defences were prepared. But great gaping holes existed in the front line: battalions had lost touch with each other; companies lost touch with flanking companies and headquarters lost touch with forward troops. All through the night, the assaulting troops worked frantically to improve their defences, based not on any ground taken because of its tactical importance, but on the convenient and muddy ditch. Their efforts were hindered by the Germans, who counter-attacked frequently, not with major offensives but with heavy raids, designed to probe for weaknesses and launched with their much better knowledge of the ground.

These raids would follow a similar pattern. Under the cover of the persistent artillery fire, which fell throughout the night on the well registered targets of the old German trenches and the muddy drainage ditch, the Bavarians would sneak out in smallish groups. Short of the Australians' position they would halt waiting for the artillery to lift. Then, in the few minutes between artillery rounds, the Germans would jump into the trench and work their way along until they came across the Australian defenders. As often as not, a brief but violent mêlée would follow, in which the Germans would hurl their hand bombs around the corner of a trench and scamper back to safety. If the Australians caught a glimpse of the attackers, it was a coal-scuttle helmet silhouetted against the skyline just metres away. For a few short hours, the impersonality of the killing disappeared; war took on an intensely personal and individual nature.

Sergeant Williams, still well to the rear of the forward positions, learned that his brigade, the 14th, had carried its objective, but that it was doubtful whether it could hold on, because the Australian 15th Brigade and the British had failed to gain a foothold in the German lines.

Elliott had realised the extent of the failure in his sector within an hour of the commencement of the assault. Early in the battle Haking had been told that his centre brigade had somehow managed to capture part of the Sugar-loaf. Confidently, Haking ordered the hold on the Sugar-loaf be strengthened to help Elliott's brigade, but that order could not be obeyed. No British troops, not even the smallest party, had managed to penetrate the German wire.

As the corps commander, probably Haking was suffering most from the paucity and inaccuracy of the information being fed back. By 8 p.m. he knew that the Australian division had achieved two-thirds of its objectives, extending from the left towards the right, with the situation becoming more obscure and the information less reliable on the right of the Australian attack. From his British divisional commander, Haking knew that some limited success had been achieved on the extreme right of the assault, where the British troops had made the same limited gains as the Australians on the left.

In the centre however, no gains had been made. Here the British battalions virtually ceased to exist as formed bodies. Because of these failures, and the apparent successes on the flanks, the British brigade commanders sought to attack the Sugar-loaf once again, with the small forces left at their disposal. Their attack was planned for 9 p.m. Could the Australian 15th Brigade help?

Elliott discussed the British request with M'Cay. Elliott could scratch together a small force, two companies of the 58th Battalion under, in his own words, 'a splendid Duntroon boy', Major A.J.S. Hutchinson. Not yet 20, Hutchinson had been born in Victoria where his father was a clergyman. Shortly after 8 p.m. Elliott personally briefed Hutchinson, directing him to attack in support with the British at 9 p.m.

At 8.20 p.m., Haking was visited by a liaison officer from the British 61st Division who brought the melancholy news of the failure on the British front. The liaison officer also had news of the planned 9 p.m. attack. Immediately Haking countermanded the order for this attack, and issued orders to withdraw the 61st Division for a renewed attack the following day. The British corps commander also ordered M'Cay to consolidate the trenches captured on the Australian left, withdraw any isolated parties on the right, and not to make any further attacks on that area during the night. Under the circumstances these were sensible and reasonable orders.

Haking's orders were passed to the British brigades by the 61st Division commander, Maj.-Gen. C.J. McKenzie, in sufficient time to stop some of the British troops going forward for the planned 9 p.m. attack. But no similar order was ever passed to the Australian 5th Division. The only message logged in the diary reads simply 'Under instructions from the corps commander am withdrawing from captured enemy line after dark'.

There was no message that the proposed attack had been countermanded; no suggestion that the Australian troops under Hutchinson were on their own. Bean remarks that it is possible Hutchinson's attack might have been stopped if the message had been passed.

> Had the several brigades, as in later battles, been in direct communication with each other and maintained liaison officers at each other's headquarters, this would certainly have been the result. But apparently there was a failure at the headquarters of the 5th Australian Division to grasp either the meaning of the message or the importance of sending it on to General Elliott.

Here, Bean is rather unfair to the staff of the 5th Division headquarters. It was not until 9.10 p.m., when Haking's order was received, that the information about the cancellation of the attack finally reached M'Cay. The fault lay with the staff of Haking's corps headquarters, who did not transmit their commander's orders to the Australians for almost an hour. By then, of course, Hutchinson's assault had begun.

On his way to the jumping off point, Hutchinson collected some survivors of the 59th Battalion, but despite these eager reinforcements, the assaulting force was still pathetically small. Moreover, it was attacking without artillery support. Planned as a device to help the British assault, it no longer had any real purpose. Not knowing this, Hutchinson pressed on. His force was about two-thirds of the way across No Man's Land before the German defenders opened fire. The first bursts were well aimed. Men crumpled into heaps or scattered in search of cover. Hutchinson, realising that his assault had been broken, rose to inspire his troops. This effort proved to be in vain. The young officer fell, almost on the German wire. Seeing him fall, his batman pushed forward to try and recover his body but he too was shot, victim of the intense machine gun fire coming from the German positions. The attack was halted; the two companies of men were almost totally destroyed.

After the Armistice in November 1918, an Australian visited this area in front of the Sugar-loaf salient.

> We found the old No Man's Land simply full of our dead. In the narrow sector west of the Sugar-loaf salient, the skulls and bones and torn uniforms were lying about everywhere. I found a bit of Australian kit lying fifty yards from the corner of the salient, and the bones of an Australian officer and several men within a hundred yards of it. Further round, immediately on their flank, were a few British — you could tell them by their leather equipment — and within 100 yards of the west corner of

the Sugar-loaf salient there was lying a small party of English too — you could tell by the cloth of his coat.

By midnight a few survivors of this ghastly, wasteful attack had trickled back to the Australian lines. Sadly, Elliott reported its total failure. Now, as well, the Germans were strengthening their counter-attacks along the left of the Australian line where the successes had been achieved. And while the Germans continued to hold the Sugar-loaf salient, those counter-attacks stood every chance of success. As Elliott wrote later, 'it became speedily apparent to everybody that in view of the failure of the attack in the centre the ground won could not be held. So word was sent to them to withdraw to our own lines'.

To the Australians on the left and in the middle, the order to with-draw was not surprising. Sergeant Williams wrote:

> Towards night an increasing number of wounded began to stream back to us. Many were in a state of exhaustion and bleeding from wounds that had not been bandaged. They told of the almost hopeless task of trying to form a trench line while the German bombing parties appeared from everywhere. We were not surprised when, about 2 a.m. our platoon officer came and told us that our troops were about to return.

Williams' section was moved to the right, and entered a bay that had been badly damaged.

> At last daybreak came, and in its light, we saw the battlefield in all its ghastliness. In the long rank grass that covered No Man's Land of yes-terday were lying the dead and wounded. Many of the latter were trying to call back to us, and in doing so made of themselves a target for the German machine gunners.

By 5.45 a.m. on 20 July, the last of the 8th Brigade, on the extreme left of the Australian line, had been forced out of the trenches they had captured the evening before. In the centre, the 14th Brigade was hold-ing on desperately. At Sailly, just to the rear of the lines where Haking had established a temporary headquarters, M'Cay and Mackenzie were attending corps commander's conference. After the failure of Hutch-inson's attack, Haking had changed his mind yet again.

At 11 p.m. the previous night, Haking had ordered the 14th Brigade to 'attack the Sugar-loaf throughout the night' but the brigade com-mander could not oblige. His trenches were being shelled continually; he could not get his shattered battalions into position. Although the attack had been cancelled about 3 a.m., now Haking was anxious it should be renewed. General Monro was also at Haking's conference that morning. As the news of the withdrawal of the Australian 8th Brigade and the perilous position of the 14th Brigade reached the corps headquarters, the First Army commander stepped in. The planned attacks would not go ahead; the rest of the remaining Australian brigade would be withdrawn.

As this conference was putting the finishing touches to this tragic expedition in military futility, only a small group of Australians was left in the old German trenches. Under the command of Captain Norman Gibbins, a 38 year old Ipswich bank manager, these troops repulsed several German attacks along the trenches with bombs and bayonets. And as the Germans continued to press their way along the trenches, Gibbins leapt on to the parapet with a satchel-load of hand grenades and ran along, dropping them on the attackers below. But even as Gibbins rallied his men they noticed the retirement of the 8th Brigade troops on their left. The task of the rear guard commander, arguably the most difficult in war, was now with this quiet, gentle, careful, almost middle-aged bank manager. Bean, who knew him well, wrote that this task 'could not have fallen to a more suitable man. Combining the gentlest of natures with a most stern sense of discipline and duty, Gibbins possessed the firmest possible hold on his men, who almost worshipped him'.

Gibbins organised the orderly withdrawal of this last band of Australians left in the German lines. The wounded went first, the more badly wounded carried out by their comrades who were still able to walk. Then went the bombers, who were physically and emotionally exhausted by their efforts. Then the Lewis gunners and finally the officers left. Gibbins cried out, 'Come on, all you gunners', but was the last to leave the trench.

Sergeant White was one of the last gunners to leave. He saw Gibbins follow his men along a sap which had been dug during the night, between the German and the old Australian lines. Just where this sap met the Australian lines, Gibbins found his path blocked by wounded. Rather than push past, Gibbins climbed out of the sap. 'I saw him just reach the top of our trenches', wrote Sergeant White, 'where he turned his head around sharply and was immediately struck in the head by a bullet and killed instantaneously'.

With Gibbins' death, the battle of Fromelles virtually ended for the Australians. There was still the task of casualty clearance. Major A.W. Murdoch attempted to organise an unofficial truce to bring the wounded back from No Man's Land but despite the almost exquisite courtesy on the part of the Bavarians opposite, could bring in only a few casualties. From the hundreds of shell holes in No Man's Land, the wounded waved and gestured for help from the Australians who had regained the relative safety of their old lines. Of the lucky survivors, Sergeant Williams wrote that gradually their senses returned to normal and 'we looked around us like men wakened from a nightmare. The ordeal of the night was plainly visible on all faces, ghastly white showing through masks of grime and dried sweat, eyes glassy, protruding and full of that horror seen only on the face of men who have lived through a heavy bombardment'.

Hugh Fitzgerald Maudsley, medical officer of the 29th Battalion, has left in his diaries an unforgettable description of the attack's aftermath, as seen by a sensitive, noncombatant officer. Maudsley established his dressing station near the front line, realising early that the casualties would be heavy and his services would be in demand. The wounded started to come in about 1 p.m.; four hours later, another doctor came down through the shell fire which was falling around his dressing station to help Maudsley. From then, until 5 a.m. the next day, was 'a nightmare. The D(ressing) S(tation) was crammed full. Outside men died wanting help . . .' The next day, Maudsley wrote, 'This was a miserable dawn. The DS was a bloody shambles . . . the padre came down last night to dispense soup to the men, and incidentally to us. That kept us going. The awful part is that the news is bad . . .' Later that day, the wounded coming in presented another problem — gangrene. 'It was frightful dressing them.'

For the senior officers, spared the ordeal of fighting, the aftermath was almost as ghastly. Brig.-Gen. Tivey, commanding the 8th Brigade, could not hold back his tears. 'Above all', wrote Captain Ellis, 'he was characterised by a loving attachment to his men, and he was deeply moved as he picked his way carefully through the front line among the bodies of the men he had loved so well'. Bean came forward on 20 July and saw Elliott and the other brigade commanders. Of Elliott, Bean wrote: 'I felt almost as if I were in the presence of a man who had just lost his wife. He looked down and could hardly speak . . .' A.W. Bazley, Bean's assistant, wrote: 'No one who was present will ever forget the picture of him, the tears streaming down his face, as he shook hands with the returning survivors'.

Haig's headquarters sent an appreciation to Monro 'of the gallant efforts made by troops of the First Army in the minor offensive . . .' Those words 'minor offensive' again. In this 'minor offensive', the 5th Australian Division lost 5,533 men in less than 24 hours. The 61st Division, admittedly weaker, lost 1,547. The total German losses were

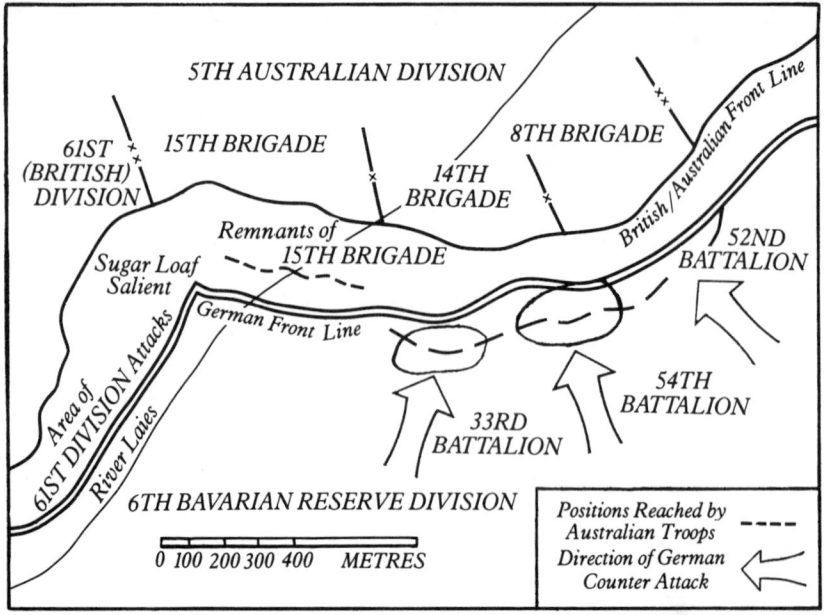

Fromelles battlefield, 9 p.m. on 19 July 1916.

less than 1,500. In detail, the Australian losses were truly appalling. For example, in the 60th Battalion, only one officer and 106 other ranks — out of a strength of 35 and 970, answered the roll call on 21 July.

The Australians felt let down by the British 61st Division. Sergeant Williams was disparaging about the fighting qualities of the Tommies: so were other Australians in their letters home. Even years later, this feeling of being let down was reinforced by the casualty figures, almost as if they were the results of some ghastly sporting fixture: Australia, 5,533; England 1,547. Yet the simple analysis of the figures overlooks that the 61st Division, a sad and depleted formation even before the battle, was at only half-strength and demonstrably unsuited for battle. But the Australians reserved their most bitter criticism for the British staff. In Williams words:

> Can the XI Corps staff absolve themselves when the 61st Division had been almost swept out of existence by the fire from this strong point on their flank, of committing the 15th Brigade to the attack again on the assurance that the 61st Division was to make another attempt on the strong point — whereas the 61st failed to make the attempt? The 5th Division was sacrificed on the altar of incompetence.

Despite its horrendous cost, the attack achieved nothing. Bean confided to his diary on 20 July:

> We wanted . . . to make the German think we were attacking there —
> so that he would hold his troops there. As a matter of fact we have proved
> to him . . . that we intended nothing serious — he was in doubt until we
> attacked. We have now given him the information. He could now, if he
> wanted, withdraw half the men who are on that front. And we have put
> out of action a fine division.

Years later, when Bean wrote the official history, he modified his language, but not his criticism.

> In spite . . . of consolatory messages received by the 5th Division from
> the high commanders . . . that, through its effort, the Germans would
> certainly be prevented from moving troops from that area to the Somme,
> the actual result was to inform the enemy that only a feint was intended.
> The normal inference would be that he could now move his troops
> without fear.

Ironically, early in the battle the Germans obtained a copy of Haking's orders from a dead British officer. Almost from the beginning they knew the attack was a feint.

In his after-action reports, Haking attempted to blame the fiasco upon the newness of the troops. 'The artillery preparation was adequate' Haking wrote.

> There were sufficient guns and sufficient ammunition. The wire was
> properly cut and the assaulting battalions had a clear run to and into the
> enemy trenches,. The Australian infantry attacked in the most gallant
> manner, and gained the enemy's position, but were not sufficiently trained
> to consolidate the ground gained. They were eventually compelled to
> withdraw and lost heavily in doing so. The 61st Division was not suffi-
> ciently imbued with the offensive spirit to go in as one man at the
> appointed time, some parts were late in deploying. With two trained
> divisions the position would have been a gift after the artillery bombard-
> ment.

In a later report, Haking wrote that the Australian attack was carried out in an exceptionally gallant manner. 'Their difficulties on the right flank were caused by the failure of the 61st Division to carry the Sugar-loaf.'

Again, however, Haking attempted to blame the failure of the infantry for the failure of the attack. But, added Haking, 'I think the attack, though it failed, has done both divisions a great deal of good'. Added Elliott with acerbity, 'The idea that an experience such as that could do the PBI [Poor Bloody Infantry] good appears to be a unique conception'.

Elliott certainly had no illusions why the attack had failed with such disastrous results. For the aggressive Australian, the attack had no redeeming quality except for the wonderful bravery shown by the officers and the men.

> The whole operation was so incredibly blundered from beginning to end that it is almost incomprehensible how the British Staff, who were responsible for it, could have consisted of trained professional soldiers of considerable reputation and experience, and why, in view of the outcome of this extraordinary adventure, any of them were retained in active command.

Much of the blame for the Australian losses was thrown on to M'Cay, unfairly according to both Bean and Elliott. According to Elliott, Haking sheltered behind Monro's weaknesses, and having laid the blame on the infantry's alleged shortcomings, particularly his own British Tommies, got away with it and retained his command until the end of the war.

Not surprisingly, the British official history is much less critical of Haking than either Bean or Elliott. Edmonds did not discuss Haking's plan, except to say that the pity of the action was that it need not have been fought, since the First Army had perfect liberty to cancel it. 'To have delivered battle at all, after hurried preparation, with troops of all arms handicapped by their lack of experience and training in offensive trench-warfare, betrayed a grave under-estimate of the enemy's powers of resistance.' Edmonds however, disagreed with Haking's reasons for the failure.

> The utmost endeavours of the artillery were unable either to subdue the German batteries or to 'reduce the defenders to a state of collapse before the assault' so the infantry, advancing in broad daylight, paid the price. Even if the German defences had been completely shattered by the British bombardment, and the infantry assault had succeeded, it would probably have proved impossible to hold the objective under the concentrated fire of the enemy's artillery directed by excellent observation. Such a situation had arisen only too often during the minor engagements fought earlier in the year.

In September 1927, when Bean was working on the third volume of the official history, he also turned to Haking's explanations for the failure of the attack and examined them in detail. He wrote that Haking's reasons for the failure — the newness of the infantry — could hardly be accepted because it ignored the additional factors:

> That the German riflemen and machine guns fired both through and after the bombardment; that the losses at starting were consequently enormous, especially in officers; and that the objective which Haking had set for his force proved to be a series of abandoned and water-filled trenches and ditches. The verdict of the military student will much more probably be that the well-known difficulties of a narrow-fronted offensive in trench warfare had been too lightly faced . . . the troops were admittedly raw; but it may be doubted if any infantry in the world could have crossed where the 15th Brigade failed . . .

Bean and Edmonds exchanged their chapters on the Fromelles battle. Edmonds attempted to defend Haking, and criticised Bean's draft, arguing that the doubts of officers such as Major Howard had no place in an official history. Edmonds also offered to send to Haking drafts of Bean's chapter of Fromelles, but there was no reply from the retired general. After a long and fruitless correspondence, Edmonds informed Bean that Haking would not comment on the battle. Added the British historian, 'I don't think he [Haking] was much use after his wound . . . in 1914'.

Elliott was also a trenchant critic of Haking. In July 1930, he lectured on the Battle of Fleurbaix (as it was then known). By then a major-general in the militia, Elliott had no compunctions about criticising the British command, and particularly Haking. After a lecture in Canberra in July, the Melbourne *Age* accused him of making 'an amazing outburst' against British inefficiency. In October, when Elliott delivered basically the same lecture to the Melbourne branch of the United Service Institution, he said he had made no such charge. He made no criticism of British inefficiency at Fromelles '. . . but one general of strong personality and little ability seems to have been allowed to run this battle without control which produced such disastrous results'.

The furore in Australia which followed Elliott's lecture produced its own reaction in the Australian army. A copy of Elliott's lecture notes was sent to Lt.-Col. Vernon Sturdee, then an Australian officer on the general staff at the War Office in London. Sturdee was told there was no authority in Australia to comment on it. '. . . we will be glad if you will give it to someone at the War Office who was associated with Generals Monro and Haking, and ask them if they would be good enough as to criticise it ... It was a very interesting and instructive lecture and if correct, very illuminating.' Sturdee also sent a copy of Elliott's lecture to Basil Liddell Hart, the military correspondent of the London *Daily Telegraph*. If someone associated with Monro and Haking ever commented on Elliott's lecture, however, their comments do not survive.

Indeed, it seems that a strange reluctance to face the facts of the battle of Fromelles pervaded all the British accounts from the very beginning. Even the communiqué isued on 20 July described the action in less than accurate terms. 'Yesterday evening, south of Armentières, we carried out some important raids on a front of two miles in which Australian troops took part. About 140 German prisoners were captured.' In the privacy of his diary, Bean fumed. 'What is the good of deliberate lying like that?' he wrote. The communiqués certainly did not fool the Germans; they knew the extent of the British and Australian offensive and their own communiqué was much more accurate. They also marched some 400 Australian prisoners through the city of Lille. 'Some important raids' which produced 400 prisoners?

Not only did the battle of Fromelles shake the Australian soldier's confidence in the British counterpart; the communiqués shook his confidence in official reports. 'The main facts', wrote Bean, 'soon became known in Australia, and went far to shake the confidence of part of the public in British official statements, which at first had been accepted as invariably true.'

As far as the 5th Division was concerned, it was virtually finished as a fighting force and took no further major part in the war until nearly the end of 1916. As Sergeant Williams wrote, it had been sacrificed on the altar of incompetence.

Sadly, the futility of the battle — if not its result — was foreseen by Brudenell White two days before the assault began. On 17 July he told Bean:

> I hate these unprepared little shows. What do we do? We may deceive the enemy for two days; and after that he knows perfectly well that it is not a big attack, and that we are not in earnest there. We don't get anything that does us any good — the trenches are hard to keep, and it would mean the breaking up (the crippling) of two divisions.

White might not have known how prescient his words were, but two days later, as the ill fated assault at Fromelles was about to begin, he found himself intervening in yet another hurried and ill considered operation.

9

A Powerful Accession of Strength

In the course of the forbidding central period of the Battle of the Somme, Haig's army received a powerful accession of strength and a potent new weapon. The accession of strength was marked by the entry into the battle of the 1st Australian Division opposite Pozières on July 20th.
John Terraine in 'Douglas Haig, The Educated Soldier'.

In late May and June 1916, Hughes and his predecessor as Prime Minister, Andrew Fisher, now the Australian High Commissioner, visited the Australian troops of the 1st and 2nd Divisions who had arrived in France from Egypt. For the soldiers, even those who had heard Hughes' fulsome tribute in London on 25 April, the Prime Minister's visit was just another break in the tedium of training. At Fleurbaix, he addressed the 1st Brigade in an apple orchard, speaking from the back of a waggon and calling the soldiers in around him in the manner that Bernard Law Montgomery was to use to such effect in the later war. Iven Mackay, later to command the Australian Second Army in 1942, had already developed a healthy disregard for politicians. On 31 May 1916 he noted in his diary, 'We are to be visited and, I suppose, harangued, by Billy Hughes'. Hughes told the soldiers that the thoughts of the people at home were always with them, and that neither they nor their dependants would ever be forgotten. The troops were not amused when Hughes arrived several hours late for the parade. After his address, the Prime Minister noticed an old parliamentary colleague in the front ranks. W.J. Johnson was, despite his advanced age, then serving as a private in the infantry. Hughes had been fêted throughout the British Isles, receiving freedoms of cities, honorary degrees from universities and membership of the Privy Council from the King. Private Johnson stepped forward, stuck out his hand to his Prime Minister and asked, 'Well Billy, have they made you a doctor of divinity yet?' Hughes' reply is not recorded; three weeks later Johnson was killed at Pozières; on 14 September, the Labor Caucus passed a condolence motion for their late member.

Hughes also saw Haig, and pressed without success for the formation of an Australian army. In his biography of Gough, Farrar-Hockley claims that Hughes also told Haig he hoped the Commonwealth divisions would not be committed precipitately to a battle involving heavy losses. No mention of this hope — reasonable enough, for an Australian Prime Minister to express — can be found in the correspondence between Hughes and Haig; nor can any mention of it be found in Haig's published diaries. L.F. Fitzhardinge, Hughes' biographer, does not mention it, nor does Terraine, nor does Bean, who devoted several pages of the official history to the meeting and its subsequent correspondence, while Farrar-Hockley's notes and acknowledgements leave the researcher none the wiser as to the origin of his statement. Perhaps Farrar-Hockley's point in mentioning Hughes' hopes is contained in this sentence: 'Though the Commander-in-Chief approved of Gough's spirit, he was not altogether content to see it combined with that of the Australians'. As we have already seen, Gough was an impatient and impetuous commander, ill-suited for the command of an army, where a measure of detachment and delegation is required. He preferred control of the battle himself rather than work through his corps commanders.

Haig had first met the Australians in March 1916, when he inspected the 2nd Division:

> The men were looking splendid, fine physique, very hard and determined looking. I spoke to all the Company commanders. I found one or two old acquaintances who had been in South Africa with me . . . The Australians are mad keen to kill Germans and to start doing it at once! I told the Brigadier to start quietly, because so many unfortunate occurrences had happened through being in too great a hurry to win this campaign!

On 20 July as the Australians moved into the line opposite Pozières, Haig noted in his diary: 'I told Gough to go into all difficulties carefully, as 1st Australian Division had not been engaged in France before and possibly over-looked the difficulties of this kind of fighting'. Two days later, Haig repeated his warning to the Reserve Army commander. 'I visited General Gough after lunch to make sure that the Australians had been given only a simple task. This is the first time that they will be taking part in a serious offensive on a big scale against the German forces.'

Pozières had been an optimistic objective on that first terrible day. Fourteen days and two great offensives later, Pozières — the key to the area, in Rawlinson's words — still lay in German hands. In the centre of the Fourth Army's second offensive, the Scots and the South Africans had taken the clump of battered and broken trees known as Delville Wood at appalling cost. But to the north-west, High Wood with its forward defences at Bazentin-le-Petit and Bazentin-le-Grand still blocked any further advance while Pozières held up the left flank. Pozières, indeed, was still the key, for Rawlinson's army had crossed the high ground to the south and had captured part of the German second line.

But Haig was determined to exploit the limited successes made on Rawlinson's right and centre. The Fourth Army commander was ordered to strike eastwards towards the shattered villages of Ginchy and Guillemont. Haig never shared Rawlinson's tactical opinion of the importance of Pozières. The strongpoint, based on the remnants of the village astride the Albert-Bapaume road and at the head of the Sausage and Mash valleys was, at best a sideshow and at worst, a minor irritant on the Fourth Army's left flank. Besides, the Commander-in-Chief believed that successes in the centre of the Fourth Army's sector would eventually make Pozières vulnerable.

In his despatches later, Haig wrote:

> West of the Bazentin-le-Petit the villages of Pozières and Thiepval, together with the whole elaborate system of trenches round, between and on the main ridge behind them, had still to be carried. An advance further east would, however, eventually turn these defences, and all that was required on the left flank of our attack was a steady, methodical, step-by-step advance as already ordered.

'Steady, methodical, step-by-step advance as already ordered.' Those words have a comfortable, almost reassuring ring; to do so would seem to require nothing out of the ordinary, nothing too spectacular, nothing too dangerous. Yet attacks launched in obedience of those orders achieved nothing except the widespread loss of life. Between 13 and 17 July, British troops attacked Pozières on four separate occasions without success and at huge cost. Haig was nothing if not methodical; as Bean said, he believed 'that a mediocre plan consistently followed is better than a brilliant one frequently changed'. But these attacks were never given the amount of artillery support needed for them to succeed. They were piecemeal attacks, with little thought as to their reason or their execution. Had Pozières been captured during the vital middle stage of the battle, however, the advantages to the British would have been immense. Great sections of the German second line defences would have been breached; a firm base and secure flanks for an assault northwards along the ridge line to Thiepval would have been gained; British artillery would have been able to use Mash Valley, thus bringing field guns in range of Thiepval for the first time and the British would have had observation from the high ground of the ridge over a wide area of the enemy's rear positions.

Whether Haig's persistence with pressing home the attack in the centre of the Fourth Army area derived from his own stubborness, or whether it was a reaction to Joffre's demand on 3 July that he attack 'Thiepval and Pozières' will never be known. The published extracts from his personal diary skip from 3 to 22 July; Terraine gives us few clues, except to say that the cost of the 14 July attacks was 9,000 men:

> half the rate of loss of July 1st, and with far more to show for it. But the German policy of counter-attacking furiously to gain every scrap of lost ground turned the three woods (Bazentin-le-Petit Wood, High Wood and Delville Wood) into bloody battlegrounds. With help on the flanks on the 14th, they might have been seized, and much suffering might have been spared. It was not forthcoming. Gough's Army was still too weak; the French preferred to make their effort elsewhere.

Certainly Haig was right to reject the idea of a frontal attack on the strong Thiepval-Pozières position early in July. But once the advances had been made in the centre of Rawlinson's area, Haig could easily have directed the thrust of his attack northwards, coming in on the flank of the strong German positions. Equally, however, it is possible to ask whether Haig should have continued the fighting on the Somme at all after mid-July. On 11 July Falkenhayn ordered that all offensive operations at Verdun cease; Haig himself noted in his diary on 3 August that pressure on Verdun had eased.

Once again Haig was confronted with the problems of coalition war. To abandon the eastward thrust and turn north, first taking out the Pozières-Thiepval position and then continuing northwards against the Germans facing the Third Army, would also have conflicted with the French view of the Somme offensive. Although Falkenhayn had ordered on 11 July that the Crown Prince's Army should 'henceforth adopt a more defensive attitude' and indeed, the offensives against Verdun had abated, the French could never be sure that the pause would be permanent.

By this stage of the Somme battle, however, Haig must have known that his original ambitious plan of penetration to the heights of Bapaume-Péronne had failed. Possibly Foch argued to the British Commander-in-Chief that the French armies would soon be able to play a greater part in the battle; that, if the temporary abatement in the fighting at Verdun did prove to be permanent, the French might well be able to contribute more troops; that the original plans made by Joffre and Haig might just be capable of fulfilment. Yet, apart from the offensive launched on the opening day and the battle on 15 September, the history of the Somme campaign is marked by a pronounced lack of co-operation between the French and British armies. For that lack of co-operation, Douglas Haig — a man who believed there was little to be learned from his French allies and who disliked them intensely — must take his share of opprobrium.

Haig's command of the battle during this crucial middle stage — what Farrar-Hockley called a 'bloody slogging match' — has a curious, almost ambiguous lethargy about it. Duff Cooper's biography tells us that in his diary, Haig daily recounted the details of the last day's fighting, 'the painful inch gained here, the painful inch lost there. Daily he visited the subordinate generals most nearly concerned and discussed with Rawlinson and others plans for the future'. Details, certainly, but no plans for the future, no appreciations for possible operations or offensives, no suggestion of any other tactical approach except a macabre and tragic blind faith in reliance upon the effectiveness of the 'wearing-down fight'. Even the war diary of his GHQ is oddly reticent about the extent of the fighting and the opportunity to end this 'bloody slogging match'. It almost seems that Haig, bemused by the magnitude of the task ahead of him and stunned by the fighting thus far temporarily lost the ability to see opportunities or alter his plans.

The final British attack on the Pozières strong point was carried out at midnight on 16 July in 'thin low, driving black fog, as cold as October'; indeed, the same weather that same day had forced the postponement of the attack at Fromelles. The harsh experiences of the previous 16 days had taught this new British army something of tactics. A day-long artillery bombardment fell on the German positions, lifting about ten minutes before midnight. Then, in the darkness and rain, troops of the Gloucestershire Regiment and the Royal Munster Fusiliers attacked towards the north-east while the Welch Regiment bombed in from the right. These resourceful troops reached a point in the German trench system just south of Pozières village itself where they found the trenches crowded with German dead and wounded.

Quickly the attackers occupied the German positions, anxiously awaiting the expected counter-attack. None came the following day, but they were heavily shelled all through the morning. At 8 p.m. that night, a battalion of the Durham Light Infantry from Brig.-Gen. Page Croft's 68th Brigade attacked the German trench line south of Pozières. Although preceded by a heavy artillery and trench mortar barrage, this assault was quickly defeated. The advancing infantry had barely gone more than 50 metres when they came under heavy machine gun fire from at least ten machine guns in a concrete structure at the south-west end of the village and from the old German lines. Page Croft at once recognised the futility of attacking such a heavily defended position without it first being systematically pounded by heavy artillery fire. Ordering his remaining three battalions to be ready to take over from the DLI, Page Croft asked for more preparatory artillery fire. His attack was planned to start in the early hours of 18 July.

Before that attack could take place, however, Haig decided to take the Pozières sector away from Rawlinson's Fourth Army so as to allow it to concentrate on its advance further east. On 17 July I Anzac Corps was transferred to Gough's Reserve Army, and on 18 July Haig's headquarters issued the operation order for the attack on Pozières, and the new line of demarcation between the Fourth and Reserve Armies. Haig wrote later:

> On our right flank the situation called for stronger measures. At Delville Wood and Longueval our lines formed a sharp salient, from which our front ran on the one side westwards to Pozières, and on the other southwards to Maltz Horn Farm . . . This pronounced salient invited counter measures by the enemy. He possessed direct observation on it all round from Guillemont on the south-east to High Wood on the north-west. He could bring a concentric fire of artillery to bear not only on the wood and village, but also on the confined space behind, through which ran the French communications as well as ours, where great numbers of guns, besides ammunition and impediments of all sorts, had necessarily to be crowded together.

Haig's first requirement was to swing his right flank up in line with the centre. To move his right flank also meant that Haig had to convince the French to join in the assault on the left, so the junction of the two national forces was not disjointed. At the same time, Haig had to contend with a series of determined counter-attacks launched by the Germans in pursuit of Falkenhayn's stated first principle that all positions lost must be recaptured, regardless of loss. The Germans forced the British defenders out of part of Delville Wood; the British hung on in the remnants of Longueval village and at Waterlot Farm.

Haig's third great offensive of the Somme battle combined an advance by Rawlinson's Fourth Army on the wide front in the centre of the sector with Gough's Reserve Army simultaneously assaulting in the north. Rawlinson's objectives were the enemy line through the High Wood, the clearance of the enemy from the northern end of Delville Wood and the capture of Guillemont; Gough's Reserve Army was to assault Pozières in the north from two directions.

Gough had two divisions at his disposal, the 1st Australian and the 48th British Divisions. The Albert-Bapaume road divided the British

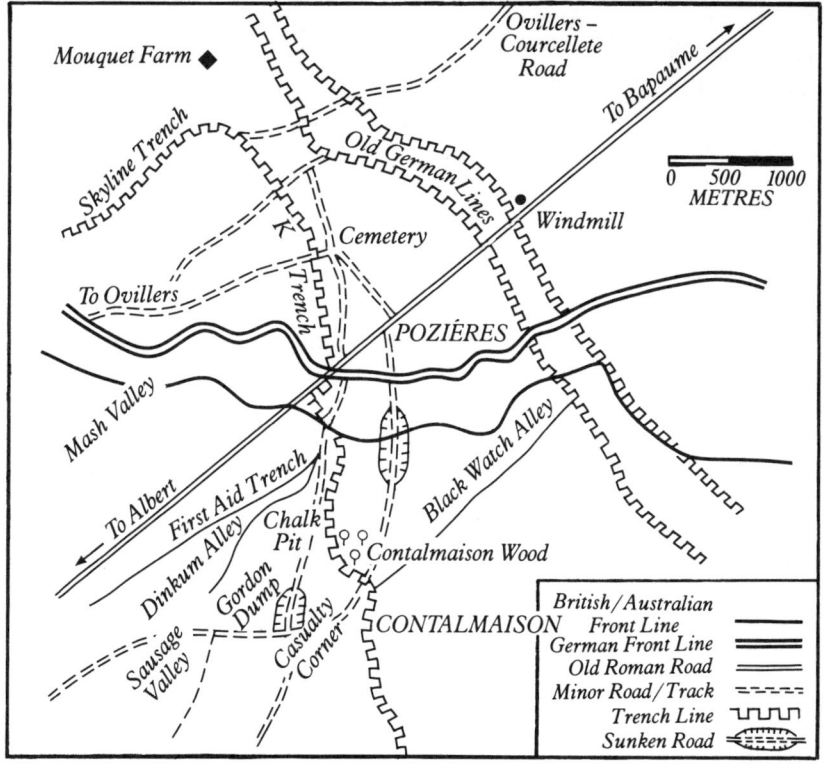

Trench lines at Pozières before the 1st Division attack.

and Australian divisional areas with the troops of the 48th holding the line from the road west to Ovillers. They were to assault the German position to their north from the south-west. 'The right of the 48th Division', wrote Edmonds, 'whose progress north of the road towards the head of Mash Valley depended, to a large extent, upon the success of the Australians attacking the Pozières bastion, was to co-operate by an attack which would keep in touch with the Australian left'.

Before the war, Pozières had been a minor agricultural hamlet, with its inhabitants working the wheat, turnip and sugar beet fields nearby. The village itself had straggled along the road, with small red brick houses backing on to orchards on both sides of the road for about a kilometre. A small gauge railway line, more of a tram track, ran through the northern outskirts of the village, dipping to the south-east and crossing the Bapaume road near where the houses ended and the fields began. To the north-west lay the village cemetery, reached by a street running at right angles to the old Roman road.

123

The tactical significance of Pozières lay in its height and position: it lay on an open part of the ridge, affording observation down Mash Valley to the west, particularly from the northern trenches around the cemetery; it provided observation down Sausage Valley to the south. From their trenches, the German defenders had clear fields of fire for their machine guns down gently sloping ground. And because of the construction of those trenches, those guns were sited to fire in enfilade. Indeed, the machine guns were sited for their optimum effect: grazing fire down the gentle slope; at maximum range, and from a flank. The Germans had incorporated the village into their second line defence system by the hurried construction of a single trench, known to the British as Pozières trench, around to the south. To the west of the village ran the German intermediate line, *Zwichenstellung*, between the first and second lines, known here to the British as K or Kay trench. To the east, over the ridge at the high point of the Windmill, (Hill 160 to the Germans), ran the roughly parallel old German lines, known as OG1 and OG2. K trench ran roughly north to Mouquet Farm, Thiepval and the Schwaben redoubt and it was from this trench that the Germans had observation down Mash Valley. The OG trenches, at right angles to the hastily dug Pozières trench, provided defenders along their length with enfilade fire positions against an attack from the southeast on to the Pozières trench and the village beyond. Any attack from this direction must first deal, or at least simultaneously deal, with the defenders on OG1. And, should this be succcessful, there was the additional problem of dealing with the defenders in the support line of OG2.

Just before the Australians moved in opposite the Germans, the British trenches lay between 100 and 500 metres from the Pozières trench. At the nearest point, the British were still beyond hand bomb range; at the furthest, there was half a kilometre of open, sloping ground. To the east of the village where the OG lines had been partially breached, the German defences almost met the British line. But the Germans still held their formidable OG lines extending about 500 metres south of the road to Bapaume and providing enfilade fire positions.

Thus, Pozières was one of the strongest points of the German line. The highest point of the Somme uplands was marked by the ruins of the Windmill, about 1,000 metres north-east of the village along the road towards Bapaume. At the entrance to the village on the Albert side, a house had been reinforced until it was almost a concrete block. The Germans called this house *Panzerturm*, the British Gibraltar. It was the key to any approach from the south, for fire from this impregnable position covered all the major approaches, as the DLI had discovered.

Gough was ordered to 'carry out methodical operations against Pozières with a view to capturing that important position with as little delay as possible'. Such an order appealed to Gough's natural impetuosity. He decided not to wait for the arrival of Birdwood and the staff of the I Anzac Corps but immediately summoned to his headquarters the commander of the 1st Australian Division, Maj.-Gen. Harold Bridgwood Walker — 'Hooky' to his officers and soldiers alike. When Walker arrived at Gough's headquarters on 18 July he was told abruptly, 'I want you to go into the line and attack Pozières tomorrow night!' Walker, who commanded the 1st Division for three years from 1915, was a quiet, self-effacing Irishman with hidden steel. As Birdwood's Chief of Staff the previous year, he had so vehemently opposed the Gallipoli operation that 'Birdie' threatened to leave him behind. Although a very competent staff officer, Walker realised that he had greater abilities as a commander and led the first division with distinction at Gallipoli after Maj.-Gen. Sir William Throsby Bridges was killed. Like Birdwood, 'Hooky' Walker admired the Australians under his command and they admired him. He was probably the best divisional commander in the Gallipoli campaign and an experienced fighting officer when he brought his division to France.

Walker realised at once that to mount a successful attack on Pozières within 24 hours was simply out of the question. No jumping off trenches had been dug, nor could they be dug in the time; artillery could not be moved into position; his troops could not be prepared and his best battalion, the 9th drawn from Queensland, could not get its companies into position in so short a time. Politely but firmly, Walker demurred. Perhaps realising the problems were arising from their commander's impetuosity, Gough's Reserve Army staff officers had told Birdwood and White at the Anzac Corps headquarters about the plan for the attack. Between them, Birdwood and White managed to persuade Gough the attack should be postponed. Lt.-Col. Thomas Blamey, Walker's senior staff officer, later remarked to Bean that White was a 'very strong determined general'. In determination, though, White conceded nothing to 'Hooky' Walker. He was soon to discover that every ounce of this determination was needed to prevail against the headstrong Gough.

According to Edmonds, the British official historian, Gough ordered Walker to attack from the 'south-east, not from the south-west. Although the position on the right of the 1st Australian Division, in the left half of the salient shared with the 1st British Division, was cramped and lacked depth, it was better to launch the assault under these disadvantages rather than advance from the south-west — i.e. up the Bapaume road — where the ground was commanded by the Germans on the Pozières ridge between the Windmill and Mouquet Farm'. However, according to Bean, the Australian official historian, Walker was given the choice of attacking from the south-west — the plan now preferred by the Reserve Army staff — or from the south-east. Bean wrote:

> If he chose the former method, his division could be allowed more space for forming up, but the enemy would be close on the left of both its assembly ground and its advance. If he preferred to attack from the south-east, his division must squeeze itself on to its assembly position from the west, since all routes to the south were already too congested by the traffic of the Fourth Army and the French.

Bean added that the accuracy of his account has been disputed, but was confirmed by the evidence of contemporary diaries.

When Bean was writing his history, he forwarded a copy of this chapter to Gough asking him for comments. Clearly his meeting with Walker was important. If Gough had ordered Walker to attack 'Pozières tomorrow night', then both Gough's judgement and his abilities as a commander were open to question. Gough replied to Bean, writing he did not believe Walker's account and claiming that he had always intended a flank attack, that is, an attack from the south-east. Yet when the chapter was shown to 'Hooky' Walker, the former 1st Division Commander was adamant: Gough had repeatedly pressed for a frontal assault (from the south-west) and had changed his mind only when one of his staff who had seen the ground, pointed out it would end in disaster. At that point, Gough had not seen the ground, nor had most of his staff who spent much of their time boar-hunting. Brudenell White, to whom Bean also referred the chapter, confirmed Walker's account of the incident. 'Hooky' Walker later recalled and described Gough's insistence on a frontal attack as 'the very worst exhibition of Army Command that occurred in the whole campaign tho' God knows the Fifth Army was a tragedy throughout'.

Walker had carried out his own reconnaissance, taking with him Blamey and an officer from Gough's headquarters. On 3 August 1916, a week after the 1st Division had left the line, Walker wrote his after-action report. Although that report gives only a hint of the clash between Walker and Gough, the preference of the 1st Division commanders is clearly stated. 'After reconnaissance,' Walker wrote, 'I preferred to attack from the south-east, because I was of the opinion that the enemy from his position on Ridge R34 Central-R34D (Pozières) would be able to menace any attack from the south-west by action against the left flank'.

On his reconnaissance, Walker pointed out to Gough's staff officer the German defences on the ridge, how they commanded the line of the old Roman road and how any assault moving on that axis would be vulnerable to enfilade fire from the left. It was this staff officer who managed finally to convince Gough, otherwise the Australians would have been committed to another disastrous frontal attack, not just into the teeth of the enemy's defences but into devastating flanking fire as well.

Walker established his headquarters in the Château Lamont, a fine old building near the village of Albert. Here in the well developed gardens and with the scent of flowers strong in the summer air, Walker and his staff planned the attack. The war had come early to Albert; the famous basilica, *La basilique Notre-Dame de Brebeires*, had been bombarded earlier in the year and now the gilded virgin, instead of standing aloft with arms and the child raised in supplication, hung precariously over the square. To the soldiers the comparison with a diver was inevitable. From the time of their arrival she was Fanny, after Fanny Durack who had won a gold medal for Australia at the 1912 Olympics.

Almost every soldier who passed through Albert and wrote home seemed to mention the falling virgin. It had become a kind of symbol, almost a mascot. Two rumours — or one rumour with two explanations — existed for it: that it would not fall until the war ended; or that its fall would symbolise the end of the war. In 1918, the Germans captured Albert and used the basilica as an observation post. The falling virgin finally fell — a victim of British artillery.

The March to the Somme sector took eight days, an ordeal for some of the Australians. Months in the line had blunted the fine edge of fitness from their Egyptian training; their feet had become soft and susceptible to blisters from the hard roads and the unyielding leather boots; the signs of boisterous nights in the *estaminets* and cafés of their billeting areas had been visible for the first day or two. One brigadier ordered his battalion commanders — in most battalions, the adjutant and the company commanders were mounted, the platoon commanders marched — to ride at the rear of their units and round up the stragglers. It was a fairly long march, Sergeant Rule remembered:

> and to make it worse either the adjutant or the CO took a wrong road and never discovered their mistake until we were almost on the top of a very long steep hill. Loaded as we were, we almost sweated blood over that hill . . . and, when the colonel turned us about and marched us down the hill again, the camel's back fairly broke. If curses ever did men any harm the lives of those two were ruined for ever.

When the Australians heard they were to form part of Gough's Reserve Army, they were dismayed, thinking they would miss out on the fighting ahead. As they neared Albert, however, they realised they would soon be participating in the Somme fighting. 'We knew we were for it,' wrote the commander of the 4th Battalion, Lt.-Col. Iven Mackay. One of Mackay's sergeants, Les de Vine of Maroubra, NSW wrote:

> We are on the way to the Somme valley, where a big push has been going on successfully since the 1st of July ... The firing line is continually moving up as we attack an objective every day. Only at one point is the advance held up, Thiepval. Many English regiments pass us who have been relieved from the front areas ... They have been very successful and are all singing as they march along, every man wearing a German helmet.

Such was the optimism and enthusiasm for battle of these anxious warriors.

The optimism was understandable. The Australians had no idea of the catastrophes which had befallen the British army in the previous three weeks. The earliest reports in the British newspapers had been optimistic: Gibbs, probably the best of the British correspondents had written for the London *Daily Telegraph*: 'It is, on balance, a good day for England and France. It is a day of promise in this war ...' Later Gibbs excused this report by writing: 'I have had to spare the feelings of men and women, who have sons and husbands still fighting in France'. But the correspondents were only partly to blame, for they had been consistently lied to by the British staff. The correspondents' fault lay with not checking the truth for themselves from the survivors of this 'day of promise'. Even so, the censors would have prevented the truth being known. As Bean wrote: 'the intermittent advances on the Somme often signified far more than they were worth; and, as the communiqués of GHQ — prepared for enemy consumption — were rose-coloured, and unfavourable comment was suppressed by the then censors, the average citizen or soldier entertained few misgivings'.

Certainly few misgivings are apparent in the soldiers' letters and diaries for this period. The veterans of Anzac knew that here in France the fighting would be different; they had hundreds of kilometres of France and then the English channel at their backs, not just a few metres of shingled beach. They also had a certain superiority, because they had been at Gallipoli. 'Have you been fighting or have you been in France?' they would ask British troops, in tones calculated to offend.

The new troops, reinforcements but no less imbued with aggression and willingness to join the fighting, were anxious they should do well. As well, many had a strong natural curiosity about the countryside through which they were passing. Marching at ease, with the loose-limbed relaxed gait that characterises and distinguishes Australian soldiers, they clomped over the cobble-stoned streets of Albert, looked up at the golden virgin and then continued along the old Roman road, the latest legionnaires in this foreign land.

They marched towards the sound of the guns, singing the old songs or whistling quietly as if to ward off the fears and the unknown of the future. Outside Albert, they had discarded their 'hats khaki fur-felt' made of the fur from the rabbits that abounded in their dry countryside. Steel helmets or 'tin-hats' had been taken from their packs and their slouch hats, that famous symbol of the Australian digger, were stored in the quartermaster's store until after the battle. They stopped for a quick brew and a snatched cigarette at the foot of Tara Hill, a treeless but grassy slope which with its twin Usna, formed a ridge astride the old Roman road and a British observation point for the battle. And as they rested on the grass, sipping their tea and drawing on the strong smoke which sustains soldiers when food is unattractive and stomach-turning, the soldiers must have reflected that this was the last of the green and pleasant ground between them and the battlefield.

From Tara Hill, it was onwards up the shallow Sausage Valley where the grass covering the surface had been stripped and worn by the constant traffic. Waggon tracks crisscrossed the gully in all directions where the iron-rimmed wheels of the transports or the iron-shod boots of the tramping soldiers had scuffed and broken the surface and revealed the white chalk on the rich, red earth. Sausage Valley itself appeared to be a kind of chaos, with troops and animals and artillery and waggons clustered in groups or huddled in old German trenches. And everywhere there was dry powdery, chalky dust, and huge black flies grown fat in the summer and on the corpses which lay in rank profusion in No Man's Land ahead. With the flies and the dust and the July heat, it might have been a busy mining camp in the Australian outback, except for the constant noise of the guns. Just below the crest were the smaller field artillery pieces, sited so their rounds — it was fervently hoped — would clear the crest line but the guns would still be invisible to the German counter-battery observers. Further down the valley were the heavier guns; ancient 4.7 inch howitzers, inaccurate to fire and a devil to serve, great noisy monsters with a blast that punctured eardrums and knocked many an unsuspecting rider off his horse.

At the head of Sausage Valley, a supply dump had been established and named after Brig.-Gen. Gordon who had so confidently predicted before 1 July that his troops could light their pipes, shoulder their rifles and march all the way to Pozières without meeting a German. That brigade, of course, had been just about wiped out in Sausage Valley, victims of the machine guns which had enfiladed this minor depression. Now, a busy track ran up its centre; a British brigade headquarters, conscious of its own comfort and safety, occupied one of the German dugouts and the British troops in reserve huddled into the holes and trenches like so many subterranean animals. Lance Corporal Eric Moorhead of the 5th Battalion, noted his observations in his diary. 'Words cannot describe the utterly smashed condition of the ground here. Unexploded shells, debris, equipment, were everywhere among the shell craters and in the mouths of the smashed dugouts were corpses.'

On the other side of the supply dump, the new track, worn by the wheels of the transport waggons and the boots of the soldiers, met the old road to the village of La Boiselle, now just a mass of tangled masonry and splintered timber. Centuries of ploughing the surrounding fields had elevated the farmlands above the road, so here where the new track met the old, the moving soldiers were protected from direct observation by a steep bank. Ahead, only a few trees of the orchards remained after the massive bombardments of the previous weeks, but the unwary British soldier could still attract a sniper or a machine gun crew by exposing his head above the crest. For this reason, and because of the aid post set up in a chalk quarry nearby, this junction was known as 'casualty corner'. Ahead was Pozières.

This, for the members of the 1st and 2nd Divisions, and later the 4th Division, was the corner of France that they had come to defend. It seemed unprepossessing, almost unimportant, for they were simply part of the great British army on the Somme. Their identity as Australian troops was important only to themselves and their politicians. For the British, federation of the Australian colonies 16 years earlier might never have happened; the 'Orstralians' were still colonials. What was this new-fangled nonsense about Dominions?

The first Australians into the line opposite Pozières — the 1st Brigade from New South Wales and the 3rd Brigade from South Australia, Queensland, Tasmania and Western Australia — moved in on the night of 19 and 20 July. They met their British guides, were led across the open ground platoon by platoon, and listened with curiosity to the dull 'plop' of German shells landing nearby. Because there was no explosion, the soldiers took these to be 'blinds' or 'duds' but they soon noticed a pungent aromatic smell hanging around parts of the track to the trenches. This was phosgene; the Australians' introduction to the gas warfare of the Western Front. Dangerous if released close to a man not wearing a mask, phosgene produced a delayed reaction on the heart, often with fatal results. As well, the Germans used tear gas with an odour not unlike that of hyacinth.

Shortly after midnight on 19 July, the Australians were in position, with the 2nd Battalion opposite the south-west end of Pozières, the 1st

Battalion alongside on its right and opposite the south of the village and the other two battalions of the brigade, the 3rd and 4th, in reserve in Sausage Valley. To the right of the 1st Brigade, the 3rd Brigade troops were strung out, some in captured German trenches, others along 'Black Watch Alley' which was 'in parts a filthy channel, half-filled with yellow liquid mud and obstructed by corpses which there had yet been no time to remove'.

Later, the Australians were to judge their British comrades by the state in which they left their trenches. In the 3rd Battalion, one company commander noted that his troops found the trench to be deep and strong and well traversed but there was no shelter of any kind except holes scraped in the forward face just deep enough to allow a man to sit up and rest in a rather crowded position. Captain J.R.O. Harris wrote:

> At company headquarters, which was a slightly deeper scrape than usual, rather like a niche in a cathedral for the accommodation of a saint's statue, I found the company commander, an Oxford don, and formally took over the trench and trench-stores. The latter consisted of a few picks and shovels and about an eighth of a jar of rum.

For three days they waited while their division commander, Walker, and his staff prepared the plan for the attack and argued with Gough for more time. Walker pointed out to the Reserve Army commander that jumping off trenches, which should be as close as possible to the enemy, had not yet been dug.

In a letter home after the battle, Blamey was to claim credit for the attack plan.

> Here in a quiet home, with a lovely garden and beautiful flowers, I can just hear the low burst of guns away up beyond Pozières. Pozières is ours, captured alone by the division. We are all very proud of the feat. Our plan, which was chiefly mine, led to a brilliant success.

Bean, who realised the complexities of Blamey's character and personality, does not ascribe full credit for the battle plan to Australia's future Commander-in-Chief. The operation order for the capture of the remainder of Pozières village (see chapter 10) was prepared by Walker 'in conjunction with Colonel Blamey now his Chief of Staff'. Perusal of the Division Headquarters' War Diary for the period does not reveal any documentary evidence to support Blamey's claim and Walker's own reports do not pay particular tribute to the work done by Blamey. It seems likely that Walker prepared the concept of the operations; Blamey carried through the detailed planning and writing of the operation order.

In the first stage of the battle, Walker planned to capture Pozières trench, a portion of the German front line between the OG 1 line and the Albert road. Another assault would capture the trenches and strong points between the Pozières trench and the outskirts of the ruined village. The third assault would put the Australians in the ruins of the houses on the southern side of the road itself. Walker issued orders for the first attack at 3.30 a.m. on 21 July, with the second attack timed to begin at 11.30 p.m. the following night, 22 July.

Even as the orders were being duplicated, a party of two officers and 100 men from the 9th Battalion attempted to seize a portion of the Old German lines on the right flank. This attack failed when the assaulting troops became involved in a grenade-throwing battle with the German defenders. With the failure of this move Walker realised he would need more time to place his right brigade in position. Initially the major assault was postponed for one hour, to 12.30 a.m. on the night of 22-23 July. Then, during the day of 21 July, Brudenell White discovered serious problems in the artillery plan which would have endangered the Australian troops. Again the attack was postponed, this time for twenty-four hours, and the brigadiers were told during the afternoon of 21 July. These successive postponements, although fumed over by the anxious Gough, gave the Australians time to prepare jumping off trenches on the right of the line.

> As the distance between the opposing line on the right was about 600 yards and as there was no ground in rear available on which to form up for the assault, it was essential to prepare trenches forward of Black Watch Alley. This was done under continuous fire on the nights 20/21, 21/22.

The artillery bombardment, systematic and carefully planned, began on 19 July and continued intermittently on the roads and barricades, the trenches and the strong points. As well, the field guns and machine guns of the Australians kept firing, preventing several German attempts to prepare extra trenches.

Eric Moorhead noted in his diary: 'The roaring of our guns shook the earth and agitated the air and lit the sky for miles and miles till as bright as day. I was on guard and had a chance of observing it all'. Troops from the 2nd Battalion, who had occupied an advanced position just 80 metres from the German lines, were able to watch the shells falling without danger. The explosions of the shells flayed the leaves from the trees, shattered and splintered their trunks and churned over the ground until it resembled a heaving, broken sea. For the first time,

Australian gunners were firing the new 'thermite' shells, incendiary rounds designed to set fire to trees and any buildings that may be left standing and protecting troops. Even through this terrible bombardment, however, the Australians could see small parties of German troops scurrying from point to point, either reinforcements or messengers.

The penultimate bombardment before the assault on Pozières could be seen for miles. The moon had not yet risen; the sky was clear and the troops in support, both in the 2nd Division and the reserve brigades, watched in amazement. Most of the firing was being done by the guns of the Fourth Army, in support of Rawlinson's central offensives. From the open area before Fricourt they saw the skyline simply alive with light. 'Flashes like summer lightning were quite continuous, making one flickering band of light; but this was away in the east behind Fricourt and Montauban. Clearly the British were doing something there.'

Bean wrote in a letter home:

> Most of these villages are marked on the shell-swept country by the trees around them. It is not that they originally stood in a woodland; but then the village is a mere heap of foundations powdered white the only relic of it left standing erect, if you except a battered wall or two, is the shredded trunks and stumps of trees which once made the gardens or orchards or hedges behind the houses . . . our heavy shells were tearing at regular intervals into the rear of the brick heaps which once were houses, and flinging up branches of trees and great clouds of black earth from the woods. A German letter was found next day dated 'In Hell's Trenches'. It added: 'It is not really a trench, but a little ditch, shattered with shells — not the slightest cover and no protection. We have lost 50 men in two days, and life is unendurable'.

Under the cover of their own artillery the Australians crept forward to their positions on the assault line, marked by pegs and tapes by small parties earlier. There they lay accepting the inevitable casualties from their own artillery rounds falling short as part of the price that must be paid for getting close. The lessons of the 1 July assault had not been lost on the Australians.*

---

*The War Diary of the 1st Australian Division, easily the best kept and most comprehensive of the divisional headquarters' diaries of this time, contains a series of 'Training Memoranda', written by Blamey who was the senior 'G' or operational staff officer and issued almost daily. They covered every aspect of warfare as it had developed on the Western Front and are notable for the lucidity and their spread of subjects.

Although the Germans fired brilliant white flares to illuminate the battlefield and warn of any impending attack, the Australians were not detected. Cleverly using the churned-over ground, they crept low, hoping the defenders' attention would be diverted by a bombardment falling to the west of the shattered village and designed to simulate an attack from that direction. That attention was not diverted completely. On the right, some troops of the 9th Battalion were seen and a machine gun opened fire; on the left, troops of the 2nd Battalion were detected in the white light of the flares and a bright red rocket, bursting into stars above the battlefield was fired as a signal.

As Private H. 'Squatter' Preston of the 9th Battalion lay out in No Man's Land, he was fascinated by the German machine fire cutting the heads off the poppies:

> . . . almost against our heads. The flashes of the guns, the bursting of the shells, the Verey lights, made the night into day, and, as I lay flat to the ground as possible I was expecting to stop one at any time. Jamming my tin helmet on my head I brought the body of my rifle across my face to stop anything that might happen to drop low. A man alongside me was crying like a baby, and although I tried to reassure him he kept on saying that we would never get out of it.

Closer and closer edged the Australians, until the forward troops of the first wave were metres from the German parapet. Troops of the 11th Battalion edged as close as 20 to 30 metres from the German position. Off to the left flank, a field gun, its wheels and harness muffled with sandbags, was dragged to within 200 metres of the front line. As a screen from enemy machine gun fire, the gun crew placed the ammunition waggon between themselves and the German trench.

For the Australians waiting to assault, the tension was almost unbearable. It 'affected the men in different ways' wrote Sergeant B.W. Champion of the 1st Battalion.

> I couldn't stop urinating, and we were all anxious for the barrage to begin. When it did begin, it seemed as if the earth opened up with a crash. The ground shook and trembled, and the concussion made our ears ring. It was impossible to hear ourselves speak to a man lying alongside. It is strange how men creep together for protection. Soon, instead of four paces interval between the men, we came down to lying alongside each other, and no motioning could make them move apart.

The artillery barrage began precisely at 12.28 a.m. For two minutes, every gun in the division fired as fast as their crews could load. This mad scramble of fire was quite unlike anything the gunners had ever experienced before. In front of the waiting infantry, the ground rose and fell, the enemy trench one continuous line of flying shrapnel. Only one Australian gun fired short, causing a few casualties on the left. The remainder poured their fire just metres in front of the waiting infantry. Then, at 12.30 a.m. the tempo of fire slowed as the gunners adjusted their targets to the old line of the orchards between Pozières trench and the village. Inevitably there was some confusion in the infantry. Some groups were slow to move, unable to distinguish between the rapid fire on the enemy trench and the sustained fire on the more distant orchards. Others were simply stunned by the overwhelming force of the barrage in front of their eyes. But as the officers rose, blowing their whistles and waving their troops into the assault, the Australian line started to rise and follow. 'Their faults', writes Farrar-Hockley with that singular British mixture of patronising condescension, 'were those characteristic of lively newcomers'. Lively newcomers, certainly; faults? So eager were the Australians that some officers had difficulty controlling their charges.

'Squatter' Preston recalled that suddenly he saw men jumping to their feet. 'Taking this to be the signal for the charge I jumped up and dashed across to the enemy trench'. At the point where Preston entered was a German doctor, whom the Australians recognised and left unharmed.

> Pte Jack Rogers, who reached the trench with me, bayonetted two Germans, and after a sharp fight the trench was cleared, and we immediately set to work to improve our position ... The trench was in good order with dugouts let into the sides. The dead bodies, which had to be thrown out, were used in building up the parapets.

Walker had planned for the first wave to capture the Pozières trench; for the second to pass through and assault the defenders in the back hedges and orchards of the village; for the third to exploit through to the line of the old road. But where the first wave had achieved success without much opposition, the troops were still spoiling for a fight. 'In the meantime', wrote Sergeant Champion, 'the next waves had gone through us, and, being over-anxious, quite a number of our waves went through with them to be in the fun'. In the 1st Battalion, Private Barwick noted later that his company was supposed to remain in the Pozières trench. '... no fear, on they went like a pack of hungry dogs now they had tasted blood ... just to show you how cool the boys were, why, some of them were walking up with rifles at the slope and singing "I want to go home".'

Gradually their officers brought these 'hungry dogs' under control. They worked on their trenches, easily now, for the artillery had pulverised and softened the earth; they brought forward their Vickers and Lewis guns and sited them carefully, preparing for the expected counterattack. Off to the right, they could hear the sounds of the battle as the 9th and 10th Battalions fought to link and turn the line. But in the ruins of the village itself, only sporadic sniper fire disturbed the digging and the machine gun siting. This provoked the Austalians, some of whom set off on 'ratting' expeditions.

In small groups, generally without the benefit of an officer or NCO, the Australians would make their way through the rubble of the village, looking for cellar doors or entrances to dugouts. Phosphorous bombs would then be dropped in, which would explode and fill the confined space with thick, choking white smoke. As the defenders emerged, coughing and spluttering, the Australians would calmly shoot them or use their bayonets at the end of a furious chase. Whether these Germans were capable of fighting or not is a moot point. Prisoners were taken — Bean says some groups numbered a score or more — but the Australians had a fairly grim attitude towards prisoners at this stage of the fight. During the assault, Iven Mackay saw 'lots of [Germans] . . . racing back towards their second line . . . Many of them remained in their dugouts, terrified and had to be bombed or bayoneted out. Some never came out. A number of the Germans taken prisoner would not, through pure fright, cross No Man's Land. They had to be killed'.

The first objective was seized easily. So effective had been the final bombardment that Pozières trench was hardly recognisable, the few defenders who remained surrendered after only the most token resistance. Only on the extreme right, where the attempt to secure the flank two nights before had failed, were the Australians faced with any great resistance. Here the Germans halted the assault temporarily with a furious flurry of hand grenades and small arms fire. The leading platoon of the 9th Battalion went to ground and for some 15 minutes or so, exchanged hand grenades with the Germans from the cover of a trench. The smaller German hand bombs, not the large, familiar stick grenades, could be thrown further than the British Mills bomb. Thus the Germans possessed the advantage. Then one member of the platoon, Private John Leak, a teamster from Rockhampton, decided that this little battle had gone on too long. Without orders, he leapt from his trench, dashed forward across the open ground and dropped three hand grenades into the German position. As soon as those grenades had exploded, Leak jumped in with his rifle and bayonet. There, his platoon commander found him some minutes later, calmly wiping the blood off his bayonet.

Within two hours, the Australians had captured the Pozières trench, but on the right, the stubborn resistance in OG1 and OG2 meant that the line was bent back, almost at right angles. Here the Germans had rushed in reserves; the assaulting troops were hampered by the lack of landmarks and the whole area was held by a complex of strongpoints and machine gun nests dotted across the broken ground. Walker's fears about the right flank were proving real.

Less than 200 metres from the trench which had held up Leak's platoon, the South Australians of the 10th Battalion faced similar difficulties. Although the fighting had also begun as an exchange of hand grenades, the Australian supply quickly ran out. The company commander ordered a bayonet charge, but before his troops were ready, he was wounded in the head by a machine gun bullet. Just on dawn, a reserve company of the 10th made its way forward, only to find their comrades on the point of exhaustion from the battle that had raged during the early hours. Arthur Blackburn, a 24 year old solicitor from South Australia, collected together a small party of the battalion bombers. Together, they assaulted one German position nearby, only for Blackburn to find that his soldiers were killed by his side. Blackburn located another machine gun post, crawled back to his trench and arranged for trench mortar fire to silence it. Then he went out into No Man's Land again, looking for the link between his battalion and the Queenslanders on the left. All through the morning of 23 July, Blackburn kept making these forays, silencing enemy machine gun posts which had been holding up the advance. Of the 70 men under his command 40 were killed or wounded but the vital link had been made. More importantly, it had held. Although the line kinked and in fact was broken, the gap was covered by the Queenslanders and the South Australians. In the initial fighting for Pozières, the casualties were heaviest here; the German defenders most resolute. For their parts in the day's fighting, Leak and Blackburn were each awarded the Victoria Cross.

During the Second World War, a French battalion commander wrote this after a battle in the Italian campaign. It is as applicable and with as much force, to the German tactics of 1916.

> Counter attacks are *the classic method* by which the Germans defend a position. A unit mounting an attack on its objective or having just occupied it is generally the object of a local counter-attack carried out by a few men but those are very well led by one or two keen officers or warrant officers. They know the ground perfectly and are well aware how effective this kind of short, sharp attack can be on partially exhausted troops who think they have definitely secured the objective.

As we have already seen, the German policy was to counter-attack vigorously, both local counter-attacks organised by the immediate defenders or massive planned assaults, such as the British had experienced further south. By the end of July, writes John Terraine, the German infantry had made not less than 67 counter-attacks. 'Probably they had made a great many more, now lost in time's obscurity — possibly twice as many. This was the texture of the battle: attack, counter-attack; attack again; counter-attack again.'

The first serious counter-attack on the Australians at Pozières came while the excited troops were still engaged on their 'ratting expeditions'. About 200 Germans no doubt led by 'one or two keen officers or warrant officers' emerged on the right flank, in a single file. Their movement was seen by troops on the right, and immediately they came under rifle and machine gun fire. The attack faltered and five minutes later, the survivors rose and hurried around behind the ruins on the north-east side of the village, to be pursued by artillery fire from the Australian batteries.

All that day, the 'ratting' and the consolidation continued. The troops went off in search of souvenirs, the spiked German helmets or *pickel-haubes* and the strong black cigars being particular prizes. In the 2nd Battalion, one digger came across a water bottle containing hot coffee. His mates cautioned him not to drink it. 'It's poisoned', they warned. The finder's reaction was simply to say, 'Well, here's luck' and gulp it down.

In the headquarters of Gough's Reserve Army, the successes of the day were recorded blandly enough.

> At 12.30 a.m. the attack of the 1st Australian Division and the 48th Division began ... At 6.30 a.m. information was received that the first objective had been gained, but that little progress was being made on the right. Both the 48th Division and the 1st Australian Division made good progress ... Two guns and about 200 prisoners were captured. The remainder of the day was spent in consolidating the line gained. Only one counter-attack was made and that but a slight one on the right. Our losses are reported to be comparatively light.

In his diary, Haig noted that a general attack was made at 1.30 a.m.*

> The 5th or Reserve Army on our left advanced well to the west of Pozières Village with the 48th Divn (Fanshawe) while the 1st Australian Division captured the village of Pozières itself as far as the Albert-Bapaume road;

---

*The attack was later in the Fourth Army's sector.

and reached within 200 yards of the windmill on the hill N E of the village, working from the S E along the ridge.

As Haig also noted, the Fourth Army had not been so fortunate. Indeed, the only success of that day — the third great offensive of the Somme battle — was at Pozières. On the British right flank, an attack by part of XIII Corps was beaten back; between Delville Wood and Pozières, an attack by the remainder of XIII Corps plus XV and III Corps failed to secure any ground. In the centre, the Scottish 51st Division ran into an impenetrable obstacle in High Wood, despite the imperturbable confidence of Rawlinson who thought the 'Boche was very tired'. There had been hopes, wrote Edmonds, that Sunday morning, 23 July, would see the whole of the Bazentin Ridge in British hands; Delville Wood and Longueval secured, High Wood and the Switch Line captured, and patrols pushing forward into Martinpuich. On the right flank, the capture of Guillemont should have prepared the way for a big allied attack north of the Somme. 'Actually no ground whatever had been gained by the Fourth Army, many factors contributing to the failure of the British plan.' Then followed something of a litany of reasons why the attacks failed.

> The existing front, with its many re-entrants and salients, was an unsuitable line from which to launch a general attack, for artillery barrages were difficult to arrange with precision; cloud and haze affected observation, thus diminishing the effects of preliminary bombardment; and the decision to assault at night brought no advantage to the face of an alert enemy warned by previous night and dawn attacks. Moreover, the various alterations of zero hour had resulted in some of the troops receiving their orders very late, whilst battalions were called upon to advance over ground which they had little or no opportunity to reconnoitre.

The Germans had not thinned out their line at Pozières but instead, had reinforced it with comparatively fresh troops, withdrawing depleted units for a rest in lines north of the village. But all of those factors applied to the Australian offensive at Pozières. Why should it have succeeded, and all others on that day have failed? The answer to that question must be in the quality of the troops used in the assault. This is not an attempt to bestow on the troops of the 1st Australian Division any particular military virtues or soldierly qualities not possessed by the British. The enormous advantage possessed by the Australians was their freshness; they had not been used in the battle before; they were fit, enthusiastic and raring to go; 'lively newcomers', as Farrar-Hockley says. And the 1st Division was, as we shall see, easily the best trained, and the most experienced of all the Australian divisions.

Edmonds concedes the exhaustion and the dispiriting effect of the three-week long battle upon the troops of Rawlinson's Fourth Army. A great proportion of their best and most experienced officers and men had already become casualties and their losses were being severely felt. As well, the War Office was keen to foster what it called an 'army spirit', where a soldier would feel his primary allegiance to the army, and not to his regiment. Considering the importance the British army had always placed on the regimental system, this seems an extraordinary *volte face*. The explanation, however, is to be found in the horrendous casualty lists which appeared after 1 July, lists which included the names of those young men who had enlisted in the 'Pal's battalions' or in the local regiment, or for the county regiments such as the York and Lancasters, or the Green Howards, or the Duke of Wellington's Regiment, recruited on a company or platoon basis from individual villages. If that platoon or company suffered heavily, the effect was felt in the small villages of the county from which it was recruited. Far better, thought the planners at the War Office, to spread those casualties around.

Reinforcements from, say a north county battalion, resented being posted to a regiment which drew its traditional recruits from the south; proud Scottish units looked askance at Sassenach recruits; young officers inculcated with regimental *esprit de corps* foolishly despised replacement officers whose badges and customs were different. Even the year before, Robert Graves noted that a reinforcement from a home counties regiment to his battalion of the Royal Welch Fusiliers was contemptuously dismissed as the 'Surrey man'. 'A heavy price had to be paid', wrote Edmonds, 'for the consequent, if temporary, deterioration in the fighting efficiency of many battalions'.

Having seen Rawlinson's Army fail so conspicuously and at such cost, did Haig think of breaking off his offensive? His published diaries suggest that no such thoughts crossed the Commander-in-Chief's mind; his despatches reveal only that he was impressed with the strength of the German resistance, the ability to launch counter-attacks and the need for 'long and careful preparation before any further successes on a great scale could be secured'. Politically — Haig was both politically aware and politically astute — breaking off the Somme offensive was simply not an option. It had begun as a 'jointive', thus any decision to stop it would also have to be made jointly with the French. Moreover, the news and the official communiqués had suggested great and telling victories. How would public opinion react if such 'victories' were thrown away?

Committed to the offensive by the dictates of coalition war, confined to the area of operations selected by Joffre simply to ensure the British participated, forced to attack before he had a sufficient supply of material and before his armies were properly trained, limited by training and experience in his tactical and strategic planning, Haig had no choice other than to continue what he had begun. His diaries, containing all the excitement of a laundry list, reveal neither doubts about the course he was pursuing nor qualms about the casualties it was costing. Haig now had to persist with the 'wearing-down' fight and hope that the advantage might turn his way with the tank, a secret new weapon soon to make its appearance on the battlefield. Meanwhile, it was on with *bataille d'usure*, although not without some misgivings on the other side of the Channel.

On 29 July Robertson, Chief of the Imperial General Staff, wrote to Haig, reflecting the misgivings apparent in Britain.

> The powers-that-be are beginning to get a little uneasy in regard to the situation. Whether a loss of say 300,000 men will lead to really great results, because, if not, we ought to be content with something less than what we are doing now. They are constantly enquiring why we are fighting and the French are not. It is thought that the primary object — relief of pressure on Verdun — has to some extent been achieved.

Haig replied that the pressure on Verdun had indeed been relieved with not less than six enemy divisions besides heavy guns having been withdrawn. As well, the successes achieved by the previous month would certainly have been prevented if the Germans had been free to transfer troops from there to the eastern theatre. Proof had been given to the world that the allies were capable of making and maintaining a vigorous offensive and of driving the enemy's best troops from the strongest positions. This had shaken the faith of Germans, of their friends, of doubting neutrals in the invincibility of Germany. He also impressed on the world England's strength and determination and the fighting power of the British race.

> We have inflicted very heavy losses on the enemy. In *one* month, 30 of his Divn have been used up, as against 35 at Verdun in 5 months. In another 6 weeks, the enemy should be hard put to it to find men. The maintenance of a steady offensive pressure will result eventually in his complete overthrow.

Haig continued that maintaining the offensive was the principle upon which the Government and the command should act.

> Our losses in July's fighting totalled about 120,000 more than they would had we not attacked. They cannot be regarded as sufficient to justify any anxiety as to our ability to continue the offensive. It is my intention (a) to maintain a steady pressure on the Somme battle. (b) to push my attack strongly whenever and wherever the state of my preparations and the general situation make success sufficiently probable to justify me in doing so, but not otherwise. (c) to secure against counter-attack each advantage gained and prepare thoroughly for each fresh advance.

In preparation for his great offensives to come he had directed his army and corps commanders to continue local attacks and secure better launching positions.

In the meantime, the Australians were to continue on from their successes of 23 July, complete the capture of Pozières village and the high ground from the Windmill to Mouquet Farm. News of their victory on the Sunday morning had spread rapidly along the line; the British 1st Division sent them a congratulatory signal. As the men of the Australian 1st Division strutted in their souvenired *pickelhaubes* and excitedly swapped yarns about the first day's fighting, they had no idea of the terrors and the casualties they were yet to endure. For the 1st Division so far, Pozières had been easy — almost too easy.

10

'Through . . . Hell Itself'

. . . we had our eyes opened when we saw these men march by. Those who watched them will never forget it as long as they live. They looked like men who had been in hell. Almost without exception each man looked drawn and haggard, and so dazed that they appeared to be walking in a dream, and their eyes looked glassy and starey. Quite a few were silly and these were the only noisy ones in the crowd.

Sergeant E.J. Rule of the 14th Battalion, describing the Australian survivors of Pozières.

Major-General 'Hooky' Walker and his largely-Australian staff regarded the capture of Pozières village as a single operation, to be completed in phases. The second phase — the capture of the northern side of the village — Walker planned for the afternoon of 23 July. Before he could put those plans into effect, Walker was telephoned by Gough and told to cease his preparatory artillery fire. According to the Reserve Army commander, the ruins on the northern side of the road had been abandoned and the position was deserted. 'These arrangements conflicted with the plans which I had made and I cancelled the previous orders accordingly', Walker wrote. Walker was reluctant to do so, because he realised the enormous advantage of quickly following up such a successful assault. It seems ironic that Gough, whose dangerous weakness was impetuosity, should have been so cautious. Basing his decision on reports from reconnaissance by the Royal Flying Corps and artillery observers on the Tara-Usna ridge line, Gough was convinced that only patrols were necessary to secure the Pozières strong point and could not resist interfering in what was eventually a divisional operation. 'I suppose the Higher Command knew its business', wrote Private Kinchington, 'but we in the line would have preferred to continue the attack, once we had the back of the enemy resistance broken. For it was only a matter of a few hours, before the German artillery, which had withdrawn to fresh positions, had our range again'.

That afternoon, Haig came forward to Gough's headquarters at Toutencourt where he approved the Reserve Army commander's plans to swing the attack northwards and to secure the ridge line between the Windmill, north-east of the village, and Mouquet Farm. Once this ridge was secured Gough would have observation positions over Courcelette and Grandcourt, imperative for any proposed assault on the Thiepval ridge. But Haig's chief concern at this stage was still that Gough's Reserve Army should continue its 'methodical, step-by-step' advance.

The soldiers occupying trenches south of the road, occasionally venturing across the line of rubble and debris that marked the ancient thoroughfare, were none too amused to be told that the Germans had gone. Small parties and snipers were still causing trouble and accounting for a few luckless and careless diggers. On the left of the Australian position, at the entrance to the village from Albert, the reinforced block house known as Gibraltar had been captured just on dawn, and 26 Germans taken prisoner. The Australians could not hold this position, however, because of the danger from the British artillery fire and so they withdrew, leaving Gibraltar unoccupied. Throughout the day here, the Germans attempted to get back into the block-house, generally moving along the line known as K trench. Had Walker's original plans not been stopped by Gough, the Australians would have easily secured both this position and the trench lines north of the road. The pause in the assault gave the Germans time to infiltrate small, nuisance parties and to launch a series of local counter-attacks.

The German determination to regain Pozières on 23 July underlined their assessment of the position's importance. Although they had only isolated parties in the village on the morning after the assault, they still held portions of the strong K trench, running roughly north-south and ending on the roadline near the Australian left and the Gibraltar blockhouse.

That afternoon, the commander of the Australian 1st Brigade, Brig.-Gen. Nevill Smyth, ordered the 2nd Battalion to capture Gibraltar. Smyth had established his brigade headquarters about 400 metres north of the Chalk Pit in Dead Man's Road, so-called because of the danger and the number of corpses that remained unburied. Before the 2nd Battalion assault Lt.-Col. Stevens, commanding the 1st Battalion and Iven Mackay commanding the 2nd, met on Dead Man's Road at the junction with the old Roman road to co-ordinate their trenches after Gibraltar had been captured. It was a desolate point, the most actively shelled in Pozières. They were surrounded by dead and dying 'amid dozens of corpses and moaning wounded, mainly German'. As the two battalion commanders crouched over the maps, ignoring the machine gun and artillery fire all around them, a messenger from brigade headquarters panted up and handed them a message, addressed 'Urgent and Secret'. It was from the Reserve Army headquarters: 'A number of cases have lately occurred of men failing to salute the army commander when passing in his car, in spite of the fact that the car carried his flag upon the bonnet. This practice must cease'. Neither Stevens nor Mackay was amused. Not that the message applied particularly to the soldiers then engaged in the fighting, for there was little risk of Gough coming this far forward, whether in his car or on foot. And, as Bean remarks, the message says little about commonsense of the staff at the Australian division and brigade headquarters who forwarded the message at that time.

Through that day, Walker moved fresh troops up, with battalions moving carefully across the road and extending the line round on the eastern flank. Officers of the 8th Battalion had been given no maps; the advance company commanders merely being told to go as far as they could. Deciding this order was dangerously vague, they determined their position by the fallen roofs of the village, still visible in the rubble. Fixing bayonets, they swept through the ruins, with their right flank on the road and their left flank in the orchards on the northern side. Still no major resistance was struck. A young schoolteacher from Wedderburn in Victoria, Private Jack Bourke* of the 8th Battalion, wrote that he scrambled over a small plough and roller and wondered where the old Frenchman was who had owned them. One of Bourke's corporals was badly wounded during this sweep. 'As he lay on the ground, making the slightest movement of his limbs, a young chap of about 19 ... remarked "Poor old Australia" A lot of meaning in that little remark.'

On the extreme right of the Australian line, a similar sweep was carried out. In this patrol, the Australians were angry; they had been suffering from sporadic sniper fire throughout the day and were determined to retaliate. The young officer leading this sweep, Lieutenant E.W.D. Laing of the 12th Battalion, later wrote that the time they had then compensated for all they suffered before and afterwards. He posted a patrol to the east to guard his flank and went straight through the ruins towards the north in a straight line. The few German defenders saw them coming, and decided they could not expect to surrender safely to such a determined looking group. One German seized a bicycle which had remained undamaged throughout the bombardment and rode off; he was probably a member of an artillery spotting party left

---

*Four days before the battle, Bourke wrote in his diary: 'Why go to war with one another? With these men we have no quarrel ... this struggle may teach us something about history'.

behind as observers. Another took three shots at the platoon commander — no doubt his aim was affected by the sight of the advancing Australians — before he was shot by an Australian.

Later, Laing wrote:

> Another tried to give himself up as soon as he saw our chaps on him. 'Come out, you . . .', yelled one of my men. I heard him, rushed back shouting at the chap to shoot the swine or I would — so he got him. Altogether we killed 6 and captured 18 down the dugouts. The men had great sport chucking bombs down any hole they saw.

When Laing finished his sweep, his company commander, Captain A.S. Vowles, came forward to supervise the new line in the right of the village. Vowles noticed a dugout which had been missed on the way through and ordered a bomb to be thrown in. After the explosion, two Australians began to descend the stairs but turned around quickly on hearing voices. Seventeen German soldiers emerged, some wounded, others shocked. They told Vowles there was a captain below. 'Tell him to come out', said Vowles. Out came a dapper officer in a long grey coat who informed Vowles, through Laing as interpreter, that his name was *Hauptmann* [Captain] Ponsonby Lyons and that his grandfather had been an Englishman. Noticing Vowles' badges of rank, Lyons asked who he was, adding, 'I am the commandant of Pozières'. Vowles' reply was admirably succinct: 'Tell him', he said to Laing, 'that he *was* the commandant. But I shall be happy to relieve him'. Lyons was indeed the commander of the *II/27th Imperial Regiment*. Lyons and his 17 comrades were also lucky; they were the only prisoners taken during Laing's sweep.

Private Bourke described one of these dugouts on the northern side of the village in a letter home to his parents.

> Two rooms were left intact, one above the other, the upper evidently a dining room, the lower a bedroom containing three wire netting beds and mattresses. On the shelves were pretty little jampots with little German men and women painted on their labels. All these little figures were dressed in blue and yellow and red like a Christmas tree . . . In a corner an officer's cap was thrown on a heap of cake boxes. These boxes were of cardboard and sewn in with calico just as the parcels come to us from Australia. The addresses were in a child's handwriting as were one or two letters. In another corner was a coat rolled up. I opened it and found it stained with blood. Right between the shoulders was a burnt shrapnel

hole, telling a tragic tale. The owner of the coat was a German and some might say, not entitled to much sympathy. Perhaps he was not, but I could not help thinking sadly of the little girl or boy who had sent him the cakes.

Now the problem remained to link up with the British 48th Division on their left. During the assault, this division had achieved some success but the British right battalion had not managed to reach the Australian left. Apart from a kink in the trench alongside the Albert-Bapaume road, the British forward lines were about 500 metres behind those of the Australians and this weakness was threatening the Australian position. Had the Germans counter-attacked at this point, the Australians might well have been isolated and the success of 23 July negated. On the right flank, the limited Australian success, and the failure of the neighbouring British to capture any of the Munster Alley trenches also left this flank vulnerable to counter-attack.

Walker wrote later that 24 July was spent in consolidating the position in the village before making a further attack.

> At 1.10 p.m. orders were received for a combined attack in conjunction with 48th Division, which was to join up with my division. Before these instructions were received, I had arranged to make a further attack on the OG trenches (to the north-east of the village) and to close the gap at the right centre in co-operation with an attack by the 1st Imperial Division on Munster Alley.

Walker says he was obliged to attack OG1 and OG2 from the west, and the eastern end of Pozières from the south. That obligation was forced on him by the failure of the flanking division to make any progress against the German defenders in Munster Alley on 23 July. Had they done so, Walker's attacks on OG1 and OG2 could have been launched from the south-west, with secure flanks provided by the Australians on his left and the British on his right. As well, because of the congestion caused by the narrow approaches to the village from the south, it was impossible for the attacks to be launched from the west and the south simultaneously. Walker also ordered two reserve battalions forward; the brigades on the right and left of the Australian line had suffered heavily, initially in the assault and later from the bombardment that was now 'methodical rather than intense'. This bombardment was preparing for the German counter-attack.

The commander of the German division holding the Pozières position had laid down his policy clearly, even before they entered the line.

> . . . not an inch of ground must be abandoned to the enemy. Every effort must be made to strengthen the position, and if the enemy penetrates, to drive him out at once by an immediate counter-attack. Sectors adjoining an attacked sector must aid by flanking fire and infantry attack without waiting for orders. The infantry will occupy the sector and ensure that rear trenches are continuously manned to act as reserves for counter-attack.

Three German counter-attacks on Pozières had failed before the evening of 24 July. Two early morning assaults, on 23 and 24 July, had failed because of the artillery and machine gun fire of the Australians; the third, on the afternoon of 23 July failed because the German artillery could not fire. Again that evening the Germans tried to dislodge the Australians. Walker's report notes it briefly: 'At 7.04 p.m. the enemy attempted a counter-attack in force along the Bapaume road. In four minutes the whole of the Divisional artillery was brought to bear, machine guns were turned on and the attack was smashed'.

'Squatter' Preston of the 9th Battalion, out on the right flank, found himself in the thick of this counter-attack.

> The enemy came over the ridge like a swarm of ants, rushing from shell hole to shell hole. Our men, full of fight and confidence, lined the parapet and emptied magazine after magazine into them. Some of the boys, anxious to get a shot at the Germans, pulled one another down from the fire-step in the midst of the fight.

Lance Corporal R.E. Adkins óf the 7th Battalion, a 28 year old farmer from Korumburra in Victoria, wrote a few lines after the battle to his mother, 'just to let you know I am alive and well . . .' Proudly Adkins told his mother that his unit had helped capture Pozières.

> The Germans kept on counter-attacking and rushing up fresh men but our boys held them easily. Our company met one of their attacks. They tried to get down the artillery trenches, what was left of it, for the artillery of both sides has chopped the ground to pieces and one could not see where the trench was. Well, they couldn't get down the trench and a mob came over the brow of the hill, in the open about 600 yards away, and we dropped them in all directions. Our artillery also picked them up very smartly and rained shrapnel and shells on them. They did not come far.

The attack Adkins described lasted about six hours, a 'real hell on earth our artillery bursting just ahead of us and their's everywhere and bombs of every kind and rifles all going at once'.

Soon the German staff learned that the ruins of Pozières village was in Australian hands; they responded by increasing the bombardment. Thus the pattern for the battle for the next seven weeks was established: attack, followed by counter-attack by the Germans, preceded by a ferocious bombardment that left strong men quivering. This is the 'true texture' of this part of the Somme fighting, the ferocious bombardments endured by the Australians as they fought to hold on to their hard-won territorial victories. Bean singles out one German 5.9 inch howitzer battery that began systematically to enfilade the trench-line south of the main road. This battery, located near Courcelette to the north-east, began by firing at the nearest Australian positions. Then, simply by elevating its range and changing direction slightly, it stepped the fire along the trench line.

> The ground had already been much shattered by the British bombardment, and though the trench walls had thus far stood without revetting, any shell bursting nearby closed them together as one might close a book, or else tumbled them in, burying and half-burying the men in loose soil. Whenever this happened, the men left unhurt were next moment digging furiously to extricate their mates; and, though these were often exhumed alive after even being completely buried, their nerves naturally had been subjected to a most violent shock.

By comparison to the smaller field artillery, the 5.9 inch howitzer fired a massive shell that could actually be seen at the top of its great parabolic arc. Almost all of the memoirs of the First World War — British, Australian and German — speak of the terrors of artillery fire. The terrors began well before the final explosion; experienced ears — not that there were many yet in the Australian divisions — could pick out the calibre of individual guns during the sporadic shelling that merely let the other side know the artillery was on its toes. In a barrage, of course, the primary explosions merged into one great roar, heard from a distance as a dull rumble, heard even in London on days when the capital was quiet and the wind was in the right direction.

As I type these words, trying to convey an experience that no Australian of my generation — not even those who served in Vietnam — has endured, the blank paper on my desk is held in place by a handful of rusty metal chunks, coated in white chalk, each no larger than a small chocolate bar. These are pieces of shrapnel, collected without much effort from the sites of the Windmill and memorial to the 1st Australian

Division. German? British? Australian? Who knows? Even today, nearly seven decades after the Somme fighting, these rich lands yield a sober harvest of grim memories.

To troops nearby, the effects of an artillery explosion were horrendous. These great metal chunks were hurled with ghastly force into soft and yielding flesh. No antibiotics existed in 1916; the wounds almost always turned septic; gangrene and amputation were often the forbidding consequences for the survivors. Those unlucky enough — or 'lucky', depending upon your viewpoint — to be at the point of explosion were all too often marked simply, 'missing, believed killed' at the next roll-call. Few traces remained, except perhaps a piece of charred boot with its grisly remains, or some scorched, shattered rags.

But the blast of such explosions could also kill slowly, rupturing the soft organs, leaving a man apparently unwounded but bleeding from every orifice. Even for those who escaped the more serious effects of the blast, eardrums would be punctured or noses would begin to bleed almost uncontrollably. In many ways, the psychological effect of artillery was just as telling as the physical result of the explosion. Men began to fear even the most remote shell burst; the time between the primary and the secondary explosions gave men time to think, to be afraid, to doubt their own self-confidence. In this passage, Lord Moran, Churchill's doctor in the Second World War and a young regimental medical officer in the trenches in the First, recounted how shelling affected him.

> At the time of this bombardment I was not too frightened. I was too stunned to think. But it took its toll later. I was to go through it many times in my sleep. I used to hear all at once the sound of a shell coming. Perhaps it was only the wind in the trees that reminded me that war had exacted its tribute and that my little capital was less than it had been. There were men in France who were ready to go out but who could not meet death in that shape. They were prepared for it if it came cleanly and swiftly, but that shattering, crudely bloody end by a big shell was too much for them. All their plans for meeting death with decency and credit were suddenly battered down. Self-respect had gone out of their hands. They were no longer certain of what they would do. It frightened more men away from the trenches than anything else.

Nothing had prepared the veterans of Gallipoli for the bombardment of 24 July. 'All that day we suffered fearfully', wrote Private Bourke.

> The guns got the range of our troops and shelled without pause. There was little use just sitting there and waiting to be knocked out, so we

started another trench 100 yards closer to Fritz' lines and there in broad daylight, with the shells just passing over our heads, the men from the bush and the town just stuck to it with a courage nothing short of sublime.

In the 2nd Battalion, eight men with shell shock reported to one officer, 'praying to be paraded to the doctor'; in the 4th Battalion, Sergeant Les de Vine wrote that nearly everyone had been buried at least once and 'we are kept busy digging ourselves out of the blown-down trench'; de Vine's commanding officer, Iven Mackay, considered moving his troops across the road, decided against it, but noted in his diary that the bombardment grew with intensity 'gradually leading with a terrifying ferocity to the worst bombardment ever experienced by the Australians'; Captain Harris wrote that the only thing for the Australians to do was 'to grin and bear it' for there were no dugouts in which to shelter. 'The wounded were so many that the stretcher bearers, who were working like heroes, could not get them away'.

At 7 p.m. on 24 July Harris's commanding officer sent him out of the company position and back to the battalion headquarters for a rest. He slept briefly and then returned to the line. Just as he was about to enter his dugout, a German 77 mm shell, commonly called a 'whiz-bang', hit the top of the parapet and exploded, killing a man who had just stepped out of the dug out, and sending Harris flying down the steps with the dead man on top of him. 'This' writes Harris, 'terminated my further interest in proceeding'.

In Harris's battalion, the wounded were being helped by a 45 year old former bushman, Private E. Jenkins, who had been one of the unit's hard cases, constantly in trouble out of the line. 'Under heavy shell fire he built a small shelter for the wounded, collecting them from their open positions in the trench and taking them one by one across to the shelter. He gave them his precious water, and refused a drink himself when more water could be brought up.' Harris believed that Jenkins kept several badly wounded men alive by his efforts. 'Every single one of these men was eventually taken out and recovered; but at the end of the day he himself, when taking a dixie of tea to the sufferers, was blown to pieces by a shell.'

Bean wrote home:

What is a barrage against such troops! They went through it as you would go through a summer shower — too proud to bend their heads, many of them, because their mates were looking. I am telling you of the things I have seen. As one of the best of their officers said to me, 'I have to walk about as if I liked it — what else can you do when your own men teach you to?'

The war diary of the Reserve Army headquarters makes little mention of the shelling being endured by the Australians. Walker's report, curiously enough, omits any mention as well. Repeated messages from the soldiers in the trenches for counter-battery fire seemed not to be getting through. In the morning of 24 July an aircraft carrying an artillery observer was sent aloft in an attempt to direct the fire of the British 12 inch howitzers; at 6.20 p.m. the British 34th Division Artillery, a neighbouring formation on the right was able to report that its front had been quiet all day but Pozières was being shelled. 'Our artillery is not replying and considerable damage is being done to trenches and rather severe casualties to men.' Effective counter-battery fire was beyond the limited resources of the Australian division artillery; it required co-ordination and fire from neighbouring corps.

Finally, at 7 p.m. on 24 July the Anzac Corps headquarters, which had taken charge of its divisions once more the previous evening, arranged counter-battery fire from a neighbouring corps which eased the German shelling. The Reserve Army also entered the picture; it ordered 12 rounds from 15 inch howitzers to be fired into Courcellette in retaliation for shelling Pozières. The difficulty in co-ordinating this artillery fire should not be laid entirely at the feet of the Reserve Army headquarters but it does seem that there was a curious lack of urgency both there and at the Anzac Corps headquarters about what should have been a relatively simple task, particularly as the neighbouring sectors were quiet and their artillery not over-burdened with missions. If the British Territorial and New Army artillery batteries were only semi-trained, then the same limitations applied to the command and control arrangements for those batteries. Admittedly observation for counter-battery fire was a problem, because the Germans still held the heights and the artillery doing the damage to the Australians was hidden well behind the lines. But at this stage of the battle, the British possessed almost complete air superiority and were able to use observers aloft to detect German gun positions and to adjust British counter-battery fire. The failure of the heavier British corps artillery to counter the German fire during this phase of the battle was to have important consequences for the senior British artillery officer at Birdwood's headquarters; it was to have terrible consequences for the Australians in their open trenches.

The reason for the German bombardment was simple: they were preparing a counter-attack that would retake the village. Previous quick counter-attacks had failed because the preliminary bombardments had not been sufficient. Now the Germans were increasing the intensity of the artillery fire and moving up fresh troops for the assault. The German *IV Corps*, which had suffered heavily, would be replaced by the *IX Reserve Corps*, commanded by General von Boehn. Once the reliefs had been completed, von Boehn's divisions would assault Pozières. This assault was timed to start at 4.30 p.m. on 25 July.

Meanwhile, Walker was still faced with his two-pronged attack. Although the German artillery fire eased at 7 p.m., two hours later it began again, clearly to hinder any preparation for a further attack. On the right, the frontal assault on the OG lines south of the Bapaume road was to be carried out by a fresh unit, the 5th Battalion largely drawn from Melbourne and surrounding districts. The plan was simple: the 5th, reinforced by two companies of the 7th, would assault the OG lines in six successive waves from 2 a.m. on 25 July. Before the assault, 6 inch, 8.2 inch and 9 inch batteries would methodically pound the German positions. Although the attack was to be carried out by night, the troops had the advantage of the old light railway line (used to carry farm produce, rather like the cane train lines so common in Queensland) which could still be dimly discerned in a landscape where most of the marks had been blown out of recognition.

This attack can only be described as 'shambolic', military slang to describe an absolute disaster. Few of the 5th Battalion officers went forward by day to see the terrain over which they would be attacking; the 'jumping-off' trench was not completed and tapes were laid instead; these tapes were placed badly, so they straggled across No Man's Land; the assaulting troops became lost getting to the starting point, including the two companies of the 7th Battalion, one-third of the assaulting force. Lance Corporal Eric Moorhead, an educated and intelligent man, left a bitter account of this action in his diary:

> Few or no explanations were given, and we were organised into parties and started off up the battered sap, carrying 200 extra rounds, two empty sandbags, two Mills's bombs, this in addition to the ordinary fighting equipment (belt and pouches, bottle and bayonet, and entrenching tools, rifle and haversack — only waterproof — etc. etc) and mess tin on back.

At Contalmaison, the 5th Battalion troops picked up boxes of bombs to carry to the front line. 'The way lay through a battered sap, corpses everywhere. Two dead Germans blocked the way, the stench was tremendous. Corpses everywhere in the sap and in the parapet. Heads and limbs protruded from the parapet, flies and maggots fed, and the stink was everywhere.' After getting thoroughly lost, Moorhead and his mates were led out into the open,

> '. . . no man knowing what he had to do and the shadow of failure already upon us. In groups, in threes, by ourselves, we crawled, none knew where, as no direction had been given, an odd bullet spattering about, waiting

for our artillery to open. *It did*. 1000 guns [here Moorhead exaggerates — the totals were considerably less] concentrating on our objective at 350 yards front. Then the fun began.'

With wild yells of 'Come on, Australia', with fierce oaths and with the old bushman's shout of 'coo-ee', the Australians launched into the attack in the direction they thought the enemy lay. The artillery fire indicated this, but it was not until a sergeant, (probably Sergeant Blair), saw the tape which had been laid to guide their progress and roared at the leading companies of the 5th to follow him were the troops sure. (Bean says Blair was unable to find the tape but Moorhead's description — 'our best sergeant, killed a few minutes later' — fits Blair.)

Blowing and gasping Moorhead wandered on till he finally flopped into a furrow. Surrounded by his mates, Moorhead realised they had taken a trench. 'There were no Huns or their dugouts in my vicinity. A few rifles and smashed equipment only being about; but our terrible bombardment had smashed everything.' In this trench, Moorhead and his mates paused, wondering what to do next.

> There was confusion, disorder, and lack of discipline, officers differed and argued. Orders had been given to two companies of the battalion to hold and consolidate this trench. Two others to get on and take the next — the counsel of an officer drunk with rum prevailed and we went on, men dropping now as Fritz got his machine guns to work. The second trench was a debris-filled furrow, along a line of trees. Here again, I met no Huns, and here again argument ensued — a captain filled to the neck with rum over rated all officers, finally blew his whistle, roared 'Charge Australia' or some such phrase, and dashed ahead again. Finally the survivors came back in a panic, calling out we must retreat, were all cut up, the Germans were on us, etc., etc. The Captain had been shot through the heart on the barbed wire.

Moorhead was right; the Germans had fled from the OG1 positions, which had been so smashed by the artillery bombardment as to be almost unrecognisable. When the first troops from the 5th Battalion reached this position, they were understandably confused by the absence of any clearly defined trench system.

Captain C. McE. Lillie (not the 'captain filled to the neck with rum') restored some order by posting troops in the OG1 line before moving forward in the second part of the assault. A 19 year old Gallipoli veteran known to the troops as 'The Pink Kid', Lillie had won the respect of the older, hard-headed soldiers during the landing on Anzac Beach; Bean described him as a 'red-headed slip of a boy whose directness of

The church at Pozières before the war. Like every other building in the village, this lovely old church was reduced to a pile of red brick rubble. The 'after' photograph was taken on 28 August 1916. Nothing in the picture so much as suggests that a church once stood on this site. (C3110 EZ96 AWM)

G. Lelong, 21, Rue St-Martin, Amiens

The village of Pozières before the war, looking towards Albert. (G1534G AWM)

An Australian Field Artillery ammunition limber, galloping up to the gun lines near Becourt during the Australian attack on Pozières. (Q899 IWM)

Australian gunners loading a 9.45 inch trench mortar in the Chalk Pit during the battle of Pozières. The shell of this weapon was nicknamed the 'Flying Pig' by the Australians. (IWM Q4092)

Above

A section of the trench line known as OG1. The sandbagged entrance to one of the many dugouts in these trenches can be seen at the top of the photograph. On the nights of 29 July and 4 August, troops of the 2nd Division attacked this section of the German lines from west to east, or left to right in the photograph. Until this system was taken, the Australians had to contend with an exposed right flank. (E7 AWM)

Below

A carrying party of the 7th Brigade passing the fortified blockhouse known as Gibraltar. The Germans had strengthened the original house with concrete; the effect of the British and Australian artillery was to destroy the house but leave standing the concrete fortifications. (EZ98 AWM)

Above
Stretcher bearers of the 2nd Division bringing out a wounded man from one of the many assaults on Mouquet Farm. This photograph was taken on 28 August 1916 near the old Pozières cemetery. Stretcher parties were rarely fired on by German machine gunners or snipers but no such immunity existed from German artillery. (E4947 AWM)

Below
The cross road leading to Casualty Corner. All traffic along the road to Pozières passed through this point. (EZ84 AWM)

Men of the 5th and 6th Brigades meet at Casualty Corner on 1 August 1916. Note the way the uniform jackets are open and sleeves are rolled. In a British regiment, such informality was forbidden. (EZ74 AWM)

Above
Brigadier-General Gellibrand (in slouch hat) and his staff at breakfast in a shell hole at Sausage Valley on 1 August 1916. Note the teapot and plates, luxuries for the front-line troops. (Q922 IWM)
Below
British artillery officers outside their dugout in the Carnoy Valley during the Battle of the Somme, July 1916. (Q4006 IWM)

speech and manner the men had resented, [he] came out of the battle one of the most popular fighting officers of the force'. It seems that the captain of whom Moorhead was so critical did not hear Lillie's order, or chose to ignore it. Only a few men were left in OG1 as almost the whole of the force swept forward. Again the OG2 lines were recognised only by the scraps of abandoned German equipment. Here Lillie ordered his troops to dig in.

Moorhead records that he dug feverishly with his entrenching tool

> ... as daylight was approaching and with it, the enemy's artillery fire. Meanwhile in our mad rush for the second (OG2) line we had omitted to look to our flanks and the Huns were coming on our left rear in a bombing attack. Our bombers attacked them vigorously and a great struggle ensued, our men throwing from on top of the trench and Fritz chiefly from below.

In fact, the Germans were coming along the OG1 line which the Australians had just captured but had virtually vacated.

At daylight, Moorhead's group was ordered to stop digging-in. The young lance-corporal thought that this was because they were in the wrong position, but the reason for the Australian move was more serious. Only a few troops had been left in the OG1 trenches and now the Germans were beginning to move down and threaten the advanced positions in OG2. The bombers from the 7th Battalion, who were supposed to have been part of the 5th Battalion attack, still had not turned up. Lillie sought reinforcements from his commanding officer who was only five minutes away, but was told there were no troops available. Lillie was told that he must make up his mind to hold OG2 or to pull back and retake OG1.

Off to his right, Lillie could see German flares rising as they prepared for an attack from that direction. He knew there were parties of Germans behind him. Now, he risked being caught between the two. A small party of the 5th had been working on a communications trench between the OG1 and OG2 lines. Lillie's men used this trench to regain the OG1 position. 'We set to work' wrote Moorhead, 'to improve the terribly battered trench, Hun equipment was everywhere, and some of the chaps actually stopped to open the Hun's packs, and put on some clean shirts, etc. These packs were filled with splendid clothing, the owners evidently being new drafts'.

Indeed they were new drafts, part of the fresh troops the German commander was planning to use in his own counter-attack. The Germans had been in the process of relieving the troops in the OG1 lines when the Australian attack began, and this largely accounted for the absence of German troops in the trenches during the initial assaults. The Australians' position in the OG lines was jeopardised by the failure of the British troops on the right to secure their objectives. Walker wrote:

> As the 1st Imperial Division failed to attack Munster Alley, the 5th Bn was promptly attacked by very heavy bombing parties from both flanks and had to give way in OG2. It held firm to most of the ground won in OG1, and assisted by the pioneers, put a 'T' head in to obtain sufficient frontage to deal with the enemy bombing.

At dawn the Australians were still in a precarious position. Cut off from their main forces, opposed by Germans on two sides and low on ammunition and bombs, they were vulnerable to any concerted offensive by the Germans. Yet their position was not realised by the brigade and division commanders, much less by Gough at Reserve Army headquarters or indeed, by Birdwood's corps headquarters. An aircraft, sent to establish contact with the Australians and determine their position, was shot down. 'We burnt flares', wrote Moorhead, 'to indicate our position, sent back messengers to our original front line for more bombs, flares, etc, etc. We were of course, disconnected from our front line but we heard at length that our pioneers were feverishly digging a communications trench towards us'.

The German attempt to retake the OG1 led to one of the most desperate bomb fights in the history of the AIF. Once again, the Australians were at a disadvantage; the smaller German hand bombs could be thrown further. 'It was bombs at the double — machine guns at the double — carriers at the double — more bombs at the double — strings of men going up.' Behind their hastily-erected barricades, men hurled Mills bombs until their arms simply gave out; others jumped forward, using the shell holes as cover, with a handful of bombs; one officer recalled seeing a sergeant, stripped to the waist, throwing grenades for an hour, with German bombs bursting all around him. 'One of these missiles seemed to explode almost on his chest, but he took no heed. His body covered with blood, he led the fight until he was forced to drop out through sheer exhaustion.' Of this battle Sir Arthur Conan Doyle later wrote:

> It was a most bloody and desperate conflict which swung and swayed down the long ditches, and sometimes over the edges of them into the bullet-swept levels between. Men threw and threw until they were so arm-weary that not another bomb could be lifted. If ever there were born natural bombers it must surely be among the countrymen of Spofforth

and Trumper — and so it proved at that terrible international by Pozières village.

Whatever this fight was, it certainly was not cricket.

There was little finesse about these tactics; little thought or application of skill; simply a matter of brute force and ammunition supply as both sides struggled for about 40 metres of trench line. The efforts of the pioneers almost defies belief. Without the recourse of retaliation, they simply had to dig trenches under fire, to throw out a 'sap' towards the enemy line and then extend it at right angles so that more bombers could be crowded in. And all the time under mortar artillery fire, and with explosions from hand bombs all around.

'The bombing fight on our left flank nearest the Germans continued', wrote Moorhead, 'till we gained the mastery and now fresh interest came'.

> Fritz came at us from the front. The nature of the ground prevented our seeing the size of the attack; but our artillery shattered it before it reached us. When the Huns came into view over the crest in twos or threes or singly, some with packs, probably filled with bombs, others with fixed bayonets, we lined the parapet like an excited crowd and blazed like hell at them, knocking them over like rabbits, not a man getting away so far as I could see. The range was about 400, and as each man appeared he got 100 bullets in him. One officer appeared and waved his men forward in a lordly way, and then collapsed like a bag, filled with our lead. I fixed about 30 rounds and did my share.

A grim incident made Moorhead and his mates roar with laughter. 'One unfortunate Boche having run the gauntlet of our rifle fire was getting away apparently only slightly wounded when one of our shells burst on him as though aimed, and he went up blown to pieces. Well, we cheered and laughed at the happening as though it was the funniest thing in the world.'

On the extreme right of the Australian position, the 10th Battalion suffered similarly. It had captured a strong point in the OG1 line, but was forced to withdraw to near the junction of OG2 and Munster Alley. North of the Albert-Bapaume road, the 8th Battalion, reinforcing Smyth's 1st Brigade pushing steadily through the village, secured a position near the cemetery and occupied a line along the northern edge of the village. This operation was nearly compromised from the beginning, because of a silly mistake by the Australian Divisional Headquarters in the date of the operation order. The brigade commander, reading the date on the first signal he received, thought he had an extra day to plan his attack and dismissed the battalion commanders. It was not until midnight on 24 July shortly before the attack was due, that he learned of the mistake.

Somehow the battalion commanders were found, new orders were issued and troops prepared for the attack. Mackay, one of the battalion commanders affected, noted that he was 'not too upset by the change in plan'. He dictated his orders to his company commanders in the dark, with not so much as a candle to relieve the gloom. As this solemn little orders group was in progress, the other officers of the battalion collected their troops and brought them around to the jumping off point. Even so, many were late getting into position and did not move off until 20 minutes after the barrage had lifted. The careful language of the after-action report conveys only some of the difficulties of this action. Walker wrote:

> The 4th Battalion bombed steadily along the whole of the western side of Pozières for nearly 700 yards, driving the enemy before it. One company of Germans was unable to stand the pressure and fled from the trenches across the open. They were caught by the fire of the machine guns which were supporting the attack by traversing the parapet and lost heavily. Posts were established along the enemy trenches about 300 yards in advance and one patrol pushed along the main trench towards Mouquet Farm.

As the bombers from Mackay's battalion pushed forward along the K trench, the troops of the 8th Battalion were making similar progress on the right. In the 4th Battalion, the bombers were collecting discarded German grenades, as well as early morning coffee and rum which had been brought forward. About 6 a.m. on 25 July the two battalions linked north of the Pozières cemetery; effectively now the Australians held the village and most of the northern approaches. Again, however, the Australians' position was compromised by the British failure on their left. Walker says simply, 'The 48th Division on our left had not got in touch with us'. An attack by the 7th Warwicks, which was supposed to have captured a nearby German strong point in support of the Australian effort, failed during the night when the troops could not reach their starting point; another attack at midday on 25 July also failed. It was not until the early hours of the following morning, 4 a.m. on 26 July that the Australians and the soldiers of the Warwickshire Regiment finally met.

The battalion war diaries for this period are necessarily terse. The 4th Battalion diary simply records that their attack was 'entirely successful'. One officer recalled that Mackay did not take stupid risks. 'But he had a knack of turning up where things were hottest. He carried a rifle as well as his pistol, and you could see Mills bombs bulging in his pockets. You knew everything was under control once he arrived. A safe feeling. I guess it's all part of leadership.' That leadership was to be sorely tested during the next hours.

At about 8 a.m. on 25 July, as the Australians were consolidating their newly won positions north of the Albert-Bapaume road, the German bombardment began with renewed violence. 'A heavy hostile counter-attack was launched at about 8.30 a.m.', Walker reported. 'It was crushed by artillery and machine gun fire.' This counter-attack was badly organised. The Germans had been first seen on the crest near the Pozières Windmill advancing south and were immediately subjected to heavy machine gun and artillery fire. The Germans broke, changed direction and headed west.

The Australians were lucky that morning. Through a series of serious errors, the Germans launched three separate, small-scale counter-attacks which, even against the weakened and battered Australians, did not succeed. Part of the problem was the German division commander's unfamiliarity with the area; part was the absence of information flowing back to him; part was an understandable anxiety on the part of all the German subordinate commanders that positions lost should be immediately counter-attacked. But the Germans were not the only ones advancing from a direction in the rear that morning. On the eastern outskirts of the ruined village, about 200 metres ahead of the forward troops in the OG1 lines, one small group of Australians withdrew under the heavy bombardment. A neighbouring battalion commander noticed the withdrawal and reported that the battalion was retiring 'badly shaken'. This simple mistake was to cause ill-feeling between the two battalions for months to come.

By 10.15 that morning of 25 July, all these counter-attacks had failed, crippling a German regiment in the process. With the German withdrawal ended the Australian artillery fire; only the remorseless pounding of the German bombardment on the village continued the pattern of the previous day. During that morning too, the 3rd Battalion attempted to advance from south of the Albert-Bapaume road and link with the 8th on the northern edge of the village. The first two officers to whom the task was given were killed even before they could reach their troops; the commanding officer, Owen Howell-Price, then only 24, took the remnants of his battalion forward himself.

Except for a couple of intervals, the bombardment continued all day. A relatively fresh battalion was moved forward on to the northern edge of the village, and managed to slip through a pause in the shelling almost unscathed — almost, that is, except for the last platoon which was caught in the full fury as they made their way up the Chalk Pit road. This platoon lost its commander and more than half its men.

Again, the Reserve Army diary gives little indication of the sufferings of the troops under its command. 'July 25: considerable heavy shelling went on all day, particularly south of Pozières. During the day there was little to report elsewhere than at Pozières ... There was heavy shelling in Pozières all day.' Bean's letters home and the diaries and letters of the soldiers give us a better indication. After the morning attack was beaten off,

> Again the enemy's artillery was turned on. Pozières was pounded more furiously than before, until by four in the afternoon it seemed to onlookers scarcely possible that humanity could have endured such an ordeal. The place could be picked out for miles by pillars of red and black dust towering above it like a Broken Hill dust-storm.

In the 1st Battalion, a former NSW farmer, Archie Barwick, scribbled his impressions of the bombardment. He counted 75 9.2 inch or larger shells falling on an area of less than four acres within five minutes.

> All day long ground rocked and swayed backward and forwards from the concussion ... like a well built haystack ... swaying about ... men were driven stark staring mad and more than one of them rushed out of the trench over towards the Germans, any amount of them could be seen crying and sobbing like children their nerves completely gone ... we were nearly all in a state of silliness and half dazed but still the Australians refused to give ground. Men were buried by the dozen, but were frantically dug out again some dead and some alive.

Private Jack Bourke saw men 'trembling like leaves ... one kind of shock affects the nerves, the other the head. With steel nerves a man might be calm. That day, for its awful terror and my escape I shall never forget'. Private Vincent Bowman of the 9th Battalion noted simply: '25/7/16: Another terror of a day. Stood to all night ... being shelled to pieces. Satisfied that it is not the taking of a position that counts, but the holding of it'.

During the infrequent pauses in the shelling, stretcher bearers — the men who 'should be wearing halos and wings', according to one Australian soldier — collected the wounded, helping them back to battalion aid posts. 'Squatter' Preston thought the stretcher bearers worked heroically. 'On one occasion I was watching two stretcher bearers carrying a wounded man on a stretcher when the rear man was shot. Another man who rushed up and took his place was immediately shot, as was the front bearer and then the wounded man.' In the 4th Battalion, Chaplain McKenzie used the pauses to bury the dead. In the warm night air, the stench of decomposing bodies was overwhelming.

The troops of the 1st Australian Division were reaching the end of their tether. All through 25 July the German bombardment continued, but still the division held on. Indeed, in the early hours of 26 July reinforcements from the 2nd Division attempted a surprise raid on the OG lines but this, too, failed. Any sudden movement of troops on either side brought about a renewal of the bombardment, growing in intensity each time for this was virtually the only sector of the Reserve Army front in which there was any activity. The commanding officer of the 12th Battalion, Lt.-Col. Charlie Elliott, wrote later the battalion had experienced many hurricane bombardments, lasting a half-hour or more, of far greater intensity. 'But I do not remember any other so severe for such a long time ... In the evening when I went up to arrange for our relief by the 19th Battalion, I could hardly find a trace of the trenches that had been so well dug the previous day.'

In the 5th Battalion position, Moorhead had remained on the parapet for the greater part of the morning of 26 July, but as he put it, 'few Huns came into view'. With the communication trench came rations and rum, their first issue for 16 hours. Moorhead spent another anxious night waiting for a German counter-attack, but none came.

> ... to our joy a relieving party belonging to the 2nd Division turned up. We made our way down a communication sap. This was literally heaped with the corpses of the men who had dug it for us, huddled everywhere, killed by shell fire, some lying head first, all in contorted attitudes, and ghastly even to my hardened nerves in the dim light.

The 5th Battalion survivors were kept huddled in the sap all day, enduring bombardment after bombardment. Moorhead wrote:

> At last we got the order to move, and we crawled and ran down the battered, wretched, and corpse-ridden communication sap, and finally got out into the road near Contalmaison, and filed down it. In small parties, dirty, unshaven, worn-out, dusty and nerve shaken, it felt like getting out of hell; and our gloom with our losses, which were heavy, was lightened by the words of approval from our mates along the road.

Again, the Reserve Army diary records the following days's events with sanguinity. 'July 26th. During the day the Germans continued to shell Pozières very heavily and also to barrage the country south of that village, thus causing considerable difficulty in supply. Notwithstanding this the work of consolidation went on well. There was nothing else to record on the army front.' And again, the records kept by the men experiencing that shelling provide a stark contrast with the dispassionate tone of the War Diary. In the 6th Battalion, Second Lieutenant Mathew Absom, who was one of the few officers left in his company, noted in his diary:

> 26/7/16. Continued work on trench until afternoon when enemy bombarded us heavily. Our own artillery took a long time to reply. An aeroplane came over and passed the word back to the batteries. They soon opened up. One big 12 inch gun from Albert opened up sending over the occasional shell which made a noise like an express train overhead and smashed up the Hun's line in a fashion that was beautiful to behold.

Lt.-Col. Bennett, commanding the 6th Battalion, reported at 4.05 p.m. that his men were being shelled. 'They cannot hold on if attack is launched. The firing line and my headquarters are being plastered with heavy guns and the town is being swept with shrapnel. I myself am OK but the front-line is being buried.'

Some hours later, Lt.-Col. Jess, commanding the 7th Battalion, reported that it had been impossible to construct adequate trenches, 'owing to the pulped nature of the ground. Those that were constructed NE of Pozières are wiped out, and men are so dazed they are incapable of working or fighting. Consider relief imperative as we could not resist attack if this is the preparation of it. 6th and 8th Battalions endorse this'. This message was sent by the battalion signallers, then, taking the telephone himself, Jess spoke directly to the brigade headquarters. If the smoke and dust hanging over Pozières prevented the artillery observers from seeing the German attack, then they must simply turn all the guns on to the German firing line.

Soon the Australian artillery was systematically raking the German line but it was another 90 minutes before the German bombardment stopped, and then only briefly. Jess' brigade commander, Brig.-Gen. J. K. Forsyth, was worried that the forward battalions were about to break. 'Men must and will fight if necessary', he told Jess. A terse battalion commander replied: 'No movement by officers or men in shelled areas to retire has been made. Men have stuck to crater holes and no one will move in a rearward direction. Messages were sent to enable brigade headquarters to realise the seriousness of the position'.

Throughout the battle, it was not unusual for brigade headquarters — perhaps 1,000 metres at most behind the lines — to be ignorant of the condition in the trenches. On the previous day, the battalions pleaded with brigade and divisional headquarters for counter-battery fire, but the combination of haze and smoke meant those appeals were late getting through.

Bean wrote:

> No attack followed this tremendous bombardment. It is now known that the enemy had adopted a plan seldom if ever afterwards applied in the experience of Australian troops — that of laying down a day long barrage, not in preparation for any intended offensive, but simply with the object of inflicting damage and loss. The bombardments of July 24 and 25 were intended to make the village '*sturmreif*' ('ready for assault'); but after the utter failure of the attempted assault on the afternoon of July 25, it was decided not to attack again, but to bombard Pozières and its approaches throughout the 26th, the special feature of the operation, however, being a sudden synchronised 'crash' by the artillery of three [German] divisions after an interval of silence.

The decision to relieve the 1st Division had been taken during 25 July. That night, the 5th Brigade of the 2nd Division moved in to relieve the 3rd Brigade on the right and the 2nd Infantry brigade (minus the 5th Battalion which had already been committed), relieved the 1st Brigade which had taken place in the original assault two days before. Of the 1st Brigade however, Mackay's 4th Battalion was left holding the line until the patrols and the bombing parties of the British divison could link up. The 4th Battalion had suffered heavily, with Mackay reporting 'Losses now heavy, many men are buried and suffering from shell-shock. Stretcher bearers and runners very tired'. It was just as well the expected counter-attack on 26 July did not eventuate. Indeed, never again did the Germans adopt such a curious plan; a day-long artillery bombardment designed not as preparation for an infantry attack, but merely to inflict damage and loss. Their failures of the previous days had made this new German formation cautious.

Battalion by battered battalion, the survivors came out of the line. Some had endured four days of bombardment, the like of which they had never experienced before. They had captured a German strongpoint that had stoutly resisted previous attempts by the British and they had held on to their territorial achievements. During the fighting, virtually the rest of the British line on the Somme — with the exception of Delville Wood — was stationary; only the Australian sector was active in 'step by step methodical operations'.

The result of this was to free the Germans to concentrate their artillery resources upon the shoulder of the ridge on which the village of Pozières had stood; the Germans, who regarded the capture of the Windmill heights with well-merited apprehension, could saturate each narrow Australian attack, each 'step by step methodical advance', with devastating quantities of artillery and allocations of ammunition.

The Germans responded so violently not just because of the general order about counter-attacking lost positions. They realised the tactical significance of the Pozières Ridge; they thought that, because the remainder of the front was relatively quiet, that this was the major British effort. Few of the contemporary German accounts suggest that their authors realised this offensive was subsidiary to Haig's total plan, long held and little amended.

Sergeant Rule of the 14th Battalion was in Warloy when the troops of the 1st Division came through. They had already been out of the line for one night.

> Although we knew it was stiff fighting we had our eyes opened when we saw these men march by. Those who watched them will never forget it as long as they live. They looked like men who had been in hell. Almost without exception each man looked drawn and haggard and so dazed that they appeared to be walking in a dream, and their eyes looked glassy and starey. Quite a few were silly, and these were the only noisy ones in the crowd.

Bean wrote that the Australians of the 1st Division who rested at Vadencourt Wood one day out of the line 'were utterly different from the Australian soldiers of tradition. The bright spirit and activity seemed to have gone out of them; they were like boys emerging from long illness. Many lay quietly apart from the others, rolled in their blankets under the trees, reading books, smoking, writing home letters'.

The casualties of the 1st Division were 5,285 officers and men: 4,937 infantry: 113 engineers; 180 pioneers; 30 artillery. The fighting strength of an infantry battalion was its four rifle companies each with about 200 men and 5 officers. Against this, the casualties of the battalions were particularly horrific: 1st Battalion, 473 men and 13 officers; the 2nd 500 and 10; the 3rd, 484 and 13; and the 4th 388 and 14. In the 3rd Brigade, which endured slightly less in the shelling, the casualties were slightly lower. The 9th Battalion lost 299 men and 17 officers; the 10th, 315 and 12; the 11th, 511 and 18 and the 12th, 407 and 14. In the 2nd Brigade, which was originally in reserve, the 5th Battalion suffered most heavily and then because of its early role. It lost 458 men and 13 officers, while the 6th lost 183 and 7; the 7th, 326 and 8 and the 8th, 321 and 15.

Not reflected in these figures are the 'shell shock' casualties and those who, in Bean's words, 'had come through actually untouched, [in which] constant fear and physical fatigue are combined to produce effects which in peace time would be labelled "nervous breakdown".' One tally of shell shock victims, although not complete, reveals the extent of this disability: 11 on 22 July; 31 on 23 July; 72 on 24 July; 205 on 25 July; 57 on 26 July. It afflicted officers and men alike. In Mackay's battalion one officer, decorated for bravery at Gallipoli, was found cringing in a corner throughout the bombardment. Although repatriated to a training battalion, this officer begged Mackay for a chance to return to the battalion. Mackay relented, only to find the man had cracked again in a few days.

Others simply went mad, or shot themselves — not necessarily the same thing. One runner for the 3rd Brigade headquarters lay down for a rest on 24 July after a particularly strenuous barrage. One of his mates came into the brigade commander and said simply, 'X has had an accident with his rifle, sir — shot himself. He had found it more than he could bear, put his rifle to his head and "went out" uncomplaining'.

The strain on the runners was indeed terrible. In his report Walker paid tribute to their 'wonderful spirit of self-sacrifice'; Smyth, commanding the 1st Brigade recorded two such examples. One appeared at Smyth's headquarters, delivered his message and then died quietly from wounds he had received on the way. Another, from the 2nd Battalion, was hit by an artillery burst as he crossed the point where the sunken road through the Chalk Pit cut the main Albert-Bapaume road. 'He died with the message held high in the air between his fingers. Twenty minutes later, a party crossing the road, came upon him still holding the paper, and carried it to its proper destination.'

With the runners, stretcher bearers evoked the greatest admiration of their mates, as we have seen from Preston's comments. Bean thought they 'were moved by an inward desire to show to the combatant troops that they shared the worst dangers'. More prosaically, Walker noted in his report that the 'establishment of stretcher bearers was quite inadequate for the large numbers of casualties inflicted in an action in modern war and a great many were borrowed from other ambulances'.

Walter George Molyneaux Claridge, later of the 22nd Battalion, and formerly a woolclasser from Glen Iris in Victoria, wrote to his parents on 10 August 1916 from the Number 4 London General Hospital, Denmark Hill.

> After your loving words I could not have turned coward, though God knows what we went through was Hell itself. We just had to grit out teeth and go ahead and do the job. I am not going to tell a lie and say I wasn't afraid because I was and who wouldn't be with Death grinning at you from all around and hellish 5.9 inch shells shrieking through the air and shrapnel dealing death all around. I don't know how I stood it so long

> without breaking but I knew you would be ashamed of me if I played the coward, so I kept straight on at the head of my platoon.

Claridge was a platoon commander in the 8th Battalion. He told his parents that from Sunday night 23 July to Tuesday afternoon 25 July, 'I wasn't touched although I was buried three times. I was very thankful to get my wound as it got me out of the firing line for a rest'. In the 1st Pioneer Battalion, Private George Angus, a 22 year old Victorian blacksmith, also wrote home to his parents, describing the battle he had just left. 'I tell you', he wrote on the bottom, almost as an afterthought, 'it makes different men of us over here. It makes you stop to think'. It was Angus' last letter home. He was killed in action on 21 August.

On 25 July, at the height of the bombardment, Haig visited Birdwood at the Anzac Corps headquarters at Vignacourt, some 30 kilometres behind the lines. His diary entry for that night is fascinating:

> The situation seems all very new and strange to Australian HQ. The fighting here and the shell-fire is much more severe than anything experienced at Gallipoli. The German, too, is a very different enemy to the Turk! The hostile shelling has been very severe against Pozières today and owing to clouds our observation was bad and our counter-battery work could not be carried out effectively.

Haig moved quickly to remedy this. Brig.-Gen. Cunliffe Owen, who had been Birdwood's chief artillery officer since the landing at Anzac was sacked, although he was not replaced until some days later. Haig noted:

> I spoke to Birdwood about his CRA., Brig.-Gen. Cunliffe Owen ... I also saw Cunliffe Owen and explained how sorry I was to have to move him, but in the present situation I would be failing in my duty to the country if I ran the risk of the Australians meeting with a check through faulty artillery arrangements.

Haig's concern for 'artillery arrangements' is commendable, but his sacking of Cunliffe Owen — indeed with most of the Corps artillery staff, as it happened — was less than fair. The Australian division had been launched into battle without the benefit of its parent Corps headquarters; at the height, the Anzac Corps headquarters was expected to pick up the pieces caused by Gough's impetuosity and restore them to some kind of order. It is significant that Walker's report praises the performance of the Divisional Artillery, but is silent about the performance of the Corps gunners, both Anzac and British.

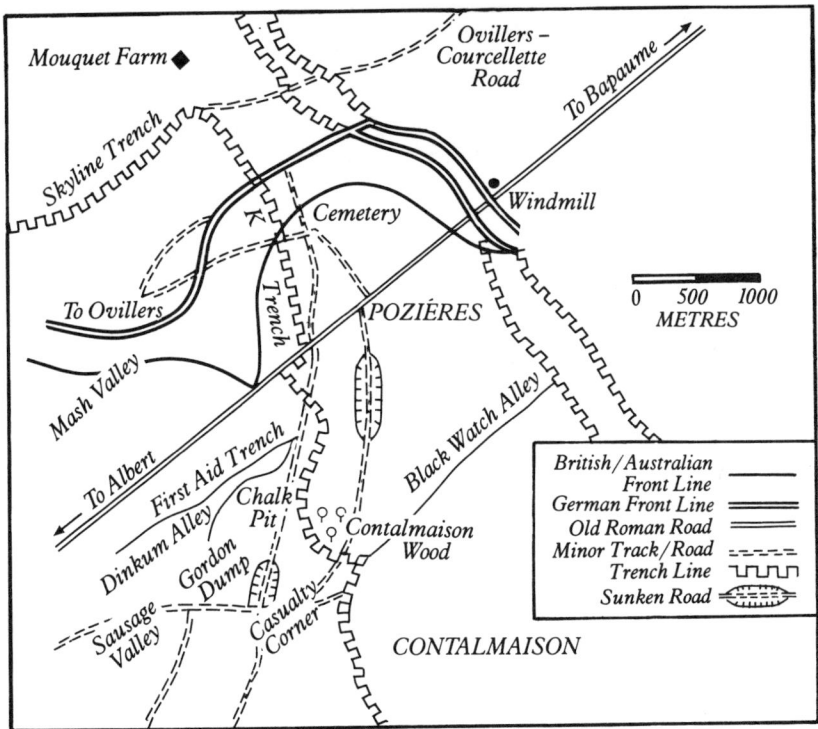

Trench lines at Pozières after the 1st Division attack.

With characteristic charity, Bean does not mention Cunliffe Owen's sacking, except in a fairly roundabout fashion. But the artillery arrangements for the early part of the Pozières attack were unnecessarily complicated by the lack of the Anzac Corps Artillery headquarters. Indeed, the artillery planners for Walker's original attack, drawn from the Reserve Army headquarters, the neighbouring British X Corps and the Australian divisional artillery, managed to plan one barrage which, if fired, would have fallen squarely upon the Australians. The credit for discovering this blunder belongs to Brudenell White, who, although not directly concerned, was worried about the possibility of error in the rapidly planned operation. It was not to be the first time that Brudenell White was concerned about apparently haphazard British planning. On 27 July as the 1st Division rested, Birdwood wrote to Walker. 'Birdie' hoped that the rest would be a 'fairly long one, but which I fear may be comparatively short'. The Anzac Corps commander described the taking and holding of Pozières as a 'really magnificent bit of work ... the worst of it is that I am afraid we must all of us look forward to a continuous series of such strains during this stage of the fighting'.

11

'Conceited Colonials'

The word 'retire' is absolutely forbidden in this division, and some other phrase has to be used where any withdrawal is required.
Maj.-Gen. J. G. Legge, GOC 2nd Australian Division, 1916.

N ow it was the turn of the 2nd Australian Division. Unlike the 1st, this division had not been torn asunder when the AIF doubled in 1916. It had been formed late in the previous year in Egypt from reinforcements for the peninsula; it had arrived on Gallipoli too late to take part in any major operation except the withdrawal; its officers and men possessed great enthusiasm and sketchy experience, qualities potentially dangerous in those proportions. Of course, with the right leaders such qualities need not necessarily be dangerous: experience is soon gained and enthusiasm is all too easily lost. But in one fundamental quality, the 2nd Australians compared less than favourably with other AIF formations of the time. That quality was leadership. Field Marshal Viscount Slim thought commanding a division was good fun. 'It is one of the four best commands in the Service ... because it is the smallest formation that is a complete orchestra of war and the largest in which every man can know you.'

The commander of the 2nd Australian Division, Maj.-Gen. James Gordon Legge, was not well known to his troops. Nor was he, in Bean's circumspect description, 'conspicuously a fighting leader'. Of course, Legge could have been a competent commander, without being either well known to his troops or a conspicuous fighting leader. But the performance of the division suggests otherwise.

Legge was born in 1863, educated in England and at Sydney Grammar School. He studied arts and law at the University of Sydney, later qualified as a barrister and served in a militia regiment. In 1894, he transferred to the fledgling Australian permanent army, served in South Africa and by 1909 was a lieutenant-colonel although he could not add the post-nominals 'p.s.c.' (passed staff college) to his Sydney University MA and Ll.B. In an early *Who's Who* entry (then largely prepared by the subject), Legge notes he was 'specially engaged for 3 yrs on organisation of Universal Mily. Training in Aust.,'. Indeed, Legge was largely the Australian architect of the Kitchener plan which extended compulsory militia service and led to the establishment of the Royal Military College at Duntroon. At the time, Legge was Quartermaster-General; his work with Kitchener caught the eye of Sir George Pearce, then Minister of Defence, who marked him for special advancement.

Pearce had noted Legge's abilities as an administrator; abilities that were needed in the early days of the war when the AIF was raised and Legge was Chief of the General Staff. When Bridges was killed at Gallipoli after just three weeks of the campaign, Pearce appointed Legge to command the 1st Division. That appointment was made without the benefit of consultation, either with Birdwood, or General Sir Ian Hamilton, a mistake which Pearce later regretted. As well as commanding the 1st Division, Legge assumed Bridges' other powers over the AIF. Not surprisingly, the decision infuriated the brigade commanders, Monash, Charles Chauvel* and M'Cay. Legge was their junior and had not served in the campaign. So far as Monash and M'Cay were concerned, Legge was also a professional soldier.

In the reaction to Legge's appointment, we can discern the strains between the militia and the professional officers which have bedevilled the Australian army: suspicion and resentment on both sides have characterised the relationships between the enthusiastic amateurs and the dedicated professionals. But relationships in 1914 should not have been as awkward as they were between 1939 and 1945. Chauvel's biographer tells us that in 1914 few senior officers had handled a brigade for more than a day or two, and this was as true of regulars like Chauvel as it was of militiamen like Monash. 'So it was hardly surprising that doubts were voiced at various levels about the fitness of Australian officers for higher command and that the idea prevailed among British generals that the AIF lacked officers capable of commanding brigades and divisions.'

It must be said, however, that Pearce's appointment of Legge was entirely reasonable; here was an Australian politician exercising the right to appoint an Australian officer to command an Australian division as part of the Australian Imperial Force. But while the appointment was proper, the choice was uninspired. Legge's personal lack of popularity (sadly, not uncommon of competent administrators), exacerbated the feelings of jealousy held by both Monash and M'Cay. There were mutterings about resignations and Birdwood was forced to intervene. According to Bean: 'Birdwood urged that resignation was not to be thought of in war and that, if they suspected their new commander was

---

* Later to command the Mounted Division in Palestine.

unequal to the task, their part was as far as possible to stand by him and help him through'.

In his assessment of Legge, Bean is guarded:

> He was a leader concerning whom opinions varied. The administrative branches of his staff were strongly impressed by his ability and made no secret of their admiration; on the other hand, his general staff, originally composed entirely of British officers, had criticised him somewhat freely as tending to impracticable theories and changing enthusiasm . . . he was a thorough Australian at heart and principle. The country owed to him, more perhaps than to any man, its fine system of compulsory military training.

Bean goes on to note that Legge had a son killed fighting as a private in the 2nd Division in 1918, 'whom he might easily have raised to the rank of officer or employed in moderate safety on the staff'. A modest tribute indeed, from an historian who knew and understood the politics of the AIF well, even though his knowledge was largely that of the interested observer rather than the enthusiastic participant.

After Legge's appointment to the 1st Division, M'Cay, arguably the best of the Australian brigade commanders in 1915, was given the task of moulding the Australians in Egypt into the 2nd Division. Before he could take command, however, M'Cay was injured and had to return to Australia for medical treatment. Fortuitously as it happened, for Birdwood was able to divert Legge to Egypt in M'Cay's place, and install 'Hooky' Walker as commander of the 1st Division.

Legge had several experienced Australian officers on his staff in the new 2nd Division, including Blamey, Major John Gellibrand, Lt.-Col. G. C. Elliott and Lt.-Col. A. Sutton. He required more, but was told there were none to spare in the AIF. Forced to look elsewhere, Legge took several British staff officers from a pool in Egypt. This combination of British and Australian officers was not unusual in the AIF, but it proved unfortunate in the 2nd Division. Even months later, British officers continued to fill the general staff positions — Blamey was the chief administrative officer* — and there was marked friction between the staffs of the divisional headquarters and the brigades.

By comparison to the 2nd Division headquarters, the brigade staffs were almost happy families, many continuing pre-war militia associations into the AIF. The 5th Brigade was commanded by the former secretary of the Water and Sewerage Board in Sydney, Brig.-Gen. William Holmes, a keen militia officer who had served in South Africa. A

---

* Even so, Blamey managed to find his way back to the 1st Division headquarters.

man of undoubted personal courage, Holmes was fond of visiting his troops in the front line wearing (against specific orders) his red-banded cap.* Holmes also appreciated the qualities of Sydney University graduates so much that they represented a significant proportion of officers in his brigade, thus beginning another Australian military tradition.

The 6th Brigade was commanded by Brig.-Gen. John Gellibrand, a Tasmanian orchardist who had served in the British army, and fought as a company commander at the relief of Ladysmith. When his battalion, the 3rd Manchesters, was disbanded in 1906, Gellibrand went to the staff college at Camberley as a student, graduated well and was posted to a staff job in Ceylon. Before this posting was completed, however, Gellibrand was placed on half pay. He resigned his commission and was gazetted out of the British army. Gellibrand went back to Tasmania and was quietly growing apples when the war began in 1914. Initially he had difficulties in joining the AIF but Brudenell White, who had been a fellow student at staff college, persuaded Bridges to take this unconventional, almost Bohemian orchardist. Bean, like his friend Brudenell White, was an admirer of Gellibrand and left this glowing description:

> He was a direct speaker of the truth, never whittling down a fact or mitigating the sharp edge of a report to please a superior. 'There comes a day in the life of all young officers', he used to say, 'when a superior will ask them for their opinion. If the youngster gives an answer which he thinks will please, he is done; he is useless. If he says straightly what he thinks, he is the man to get on'. It was a constant wonder, to those who knew in Gellibrand one of the best and ablest officers in the army within the experience of the Australians, how a man with these qualities and with staff college training could have been allowed — much less almost compelled — to slip out of the British army. It was standing evidence of the hopeless defects in a system which elected a staff much on the principles of a hunt club. Gellibrand did not play polo at the staff college; he was not a good rider; he had no skill at games; he kept largely to himself; he read voraciously.† Men of this type found it no easy matter to achieve success in the old British army.

---

* Holmes' soldiers did not always appreciate their commander's personal courage. His red-banded cap was conspicuous and responsible for attracting enemy artillery, drawing the crabs as they said, on to their positions, often after the brigadier had left.

† In New Guinea during the Second World War, 'Jo' Gullett wrote to his mother asking for a number of serious books. Lady Gullett discussed the choice 'with her old friend, that most erudite, eccentric and charming of professional soldiers, General Sir John Gellibrand.' The books were sent and read, a habit 'Jo' Gullett maintained for the rest of the war.

Although of markedly differing personalities, Gellibrand was similar to H. E. 'Pompey' Elliott in this respect: both would have been difficult subordinates. But both had the ability to inspire troops under their command, Gellibrand by a remarkable leadership style in which he set himself only slightly apart from his soldiers. He wore the same uniform (by choice not affectation) and endured the same hardships. His headquarters functioned more as a co-operative venture than a military hierarchy with the commander sitting back and discussing the problems with the staff and with his unit commanders; at the same time, he was not above intervening personally to ensure his standards were being met and his orders carried out.

The third brigade, the 7th, was comprised of troops from the lesser-populated Australian states, containing in Bean's words ' ... an unusually high proportion of country men — the Queenslanders and Western Australians, largely from the mining fields and stations outback. It would therefore, other things being equal, be expected to be the hardest and most effective of the three'. Its commander, Brig.-Gen. John Paton, a former Newcastle merchant and another enthusiastic militia soldier, had taken part in the operation in German New Guinea, and had commanded the 25th Battalion, now part of his brigade. But this was a brigade with problems, particularly among the regimental and battalion commanders, with rivalries and petty jealousies simmering below the surface. This formation was suffering from poor selection by the boards which had been established as a reaction to the accusation of 'cronyism'* in selecting officers for the First AIF. One battalion history noted that commanders were forced by 'compromise and adjustment' to secure their best team, often having unsuitable officers foisted upon them. The lack of suitability was felt particularly at company and battalion commander level; it was to reveal itself tragically in the coming battle.

The 2nd Division relieved the 1st Australian Division during the night of 27 July. Gough had already explained to Birdwood his theory for the offensive: it was to keep attacking with moderate numbers. That way, the Germans would be kept off balance. 'Once we allow him to get his breath back', Gough told Birdwood, 'we shall have to make another of these gigantic assaults by which time all the German defences will have been repaired and strengthened. I think our way keeps down casualties and brings the best results.' Formally, the orders were that: 'II (British) and Anzac Corps were to work systematically northwards, rolling up the German line from about Pozières to about Grand-

---

*The notion began to spread that the selections were being made by a coterie of the Australian Club in Sydney.

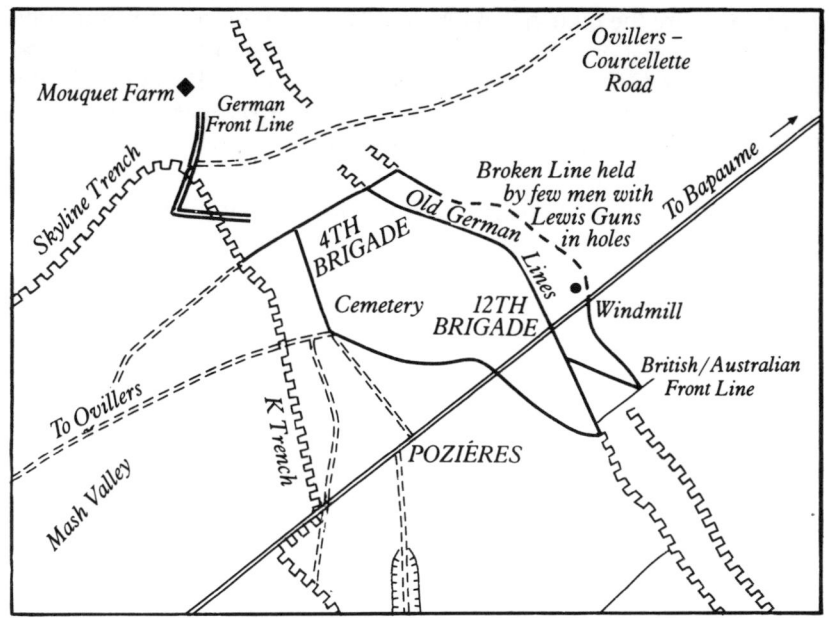

Australian lines after 2nd Division attack on the night of 28/29 July 1916 and Australian lines after 2nd Division attack on the night of 4/5 August 1916.

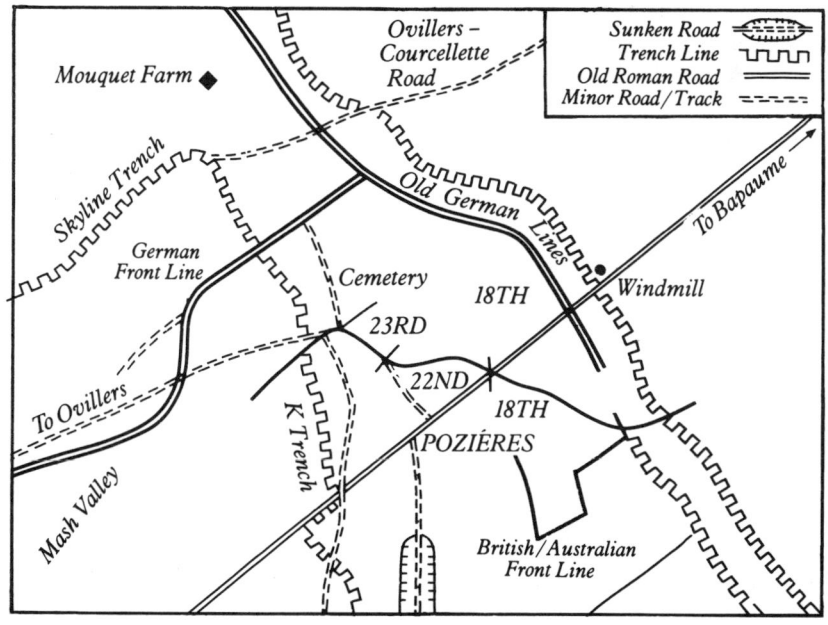

court; to secure the high ground N. and N. E. of Pozières and Thiepval; to obtain observation over Courcelette and Grandcourt; to cut off, capture, or kill the German garrison in the Thiepval area'. Birdwood clearly understood Gough's need for urgency. The Corps order was issued at 8.30 p.m. on 26 July, with the artillery plan for the attack already framed.

Although the timing of the attack was to be left to Legge, the other details were clearly laid down by Gough's headquarters through the Anzac Corps. As part of working 'systematically northwards, rolling up the German second line', the 2nd Australian Division was to attack and capture the Old German lines and the Windmill.

> The 2nd Aust. Div. will make an attack on the German positions north and north-east of Pozières on a night and at a time to be determined by GOC, 2nd Aust. Div. The definite objective will be the German second line known as OG1 and OG2 from the vicinity of the Bapaume Road to R34 central and from the ridge north of the Cemetery from R34 central to R33.d.4.3.inclusive.

Thus the division had to capture that portion of the OG lines still held by the Germans south of the Bapaume road, as well as a heavily defended trench line, formed by improving a sunken road between Ovillers and Courcellette, north-west of the village, and the OG lines north of the Albert-Bapaume road. 'The preliminary steps for this attack ... will include — the preparation and occupation of advanced strong posts towards the new line; arrangements for assembling and forming up the troops destined for the attack; preliminary reconnaisance by unit commanders.' For artillery, Legge was given the guns of the 1st Division to continue cutting the German barbed wire, as well as the guns of the neighbouring corps and divisions which, in line with Haig's 'methodical, step-by-step' approach would not be employed in support of their own formations at the time of the assault.

Legge had been presented with a suggested plan for the capture of the old German lines prepared by Gough's headquarters. This plan, however, lacked both intelligent thought and imagination; it proposed a bombing assault from the south, an approach that had been tried and had failed. Again it was Gough's enthusiasm for quick action that dominated his thinking and permeated through all the formations under his command. However, Brudenell White, worrying over the 2nd Division at Corps headquarters, opposed the British plan, and argued that the attacking brigade would use up its four battalions in the first sector. But White could not influence the rest of the 2nd Division planning; he allowed, according to Bean: ' ... his grave misgivings to be overborne by the pressure and confidence of Maj.-Gen. Legge'. Here we see the inexperience of both Legge and his staff; whereas the wiser and more experienced 'Hooky' Walker had managed to resist Gough, Legge could not. And his staff, who had no experience in planning such actions, were unable to advise their commander to take his tasks more slowly. The British official historian gives us only a tantalising glimpse of the pressures on Legge. 'Although anxious to afford the enemy as short a respite as possible, General Gough judged it advisable to leave the actual day and hour of the assault for the corps commander to determine. Following the Anzac practice, the decision was thus left to the divisional commander.'

The key to the position was still the high ground of the Windmill, Hill 160, belonging to the Germans. The OG lines, which had proved so stubborn an obstacle in the 1st Division's separate attacks, ran roughly parallel in a north-west direction between the village and the Windmill site. If these trenches could be taken, and the Germans forced off the high ground of the Ridge on to the reverse slope, the British would have observation over the terrain between Bapaume and Grandcourt.

The 6th Brigade moved into the ruined trenches on the northern side of Pozières, with the 24th Battalion on the left, the 22nd Battalion in the centre and the 19th Battalion on the right. The Australian trench line ran north-west, except for a section of the 19th Battalion line which was dug in along the line of the old Roman road through the village. South of the road, the 5th Brigade occupied sections of Pozières Trench, and Black Watch Trench, with the 17th Battalion on the extreme right in the captured portion of the OG lines near Munster Alley, the 18th Battalion in the centre or Pozières Trench, and the 19th in Long Drive, a communications trench running towards the north. Later, Legge wrote:

> The front taken over was an irregular line through the northern outskirts of Pozières and connected with the 23rd Division on the right and the 48th Division (subsequently the 12th Division) on the left. There were trenches in places and strong points, but not a continuous line. Some communications trenches had been dug but were much battered in by hostile artillery fire.

From their positions in the battered trench lines, the troops of the 2nd Division were able to make out the OG lines. The chalky parapets were clearly visible north of the village, where the trench lines snaked over the Ridge between 450 and 650 metres away on the near horizon, near the Windmill. The slope of the Ridge was gradual; the Germans might have been only 10 metres higher over those 640 metres of ground, but the height was sufficient to give them excellent observation over the Australian trench lines, the pitted and cratered fields and the battered, broken hedges and orchards. The village itself had ceased to exist, so heavy had been the artillery fire. Bean's description is vivid:

> The powdered debris of houses and earth was spread like ash six feet deep over the surface, as featureless as the Sahara, and level except for the shell craters which lay edge-to-edge like the scratchings of gigantic hens in an endless ash heap. Each fresh salvo flung up rolling clouds of this dust and rearranged the craters. Except for two fragments of German concrete every vestige of building above earth level eventually vanished. Visitors shocked by the destruction of other Somme villages were un-impressed at Pozières because it had simply become an open space, marked vaguely by tree-stumps, but with no other sign that a village had been there.

The bombardment did not slacken with the arrival of the new troops. The Reserve Army Diary for 27 July again blandly notes that: 'The enemy shelled Pozières during the day and did considerable damage to our trenches in that vicinity'.

Moving up through Sausage Gully, Private Arthur Whitear of the 24th Battalion was astounded at the increase in our artillery and air force: 'Our guns are wheel to wheel and our airmen in charge of the air. No Hun planes can get through. This, of course, spells confidence to men who are about to take part in a battle of this magnitude'. That confidence, however, was not to last long. Because of the appalling bombardment endured by the 1st Division, the handovers to the reliev-ing troops were perfunctory. The new troops were horrified by the destruction, by the unburied dead of both sides: 'dozens and dozens . . . all distorted and frozen looks of horror on their faces'. The old troops were only too pleased to be moving out, even the sketch maps in the two divisional war diaries at the time of the handover have discrepancies and differences. There was little opportunity for the new troops to reconnoitre the ground over which they would soon be expected to attack. 'The 28th Battalion', wrote Major Arnold Brown, 'entered the fight knowing nothing of the position. Not an officer or man had had a daylight view of the objective which the battalion was set — an error in tactics that was later corrected'.

This was not the only tactical error to be made in the planning of the 2nd Division attack. Like the British commanders in the early stages of the Somme battle, Legge optimistically relied upon his field artillery, the lighter guns, to cut the German wire. These thick wire entangle-ments, up to 50 metres wide and covered by well sited machine guns, lay between the Australians and the Germans in the OG trenches. Although Legge had a generous allocation of both heavy and field artillery, he did not use the larger calibre guns to fire on the wire. Since the first day of the Somme fighting artillery commanders began to rethink their techniques for wire-cutting. Warnings about the failure of field artillery firing low-burst shrapnel to cut wire entanglements began to appear in various training memoranda; certainly the general and artillery staffs of the 1st Australian Division were aware of the problem. Yet Legge was confident that his field artillery could cut the German wire sufficiently to enable an assault on the night of 28 July and Brudenell White, who normally supervised operation plans submitted by subordinate formations, made no recorded objection.

Birdwood's orders to Legge included an instruction that jumping off trenches be dug. This would allow the assaulting troops to assemble 274 metres nearer their objective, instead of making a 640 metre assault over open ground against heavily prepared positions; a plan which again the events of 1 July had demonstrated to be fatally flawed. 'Troops will be advanced as close as possible to the objectives prior to the assault.'

This order was simply incapable of being obeyed — at least in the time Legge had available for his attack. The enormous bombardments of the previous days had destroyed the trench that had been constructed and no connected trench existed around the north of the village. It is difficult to blame Legge, Birdwood or White. All the senior commanders of the AIF were aware of the importance of assaulting troops getting as close as possible to the enemy; a warning issued by Haig's GHQ that no attack could expect to succeed if the starting position was more than 182 metres (200 yards) from the objective had been widely circulated; the success of the 1st Division assault, where the troops were only metres away from the German parapet when the barrage lifted, was still clear. But anxiety to attack quickly overrode these sensible precautions.

Gough and his headquarters cannot escape criticism. Although Gough was under no great pressure from Haig, the insistence by the Reserve Army commander that the attack go ahead as quickly as possible made Legge's position clear; the latter was the subordinate commander with an order to obey. Legge needed more time, both to allow his artillery preparations to go ahead and to dig jumping off trenches so his assaulting troops would not have to move over open ground with a slight uphill slope and into the teeth of German defences. Time was also needed to allow the divisional commander's orders to be issued to the brigadier-generals; for the brigade commanders to issue their orders; for the battalion commanders to do their reconnaissance and issue their orders; for the company commanders to make their plans, issue their orders and if possible, to take their platoon commanders cautiously forward and show them the ground over which they would be attacking. At the end of the long chain of command which began in Gough's château were the private soldiers sitting in trenches and wondering what they were expected to do. The soldier needed to be told, to understand what was expected of him and what support he could expect from his mates. Under pressure from Gough, Legge had simply not allowed enough time for a division that was new to battle.

One by one, the factors mounted against success: the sanguine confidence in the artillery, even more misplaced because the dust raised by the German shelling of Pozières and the mid-summer haze made observation almost impossible; the inability to get assaulting troops close to the enemy position; the rushed preparations; the lack of time for planning, orders and reconnaissance.

Add to these factors a fresh enemy, new to the line, with a clear conception of the value of the ground he was defending, expecting at any time to be attacked and able to watch the Australian preparations. One German observer had reported that trenches were being dug in front of Pozières. These trenches could have only one major purpose; a jumping off point for an attack on the high ground of the Windmill. So, on 26 and 27 July, the ruined village and the trenches were comprehensively bombarded. The German artillery commanders realised that the bulk of Australian troops would be concentrated in an assembly area, somewhere to the rear of the forward lines, waiting for the attack. This bombardment fell most heavily on these support lines where one company of the 24th Battalion was virtually annihilated. Here the Australians had no dugouts in which to shelter, no overhead protection. They had to sit in exposed trenches, endure the shelling, and wait to be killed or buried. During the shelling, one officer, passing along the trench, noticed four men playing cards. Above them, on the parapet, was the body of their sergeant who had earlier been playing with them. When the officer returned soon afterwards, the four men were dead. 'It was perfect Hell', wrote Lance Corporal Cohen of the 24th Battalion. 'Two minutes before I was hit 50 men [were] left out of my company of 220 strong. When I was hit, 18 others were hit at the same time.'

Legge's attack order was issued at 2 p.m. on 27 July. 'The 2nd Aust. Div. will attack the German positions north and north-east of Pozières on the night of 28/29th inst.' Later in a report, Legge detailed the problems encountered during the preparation for the attack. It makes depressing reading:

> The artillery programmes were carried out, but, owing to the range, and to the fact that observation could not be obtained, it was not possible to

ascertain to what extent the wire had been cut. During the evening and night of the 27th, the followiing preparatory work was commenced or attempted.

(a) opening-up broken communications trenches . . .

(b) construction of strongpoints . . .

Little progress was made, however, owing to heavy shelling, men losing their way because they were new to the locality, and there were no large scale maps showing existing trenches, and the consequent confusion.

That night the Somme front would be relatively quiet, except for an attempted recapture of Delville Wood and Longueval by the Germans who had been evicted from both strongpoints during fierce fighting the day before. No other major British offensive was planned; Legge's Australians had centre stage. In the failing light, the men of the 7th Brigade filed smartly up Sausage Valley, moving quickly and quietly. Part of Legge's preparation was not to signal his intentions unnecessarily by a special bombardment. The gunners were originally ordered to fire their normal allocation of rounds on dusk but Legge, fearing that this would arouse German suspicions, ordered steady fire until 12.14 a.m., just one minute before the assault. Then the Australian brigades would fire a more intense rate for one minute on the first objective, lifting then and shifting to the second. This fire plan, prepared by Legge and his artillery commander, had one flaw: it ignored the fact that the Germans maintained their sentries during so-called normal artillery bombardments and that the 7th Brigade, which had the greatest distance to move, would be exposed for at least 10 minutes.

> Routes were reconnoitred by each Brigade during the afternoon and arrangements were made with guides to be furnished by the 5th Bde. (who occupied the front line) to the 7th Bde., who were to assault in the centre. During the night of 27th/28th July, patrols from the 5th and 6th Bdes reconnoitred enemy's wire. They reported that it was 'still strong in places though knocked about'. An advanced fire trench along the tramline north-east of Pozières was dug during the night and occupied by 5th Bde. . . . Further reconnaissance of routes and forming up places was carried out on the morning of 28th July. Brigades, as far as they were able to, ensured that the objectives and tasks were explained to the troops detailed for the attack.

Paton's brigade, still waiting at Tara Hill, had the most difficult task, yet all this commander could do was bring his battalion commanders forward and point out to them the ground over which their troops would be expected to attack. There was time for some of the company and machine gun commanders to come forward and attempt to identify landmarks from the inadequate trench maps. But for the platoon commanders, upon whose shoulders the responsibility for the attack rested once the troops 'hopped the bags', there was no time for reconnaissance. Their perspectives were limited by the trench walls as they moved up and by the hurriedly pointed out objectives before the main, mad scramble.

Legge planned for the right brigade, the 5th, to attack the OG lines between the left of the neighbouring British 23rd Division and the Bapaume road; the centre brigade, the 7th, was to attack north-east towards the OG lines, while the 8th, the left brigade, attacked northwards on to the old communication trenches. The most important attack was that of the 7th Brigade, which had to capture the OG lines between the Ovillers-Courcelette road and the Albert-Bapaume road.

Again Legge's report gives us the essentials of the attack. Of the right brigade, he wrote:

> The 20th Battalion, on leaving their trenches to form up in No Man's Land shortly after 11 p.m., were evidently observed by the enemy for they came under heavy machine gun fire and, about a quarter of an hour later, under artillery fire in which gas shells were used. They reached the line decided on as a 'jumping off' place by 12.15 a.m. but could not reach OG1 on account of the hostile MG fire. Meanwhile the 17th Battalion were also discovered by the enemy after two waves had moved out: the ground moreover was so lit up by German flares that their fire was very effective. On discovering that the 20th Battalion were unable to advance the 17th Battalion were compelled to withdraw.

This particular part of the attack seems desultory, almost an afterthought to the grand divisional plan. Except for a handful of trench mortars which were to fire a few bombs for just 5 minutes after the northern attacks had begun, Legge and his advisers allocated no artillery to this particular assault. Yet this was the approach urged on the Australians by Gough's headquarters, the approach which might well have been adopted by Legge had not Brudenell White intervened. Here the Germans, whose appreciation of the tactical situation was as literal as that of White, were waiting and prepared. They had flares and rockets, sufficient to turn night into day; they had well-sited machine guns, with interlocking arcs of fire that made any movement above the cratered ground virtually impossible; they had good and immediate communications with their artillery so that any signs of an impending attack could be met with devastating concentrations of fire. All of which happened to the battalions on the right of the Australian attack. Their efforts failed, as would have any stronger effort. For the survivors, all that remained was to cower in shell holes and make their way back when the firing had died down.

The main burden of the attack fell on Paton's 7th Brigade, with its heavy preponderance of troops from the smaller, less-populated States. Paton had a wide objective to cover in his assault; he was forced to use three battalions initially, with just one in reserve. Despite the problems of moving so many troops through crowded communications trenches at the same time, Paton's brigade managed to reach their allotted forming-up places in time. Once launched into the assault, however, every thing seemed to go wrong at once.

Legge had planned a ferocious artillery barrage on the German trenches at 12.14 a.m., just one minute before the assault was due to begin. He was worried about the risk of retaliation from the German artillery if the intense fire began any earlier. During the troops' approach to their jumping off points, only light artillery fire fell on the German positions. The Germans fired flares which continually lit the area; the attackers were seen; the defenders were ready. As well, within the 2nd Division, the attacking troops were supposed to wear small plaques of bright tin, sewn into the middle of their tunics or strapped on to their packs, as an aid to identification. Not surprisingly, the troops hated wearing such devices, which caught the moonlight or the flash from a flare, and attracted attention. No evidence exists, however, that the Germans noticed these plaques; their records say merely that 'concentrations of troops were seen'. Before the attack, the divisional staff had reconsidered the value of these plaques and, while insisting that the troops still wear them, conceded that they might be covered for the assault or at night. Orders to this effect were issued, but did not reach the attacking battalions in time.

Legge's report makes melancholy reading: 'While moving forward to get close under the artillery barrage, the troops were discovered by the enemy, who met them with flares and heavy MG fire from 5 to 8 minutes before 12.15 a.m.' The 28th Battalion reached the wire but found it strong all along their front. They endeavoured to cut it but were then under close bomb, MG and rifle fire.

> No openings could be found . . . The next Battalion — the 25th — found openings in the wire and got through first into OG 1, where the enemy were overcome after a bayonet fight, and then portions of two coys appear to have reached OG 2 . . . The other two companies of this Battalion were unable to get through the wire and lost heavily. All the Company officers except one in this battalion were hit, chiefly while trying to get through the wire.

> If you want the old battalion,
> We know where they are
> Hanging on the old barbed wire.

Few of the personal accounts of the war deal at any length with barbed wire; it has been left to the war poets and the songsters to remind us of its horror. Even in its agricultural use, this easily erected barrier has a deceptive malignancy.

Barbed wire, both German and British, impinged constantly upon the conciousness of the First World War soldiers; the German wire was a ubiquitous barrier to be surmounted. Assaulting troops hoped that it had been well cut but often, even the best-aimed artillery fire simply made the obstacle more difficult to pass. Even in the quiet sectors at quiet times, there were constant wiring parties, repairing or improving the barriers that lay in rank profusion between one line of straggling trenches and the other. Here, on the gentle Somme uplands between the pulverised village of Pozières and the old Windmill, the wire was thick and formidable, 50 metres across, with strands as thick as a man's thumb and great jagged barbs that plucked at clothing, or entangled webbing, or simply impeded movement so that the struggling soldier, ensnared like an insect in a web, became an easy target for the machine gunners.

> A man of mine
> Lies on the wire.
> It is death to fetch his souless corpse.

Not only was there wire in front of OG1, but the Germans had erected further barriers between OG1 and OG2, so that any attack which managed to penetrate the first line of trenches still had obstacles to conquer before the second line. This wire remained unaffected even by the artillery fire because it could not be seen by the observers and its existence was unknown to the assaulting infantry.

The story of the attack by Paton's brigade is brief and bitter; and the sad, almost apologetic words of Legge's report give us no real understanding of the confusion endured by the soldiers. In the soldiers' accounts of the offensives, there is a dullness, almost a kind of mental insensibility, compounded of shock and violence and simple exhaustion. The troops were curiously ambivalent about night attacks, for they realised that darkness provided some cover if their movement above the ground remained otherwise undetected. The young company and platoon commanders however, hated and feared night assaults for they had the added responsibility of finding and maintaining their direction over rough, pitted ground. One such officer was Walter Grantlee Boys, a master draper in the family company from Maryborough, Queensland, aged 26, and a company commander in the 25th Battalion. On 2 August 1916, Boys wrote to his family:

> That I'm alive and have the chance of writing to you once again is a miracle. I've had an experience which I never again wish to have. My company was ordered into the attack on . . . It was a big attack, with a charge of 700 yards. I cannot explain the feeling I had for about 12 hours before the charge. I had sole command for my portion of the attack of about 250 men. I had to march on a compass bearing for about three miles before I got to the debouching point through a perfect hell of fire . . . as soon as I began to move I lost all nervousness and felt I could cope, I would like to give you full details of the battle which was the biggest and fiercest battle fought in the whole world, even worse than Verdun, so they say.

Boys' company had assembled in a slight depression known as Tramway Trench, the old agricultural rail line. Nearest the Bapaume road was the 28th Battalion, with the 25th in the centre and the 26th on the right. Although the troops had been warned to stay away from the line of the Roman road if possible, it was impossible for Paton to assemble his brigade without having part of his force on or near it. 'During the move forward', wrote Major Arnold Brown, 'all was quiet, but just as the leading company approached the communications trench, "Centre Way", the first casualties occurred — a shell landed near the head of D Company, and Major Welch, and two of his men were killed. On reaching the front line, the companies filed smoothly out to their respective positions on the jumping off tape. The right flank of our objective was the Windmill site'.

Except for the occasional burst of machine gun fire off the right, it was quiet before the final barrage. The troops lay in this shallow depression, waiting for the order to move. In the 28th Battalion, the commanding officer walked up and down the line, quietly joking with the men, 'inspiring confidence among all as only a soldier and a leader could do. At the last moment the colonel took up his position at Bn Headquarters — an improvised shelter in the front line'. Once the assault was launched, this commanding officer — or any other — could do little. It was then the responsibility of the company and platoon commanders because no means, apart from runners, existed for getting orders forward swiftly. Realising this, some battalion commanders took the opportunity to establish their headquarters in safe areas well behind the jumping off points. The commanding officer of the 28th was an exception.

As planned, the first waves moved off before the 1-minute intense barrage. The difficulties encountered by the junior leaders were immense. Because of the ground, the forward troops had to fan out, expanding the line laterally as they moved forward. On the right flank, the 28th Battalion could follow the line of the old road, but in the centre there were no landmarks. Inevitably, the troops lost touch in the confusion and the darkness; great gaps appeared in the advancing line.

It was a long uphill assault and all the time the troops were moving, the Germans were watching and waiting. Brown wrote that once the Australian barrage began, the German reply was swift. 'Then bursting shells lit up the darkness, and the advancing men fell fast under a terrific rain of shrapnel and HE, and a withering machine gun fire.' Boys, in the neighbouring 25th Battalion, was with the first wave. '. . . my word my men fought well. They fell about me like flies but on we went . . . the smell of powder and the din of guns and bombs nearly turned my head. Owing to the German barbed wire . . . my men could not get through and the Hun brought his Maxim guns on to us . . . '

The intense barrage had not lasted long enough. It suppressed some of the fire from the OG1 positions, but the Australians still had a long way to go before they were in the forward trench line. And they had still to surmount the barbed wire. Now the flares were rising thickly from the German support lines, silhouetting the Australians as they struggled with the uncut wire. Some used wire cutters; some attempted to bash their way through with butts of rifles; others wrenched at the stakes with their bare hands. Brown wrote that the survivors of the German machine gun fire ran up and down the wire in search of an opening, others tried to climb over, but all failed.

In the 28th Battalion only one company commander survived this attack. As the successive waves moved up, still trying to maintain their 45 metre interval, they were puzzled to see their mates lying on the ground near the wire, as if waiting to assault. It was not until these troops reached the wire themselves and also came under heavy fire, that they realised the 'waiting' troops were, in fact, dead.

In the centre, some of the 25th Battalion troops actually found gaps. One Company, led by a former Townsville journalist, Captain J. E. Nix, managed to make their way through the wire in front of OG1 and discovered the trench line was virtually deserted. Pushing forward, Nix waited until the intense barrage on OG2 lifted and rushed the second trench, only to find it crowded with Germans who had withdrawn and were sheltering, waiting to counter-attack. Nix was fired on from 27 metres by a German machine gun. His attack, which had probably penetrated further than any Australian assault that night, faltered and failed. Most of the assaulting force in the centre lay behind them, in the shallow saucer-shaped depression which the Germans could cover from the high ground on the rim. Despite the efforts of their platoon and company commanders to get them up and moving the men were down and staying down. Nix withdrew, bringing with him only 8 men from the 200-plus company he took into the attack, of which 50 were left to assault the OG2 position. Boys wrote later that he was forced to retire. 'I gave the order to retire very much against my will.' Off to the right, near the Albert-Bapaume road, a similar order was given; it ran quickly along the line from battalion to battalion. As Bean noted: 'Apparently few officers had been left in action to question it, and, though attempts were made to check the movement, part of the 25th and most of the 26th fell rapidly back across No Man's Land'.

In his after-action report, Legge wrote:

> At this stage an order to 'retire' appears to have been given. The Battalion Commander cannot say where it originated. The Brigade Commander considers it may have been given by an officer who did not live to return. The word 'retire' is absolutely forbidden in this Division, and some other phrase has to be used where any withdrawal is required.

It will never be known whether Boys' battalion commander knew that one of his officers had given the order to retire, nor will it ever be known whether Paton, a wise and sensible commander, simply protected his officers from an unsavoury 'witch-hunt'.

Probably the most terrible point in a battle for a commander is where he realises that all chance of success has gone; that his troops are depleted by casualties; that his support has failed and that his task is hopeless. At the same time, duty and honour oblige him to press on 'at all costs'. No such obligation imposed itself on Boys. Under the circumstances his order to retire was sensible and reasonable, probably the only order he could and should have given. There was no point demonstrating, by the loss of further lives, that this attack was senseless and impossible. That had already been made clear. Besides to whom could Boys refer? His battalion commander was not with him in the attack; there was no way of communicating with his headquarters. It was Boys' decision to make. He made it.

The survivors of Boys' company got back that night. 'But I had to see all my men from the German lines before I could leave and at daybreak I found myself about 30 yards from his trench.' There Boys lay, for 20 hours 10 minutes, with no water in the heat of the sun, not daring to move for fear of attracting attention from the German sentries nearby, with dead and wounded all around him, and with a bombardment falling on the German positions. 'Somehow God watched over me, and I got through all right.' Boys used the 20 hours to note details of the German wire and the effect of the renewed bombardment on it. He was slightly wounded, and offered a staff job, but turned it down to return to his men and his friends. He had seen one of his best friends, Lieutenant Vic Warry, another Maryborough man, killed nearby.

> Poor Vic Warry was killed beside me. He fought splendidly and was right on top of the Germans when he went down. I nearly went mad when I saw him killed. Poor Vic, he died at the head of his men like a soldier. I am writing to Mrs Warry when I get settled a bit, but I would like you to tell her that I was beside him when he fell and he was as brave as he could be. When I look back at what I have gone through, it makes me shudder and I feel sure that many prayers are being sent up for me otherwise I should never have pulled through. I am too upset to write any more just now but I will write you a long letter when I get back . . . Don't forget to pray for me . . . it is absolute hell . . . anyhow, I've had the honor of being in the biggest battle in history. I expect to get a decoration out of it.*

On the left, Paton's brigade, the 6th Brigade, enjoyed some success. This was a much smaller attack, with just one battalion making the assault. In fact, this battalion actually overran its objective — again the shattered ground made navigation almost impossible — but later came under heavy and accurate machine gun fire. This success, however, was useless without corresponding gains in the centre and and the Australians here were withdrawn to avoid having a flank which was too exposed. Even so, the casualties for this limited success were severe — 7 officers and 326 soldiers — including one young officer, Lieutenant R. G. 'Goldie' Raws.

But the attack had taken other tolls. The German intelligence officers who examined the Australian prisoners (of whom there were about sixty belonging to the 6th and 7th Brigades) were highly impressed with the bearing of a few old Gallipoli hands among them — but not with that of the majority. These it was noted, were almost all young reinforcements, with little training. Some of them said they were tired of the war and glad to be made prisoners. It is fair to add that, according to German accounts, about half were 'more or less' wounded, and all had emerged from a terrible operation which they knew to have been mismanaged. Many had run into their own barrage as well as the enemy's; and those on the Australian left, had, according to their own

---

* Boys was not decorated. He was killed in action two days after that letter was written.

statement: ' . . . been mistaken by the British troops for Germans, and [had been] fired on from the rear'.

The 2nd Division lost 3,500 men in the attack and in the two days in the line before. The attack itself had achieved almost nothing, a gain of a few hundred metres which was handed back later because it was so precarious. Arnold Brown thought it was an attack 'so complete in its stark tragedy that it should never have been undertaken'. Brown was right: the planning and preparation for this attack was so bad that it was doomed to failure from the beginning. The causes of the failure were many, the inability of the artillery to cut the wire; the failure to prepare protected jumping off trenches; the infantry assault across hundreds of metres of exposed, broken ground; the confusion among the inexperienced troops and officers at night; the inability of the artillery to suppress the enemy fire.

After the failure came the recriminations. The Reserve Army War Diary noted the attack briefly:

> During the night the 2nd Australian Division attacked OG1 and OG2 at 12.15 a.m., but in no case, owing to the severity of the hostile artillery and machine gun fire, did they succeed in gaining their objective. The Germans sent up many flares and opened machine gun fire as the lines started to go forward to the attack; nevertheless part of the Right Brigade succeeded in reaching OG2, from which they were eventually driven out. The Left Brigade reached its objective and retained it . . . Our casualties were not heavy.

On 29 July, Haig noted in his diary that the:

> . . . attack by the 2nd Australian Division upon the enemy's position between Pozières and the Windmill was not successful last night. From several reports, I think the cause was due to want of thorough preparation. After lunch I visited HG Reserve Army and impressed on Gough and his GSO (Neil Malcolm) that they must supervise more closely the plans of the Anzac Corps. Some of their Divisional Generals are so ignorant and (like many Colonials) so conceited, that they cannot be trusted to work out unaided the plans of attack.

There was only one 'Colonial' General in Birdwood's Corps; Haig's criticism was directed squarely at Legge.

After visiting Gough's headquarters, Haig went on to the Anzac Corps headquarters at Contay where he saw Birdwood and White. 'The latter', Haig wrote, 'seems a very sound capable fellow, and assured me they had learnt a lesson, and would be more thorough in future. Luckily, their losses had been fairly small, considering the operation and the numbers engaged — about 1,000 for the whole 24 hours'.

Terraine tells us that 'Birdwood never found favour in Haig's eyes'; Birdwood had been a Kitchener protégé, sufficient in itself to make him suspect in Haig's eyes. Birdwood had also been an enthusiastic supporter of the Dardanelles campaign, which would also have diminished further his standing with the Commander-in-Chief. With these feelings apparent, and with a comprehensive failure to be explained, the atmosphere at the Anzac Corps headquarters that Saturday afternoon must have been somewhat strained. 'You are not fighting Bashi-Bazouks* now', Haig said to Birdwood and White. 'This is serious, scientific war, and you are up against the most scientific and most military nation in Europe.' On a large wall map, Haig then proceeded to point out a number of omissions, to his mind, in the artillery and other preparations. According to Haig, these omissions were due to Legge's over-confidence. The Commander-in-Chief would have no such rough-and-ready methods in France.

Haig had some cause for this criticism. Just before the 2nd Division attack he noted in his diary:

> ... the Australians had at the last moment said that that they would attack [the Windmill] without artillery support and that 'they did not believe machine gun fire could do them much harm!' Birch [General Sir Noel Birch, Haig's chief artillery adviser] at once saw Gough and arranged that the original artillery programme should be carried out. The Australians are splendid fellows but very ignorant.

As Haig stood before the wall map, pointing out the inadequacies and the faults in the divisional attack plan, it was White who came to Birdwood's rescue. Bean wrote that: 'White knew that the formation of an adverse opinion by Haig could seriously affect Birdwood's future in the British army'. By then, of course, it was probably too late; Haig had formed that adverse opinion, but White was not to know.

> ... while the Commander-in-Chief was indicating, one after another, the supposed defects in the preparations, White's resentment was mounting. As Haig finished and turned from the map, White, despite a warning sign from Haig's chief of staff, brought the Commander-in-Chief to look at the map again. There had been defects, he admitted; but 'Look here, sir', he said, pointing to the map, 'you said this . . . and this . . . and this

---

* Nineteenth century Turkish irregulars — hardly an accurate description of the Turkish army in 1915.

. . .' and he took item by item the supposed blunders. 'But what actually happened was this . . . and this . . . and this . . .' And he showed that the course of events was almost completely different. As he ended, he was prepared for an explosion. Instead, Haig laid his hand on the Australian's shoulder. 'I dare say you are right, young man', he said kindly.

Haig's information about the reasons for failure had been almost wholly inaccurate; it had been supplied by Gough and his headquarters. The entry in the Reserve Army War Diary, quoted previously was clearly incomplete and wrong: it noted the division's casualties as 'not heavy' which Haig used as the basis for his diary entry that night of 'about 1,000 for the whole 24 hours'. And Haig did not bother to go forward to Legge's headquarters and discover for himself why the attack had failed.

Legge set out the reasons why his attack had failed in his after-action report.

> Troops must be able to reach their assaulting positions undiscovered. In this case the enemy's flares enabled him to see the movement of troops and to prepare accordingly. Where time permits, deep trenches in which to assemble are the remedy. Where time does not permit, a continuous and heavy bombardment to prevent the enemy looking over his parapet with impunity is the only alternative.

It would have been impossible for Legge to say that he had not been given sufficient time to prepare his attack properly. The senior commander always has the option of applying the time, and there was no particular urgency about this attack. Gough did not have to co-ordinate the 2nd Australian Division assault with any other major offensive on the front at the time. All he had to do was carry out Haig's plan of the methodical, step-by-step advance. Yet, even in the guarded phrases of his after-action report, Legge is able to make clear the problems he faced because of Gough's insistence that the attack be carried out quickly.

> Time is necessary to enable the enemy's wire to be well cut in numerous places. These places must be known to the assaulting battalions. In this case our patrols the previous night had only been able to discover that the wire was knocked about, but was still an obstacle. It was hoped that the wire-cutting of the 28th inst would have increased the gaps and made new ones. As the artillery were unable to get good observation on the wire, the result of their fire could not be ascertained. The patrols being unable to explore the wire in front of OG2, its state could only be guessed.

Finally, Legge examined the problems caused by assaulting without waiting for deliberate preparations and full reconnaissance.

> In such a situation, it is preferable to attack in daylight under cover of intense artillery bombardment and smoke barrages. The men can then see what they are doing and can co-operate with each other. At night this is not possible though a high state of training in night operations undoubtedly minimises the difficulties of co-operation.

Even before the Commander-in-Chief made his way to the Anzac Corps headquarters on the afternoon of 29 July, Birdwood and Legge were planning another attack. That morning, the corps and divisional commanders met at Contay with their respective chiefs of staff, White and Lt.-Col. A. H. Bridges, cousin of the W. T. Bridges, who had been killed at Gallipoli while commanding the 1st Division. According to the latter's biographer, A. H. Bridges was; ' . . . like the 2nd Division commander in temperament and theoretical outlook — both aspects which made Legge one of the most unpopular generals at the front'.

Legge wanted to redeem himself and his division. He pointed out to Birdwood that, although his division's casualties had been heavy, he still had more than 10,000 infantry soldiers. The greatest concern was the 5th Brigade, which had been suffering heavily during the four days it had been in the line and its two assaults on the OG lines south of the Bapaume road.

When Legge suggested to Holmes, the brigade commander, that his troops be relieved by two battalions of the 4th Division, the latter replied: 'I understand from you that you are going to take the position with the 2nd Division. That being so, it is my desire, and, I am sure, the wish of all, that the whole of the battalions of my brigade should remain and play the part allotted to them.'

Despite Legge's intentions and Gough's enthusiasm, however, no attack was made the following night. The first attack had failed because of lack of preparation; now, as the division was slowly recovering from the effects of the battle, there was no time for preparation for an attack barely 24 hours later.

After the conference, Bridges signalled the units of the division on behalf of his commander:

> The fine attack made last night did not meet with the success it deserved. The Divisional Commander appreciates the efforts of the Division and desires Commanders to convey his congratulations to all ranks. The task set to the Second Australian Division must be completed, and the enemy's position captured. Commencing forthwith the hostile trenches and wire

will now be subjected to a far more intense bombardment which will be almost continuous till the next assault takes place.

This 'far more intense bombardment' was to be a game at which two could play.

For two days, a relative quiet settled over the ruined village of Pozières, almost as if each side was ruefully licking its wounds, waiting and wondering when the next blow would come and who would strike it. The relative quiet was, however, confined to daylight hours. At night, the British and Australian artillery fired in accordance with the plan being worked out for the next phase of the offensive — and the Germans replied. And in the middle, caught in open, exposed ground with earth the consistency of fine talcum powder, were the infantry, unable to dig and unable to shelter.

Yet they had to dig. After the disaster of the 29/30 July attack, Brudenell White exercised a much closer supervision over the preparations of the 2nd Division. For the guidance of both Legge and Bridges, he prepared a detailed and careful appreciation which covered the points of failure in the previous attack. These survive, in the form of Legge's own report, although without the divisional commander's acknowledgements of their origins. White saw six main preparations necessary before any fresh attack was launched:

> the construction of an assembly trench parallel to the objective and about 200 to 250 yards distant. To be wide enough and deep enough to hold the first two waves.

> the construction of communication trenches up to this and of saps in advance of it with strong posts.

> the improvement of the fire trench along the tramline to hold the third and fourth waves and a small garrison to remain in it.

> a further reconnaissance of the hostile wire, and further wire cutting by artillery and M(edium) T(rench) mortars.

> heavy bombardment of the enemy's position including that portion south of the BAPAUME road which had been omitted from the previous bombardments.

> organisation of the back area roads, trams and dumps, with a view to relieve the men of some of the carrying, pack horses and mules being substituted forthwith.

White insisted that the whole operation 'be undertaken deliberately. The actual date will be determined by the progress of preparation'. Quite clearly, those preparations could not be carried out in less than 24 hours. In all, the Australians had to dig some 1200 metres of jumping off trenches, a daunting task under the best of circumstances, even without being shelled.

Meanwhile, Haig was being forced to adopt the 'wearing-out' process advocated by Joffre. Of this second month of the Somme, the British official historian wrote:

> It was a period of bitter fighting when hardly any ground was gained and the struggle became, more than ever, a grim test of endurance. There was little to encourage or inspire the troops of all arms who fought on the Somme in August: subjected to heavy losses, great hardships, and tremendous physical and moral strain, they had only their own dogged spirit to maintain them.

Haig was convinced that the strength of German reinforcements made it impossible to achieve any major breakthrough on the Somme front. On 2 August, Haig issued a directive to both Rawlinson and Gough which set the future course of the battle.

The first priority, according to the Commander-in-Chief, was to continue the offensive in close co-operation with the French.

> The present situation is that the enemy had brought up considerable reinforcements of men and guns, and can continue for some time still to replace tired troops. He has also strengthened, and continues to strengthen his positions; and he has recovered to a great extent from the disorgani-sation caused by the success of the Allied attacks last month. In conse-quence, although most of his troops in our front have been severely handled and must be somewhat tired, they are still too formidable to be rushed without careful and methodical preparation; and they may even prove capable of developing strong and well-organised counter-attacks, prepared and supported by the heaviest artillery fire that the enemy can develop.

Haig's words have a special relevance to the Australians of the 2nd Division: the acceptance of the need for 'careful and methodical prep-aration' and the concern about counter-attacks and the effect of the German artillery.

Haig saw two future tasks for his army commanders: '. . . preparation for the delivery of fresh attacks, combined with strengthening our po-sitions against the danger of counter-attacks on a formidable scale.

Provided we have done all we can to be ready for them such counter-attacks should cost the enemy dear without attaining their object'. But the Commander-in-Chief also had some words of caution for both Rawlinson and Gough:

> To enable us to bring the present operations (the existing phase of which may be regarded as a 'wearing-out' battle) to a successful termination, we must practise such economy of men and materials as will ensure our having the 'last reserves' at our disposal when the crisis of the fight is reached which may — and probably will — not be sooner than the last half of September.

In particular, Haig was insistent that no attack should be launched until the responsible commanders were satisfied that everything possible had been done to ensure success. But to see this phase of the Somme fighting merely in terms of a 'wearing-out' fight, part of the ghastly battle of attrition, is not fair to Haig. He wanted the whole of the Morval-Thiepval Ridge captured in preparation for the planned September offensive. But then, Haig had been promised the first of the new tanks, the 'potent new weapon'. The methods by which these tanks were employed is outside the scope of this narrative but it is fair to say that Haig realised their importance and their potential, was bitterly disappointed that so few were available for his September battle and pressed without success for substantial increases in their numbers.

Haig's instructions to Gough were designed to prepare for this crucial battle in September.

> For the present, operations west of Munster Alley will be restricted to careful and methodical progress designed to gain possession of Windmill Hill above Pozières, of the enemy's main second line trenches running thence north-westward to about Mouquet Farm and of the enemy's trenches on the spur between Mouquet Farm and Ovillers-la-Boiselle. Each step in the progression must be thoroughly prepared, and no attack is to be made unless and until its success has been ensured so far as forethought and careful preparation can do so.

So much for Haig's written orders. Although these make clear the Commander-in-Chief's apparent concern that attacks not be launched without 'forethought and careful preparation', Haig was still applying pressure to Gough over the Reserve Army's operations, and particularly over the 2nd Australian Division's part in them. Because the required preparations had not been completed Legge's attack was postponed several times from 30 July to 1 August and then again to 3 August.

The British official historian notes simply that much more time was needed for proper preparations and the end of July arrived before they were completed.

Although the attack was ostensibly being planned by Legge, it was White who was making the crucial decisions. Each day, the Chief of Staff at the Anzac Corps Headquarters ordered aircraft to photograph the preparations; each night, he studied the results of the reconnaissance at his headquarters. White realised that more time was needed. On 2 August, Legge and Bridges were confident their division could attack the following day, but White suspected otherwise. He ordered fresh photographs to be taken, and visited the brigade headquarters to check personally on the preparations. That night, White rang Gough's headquarters and informed them the 2nd Division would not be attacking the following day. White was told the Reserve Army had ordered the attack for the following day and it would go ahead. 'Well, you can order them to attack, if you like', replied White, 'but I tell you this . . . and this . . . and this . . .'. Carefully White listed the reasons why the attack should not go ahead. Gough agreed with White: the attack would be postponed until Friday, 4 August. A relieved White passed this decision on to the 2nd Division where it did not meet with universal approval. Bridges noted that 'This gives us a bit more time for preparation, and more time to the Boche too!'

The following day, Haig met Gough near the Reserve Army headquarters at Toutencourt. In his diary, Haig noted that the Australian corps had again put off their attack. 'From what [Gough] said, I concluded that the cause was due to the ignorance of the 2nd Australian Division, and that the GOC Legge was not much good. Gough had called for his reasons in writing why the delay had occurred.'

Not only had Gough asked Birdwood why the delay had occurred, but he also wanted to know the Anzac Corps Commander's opinion of Legge's ability. Sensibly, Birdwood kept this letter from Legge until after the battle, but replied that in accordance with the Australian Government's policy of appointing commanders, he thought Legge should have a fair chance.

Later, Legge argued that the original estimate of when the second attack would take place was dependent upon the preparations not being seriously interfered with by the enemy.

> Work was delayed and hampered each night by severe hostile artillery bombardments and barrages were incurred by the working parties — partly while getting up the communications trenches to the site of the work and partly while doing the work. Much of the work too was broken down by the enemy fire and had to be done again.

Bean, who had been able to move no further forward than the Brigade headquarters so far, on 31 July managed to get into the ruins of Pozières. The following day, he wrote home that he knew of nothing approaching the desolation of Pozières.

> Perhaps it is that the place is still in the thick of the fight. In most other places behind battlefields that I have seen there are the signs of men again — perhaps men who have visited the place like yourself. There is life, anyhow, somewhere in the landscape. In this place there is no sign of life at all. When you stand in Pozières today, and are told that you will find the front trench across another hundred yards of shell holes, you know there must be life in the landscape. The dead hill side a few hundred yards before you must contain both your men and the Germans. But as with most battlefields, where the warmest corner is, there is the least sign of movement. Dry shell crater upon shell crater — all bordering one another until some fresh salvo shall fall and assort the old group of craters into a new one, to be reassorted again and again as the days go on. It is the nearest thing to sheer desert that I have seen since certain lonely rides into the old Sahara at the back of Mena Camp two years ago. Every minute or two there is a crash. Part of the desert bumps itself up into huge red or black clouds and subsides again. These eruptions are the only movement on Pozières.

Ever the fastidious, diligent reporter, Bean inspected the entire Australian front on 31 July, from the cemetery on the left to the tramway and copse on the right, at the east end of the village. 'One could look out on the cup [the wide shallow depression lying between the Australian and the OG lines] . . . The men were lying crowded on the floor of these narrow trenches, and one had to step over them — but on the whole the trenches were good . . .' The 19th Battalion occupied trenches astride the road at the eastern end of the village. Bean thought the men looked:

> . . . dreadfully tired. They had been in for seven days and were nearly at the end of their powers. In a deep dugout I found little Sherbon [Major I. B. Sherbon, of the 19th Battalion] — he had his machine gunners down there resting. They have had no fight — they have simply had to hang on in the line cut (i.e. traversed) by the German barrage. The southern end of it by the road is quite knocked to bits — they can't keep men there at all . . . they are quite cut off from right and left except for journeys overground. There they live and are slowly pounded to death . . .

For a description of what it was like to be 'slowly pounded to death', we have the letters written home by another journalist, then serving as a lieutenant with the 23rd Battalion. John Alexander (Alec) Raws was, in many ways, an improbable infantry subaltern. In 1916, he was 32 and unmarried. Although originally rejected for service in the AIF because of his small physique, he had been captain of the First XI at Prince Alfred College in Adelaide and captain of the St Kilda Tennis Club in Melbourne. Raws was a sensitive man, and his letters give us a fascinating picture of the infantryman's life in the First World War. Had he survived the war and written more fully of his experiences, Raws might well have produced accounts comparable with those of Robert Graves and Siegfried Sassoon. His letters written before the battle of Pozières contain references to his doubts about the conduct of the war, his own self-perceived lack of bravery, his love for his parents and his admiration of his younger brother 'Goldie', who had joined the army before him and was serving in the same battalion. Before he moved up, Alec Raws wrote:

> Tomorrow I shall be in the midst of it all. There is something humorous in the situation, when I actually come to it. John Alexander Raws, who cannot tread upon a worm; who has never struck another human being except in fun; who cannot read of the bravery of others at the front without tears welling to the eyes; who cannot think of blood and mangled bodies without bodily sickness — this man, I, go forth tomorrow to kill and maim, murder and ravage. It is funny.

That last comment was hugely ironical, for Raws could find no source of humour in his experiences.

On the night of 31 July, Raws' battalion, then reduced to about 200 men, was sent back into the line to try and dig the necessary jumping off trenches. To do so meant a march of almost 5 kilometres, under shell fire all the way, before they reached the front line. Then the troops had to go out into No Man's Land. Raws was posted in the rear to prevent straggling. On the way up, the shelling was so intense and the ground so broken that about half of the party had become separated. 'I went up from the rear', wrote Raws, 'and found that we had been cut off, about half of us, from the rest of the battalion, and were lost. I would gladly have shot myself, for I had not the slightest idea where our lines or the enemy's were, and the shells were coming at us from it seemed, three directions. As a matter of fact that was right'.

Terror-stricken, Raws and his party lay down along a bank.

> The shelling was awful. I took a long drink of neat whisky and went up and down the bank trying to find a man who could tell us where we

were. Eventually I found one. He led me along a broken track and we found a trench; he said he was sure it led to our lines, so we went back and got the men. We eventually made our way to the right spot, out in No Man's Land. Our leader was shot before we arrived, and the strain had sent two other officers mad. I and another new officer (Lieutenant Short) took charge and dug the trench. We were being shot at all the time, and I knew that if we did not finish the job before daylight a new assault planned for the next night would fail. It was awful, but we had to drive the men by every possible means and dig ourselves. The wounded and killed had to be thrown on one side — I refused to let any sound man help a wounded man: the sound men had to dig . . .

Raws thought it impossible later that he had said the 'most dreadful things to broken men to shake them into activity'. But he did, and he remembered doing so clearly.

Shortly before daybreak, Raws was ordered to leave the trench he was digging by another officer, 'hopelessly rattled', he wrote. Although the officer might well have been rattled, the Australians had been ordered out of the forward positions before the bombardment timed to begin at 3 a.m. Raws took it on himself to insist the men stay and told them bluntly that anyone who stopped digging would be shot. 'We dug on and finished amid a tornado of bursting shells. All the time, mind, the enemy flares were making the whole area almost as light as day. We got away as best we could.'

On the way back, Raws was buried twice with the dead and dying.

The ground was covered with bodies in all stages of decay and mutilation, and I would, after struggling free from the earth, pick up a body by me to lift him out with me, and find him a decayed corpse. I pulled a head off — was covered with blood. The horror was indescribable. In the dim, misty light of dawn I collected about 50 men and sent them off, mad with terror, on the right track for home.

Two soldiers stayed with Raws and helped him back with the only unburied wounded man they could find.

The journey down with him was awful. He was delirious — I tied one of his legs to his pack with one of my puttees. On the way down I found another man and made him stay and help us. It was so terribly slow. We got down to the first dressing station. There I met another of our men, who was certain that his cobber was lying wounded in that barrage of fire. I would have given my immortal soul to get out of it, but I simply had to go back with him and a stretcher bearer. We spent two hours in that devastated village searching for wounded — but all were dead. The sights I saw during that search, and the smell can, I know, never be exceeded by anything else the war may show me.

One of the enduring clichés of the First World War* is the ignorance of the staff officers, adorned with their 'red badges of funk', comfortable and secure in their châteaux kilometres behind the lines, of the real conditions suffered by the regimental officers and soldiers. But like most clichés, it is fundamentally true and, in this instance, revealed by the entries in the War Diary of the Reserve Army. Such diaries provide accurate guides, not so much to how battles were proceeding, but how the officers making the entries thought they were proceeding. The Reserve Army diary for this period is remarkably consistent in revealing the ignorance of the conditions experienced by the troops under its command.

The following night, 1 August, Raws went back up to the line and stayed there. 'We were shelled to hell ceaselessly. X went mad and disappeared.'

At Toutencourt, the staff of the Reserve Army recorded the events of the day in the War Diary with their usual scrupulous care. For 1 August, the entry reads:

> The day was on the whole quiet with less shelling of Pozières, where the work of joining up our strong points is proceeding apace. Some enemy aeroplanes came over our lines for the first time for a long period. Our artillery were active in counter-battery work, and destroyed some gun emplacements near Courcelette. The Guards Division arrived in the Army area to join XIV Corps.

And, for the following day: 'During the night the 2nd Australian Division made 100 yards progress towards the German 2nd line . . . There was some shelling of our communication trenches S of Pozières . . . The day was very quiet except for our artillery who did a lot of damage to the enemy's gun positions and ammunition dumps . . .'

Even Bean, whose magnanimity extended beyond that expected of the official historian, remarked that 'no one in rear — not White, or Legge, or Birdwood, Gough, or Haig — though they realised that Pozières was being heavily shelled, had the faintest conception of the conditions in which the work on that now naked height had to be carried through'. For the troops of the 2nd Division, the days between

---

* Indeed, of all wars, as Shakespeare points out in *Henry IV*, Pt I, Act I, Scene III. The feeling between the regimental and staff officer is as old as war itself.

their two assaults on the Windmill and the OG lines were probably the worst experienced by the AIF in the entire war.

> The shelling at Pozières did not merely probe character and nerve; it laid them stark naked as no other experience of the AIF ever did. In a single tour of this battle divisions were subjected to greater stress than in the whole Gallipoli campaign. The shell fire was infinitely worse than that subsequently experienced in the Third Battle of Ypres . . .

The Germans called it *trommelfueur*, drum fire, and it did, indeed, resemble the swift roll of a kettledrum. Bean wrote home:

> Strong men arrive from that experience shaking like leaves in the wind. I have seen one of our own youngsters — a boy who had fought a great fight all through the dark hours, and who had refused to come back when he was first ordered to — I have seen him unable to keep still for an instant after the strain, and yet ready to fight on till he dropped; physically almost a wreck, but with his wits as sharp; and his spirits as keen as a steel chisel. I have seen other Australians who, after doing glorious work through thirty or forty hours of unimaginable strain, buried and buried and buried again and still working like tigers, have broken down and collapsed, unable to stand or to walk, unable to move an arm except limply, as it were string; ready to weep like little children.

For poor Alec Raws, the horrors of the bombardment were magnified by the uncertainty about his brother Goldie, who had taken part in the abortive attack on 29 July and had not been seen since. As best he could, Raws searched the area where his brother had disappeared, going out frequently into No Man's Land to check the identity of the corpses in Australian uniform. He hoped that Goldie had been taken prisoner but suspected from the beginning that his beloved younger brother, a veteran of Gallipoli, had simply disappeared in the churned-over country.

On 4 August, Raws wrote:

> from the battlefields of the Great Push with thousands of shellings passing in a tornado overhead and thousands of unburied dead around me. It seems easy to say that, but you who have not seen it can hardly conceive the awfulness of it all . . . One feels on a battlefield such as this that one can never survive, or that if the body holds the brain must go forever. For the horrors one sees and the never-ending shock of the shells is more than can be borne. Hell must be a home to it. The Gallipoli veterans say that the Peninsula was a picnic to this push . . . My battalion (23rd) has

been in it for eight days and one-third of it is left — all shattered at that. And they're sticking it still, incomparable heroes all. We are lousy, stinking, ragged, unshaven, sleepless. Even when we're back a bit, we can't sleep for our own guns. I have one puttee, a dead man's helmet, another dead man's gas protector, a dead man's bayonet. My tunic is rotten with other men's blood and partly spattered with a comrade's brains. It is horrible, but why should you people at home not know?

Raws told his brother-in-law that he was all right.

I have had much luck and kept my nerve so far. The awful difficulty is to keep it. The bravest of all often lose it. Courage does not count over here. It is nerve. Once that goes one becomes a gibbering maniac. The noise of our own guns, the enemy's shells and the getting lost in the darkness . . . the great horror of many of us is the fear of being lost with troops at night on the battlefield. We do all our fighting and moving at night and the confusion of passing through a barrage of enemy shells in the dark is pretty appalling . . . The sad fact is that one can see no end of this. If we live tonight we have to go through tomorrow night and next week and next month. Poor wounded devils you meet on the stretchers are laughing with glee. One cannot blame them. They are getting out of this.

On the night of 4 August, the 2nd Australian Division attacked again. Because of the problems of a night attack, so apparent on 29 July and so vividly described by Alec Raws and Walter Boys, this attack was planned to begin at 9.15 p.m. just on dusk, when the line of the German trenches would still be visible and the untidy mound that was formerly the Windmill was clear on the skyline. But a dusk attack meant a daylight assembly, hence the need for the deep forming-up trenches. The digging parties had done their job well under the most appalling conditions; the assaulting troops were able to assemble and form up for the attack without being detected.

Again Legge had an abundance of artillery; the heavy artillery of the Reserve Army, the II, III and Anzac Corps; the lighter guns from the 25th, 34th and his own 2nd Australian Division, supported by two brigades of the 1st Divisional Artillery. The plans for the artillery bombardment were co-ordinated by Brig.-Gen. W. J. Napier, who had replaced the hapless Cunliffe Owen and who worked closely with White. Ten batteries of heavy howitzers from the Anzac and II Corps alone each put four destructive bombardments, lasting an hour each time, on the German lines each day. Trench mortars and lighter field artillery, pounded the closer positions; additional heavy guns were ready to fire counter-battery tasks once the German guns began to fire. Napier managed to incorporate an element of surprise, which had probably been considered impossible. Targets were meticulously selected; fire plans carefully co-ordinated; the whole effort orchestrated by Napier, culminating in an intense barrage on the first objective, at 9.15 p.m., dwelling there for three minutes, then switching to the second objective for another three minutes and then firing an intense counter-battery bombardment against all the known German gun positions.*

Mindful of the damage that had been caused to the previous attack from isolated German machine gun posts in advance of the main trench line, Legge ordered his own divisional guns to fire on No Man's Land and the area between the OG1 and OG2 lines before the attack was due to begin. Apart from a more careful and comprehensive artillery plan, and the construction of jumping off trenches, the plan of attack was basically the same as that of the night of 29 July. Indeed, the 20th Battalion was attacking the same trench line for the third time.

As we have observed, no plan, however well considered, survives contact with the enemy. But just as so many things had gone wrong on 29 July, now all the planning and preparation seemed to pay off. Again the main burden of the attack fell on Paton's 7th Brigade in the centre. So close to the barrage were the troops of this brigade that they met the Germans coming out of their dugouts. The 25th Battalion troops, arriving in their jumping off trenches, had found them occupied by troops of the neighbouring 26th. This muddle was soon sorted out and although the first two waves were somewhat disorganised, they managed to get within 20 metres of the German trenches before the barrage lifted. The speed and violence of the assault had worked; the defenders had no chance to man their machine guns before the Australians, cheering wildly, were on them with bayonet and bomb. The Australians quickly moved their machine guns forward to cover any counter-attack and consolidated the line. The contrast between the two assaults — 29 July and 4 August — is fascinating.

That the attack succeeded in all sectors was as much a tribute to the leadership and initiative of the young regimental officers and NCOs as it was to White's careful overseeing of the operation. One such officer was Major Murdoch Mackay, a 25 year old Victorian barrister of the 22nd Battalion. Mackay was a stubborn, somewhat opinionated young

---

* I can find no suggestion that either Legge or White considered the possibility of a dawn attack. Apart from the disadvantage of being silhouetted against the rising sun, the attackers would have been able to assemble by night, consolidate in the daylight and any German counter-attack would have had to be made in clear visibility. Later in the war the Australians realised the inestimable advantages of the dawn attack.

man; '. . . of the stuff,' Bean wrote, 'which makes good leaders but difficult subordinates'. So difficult was this subordinate in fact, that his battalion commander seriously considered sacking him and his brigade commander, Gellibrand (with whom he had also differed over points of law and courts-martial) thought twice before promoting him, although he admitted later that he was thankful for the decision he had made.

Mackay's battalion had become confused and mixed with the 26th. To make the confusion worse, the battalions were of different brigades. Murdoch Mackay took charge, led his troops across open exposed ground in a terrible fire of shrapnel to reach the right jumping off position. Only part of the battalion had arrived, the remainder were milling around in the confusion of the communications trench. At 9.30 p.m. when the attack had been underway for 15 minutes, Mackay reached the forward positions. With a simple, 'Come on, boys', he assumed command of the 22nd Battalion troops and led them across open ground. Off to the left flank, a single German machine gun that had been overlooked or missed in the bombardment opened up, the only gun to do so at close range with direct fire at any part of the 2nd Division attack.

Although this gun caused heavy casualties on the way across, the survivors fought their way into the OG1 lines. 'They were in too great number to be stopped', said a captured German officer later, '. . . fine strong lads'. Mackay was among the casualties. He was killed just metres from the OG1 line. Without his swift actions in taking charge of the split battalion and in the leading of the attack, the assault here would have failed. And failure on this flank, the northern-most point, would have compromised the entire divisional attack.

On the right near the Albert-Bapaume road, the bombardment had virtually obliterated the German trench lines. Major Arnold Brown wrote that the 28th Battalion had regained its spirit and were more than determined to show their qualities.

> Zero hour was heralded by the same terrific shell and machine gun fire, and the battalion moved to the attack in the same formation as previously. 'B' Coy (Capt. Foss) and a bomb platoon remaining in support; but bound by a timetable to move forward immediately OG1 was in our hands. No one, I know, will contradict me in the statement that the shell-fire at Pozières was never at any stage of the war surpassed in volume or intensity, at least, not by British troops; though the Germans might have had the experience at a later date.
>
> According to schedule, the storming troops took possession of OG1 and then moved straight forward to OG2. During these few minutes, I was sitting in the front line with Major Leane.

> To the second Foss and his men moved forward through a terrible barrage to the support and occupation of OG1. Casualties were so heavy that a greatly reduced B Coy got through to occupy the position.

Maitland Foss, who had already developed a considerable reputation in the AIF for leading raids, pushed his troops forward and established a small machine gun post near the Windmill. As well, the position was covered by several Vickers machine guns. At last the Australians had captured the high ground of Pozières, this 'key to the Somme', 36 days after the original offensive had been launched.

It had taken the infantry less than an hour to complete their main task, although on the left flank a single German machine gun post continued to hold out until the following afternoon. The fighting continued throughout the night however, with odd violent actions here and there as both sides wrestled for sections of torn and battered trenches. Invariably, in the confusion and with the rudimentary communications, there were mistakes: one battalion commander thought the battalion on his right was not occupying the OG2 trenches and so omitted to extend his line along, creating a gap. This gap was quickly discovered by the Germans who launched a counter-attack about 4 a.m., just on dawn. This failed. The Germans tried again, further round on a flank. This attack failed also. On the eastern slopes of the Pozières Ridge, the Australians could see the flashes of German artillery fire, the first time they had seen the muzzle flash of the guns firing at them. Just before midnight, five great explosions behind Courcelette threw debris hundreds of metres into the air, clearly visible in the violent sudden light.

The Germans were destroying artillery ammunition lest it fall into the hands of the advancing British. The light, lasting fully five minutes, provided a brilliant and bizarre backdrop for the struggles on the ridge.

The First World War is often thought of as an artillery war, a war of remote-control destruction. For the gunners, perhaps it was, although they lived and died with the constant fear of counter-battery fire obliterating their gun positions. For the infantry soldiers, the war took on an intensely personal nature, almost an individual struggle, man against man, bomb against bomb, bayonet against bayonet, even — unlikely as it may seem in this massive conflict — pistol against pistol.

One such exchange occurred during a German counter-attack on 'The Elbow', the point where the OG lines changed direction from north-west to west, along the ridge line. Captain Percy Cherry, a Tasmanian apple grower who had celebrated his 21st birthday just two months before, was commanding two detachments of Vickers machine guns sited to cover the northern approaches to the Windmill. Just after dawn, Cherry saw a small party of Germans approaching, led by an officer waving a revolver. Cherry ordered his guns to fire; the Germans, not realising where the fire was coming from, bunched offering the Australian gunners a better target. Again the Australian gunners fired and the Germans, now much depleted, pressed on, dashing from shell crater to shell crater, all the time closing the distance between them and the Australian gun positions.

It is this aspect of warfare that makes the infantry's role — 'to seek out and close with the enemy, to kill or capture him' — so personal. In the Second World War, a French infantry battalion commander described it thus:

> In an attack, there comes a moment when the infantryman gets close to the enemy lines, all support ceases, and he must mount the charge that is his last argument, his sole *raison d'être*. Such is the infantryman's war ... [and] the object of his training should be to prepare him for what one might call 'the battle of the last hundred metres'.

The Germans attacking Cherry's machine guns were, indeed, within this 'last hundred metres', bombing his gun positions, wounding his gunners. Cherry and the German officer were fighting their own private war, dodging from shell hole to shell hole, loosing off shots from their revolvers. At one point, they rose simultaneously, fired simultaneously, each hitting the other. Cherry was saved by his helmet; the German was mortally wounded. The Australian officer crossed to his opponent's hole. From his pocket the German took a bundle of letters and, in good English, asked whether Cherry would have them censored and posted. Cherry agreed. With that promise, the German handed over the letters saying, 'And so it ends' then died at Cherry's feet.

The Australians were not immune from the propaganda about the 'bestial Hun', nor were they overly sympathetic towards their opponents. But the more sensitive, thoughtful among them realised that the life of an infantryman in the trenches, whether he was wearing khaki or field grey, was the same. Still, the Australians rejoiced in their own abilities, basked in their self-confidence and regarded most other troops, enemy and ally alike (with the possible exception of the Scots) with ill-disguised disdain. But that did not prevent odd instances of humanitarian behaviour, such as Cherry's agreeing to post his former foe's letters, or Bourke's concern about the inhabitant of the dugout in Pozières. 'It is very funny', wrote one officer about this time, 'how one watching the effect of our guns on the German trenches, remarks "good oh" as their parapet and dugouts fly up in the air; one does not think till afterwards that some poor devils may be flying up with it, who are just as anxious for the war to end as we are'.

The Reserve Army's War Diary entry for 5 August gives us a neat summary of the previous night's fighting:

> At 9.15 p.m. on the night 4/5th the 2nd Australian Division attacked the German 2nd line trenches from the Bapaume road to R34 central. The whole objective was gained with comparatively little loss, the attack coming as a surprise to the Germans, who were all ready for a relief.
>
> The 12th Division also extended its gains, and gained touch with the left of the 2nd Australian Division. It was reported that a fair number of prisoners had been taken. The attack had been preceded by a steady observed bombardment of the objectives with heavy artillery; all wire had been cut; and several short intense bombardments without attack on the preceding days deceived the enemy so that he was unprepared for this attack, which followed on a short intensive bombardment. Good counter-battery work, too, had reduced the fire of the enemy's artillery considerably.

Gough came forward to Birdwood's headquarters, and congratulated the Australians on having 'inflicted a severe defeat on the enemy and secured us most valuable ground'. Haig telegraphed the Anzac Corps headquarters: The attack was of 'very considerable importance and opens the way to equally valuable success to be obtained by similar careful methods of preparation, and gallantry and thoroughness in execution'. For Haig, however, this attack and the assault on Pozières village itself were still minor operations. 'Our line was brought to the crest of the ridge above Martinpuich, Pozières' Windmill and the high ground north of the village were secured, and with them observation over Martinpuich and Courcelette . . .' And the Commander-in-Chief was still dubious about the worth of the Australians; he was uncomfortable 'about the extraordinary system by which discipline was maintained in their ranks'.* He was lectured by Gough on the staff officers at GHQ who engaged in 'tittle-tattle' when they had no real idea of the worth of the Australians.

---

* Australian soldiers did not polish their badges and buttons, had a robust attitude towards paying military compliments and were not executed for desertion — all to Haig's displeasure.

Both John Terraine and Duff Cooper have attempted to show how much Haig thought of the Australians under his command, despite his original doubts about their abilities. 'His over-riding inclination', Terraine writes, 'was to think well of them, to believe in their success; when he made sharp criticisms, it was disappointment, more than anything else, that incited them'. Duff Cooper tells us Haig learned to appreciate the splendid qualities of the Australians during this period:

> Although the fighting and the shell fire were far more severe than anything they experienced in Gallipoli, and although they found the German a very much more formidable foe than the Turk, their high courage and their high spirits remained indomitable . . . A tendency to underestimate dangers was their only failing.

Fine, gracious tributes, indeed.

One need only ask now why Haig did not find a better use for these Australians, with 'their high courage and their spirits', than repeated attacks on narrow fronts as part of minor operations in the 'steady methodical, step-by-step advance'. In a conversation with White, Bean said he hoped the assault on the Windmill was preparation to bring the British forces into position to make another attack on a wide front. 'I'm afraid there doesn't seem to be any sign of it', White replied. 'They seem to be content to let each little lot plan its own attacks.' In this sentence, White captured the essential weaknesses of Haig's tactics and control in this 'forbidding central phase': the inability or reluctance to adapt his original plan; his lack of direction to his subordinate commanders, particularly Gough, apart from the issue of a few trite maxims; his failure to see the opportunities offered by the capture of Pozières' Windmill. Certainly his opponents had no illusions about the importance of the feature they called Hill 160.

Pozières Heights was of paramount importance to the Germans, despite the strong flank position they held at Thiepval. Indeed, it threatened this strongpoint, on which so much of the German defence in this sector of the line was predicted. On 5 August, the Commander of the First German Army, General Fritz von Below, issued an order which left his subordinates no room for doubt.

> At any price Hill 60* [the Pozières plateau] must be recovered, for if it were to remain in the hands of the British it would give them an important advantage. Attacks will be made by successive waves 80 yards apart.

---

*A translation mistake. A copy of von Below's order was captured during a German counter-attack on the Windmill feature two days after it was issued.

> Troops which first reach the plateau must hold on until reinforced, whatever their losses. Any officer who fails to resist to the death on the ground won will be immediately courtmartialled.

The Germans felt they had come dangerously close to losing even more ground in this sector on the night of 4/5 August. The Australians had attacked at a time when the German batteries around Courcelette were short of ammunition; when the troops were tired and being relieved; when the effects of the British and Australian preparatory bombardments were being felt. 'If the enemy's attack had continued', wrote one German officer, 'Courcelette would have been lost'. 'Are you in Courcelette?' asked one young German officer at his interrogation. Nothing much in the way of German forces or positions lay between the Australians on Pozières Ridge and the village 3 kilometres ahead. Here, the German third line was still largely chinagraph marks on headquarters' maps. Arnold Brown wrote in 1932:

> I cannot understand to this day why we were not sent forward, at least in the form of a raiding party; but I presume there were good reasons. But during the afternoon of August 5, when the enemy was so disorganised that barely a shot was fired, we had to sit and suffer the sight of enemy machine gun teams limbering up and drawing their field guns to safety, later to again rain shells on us. It was not long before that happened.

In the 24th Battalion Lance Corporal Whitear was similarly puzzled. 'We saw German artillery men limber up and get two field guns safely away because we were not allowed to go further forward and capture them. Attacks have to be made to plan.'

Indeed, attacks have to be made to plan. Although the Australian success was significant, it was still very narrow, a mere divisional front. And Gough's orders were not to continue eastwards, but to shift the direction of his attack northwards, attacking the strong Thiepval position along the ridge line. Even before the last fighting of that night had died away, Gough was pressing for a northward move. Birdwood came forward from his headquarters to press Legge who, in turn, sent Gellibrand forward. Could the 6th Brigade assault and capture the next trench line to the north?

The artillery fire was terribly systematic: first the German gunners would register their targets on one point along the trench, easily determined on a map. Then, carefully and methodically, the concentrated artillery fire would move along the trench from flank to flank, down a communications trench, to the support line, then along that line to another communications trench and so back to the front line. Or else, two batteries would work in unison with their fire crossing, parting to follow the same pattern in opposite directions and then re-crossing again. No portion of the trenches escaped the fire; no one in the trenches escaped the billowing dust and the choking smell of cordite and the terror of waiting for the rounds to fall. 'It was', said one soldier later, 'like waiting your turn at the bar'.

Again, the Reserve Army War Diary gives only a bare account. For 6 August, it records:

> There was nothing to report during the night: things were generally quiet except about Pozières, where the shelling was heavy. . . . A good many casualties were caused by shell fire during the night. There was heavy and continuous hostile shelling all day about Pozières and near the Windmill a battalion was withdrawn to avoid casualties, leaving posts with Lewis guns out in front. On the rest of the front all was quiet.

It is probably unfair to expect that such a diary, recorded in haste and rarely amended, should convey anything other than the barest and blandest details. Yet, recurring almost as a nagging variation on the same theme, is the gulf between the record and the reality. In any army headquarters, with its legions of busy staff officers — perhaps not Siegfried Sassoon's 'fierce and bald and short of breath . . . scarlet majors' — there could be little concept of the meaning behind such phrases as 'heavy shelling', 'heavy and continuous shelling'. A year later, after four months of fighting in the Ypres salient, an officer from Haig's GHQ came forward. As the staff car approached the morass of swamp and mud of the battle zone, this officer became increasingly uneasy and then burst into tears. 'Good God', he asked his companion, 'did we really send men to fight in this?' That officer's ignorance of the conditions at Ypres was matched by the Reserve Army staff's ignorance of the conditions at Pozières.

The German gunners had few distractions. As the Reserve Army Diary remarked, elsewhere on the Somme front it was quiet; attention was focused on the Pozières Ridge. At noon on 5 August, the commander of the Anzac Corps artillery asked politely whether his guns were still required, as they had been firing all night and into the morning. Equally politely, he was told they were still required, because the infantry had been enduring the German bombardment and were suffering severely. Brown noted that during 5 August the troops worked on their newly captured positions. 'About 7 p.m. the enemy commenced a most terrific shell fire, which blew our newly made position to smithereens. He counter-attacked in the early hours of August 6, but it was half-hearted, and was blocked entirely by our artillery and machine guns before it reached our positions.'

Brown's own account is almost excessively modest. By then, his battalion was so weak and depleted that it could not hold a continuous line of trenches. Instead, it held three separate points in the line. As well, the battalion commander, realising the extent of the German artillery fire which would inevitably follow the capture of the heights, ordered his front trenches to be thinned out as much as possible, so as to avoid unnecessary casualties.

Most of Brown's battalion withdrew that second afternoon. They lost heavily during the withdrawal itself, and were distressed at having to leave their wounded behind. During this withdrawal, the battalion lost Captain Maitland Foss, 'soldier, gentleman and leader — a man who would have risen high in the service had he survived', wrote his friend Arnold Brown. Foss had led some of the first trench raids made by the Australians in France; he had pushed forward on this feature further than any of his comrades; now, during this final difficult phase, he was mortally wounded. His wounding, and death six days later, cast a pall over the entire battalion.

The withdrawal meant only a short respite for the 28th. The battalion was not to be rested well out of the line; instead, it moved to the next sector to the north, and relieved the 25th. But it was virtually finished as a fighting force, down to fewer than 100 men and just two officers. The battalion it replaced was in an even worse state. Late on the afternoon of 5 August, Paton told the divisional headquarters that the 25th Battalion was reduced to just one officer and 29 men. The 27th could muster only 100 soldiers, some badly wounded but still remaining on duty. The fourth battalion had about 200 men left.

Now, some of the strains in the command structure began to emerge. An exhausted Paton urged that his brigade be relieved, although he undertook to keep holding a reduced frontage in the line. This request was shuffled from Legge's headquarters to the Anzac Corps and then passed on to Gough's Reserve Army headquarters.

Birdwood had already pointed out to Gough that the attack could not proceed without fresh troops; Paton's message was sent to reinforce that point. It seemed to take an inordinately long time for the decision to be made to relieve the entire 2nd Division. Two full days elapsed before its infantry was out of the line and on the road to the rest areas. In its twelve days, the division had suffered 6,846 casualties, killed, wounded and missing in action. Many were also suffering serious shock; Bean saw wounded sitting in front of Vadencourt Château trembling like an 'aspen leaf — a sure sign of overstrain by shellfire'. Even as the battalions moved out of the line, the troops were not safe from the seemingly ubiquitous artillery. On the night of 7 August, the 6th Brigade was halted on Tara Hill, between Pozières and Albert. The headquarters officers of the 24th Battalion — commanding officer, Lt.-Col. Russell Watson; the second in command, Major Charles Manning; the adjutant Captain William Tatnall; the assistant-adjutant, Lieutenant J. B. N. Carvick and the regimental medical officer, Captain H. F. H. Plant — were sitting around in an old gun pit when a single artillery round burst among them. Watson was pulled out unconscious; the others were killed instantly. Charles Manning had been a friend of Bean and had preceded the official historian as associate to Mr Justice Owen of the NSW Supreme Court. 'Poor old Manning — it is horrible ... He was buried in Lone Pine, was through a dreadful bombardment at Pozières — and lived through it all to be killed the very night they came out.' Carvick had been a popular battalion officer. In the first assault, Arthur Whitear remembered Carvick as being 'most brilliant in his leadership, who constantly called "come on, 24th", and who did a lion's share of digging in the captured position'.

The enormity of the killing and the destruction took days to sink in with the exhausted and battered Australians. The fearful nightmares of the previous days exacted their toll; the troops sat quietly, or smoked, or wrote home, trying to convey their experiences with paper and indelible pencil. Alec Raws thought many of his experiences unbelievable, having a remote, almost dream-like quality. Perhaps the careful and meticulous journalist thought that by recording these experiences in detail in his letters home, he might both preserve them and ensure that the dream was reality. During the battle, Raws had other props. 'I found my little whisky flask invaluable', he wrote in one letter. In one letter to his sister, Raws wrote that there were things he could not tell his father and mother. 'I write to you because you are more my kindred spirit than any other ... and because in a letter from you I read the other day out on the battlefield, you asked me to tell you the psychological side of battle.' Raws told his sister that their brother Goldie was either dead, wounded or a prisoner. 'He was seen to fall and get up again and say he was all right. The battalion took the ground it was supposed to take, dug in but was not supported on the flank.' The battalion had to withdraw; Goldie fell during this stage. Alec Raws told his sister that he and others had thoroughly searched the battlefield 'but there is no sign of his body'.

Alec Raws thought that Goldie was either dead, or a prisoner, or wounded in the head and blinded. 'In the confusion ... I have been unable to discover just what has happened.' Briefly, Alec Raws' hopes were raised; another wounded soldier had reported seeing his brother in a dressing station after the action. By 19 August, however, all hopes were gone. That day, Alec wrote to his other brother; this letter has its own sense of desolation and loss. 'I have written this day to mother explaining there is no good news of Goldie. [She will be told] officially by cable. He must be accepted as missing. His death has proved a far greater shock to me than I thought possible.' Alec Raws had fainted three times since he had come out of the line, although only one time had been in public and then among strange officers.

> I was terribly glad I was never even threatened with anything of the sort during those ten days in the line. The first I ever had was quite unexpected — the night before, in an adjoining village. None of this for father, of course ... Before going in to this next affair, at the same dreadful spot, I want to tell you, so that it may be on record, that I honestly believe Goldie and many other officers were murdered on the night you know of, through the incompetence, callousness and personal vanity of those high in authority. I realise the seriousness of what I say, but I am so bitter, and the facts so palpable, that it must be said. Please be very discreet with this letter — unless I should go under.

Four days later, Raws went back into the line. While conferring with three other officers, an artillery shell burst nearby. All four were killed. Raws died of concussion, his body had not a visible mark. He was buried where he fell, with a neat white cross to mark his grave.

12

Counter-attack

An officer came blundering down the trench: 'Stand to and man the
fire step! On he went . . . Gasping and bawling, 'Fire step . . . counter-
attack!'
Then the haze lifted. Bombing on the right
Down the old sap: machine guns on the left;
And stumbling figures looming out in front.
'O Christ, they're coming at us!'
Siegfried Sassoon, Counter Attack (London, 1968).

The First Australian Imperial Force, doggedly and proudly egal-
itarian, had few genuine heroes. Men were admired and respected for their courage and their leadership, not necessarily
for the bits of ribbons on their breasts or the badges of rank on their
shoulders. Courage and leadership cannot be accurately measured in
terms of medals or rank. Too many brave actions had gone undecorated
or been otherwise unrecognised by military officialdom; too many awards
were often, or so it seemed to the soldiers in the field, made to the
wrong men.

Leadership distinguished the AIF at all levels. Not merely the formal
leadership bestowed by rank and appointment, but the leadership ex-
hibited by the ordinary soldiers. According to Bean, the success of any
citizen volunteer army like the AIF depended on the proportion of
strong independent men in its ranks; men who, when they heard a
desperate call to withdraw during some fierce fighting, would resist and
demand to know who gave such an order. Bean wrote:

In the Australian force the proportion is unquestionably high — it may
amount to 50 per cent or more. I have seen them going up against a rain
of fire and the weaker ones retiring through them at the very same time
— the two streams going in opposite directions and not taking the faintest
notice of one another.

212

Of such strong independent men are heroes and leaders made. In recent years, few subjects have attracted as much attention, as much debate and as much theorising in military literature as the subject of leadership. Young officers and NCOs have the benefit of such marvellous common sense contained in Slim's talks on leadership and courage, General Sir John Hackett's profound essays on the subject and Brigadier Shelford Bidwell's perceptive observation that most of the commonly held views about great leaders rely largely on their public relations images. But in contrast, much leadership training has been dominated and no doubt confused by management theory and the *Harvard Business Review* approach. And such theory is distinctly uncomfortable with the idea of a 'born leader'.

One wonders how Albert (Bert) Jacka, one of the AIF's few genuine heroes, is regarded by modern military psychologists and management consultants, both in and out of uniform. Jacka was more than just a born leader; he was also an extraordinary fighting soldier. His battalion, the 14th, was simply and widely known throughout the AIF as 'Jacka's Mob', a far from modest tribute by all the AIF, but particularly by the soldiers of the 14th, who loved and admired Jacka, who envied his great courage and who deplored a miserly attitude by military authorities to decorations for that courage. They knew what Jacka was worth, not only to the battalion, but to the AIF as a whole. When that worth was not sufficiently recognised by authority, it tended to diminish the standing of other decorations and awards as well.

In that hackneyed phrase, Jacka was a legend. His progress through the ranks was not slow even for such an outstanding fighter and soldier: lance-corporal in August 1915; his second stripe arriving a day later; sergeant the following month. In November, Jacka was a company sergeant-major, the senior soldier of the company, arguably the most demanding position in any fiercely civilian AIF infantry battalion. By April 1916, Bert Jacka was a 25 year old second lieutenant. The transition from sergeants' mess to officers' mess has perplexed and challenged many soldiers; the subtle differences, distinctions of shade rather than colour, are often difficult to appreciate. Not for Bert Jacka: his authority was absolute; his confidence was unshakeable; his reputation was universal.

That reputation flowed largely from the award of the Victoria Cross to Private Jacka at Gallipoli. On 19 May 1915 the Turks attacked along most of the Australian front with the aim of driving the Australians and New Zealanders from their trenches and down to the sea. The 14th Battalion was holding the sector known as Courtney's Post. With four other men, Jacka was holding a portion of the trench. Amid the confusion, the dust and the smoke of the assaults, about a dozen Turks managed to capture a section of Courtney's Post. One hastily organised counter-attack failed. Quickly an Australian officer organised a diversion while Jacka crept around to a flank. While the defenders were distracted, Jacka made his ground, jumped into the trench, shot five of the Turks and bayoneted one more. The remaining attackers quickly scrambled out; Jacka was found minutes later with an unlit cigarette in his mouth and his face flushed with excitement. 'I managed to get the beggars, sir', he told his company commander.

Jacka received the first Victoria Cross awarded to an Australian in the First World War. His personality appealed to Bean who helped to foster the legend of this 'guiding spirit of the storm of battle'. When E. J. Rule arrived in the 14th Battalion, Jacka was CSM of D Company.

> 'Have you seen him yet?' was on all lips; the man who could point out Jacka seemed to swell with importance. To me, Jacka looked the part; he had a medium-sized body, a natty figure, and a determined face with crooked nose. His feat of polishing off six Turks single-handed certainly took some beating. At that time one characteristic above all endeared him to all the underdogs; instead of criming men and bringing them before the officers, his method was: 'I won't crime you, I'll give you a punch on the bloody nose'. It is difficult to exaggerate what Jacka's connection with our battalion came to mean to us. He was with us practically throughout the war. Not merely to us 'rookies', but to the whole battalion he was not nearly so well known at Gallipoli as he afterwards became. He was not one of those whose character, manner, or outlook was changed by the high decoration which he had received. His confident, frank, outspoken personality never changed. His leadership in his last battle was as audacious and capable as in his first ... Not we only, but the brigade and the whole AIF came to look upon him as a rock of strength that never failed. We of the 14th Battalion never ceased to be thrilled when we heard ourselves referred to in the *estaminet* or by passing units on the march as 'some of Jacka's mob'.

Rule's remarks show how clearly Jacka's personality had been implanted upon the battalion.

'Jacka's Mob' was part of the 4th Division, with two new brigades and one — the 4th (which included the 14th Battalion) — a veteran of the Gallipoli fighting. Bean says the division achieved a reputation for hard fighting 'and for the possession, perhaps, of the least polish but the most numerous war scars'. It was commanded by yet another British officer of the Indian Army, Maj.-Gen. Sir Herbert Cox. At 56, Cox was old for a divisional commander, even by First World War standards. He had commanded the Indian Brigade at Gallipoli the year before, where he had declined to accept responsibility for the two companies of Indian troops under his command who shared the Turks' religious beliefs. Monash, who had served under Cox at Gallipoli once described him as 'one of those crochety, peppery, livery old Indian officers, whom the climate had dried up and shrivelled up into a bag of nerves'. But Cox had a high opinion of Australian soldiers, confiding to his wife in 1915 that he wished he had more of them. In Birdwood, Cox also had a champion; it was Birdwood who argued that the veteran Indian Army officer be given the 4th Division after the AIF expansion in 1916. The 4th Division had a fair sprinkling of British officers in both its headquarters and its brigades, but Cox's shrewd temperament and experience helped prevent the difficulties which existed in some other mixed headquarters.

The brigade commanders were a mixed bunch. Brigadier Charles Henry Brand, commanding the 4th Brigade, was an Australian permanent officer. Like so many other officers in the fledgling army, Brand had been a school teacher with a militia commission. He had resigned this commission to serve as a sergeant in South Africa but was again commissioned, this time in the Rhodesian Field Force. After the South African war, Brand returned to school teaching in Charters Towers and in 1905, joined the permanent military forces as a temporary lieutenant. Brand's pre-war career followed a predictable and conventional path: exchange duty in India, staff and instruction postings. Bridges selected him as brigade major of the 3rd Infantry Brigade when the 1st Division was raised; he later commanded the 8th Battalion and received the first Distinguished Service Order awarded to an Australian. In June 1916, Brand was promoted and given the command of the 4th Brigade. His greeting to his new troops was, according to Bean, 'an extraordinary inept and egoistic oration'. Brand did not bother to endear himself to his troops.

By comparison, the commander of the 13th Brigade, Brig.-Gen. Thomas William Glasgow was a popular, if stern, leader. A Queensland merchant and pastoralist, Glasgow had been another militia officer, joining the Wide Bay Regiment, Queensland Mounted Infantry, while still a teenager and serving with this unit in South Africa. Glasgow was awarded the DSO as a subaltern in the Boer War. When war broke out in 1914 Glasgow immediately joined the AIF, despite having just bought a cattle property in central Queensland. Three of his six brothers also joined with him. Glasgow was made a squadron commander in the 2nd Light Horse Regiment, fought with them on Gallipoli and was given command of the regiment in August 1916. In March 1916 Glasgow was given the tasks of raising and commanding the 13th Infantry Brigade. Bean thought him to be:

... the most forcible of three strong brigadiers of the 4th Division. With keen blue eyes looking from under puckered humorous brows as shaggy as a deer-hound's; with the bushman's difficulty of verbal expression but a sure sense of character and situations; with a firm temper, but cool understanding and a firm control of men; with an entire absence of vanity, but translucent honesty and a standard of rectitude that gave confidence both to superiors and subordinates, he could by a frown, a shrewd shake of the head or a twinkle in [the eye] awaken in others more energy than would have been evoked by any amount of exhortation.

The third brigade commander was Duncan John Glasfurd, son of an officer of the Indian Army, educated in Scotland and at the Royal Military College, Sandhurst, commissioned into the Argyll and Sutherland Highlanders, once seconded to the Somali Camel Corps, a graduate of the staff college at Camberley and seconded, in June 1912, to the Australian Military Forces, where he was when war broke out. At first, Glasfurd tried hard to rejoin his regiment, but Bridges had other ideas and the 41 year old captain found himself a staff officer on the headquarters of the 1st Division. Glasfurd did well as a staff officer: he devoted himself to training in Egypt; he brought a degree of British army formality to what was still overwhelmingly a civilian force; he was, according to Bean, 'boyish, loyal and devoted, if somewhat old-fashioned'. If Glasfurd had one disadvantage, however, it was lack of command experience. Until he was appointed to command the 12th Brigade in February 1916, Glasfurd had served exclusively as a staff officer and instructor since his secondment to the Somali Camel Corps in 1904; not exactly the best background to handle the difficult civilian soldiers under his charge.

Still, the 4th Division was demonstrably a better division than the 2nd. As Commander, Cox was experienced and wise, if somewhat sardonic; the 4th had a reasonable mixture of militia and permanents as brigadiers; for staff, it had competent and careful officers. As well, the 4th Division had, because of its leavening of Gallipoli veterans, that undefinable but unmistakable quality of combat wisdom. There were sufficient old soldiers to give the formation the leadership at the lower levels of command necessary once the battles had begun. This division too, had the inestimable advantage of possessing among its subordinate units two of the best battalions of the AIF.

Once such battalion was the 14th, 'Jacka's Mob'; the other was the 48th Battalion, commanded by Lt.-Col. Ray Leane, older brother to the commanding officer of the 28th. Ray Leane's brother, B. B. Leane was the adjutant; a cousin, A. E. Leane was a platoon commander. It was known, throughout the AIF as the Joan of Arc battalion: 'Made of All Leanes'. This battalion was due to take over the most precarious section of the line, from the Windmill to The Elbow.

Leane's battalion had two tasks when it moved into the line. The first was to take over that portion of the OG trenches in its sector, linking with the remnants of Arnold Brown's company on the left. The second task was to clear the Australian wounded which still lay, crowded in the trench, victims of the ferocious artillery fire of the previous two days. Within hours, Ray Leane and his brigade commander, Glasfurd, clashed violently. Glasfurd ordered Leane to occupy the forward trenches with two companies; Leane argued that to do so would expose his troops to unnecessary risks from being overcrowded in trenches registered by the enemy artillery. The two strong officers disagreed publicly, until finally Glasfurd gave Leane a written order to put two companies forward of Pozières. Leane, a man of somewhat difficult temperament, according to Bean, ignored Glasfurd's orders.

In the 14th Battalion, Lt.-Col. C. M. M. Dare also ignored similar orders from his brigade commander, Brand. Like Leane, Dare realised that to crowd his entire battalion into destroyed, well-registered trench lines under virtual constant observation by the Germans was to invite horrendous casualties. Dare opted to hold his portion of the line with just one company, with another company to the rear in the support trench and the other two companies in reserve, out of relative harm. Curiously enough, both Leane and Dare were following the spirit of Gough's intentions. Late on the night of 5 August, the Anzac Corps headquarters logged a signal from Reserve Army headquarters: 'Army commander considers sufficient garrison for OG2 — 4 Vickers and 12 Lewis guns over the whole front now held. OG1 he considers could be held by about four times that garrison provided close touch with artillery maintained. Remainder of garrison can be withdrawn to line from which attack was made.'

OG2 was, of course, the German depth line, intended to be the Australian forward line. At that time, the infantry battalion held eight Lewis guns in the headquarters, to be deployed where the commanding officer thought fit. The Vickers (heavier machine guns) were held in machine gun companies, one company allocated to each brigade. Thus, Gough was suggesting that the OG lines nearest the Germans could be held with two Vickers gun detachments (two guns per detachment, operating in pairs) and twelve Lewis guns, but not necessarily a battalion and a half of troops. In the OG1 lines, which now became the Australian support positions, Gough suggested that the bulk of the Australian strength be concentrated. For the Australian commander, however, several problems arose from Gough's suggestion. Although the OG lines had been assaulted and captured in this sector, they were designed by the Germans to cover assaults from the west, not the east. Yet it was from the east that the inevitable German counter-attack would come.

This instruction might well be seen as merely another example of Gough's interference with what was essentially a divisional or brigade responsibility. Equally however, it is clear that by then, Gough must have had some idea* of the casualties that were being suffered by the troops enduring the almost continual bombardments in virtually unprotected trenches. Gough assessed that it was not necessary to hold this line along its length, particularly as it did not face a continuous German line. Instead, it was sufficient to hold the strong points, provided that close touch was maintained with the artillery. The Australian brigade commanders, particularly the inflexible Glasfurd and Brand, preferred to hold their troops forward, despite the inevitable casualties.

Certainly they regarded any penetration of their lines by the Germans as a grievous blow. Equally, however, they were concerned about the practicality of providing communications to the artillery. Earlier both Walker and Legge had stressed the problems of communication during all phases of their occupation; ultimately such communications depended upon runners rather than signals. Few of the Australian commanders above the battalion level were prepared to allow gaps between defended strong points, either to a flank or to the rear, and so jeopardise these communications. They feared the possibility that isolated machine gun positions — which Gough intended to be both individually and collectively strong — might be captured or shelled into non-existence without the others realising the situation. For these reasons, the Australians were crowded into the forward trenches except where commanding officers like Leane or Dare, men of conspicuous common sense and great moral courage, turned a Nelsonian eye to their orders.

The first stage of relief of the 2nd Division units by the fresh 4th Division battalions took place during the night of 5/6 August. Again, the Reserve Army diary gives us only a bald account: 'There was nothing to report during the night: things were generally quiet except about Pozières, where the shelling was heavy'. The British official historian notes that the relief was 'Accomplished with infinite difficulty, owing to the German bombardment'. Ray Leane, commanding the 48th Battalion, described it simply as his worst experience of the war and another officer said artillery fire that night was the heaviest his battalion had ever endured on relief. Moving up, the historian of the 14th Battalion, Newton Wanliss saw: 'Ghastly sights . . . scores of bodies had been partially buried in the soft earth, and bloody hands and feet protruded at frequent intervals. Boxes of ammunition and rations lay

---

*Despite the vagueness and imprecision of the Reserve Army War Diary.

scattered about where fatigue parties had been annihilated by artillery fire'. Sergeant E. J. Rule, in the same battalion, vividly remembered seeing one shell shock case: '. . . he came along, the picture of terror, and trembling from head to foot. His legs trembled so much that they just about carried him, and that was all'. The German artillery began about 7 p.m.: 'a most terrific shell fire', according to Arnold Brown. At least one battalion of the 2nd Division, the 27th, fled even before the relieving troops arrived. Leane pushed forward through the dead, dying and terrified troops to find its commander, but he had gone, pulling his men back into Sausage Gully. Gradually Leane gained some control but in the noise and the confusion and the constant horror of the artillery, it was a trying task even for this outstanding leader.

Once again, there was a huge gulf between the intentions of the orders and the ability of the troops to carry them out. Leane's battalion managed to occupy the OG1 lines, but could find no survivors of the troops who had attacked and captured OG2. One officer went forward through the barrage, looking for the second German line without much success and pushing so far forward that Arnold Brown mistook them at first for Germans. A 20 year old Victorian university student, Sergeant D. A. Twining, of the 48th Battalion, took ten of the battalion scouts forward of the Windmill, probably the most advanced troops at that time of the entire British offensive.

That morning, 6 August, a strange and silent lull fell across the battlefield. The new troops of the 48th stared in wonderment at the open country beyond them, so very different from anything they had seen in their movement up to the line between Albert and Pozières. With the daylight too, came a blessed pause in the artillery fire. Both sides busied themselves collecting the wounded which lay all around. One German stretcher bearer party approached the new Australian line, arousing the suspicion of Sergeant Twining, who stood up and gestured for the Germans to move back. They ignored him. Again Twining waved them away; again they ignored the young Australian. Finally, Twining fired one round, hitting the leading stretcher bearer. A bag, stuffed as if to resemble a body, fell from the stretcher. Twining's suspicions appeared well founded.

The lull did not last long. By mid-morning the shelling began again to continue through the day, directed by German observers in three balloons and from a number of aircraft. By 5 p.m. the shelling was as heavy as anything the troops had experienced the night before, easing around dusk and then increasing in intensity during the night. That night, the 14th Battalion slipped into position on the left flank of the 48th, with the 15th Battalion, a Queensland unit on the left flank of the 14th holding The Elbow. There Newton Wanliss wrote:

... the German artillery opened up a fearful bombardment. Their guns were innumerable, and were exactly ranged. The drum fire was incessant, and continued all night with unabated fury. 14th men had afterwards many experiences of enemy bombardments, but those who experienced this one always recalled it as surpassing anything that they ever faced, both in its fury and continuity. There were shells from the big 12 inch howitzers down to the little nerve-racking 'whiz-bangs'; there were high explosive shells with sulphur fumes which burnt immediately over head, and there were other shells with neither fumes nor smoke. There was not only a frontal fire, but an enfilade fire from Thiepval.

The very earth, lacerated and torn, rocked and dissolved under the weight and force of the metal blown into it. Both the earth and the heavens seemed rent by this concentrated effort of man's fury. Some men were blown to fragments; others were stunned by concussion alone. The appalling uproar rendered speech useless, whilst trenches were blown in, and communications severed. Most of the men fortunately found cover in some untenanted and commodious German dugouts which had survived previous bombardments.

Rule thought that for continuous shelling:

> ... this night stands out alone in all that I have ever endured ... We all sat huddled in the bottom of the trench resting against each other's knees, constantly showered with falling earth from the bursts. Quite often one of the boys would come along and tell us that their bay had been blown in and so-and-so was buried. Willing hands would quickly get to work and dig them out. To be buried alive by the earth shovelled over him by a shell-burst is just about all a man can stand, and retain his reason. We tried to be cheerful, but the jokes were very feeble.
>
> It was not a bit of wonder that men were being killed like rabbits. Every shell that got into the trench simply cleaned it out, and it was easy to see how one shell could smash up a dozen men. It was only with the greatest difficulty that I could force my way through.

Even though both Leane and Dare had reduced the number of troops that should have been moving up into the front line, the crowding in the support trenches was still heavy. 'In all my experience before or since', wrote Rule, 'I've never seen men so closely packed in a trench. This was the support line, and its left end was on Pozières cemetery'.

The German order for the recapture of the Pozières plateau — Hill 160 position — was issued on 5 August. The German preparations began immediately: heavy artillery was directed to prepare for a counter-attack on the morning of 6 August; the field artillery of three German divisions also began a most thorough and careful preparatory fire. Whether that counter-attack was made on that morning is unclear at this stage. Certainly the senior German commanders, von Boehm and Wellmann, were initially under the impression that the attack had been launched and was successful. The Australians occupying the Windmill position and south of the road reported minor attacks, which were easily beaten back with machine gun fire. By mid-morning on 6 August, largely from information brought back by their reconnaissance patrols, the Germans realised the Australians still held the Windmill. Another counter-attack the following morning, 7 August, was inevitable.

According to Newton Wanliss, the German artillery fire on the night of 6/7 August lasted about eight hours. The main targets were the OG lines, where the Australians were huddled in the inadequate protection offered by the battered and broken trenches or sheltering in what remained of the German dugouts. As well, the Germans shelled areas behind the Australian lines: Sausage Valley, which was the only approach route; Becourt Wood, or what was left of it; the slopes of Tara Hill and even Albert itself.

The main targets, however, were the OG1 lines where the bulk of the Australian defenders were concentrated. That night, OG2 was held only by small groups of men armed with Lewis guns in advanced posts. Just on dawn — the actual time varies from account to account, but with daylight saving, probably about 3 a.m. — the intensity of the barrage altered. Sergeant Rule noticed that the shells were falling further back from his position in the OG1 lines. Rule told his platoon commander who merely laughed and suggested that the anxious sergeant sit down. Rule was not put off by this suggestion. 'I'm getting my rifle and bombs ready, anyhow.' As Rule was slipping a clip of cartridges into his rifle, a soldier came running along the trench crying out: 'Jacka is killed and the Huns have got the Ridge'. Still, Rule's platoon commander was unmoved. 'The poor fellow must be off his head,' he remarked to Rule.

Rule and his platoon commander had moved up during the night. They were still unsure as to where the front was and they were reluctant to fire on men they saw in the dim morning light, not knowing whether they were Australians or Germans. It was not until a man from one of the forward positions came along the trench asking for more Lewis gun crews did Rule and his platoon commander realise the counter-attack had begun in earnest.

The order to 'Stand to' had been shouted along the lines just on dawn, probably beginning in the 15th Battalion holding the trenches due north of the village and west of The Elbow. In the noise and the confusion, however, it is not certain that the order ever reached Rule's position, about 500 metres behind. It is certainly unusual that Rule's platoon was not 'Standing to' at dawn as a matter of course; a practice that had been followed in the British and Australian armies since the Zulu Wars.

The main force of the German counter-attack, launched here by more than three battalions, fell on a sector of the trench manned by a few survivors of the 5th Platoon of the 14th Battalion, and the left flank of the 48th Battalion. The Germans attacked from the direction of Courcelette, using an old track on their left flank to guide the assaulting troops on to the objective, on a frontage of about 600 metres. The right flank of this line, still shrouded in the tricky dawn light, passed just 30 metres in front of a machine gun position occupied by Sergeant Douglas Mortimer, a Victorian grazier, and the nearby platoon position of the 15th Battalion, held by Lieutenant David Dunworth of Sydney. Few defenders had been given such an opportune target.

Rifle and machine guns from both positions opened up, and even in the dim half-light, the Germans presented easy targets. 'But we could not shoot them all', said Mortimer later, and the disciplined line of Germans swept past. On the flank, Sergeant Twining's group, now reduced to four men and a broken Lewis gun, caused a few casualties but not sufficient to check the momentum of the attack.

Without meeting any real opposition in the centre of their assault, the Germans swept over the OG2 lines. Once into the OG1, they were forced to slow down and began bombing their way along the trenches. Even so, here again the opposition was light, for both Dare and Leane had thinned out the number of their troops meant to be holding this sector. Once through the line of the 14th Battalion, the Germans hooked left and captured the remnants of a company of the 48th Battalion. These men had lost their commander early in the assault and his successor ordered the reluctant soldiers to surrender. At that point, the German attack had succeeded, despite heavy casualties on the flanks. They had recaptured a significant section of the OG2 and OG1 lines, and had driven back at least two battalions of Australians.

What followed was one of those odd, almost unreal encounters of the war, an action by a handful of men that managed to change the course of a battle. Bert Jacka was commanding the 5th Platoon of the 14th Battalion, upon whom the main force of the assault had fallen. It was occupying the southern-most position in the OG line with the 48th Battalion on its right. At dawn, Jacka had left the deep dugout where he and his men were sheltering and gone up, only to find the bombardment still heavy in his sector.

In the warmth and comfort of the dugout, Jacka's men were sleeping heavily, a reaction to the strain of the previous night. Jacka went back underground, and attempted to wake them. As he was doing so, two explosions rocked the interior of the dugout, badly wounding several of the sleeping soldiers. The assaulting Germans had reached the dug-out and rolled two grenades down the steps. Jacka immediately fired at the bomber with his revolver but realised that his men were now cut off by the German advance which had rolled over his position. He decided to round up as many unwounded men as he could find and try to make a break through the assault back towards Pozières. To do so took some little time, and as Jacka cautiously emerged, with only seven men still fit, he saw prisoners from the 48th Battalion being marched back towards Courcelette, guarded by a German party about 160 strong.*

Jacka's small group hid until the Germans and the prisoners were almost on them and then, sprang over the back of the trench and charged. Each of the eight Australians was hit immediately by German rifle fire, although at least half of the Germans dropped their rifles and fled. Australians from nearby trenches rose and joined in the mêlée; prisoners grabbed weapons off the guards; other prisoners were shot down helplessly before the guards began to fire on Jacka and his men.

Nearby, Lieutenant Dunworth led an attack on a small group of Germans who had sheltered in shell holes. It was, according to Newton Wanliss, an 'unknown experience . . . Germans were everywhere, and mixed up with our men like players in rival football teams during a match'. Jacka was wounded seven times, once by a bullet that passed through his body under his right shoulder and twice partially stunned by head wounds. Sergeant C. H. Beck of the 48th Battalion, who had joined in Jacka's attack, was killed; another sergeant from the same battalion, despite having his leg blown off by a bomb, crawled to the edge of a trench and yelled encouragement to the Australians until he, too, died.

Under Jacka and Beck, the Australians fought furiously with rifles and bayonets and fists. Jacka is supposed to have killed twenty or more Germans but despite Jacka's efforts, the result was in doubt until a platoon of fresh reserves, ordered forward by Leane, arrived and the Germans suddenly surrendered. 'This brilliant counter-attack', wrote Wanliss, 'against an overwhelming and triumphant enemy was com-pletely successful — all the Australian prisoners were released, the whole of the German escort guarding them was killed or dispersed, and in addition 42 unwounded Germans (including two officers), the

---

*That estimate is based on Wanliss' account. It is probable that the Australian prisoners were being escorted back by a company that had taken part in the initial attack and had been relieved.

survivors of the German escort, were captured'. From his position in the rear, Sergeant Rule watched the stretcher bearers clearing up the wounded and called out to one: 'Who've you got there?' 'I don't know who I've got, but the bravest man in the Aussie Army is on that stretcher just ahead. It's Bert Jacka, and I wouldn't give a Gyppo piastre for him; he is knocked about dreadfully.'

Jacka recovered and years later, told Rule what had happened:

> There were four Huns in a shell hole. All I could see was their heads, shoulders and rifles. As I went towards them, they began firing point blank at me. They hit me three times and each time the terrific impact of the bullets fired at such close range swung me off my feet. But each time I sprang up like a prize-fighter and kept getting closer. When I got up to them, they flung down their rifles and put up their hands. I shot three through the head and put a bayonet through the fourth. I had to do it — they would have killed me the moment I turned my back.
>
> I think another fellow must have fired at me, and missed. I looked around and saw a Hun who must have weighed seventeen or eighteen stone. I aimed at his belly and he almost fell on me . . . A stretcher bearer came, took off my tunic, and fixed me. I asked him to go and bring a stretcher. He went away and I never saw him again. I lay there for a long time, and then began to think of the wounded that were never found. I made up my mind to try and get back by myself . . .

Jacka crawled most of the way back towards the Australian lines before he was found and brought in by the stretcher bearers.

By counter-attacking so vigorously at precisely the right time, Jacka destroyed the success of the German attack. Of course, the platoon commander could have had no idea at the time of the value of his actions; no doubt he saw merely the Australians being escorted back and an opportunity to free his mates. But it was the effect, not the intention, that was important. Bean described Jacka's counter-attack as 'the most dramatic and effective act of individual audacity in the history of the AIF'; Wanliss, justifiably proud to be a member of 'Jacka's Mob', thought it 'a marvellous piece of work, bold in conception, brilliant and heroic in execution, smashing and demoralising to the enemy and fruitful in its results — a splendid piece of bluff carried to a successful and glorious conclusion by a handful of men who had already endured a nerve-racking bombardment of several hours'.

Rule had watched the action from a distance.

> Through my glasses I could see some of our boys standing up and firing point blank at other men. Some figures I could see on their knees praying

for their lives, and several were bayoneting Huns . . . Pretty soon all the Huns who were left got into a communications trench and were brought through us to the rear. About eighty came by us in the trench, and they were certainly the most joyful looking lot of Huns I'd ever seen. They were clean shaven and had hardly a dirty article on them. They looked as if they were off to a wedding and not a hopover.

The 4th Australian Division War Diary records that at 10.30 a.m. on 7 August, Maj.-Gen. Sir Herbert Cox assumed command of the Australian front. Gradually the entire line was reoccupied with Australian troops, with the Queenslanders and the Tasmanians of the 47th Battalion taking over from the 48th. Off to the Australian's right, the British finally secured Munster Alley, and the crest of the ridge east of Pozières, with its main approaches, was now secure. Although the Germans continued to make local counter-attacks against the flanking positions, the assault on the morning of 7 August was their last serious attempt to retake the crest line east of Pozières. Now this high ground, this 'key to the area' was secure. 'Twas a famous victory, although the War Diary of the Reserve Army noted baldly: 'About 5 a.m. the enemy attacked our lines N. of the Windmill on the E. of Pozières: they effected a lodgement, but were driven out. An attack N. of Pozières about the same time by the enemy received the same treatment. Some prisoners were taken in each case'.

13

'Mucky Farm'

[The Australians] had had enough of Gough's constant pressure with demands for energetic action by a staff believed to spend its own energy in boar hunting. The daily reinforcement of failure, with no apparent reason for the sacrifice, made them long to return to Flanders and the paternal presence of the Second Army commander.

General Sir Anthony Farrar-Hockley, The Somme (London, 1983)

In that passage, Farrar-Hockley captures precisely the feelings of the Australian troops at the end of their time on the Somme. But the soldiers were not yet generally expressing the doubts and fears so poignantly related by Alec Raws in his letters home. By the end of the first week of August 1916, the extent of the Australian victories imbued the troops with a clear sense of superiority. They were splendid victories — achieved at appalling loss, certainly, but no less victories for that. The Australians had succeeded where the British had failed. At least the sacrifices since 23 July could be measured in terms of metres gained, of objectives taken, of trenches held. From now on, there was not to be even this slight consolation and the key to success or failure would lie, not in terrain, but in human cost to both sides. For the Australians, the next three weeks were to be the worst of the wearing-down battle.

Gough wanted to swing the Australian attack north along the ridge line, and come in behind the heavily defended Thiepval Ridge position. It seems easy enough now, seventy years or so later, to sit back and criticise Gough's actions at this time. Clearly Thiepval had to be taken; for all his deficiencies as a tactician, Joffre had realised the importance of the position from the very beginning of the offensive six weeks earlier. Even today, it is possible to see the enormous importance of the position. From the top of the Ulster Tower — the memorial to the 36th (Ulster) Division which attacked on 1 July — the advantages held by the German machine gunners in the ruins of the village are still apparent; from Lutyens' Thiepval Memorial itself, built on the site of the Thiepval Château, the folds and undulations of this gentle country are revealed in stark relief. All the advantages rested with the defenders.

For the soldiers in the front lines the grand tactical plans of red-tabbed generals were, of course, both remote and obscure. The soldiers' struggles were confined to the smaller areas of trenches and positions, battered by the incessant shelling but optimistically marked on headquarters maps or reduced to a simple geometrical expression of letters and numerals.

Not that Gough proposed using the Australians in splendid isolation. His attack on Thiepval was to be a co-ordinated and detailed attack by the Reserve Army, on both sides of the River Ancre. North of the river, the divisions of his V Corps would attack to the north-east; south of the river, the divisions of the II Corps would attack directly north, on to the very strength of the German position. But these attacks could not take place unless and until the Australians extended their line along the Pozières Ridge towards Thiepval. Once that high ground had been captured, Gough had a secure right flank for his attack on to Thiepval itself.

By capturing the Windmill position, the Australians had driven a salient deep into the German front line. It bulged out, cheekily and defiantly, threatening the Thiepval fortress, occupying the high ground, dominating the surrounding countryside. This salient included the ruined village of Pozières and the high ground of the Windmill, and extended almost to the strong German position developed on the ruins of Mouquet Farm. On the Australian left, the Germans still held ground overlooking the approaches through the ruins of the village and then along the Ridge. Any movement in these trenches immediately attracted heavy artillery fire, yet this was the only route to the Australian forward position. Every soldier and every item of equipment had to pass along these trenches: food and water, ammunition, barbed wire, sandbags and wire pickets, shovels and stores. Within battalions, companies were relieved using the same routes: within brigades, battalions swapped positions along the same crowded and clearly identifiable trenches. All day and all night, the shelling continued, easing in intensity only between dawn and about 7 a.m., when the heavy ground mists, the exhaustion of the German gunners and the replenishment of their ammunition supplies combined to give a few hours of relative peace.

Sergeant Rule described how his platoon was relieved during this stage of the fighting. Although the remainder of his unit was filing out of the line, no new troops came to Rule's dugout, so he decided to wait until the following morning:

> ... when things would calm down a little, rather than go back through the shell fire, which was always pretty heavy late in the afternoon. In the morning we made a run for it, but only got as far as Pozières cemetery

when a strafe started. We were in a new trench, and it was very narrow, but if we ran before, we bolted now. One fellow, who had not fastened his gear securely, began to shed it — first his puttees, then his pack. He had the hardiness to stop and start fixing himself up; but the curses of those who were behind made him leave half his stuff in the trench.

The first phase of the July fighting had brought the Australians first to the Roman road through the village, and then across into the village itself; the next phase had secured and held the high ground of the Windmill. In doing so, however, all three Australian divisions available to the Reserve Army commander had been used, and had suffered heavily. These casualties did not surprise GHQ for, even as the 2nd Division was assaulting the Windmill position, Haig's staff was deciding to replace them with the Canadian Corps, then still in Ypres. According to the staff planners, the final Australians would leave this sector in early September.

First, however, they had to secure Gough's right flank, and this could only be done by a series of small narrow frontal attacks launched along the ridge line towards Mouquet Farm; 'Mucky Farm' or 'Moo-cow Farm' as it was called by the Australians. The farm buildings had been burned in 1914. In August 1916 little remained of the ruins except a beam or two protruding from a patch of white cement rubble. Along the ridge line between the Australian position and the ruins lay three main trenches: the first along the Ridge north of Pozières; the second through an old chalk quarry which opened towards the Australians and the third, which included the farm site itself, on the reverse slope of a small rise. Known as Park Lane, Skyline Trench and Fabeck Graben respectively, these trenches posed formidable obstacles, not only to the Australians assaulting along the ridge line, but to anyone attempting to attack up the slight indentations on to the high ground.

Gradually, the battalions of the 4th Division edged forward along the spine of the Ridge, capturing a dozen metres or so here and there, establishing small posts, all the time extending their salient. On the night of 8 August, Brand's brigade attacked and held the trench known as Park Lane, advancing behind a 'creeping barrage' timed to advance as the troops moved forward. Some of Rule's battalion, the 14th, and the Queenslanders of the 15th, actually advanced 137 metres beyond the Park Lane trenches without realising where they were, so great was the damage and so few were the landmarks.

The British troops, who were to attack at the same time and secure their left flank, failed. Several machine guns enfiladed the British line and most of the attackers died without reaching anywhere near the objective. Once again, the successes achieved by the Australians could not be exploited because of failures by the British. The Australian line was withdrawn. The next night, the Australians attacked again, this time securing an objective on their left flank and extending their front into what had previously been a British sector of the trench. That day, another factor entered the fighting. Light rain began to fall, not enough yet to turn the chalky soil into the glutinous mud that characterised the fighting around the Ypres salient the following year, but enough to make life even more unpleasant for the front line troops.

Newton Wanliss records that the men of the 14th Battalion were showing signs of exhaustion, despite the efforts of its commanding officer to rotate his companies through the line: '. . . the incessant drumfire rendered it very difficult to obtain sleep, and several had been evacuated for nervous breakdowns'. Even so, Rule thought that the 14th had not been given its proper share of work during this week:

> . . . the brigade 'hopped the bags' three times in all, but for some reason or other our battalion only had to go out one night, to straighten out a kink after the 15th Battalion's hopover. The reason for our immunity I don't know — maybe it was on account of our diminished numbers through losses in the Hun counter-attacks.

Once Park Lane had been captured, Gough determined that the next objective for the Australians should be a preliminary operation on the section of trench that included the small, open quarry on the Pozières-Thiepval road. This attack was planned for the night of 12/13 August, again to be supported by British attacks on the left flank. In the meantime, Cox planned to capture as much ground between his present position and the objective for 12/13 August. Advanced posts were flung out; the Germans counter-attacked with determination, using fresh troops. All the time, the artillery fire fell on the newly won positions. The strain on the troops was enormous. Even those in companies rotated out of the front line trenches were exposed to the bombardment, either as they waited in the support lines or toiled through the night to bring food, water and ammunition up to their mates. Now, there were no great successes to lift morale and the flagging spirits. Time after time, the battalions were launched into seemingly hopeless attacks on narrow frontages.

Even when they succeeded, the Australians found that the flanks had not moved and that the line had to be ruled off more neatly. Gains were handed back in the interests of tactical neatness. This too, has become another cliché of the First World War: Generals ordering local attacks merely to rule off a kink in the line. But an advance in one sector of the line which was not matched by similar advances on its flanks posed immediate security problems to the troops in that salient, hence the reason for the apparent obsession with 'kinks in the line'. Gough and his staff, however, did not share this particular tactical obsession; they were quite prepared to force the Australians to continue their narrow, shallow attacks effectively behind the main German lines.

Initially Gough's major assault on Mouquet Farm was planned for the night of 13/14 August. On that day, the Reserve Army commander was visited by officers from Haig's staff who warned him that the Germans had reinforced this sector with fresh troops. Gough was to be prepared for counter-attacks.

All that evening, the Germans shelled the Australian positions, for they had realised Gough's intentions almost from the beginning. By itself this was not surprising, for the failure of the British divisions on the left of the Australians to secure much new ground meant that Gough was left with just the one course: a predictable and easily re-pulsed advance along the high ground of the Ridge. The burden of the Australian attack was to fall on Glasgow's 13th Brigade, consisting of the 49th, 50th, 51st and 52nd Battalions, drawn mainly from the smaller Australian states.

Again the planning for this attack was dominated by Gough. As the divisional commander, Cox had a difficult task. He had to defer to Birdwood and particularly to Brudenell White in the Anzac Corps headquarters; as an Indian Army officer commanding an Australian division he had also to take notice of Gough, who was determining objectives for the Australian Division. Again, Brudenell White at-tempted to defuse a potentially difficult situation. With Birdwood's authority the tactful, careful staff officer suggested a plan of attack to Cox. But White's planning for this attack was hampered by the lack of information about the defences at Mouquet Farm. The farm lay in a slight hollow, in 'dead' ground for most of the observation posts around the battlefield. In particular, White's planning had to take into account a German trench line about 500 metres east of the farm position, on a slight rise. This trench line was about 400 metres from the most ad-vanced Australian position; clearly too far for troops to advance in the attack, even when supported by heavy artillery fire. 'Jumping off trenches' would have to be prepared.

Cox, however, took a rather more relaxed view of the difficulties confronted by his troops. He believed that White was being unduly pessimistic about the difficulties his division faced, and argued that he could complete the attack in one phase, rather than the two suggested by White.

Cox planned merely to surround Mouquet Farm, believing it to be of no great strength. This planning, however, was made academic by

German successes in the afternoon of 13 August. The British troops who had taken Skyline trench to the west suffered a ferocious counter-attack and were forced to withdraw. And without that trench position, any attack on Mouquet Farm itself was out of the question.

Even so, the Germans were still expecting an attack. Near Thiepval, the German *26th Reserve Division* captured some British documents which were interpreted to mean that Mouquet Farm must be captured at all costs that evening, (13 August). 'The staff of the *XIX Corps* now became aware that it was the clear intention of the British to force their way from Pozières and Mouquet Farm by repeated attacks, in order to render untenable the German position further west.' While this inter-pretation by the German intelligence officers was not strictly accurate — the loss of Skyline Trench had made such an assault virtually im-possible — it had one important consequence. From then on, the Germans assumed any movement in the British and Australian trenches near Mouquet Farm was part of the preparations for the inevitable assault. German reserves were readied and given specific tasks when the assault was launched; artillery concentrations were directed on the Australian salient and particularly the narrow neck through which all supplies had to pass.

After the British failure, Gough gave the Australians a modified objective: while the British were to attack and retake Skyline trench, the Australians were to assault and capture the trench line north of the quarry and the Fabeck Graben line to the east of the farmhouse.

This attack was planned to begin at 10 p.m. on the night of 14 August, under a full moon. The bombardment had made preparations almost impossible. 'During the evening of the 14th,' wrote the British official historian, 'the Australian front positions and communications were heavily shelled, causing such confusion and loss that a properly co-ordinated advance became out of the question.' Just how much 'out of the question' is clear from the scribbled messages in the war diaries and the signal logs of the Australian units then in the line. The incessant artillery fire, the exposed and open trenches, the mounting casualties and the looming and apparent futility of the attacks were severally taking their toll. For the first time in this battle, whole units began to resist their leaders. This was not the odd example of 'funk' or 'shell shock'; now a collective and terrible fear gripped the soldiers in the front lines. At 7.55 p.m., the battalion headquarters of the 50th Battal-ion, the left flank of the planned Australian advance, recorded the following message from one of its rifle companies:

> We cannot move. We have few tools, few bombs, no water, and the men
> are badly shaken. At present we are digging a number out. I have too

few men to take up the frontage, and after consulting the company commanders have decided to remain fast. Am notifying 13th Battalion.

It is difficult to imagine the conditions under which such a message could be sent. Here was a company commander deciding on his own volition that he would not participate in a planned attack, and that particular company commander's views were shared by Lt.-Col. A. M. Ross, the commanding officer of the 51st Battalion further round in the salient, and also by the commanding officer of the 13th Battalion. Ross also wrote a hurried note to Glasgow:

> Both 13th C.O. thinks, and it is my genuine (not depressed) opinion that it would be a mistake to press the offensive further locally in this salient. We are heavily shelled from due E. right round to N.W., and the communications are simply *awful*. It really requires some days' solid work. Water and ration-carrying is most precarious. The boys are sticking it well, but are so congested that it will be most difficult to deploy tonight. Do not worry about us, but we want WATER and digging tools always.
> Our artillery are bombarding our own front trenches (heavies!!!)

One officer of the 13th Battalion, Captain Harry Murray, reported that C Company was rattled and had only 35 men. Murray had taken the place of Captain F. M. Barton who had become lost in the mist on the morning of 11 August and was never seen or heard of again. There was little that Glasgow, as the brigade commander, could do. There was no time to come forward to the worried officers and frightened soldiers, no radio net over which to speak and encourage the men under his command. Instead, he sent messages by runner to the battalion commanders, pointing out the importance of the attacks as they had been planned and underlining the risks to the other units should one fail to cross the start line on time. Yet not all the 13th companies were rattled. On the day before, one of the 13th sergeants took advantage of a slight lull in the fighting during which stretcher bearers from both sides worked under the cover of the morning mist. He walked across to the German trench, chatted briefly with its occupants, noted its condition and walked cheekily away. From this information, the 13th knew it would be attacking a trench with numerous dugouts practically undamaged by shell fire.

One officer of the 13th, Major T. Wells, thought the battalion was 'worn out by six strenuous days at full tension'. Even so, the feeling was that this was the chance to show that the battalion was still as good as it was at Gallipoli, despite the expansion earlier in 1916. On the left of the 13th, the 50th Battalion was to take the Mouquet Farm position itself; the 13th in the centre and the 51st on the right were to assault and capture the strong trench line, Fabeck Graben, to the east of the farm.

Wells wrote:

> At zero hour — at 10 o'clock — our barrage came down but this time it was too far ahead; so far ahead, in fact, that the enemy rifle and machine gun fire was absolutely unchecked. Nothing daunted, the first wave 'hopped the bags' and sprinting through the terrific hail of bullets, actually cheered and yelled as they approached the first trench of the Fabeck Graben system. This charge was the most dashing display of reckless courage I saw throughout the war — entirely different from the dour determination of the advances in 1918.

Harry Murray, in the other company of the 13th, noted a similar success. The two companies of the 13th Battalion sheltered in the shallow jumping off trenches until the barrage began and then, as Wells described, charged forward. Here, the Australians might have been helped by the confusion in the German trench which was crowded by relieving troops. Even so, the small arms fire directed at the attackers was intense, 'the hottest fire I ever saw, even including the peninsula', according to Murray. It was the sudden savage momentum of the 13th Battalion attack that carried them into the German trenches. The C.S.M. of the attacking company, George Hardy, flung a pick he was carrying at a German machine gun crew, quickly following up with bombs and an assault into the pit. Hardy took eleven prisoners and nine bullets in his thigh.

On the flanks, however, the other Australian battalions made little progress. On the left in the 50th Battalion, Captain H. E. Armitage, a 19 year old Adelaide university student, heard an order to retire but quickly countermanded it and stopped a growing panic. Armitage gathered a small party of men around him and attempted to dig in around the open quarry, but was soon forced to withdraw away from the fire of German machine guns. On the right of the 13th, the 51st met with similar failure and Murray could not establish any contact on this flank. The 13th was on its own.

The effective command of the 13th Battalion attack fell to Harry Murray who, as a timber-getter and miner in the south-west of Western Australia, had enlisted in the AIF in October 1914. Murray was then 30, an experienced bushman who had spent six years in the militia in his native Tasmania, then moving to Western Australia in search of work. His military career is best summarised in the words of the 16th Battalion history:

To Murray belongs the honour of rising within three and a half years from a machine gun private to the command of a machine gun battalion of 64 guns, and of receiving more fighting decorations than any other infantry soldier in the British army in the Great War — rewards and decorations every one of them richly deserved.

Within a month of landing at Gallipoli, Murray had been promoted to lance-corporal and been awarded the Distinguished Conduct Medal. Because of heavy officer casualties in the British 29th Division, suitable candidates for commissions were sought among the Australians. Murray's name was submitted and recommended for transfer to the British army but Monash, then commanding the brigade, blocked the move. Instead, the former bushman was commissioned in the AIF as the machine gun officer in his original battalion of the 13th.

Later, he wrote that:

> Cowardice — or self-preservation — which is practically the same thing, is the first law of nature, and while some men may be so constituted that they require no artificial stimuli, I cannot make any such claim. I fought many a hard battle (to put it bluntly) between duty and funk, but the hardest of all, in which the decision had to be made in a split second, and while fleeing from the enemy was [at the battle of Pozières].

It became clear to Murray that the Germans were trying to cut off the small party of the 13th while at the same time attacking strongly from the front along their communications trenches.

'Immediate retreat was essential, and to effect this under such hostile pressure it was necessary to hold the enemy in check, while retreating along the captured trench, falling back successively on to a number of hastily thrown up strongpoints.' Murray and his men had run very short of hand grenades.

> . . . the cool, heady, courageous men who pressed us were well aware of our disabilities, and pushed their advantage relentlessly. Cleverly they mixed their attacks, twice trying an 'over-the-top', enveloping movement but each time a fierce and deadly response from our riflemen and Lewis gunners taught them the futile and dangerous nature of such tactics. From thence on, they relied on bombing entirely. Altogether we retired to seven successive points, we kept the enemy well in check all the time, and got our wounded away. Our men were cool, confident and grimly determined, despite the continuous pressure.

The Chalk Pit, near Pozières, another view. Note the dugouts with the sandbagged entrances and the field cookers in the foreground. (EZ112 AWM)

Above
General Birdwood (in peaked cap and Sam Browne belt) talking with troops of the 1st Division after the first spell in the line at Pozières. (Q946 IWM)

Below
The marching troops are from the 6th Brigade after their first tour in the line at Pozières. Watching from the bank are troops of the 2nd Brigade, who had already been relieved. Both brigades were to find themselves back in the line for a second tour very quickly. (EZ92 AWM)

Australian troops returning from the line. This photograph was taken near Contay in August 1916. (Q1047 IWM)

Australian wounded in a trench waiting to be evacuated to hospital during the battle for Pozières Ridge. (Q4055 IWM)

Mouquet Farm, before and after. The top photograph shows the fine farm buildings before the war. It was the country residence of a local factory owner. The Germans fortified the buildings by digging deep under the foundations. The second photograph shows the farm after the Australian, Canadian and British assaults. Although the attention is drawn to the devastation, one should also notice the fine observations afforded to the Germans over the Pozières area, which meant the German artillery fire was both reliable and accurate. (J181 E5 AWM)

Above
German shells bursting on the village of Pozières when it was held by the Australians. (G1534e AWM)
Below
A British shell bursting on the OG lines near the Windmill at Pozières on 1 August 1916. The trenches still formed part of the German front-line system. (G1534c AWM)

Above
German shells bursting on the Australian lines on 28 August 1916. The remains of the barbed wire entanglement in the right of the photograph show the effect of the continued shelling. It was through this wire that the 28th Battalion attacked on the night of 4 August. (Q909 IWM)

Below
The trench system known as 'Centre Way' running through the ruins of Pozières. The view is towards the high ground and Mouquet Farm. (EZ 100 AWM)

Above
A 6 inch, 26 cwt howitzer being manhandled through the mud near Pozières in September 1916. The troops in this photograph are British gunners who had probably been firing in support of the Australian attacks. (Q1490 IWM)

Below
Unveiling of the memorial to the 1st Australian Division, near Pozières, on 8 July 1917. This memorial, to the south-west of the ruined village, has been replaced by a stone obelisk. (Q2598 AWM)

Yet they so nearly failed. At the fourth strongpoint, the Australians' supply of bombs was exhausted. Murray could hear the

> ... excited guttural voices together with the rattle of enemy accoutrements, and I experienced the usual fierce struggle between natural promptings and duty, but *the discipline of the AIF enabled me to see it out.* [Emphasis in the original]. Even in those hectic moments I had experienced many a cold shiver, as I thought of the bayonets of the counterattacking force, because it seemed to me, as I ran, that I was almost within reach of those lethal, shining blades.

Like his men, Murray ran, but as the commander, he was also the last man out of each position. Just as his men had reached the fifth post, he saw a German bomb drop one of the two men in front of him.

> The survivor, half-dazed by the explosion, wounded superficially by metal fragments, and not comprehending what had happened, continued his flight. I jumped over the body of the prostrate man, who appeared to be dead, but just as I did so, his eyes opened and it was plain that he was alive, but how badly wounded it was impossible to say. His leg was doubled and twisted, and although he did not speak, his eyes were eloquent.

Murray then fought what he called his hardest battle, between an almost insane desire to continue running and save his own life, or to stop and help a wounded comrade, in what he called unashamedly 'the sacred traditions of the AIF'.

> Surely I must be bayoneted if I stopped for an instant. The enemy were coming up at the double, having no opposition. I often dread to think what I might have done. I was safe enough at the time, and all I had to do was keep on going; there was only a straight run of 50 yards to my mates, and despite that poor twisted leg, those mute lips and pathetic eyes, it was really only mechanical habit engendered by strict discipline that forced me to do what I did. I dropped on to my shaking knees, caught him by the arms, and pulled him on to my back. He helped like a hero with his one sound leg, and off we staggered with Fritz just coming into our bay. We outpaced him, however, largely because the impetuosity of his advance had more than once been checked. Already he had been pulled up with a jerk four times, and such things test the mettle of the bravest and most seasoned troops. At last I had reached the haven of temporary safety, and now had others to support us. I was once more among my mates, and the wounded digger was safe, for a little while, at all events.

The troops were almost at their wits' end.

> It looked as if we were to be reduced to our last resources — the bayonet — but then I heard dear old Bob Henderson's voice asking for me. He was our battalion's bombing officer, and I called out promptly, 'Here I am Bob — have you any bombs?' and back came his reply, like a returning wave, and couched in strong Australianese: 'ANY BLOODY AMOUNT! THROWERS TO THE FRONT!' ... Bob and his men exchanged deadly compliments with the enemy, beating them backwards for over 100 yards of the trench; the breathless crisis was over at last, and we retired in our own time, strolling over to the jumping off positions which were to be permanently held. This dramatic reversal enabled all of us to obtain souvenirs, as the Germans had been there in force, and Bob carried back one of the German machine guns we had captured.

Murray's account is worth including in detail for, although written some 19 years later, it is the best surviving record of what Bean described as 'one of the most skilfully conducted fights in the history of the AIF'. It was also a perfectly executed example of arguably the most difficult military exercise, the opposed withdrawal, and showed outstanding leadership and skill by a man who had been commissioned in the field without the benefit of any formal officer training. Moreover, Murray's remarks about discipline — 'a system enforced by the AIF [that] transformed thousands of men, nervy and highly strung like myself, enabling them to do work which, without discipline, they would have been quite incapable of performing' — provide a fascinating and revealing counterpoint to the opinions of Haig and his staff.

On 17 August, three days after this ill fated and abortive attack, Captain Armitage wrote home to his parents. His letter began starkly: 'Since writing to you, I've been in Hell'. Judging from his letters home, Armitage was a thoughtful and careful young man, concerned about his abilities as a commander of troops and anxious that his training of them was both suitable and adequate. 'My boys have great confidence in themselves,' he wrote, 'and from what I can gather from the old brigade, I've been right in what I have taught them . . . bomb-throwing, bayonet, fighting, trench-building, passage of information. If they fail, it won't be through lack of proper instruction.'

Armitage had reached Gallipoli with the first reinforcements for the 10th Battalion in the 3rd Brigade. Before moving into the line at Pozières, he had spent time with his old comrades who had already been through the fighting, checking their experiences against his own at Gallipoli, ensuring that the emphasis in his platoon's training was correct. Like many other young subalterns, the thought of decorations crossed his mind. He wrote to his parents that it would be nice, to win a M.C., 'but I'm not really concerned for decorations so long as my boys don't finish up killed'. His letters also reflect that serene confidence of colonial Edwardian 19 year olds. 'I will go into action with the calm assurance that I have done my duty by my men and my country. If I happen to fall, I rest content with the knowledge that I have played the game.'

Five days before this attack, Armitage was anxious. 'I'm still disappointed at being out of action. I have had the boys at concert pitch for so long. They are very disappointed.' That disappointment was soon to turn to horror. As we have noted, the 50th was on the exposed left flank of the attack. Here, the trench lines into which they moved were, in Armitage's words, 'absolutely smashed'. The 50th had moved westwards after the loss of Skyline Trench the previous night; and this move exposed the troops to even greater shell fire. 'For four and a half hours, the Huns poured shells on to us', Armitage wrote of his first night in the line. By the time his battalion was due to attack — 'a very difficult stunt' in Armitage's words — it had lost about two-thirds of its men. 'After three nights of heavy digging, we now had to go out to the left and dig in to Skyline. We got out okay . . . but Fritz spotted us and made our lives precarious with machine guns . . .' Armitage tried hard to get his men to dig in, but the bombardment and the machine gun fire made it almost impossible. Patrols which pushed out to the right flank could not make any contact with Murray's 13th Battalion; either Murray's troops had gone past Armitage's party or the latter's patrols were not going out far enough to make contact.

> I lost 43 men in a very short hour. All that night Fritz rained his shells on us and the next day too. It was terrible. I thought it would never pass. At 9 p.m. we were relieved but even then the troubles did not end. We were shelled all the way home . . . Our boys earned their name 'The Fighting 50th', four days of hell, four nights of double hell and one issue of water . . . Anyway, we've opened the way to Mouquet Farm and probably Thiepval as well.

Sadly, Armitage's optimism was misplaced. The Reserve Army War Diary gives us the bare summary of the night's events:

> During the night the 4th Australian Division made a further attack to the north of Pozières, but the right battalion was held up by machine gun fire, and their objective was not gained. The centre battalion captured a trench full of Germans, taking several prisoners. They were then heavily counter-attacked, and not being in touch on either flank, were compelled

to fall back to their original position. The left battalion were unable to advance their right flank and were also forced to fall back to their original line.

For only the second time since they had entered the battle, at Pozières, the Australians were severely checked. Although Murray's troops reached the outskirts of the Mouquet Farm defences, they were forced to retire; the gains of that night were lost even before dawn. And the battle had exhausted the 4th Division, particularly the three battalions that had taken part in the attack. In nine days, the division had lost 4,649 men, with the 13th Battalion losing 18 officers and 368 other ranks, the 48th 25 officers and 610, the 47th 13 officers and 354, and the 45th 10 officers and 438, the 50th 8 officers and 406 and the 51st 6 officers and 295. Now, it was the turn of the 1st Division again.

On 15 August, Haig visited Gough. The Commander-in-Chief was perturbed about the apparent lack of co-ordination between Gough's Reserve Army and Rawlinson's Fourth Army. Haig's instructions to his army commanders were explicit, sensible and well-considered: no longer should Gough continue his attacks without first co-ordinating these operations with Rawlinson who was planning attacks for 18 and 22 August. Any operations that Gough was planning north of the Ancre should be postponed because of a shortage of troops, but he could continue with the minor operations such as the assault on Mouquet Farm. There were other problems in the Reserve Army. Lt.-Gen. Sir Thomas Morland, commanding the British X Corps, was not aggressive enough for Gough who asked Haig to replace both commander and staff with the newly promoted Sir Claud Jacob and his staff from II Corps. About this time, Gough also managed to take a couple of days leave in England but chaffed under the enforced idleness. 'I want to get on with things', he wrote. 'We are breaking in bit by bit and we must not stop until we have made the gap. It would be terrible to ask our men to begin their attacks all over again on fresh defences next year.'

Of course, Gough was right; it was the 'steady, methodical, step-by-step advance' ordered by Haig and carried out, with scrupulous regard to orders, by his subordinate commanders. But it was not a tactical approach that endeared the senior British commanders to the Australian troops. Now, some of that ill-feeling was perhaps even rubbing off on Birdwood. Bean writes that the Anzac Corps commander knew 'and in all probability approved [of] the army commander's intentions' to keep breaking in bit by bit. In his speeches to the troops, Birdwood was always enthusiastic:

> .. they [had] drubbed the Germans and he was sure they were all anxious to get back and kill some more. Some caught his spirit; many more listened grimly to his praises, and called them by a harsh Australian name for idle flattery; a certain number suspected that the desire to furnish a success had caused him to pledge them to an impossible task.

When Birdwood visited the 1st Brigade and Brig.-Gen. Smyth called for cheers from his men; Iven Mackay in the 4th Battalion thought the response 'very ragged'. B. W. Champion was one of the soldiers on that parade.

> It was an awful bother stripping our web equipment to parade in belt and bayonet but it was a beautiful day and that certainly appealed to the boys. [Birdwood] rubbed his hands together as if he was very pleased and said 'I have some wonderful news for the 1st Brigade, beautiful stirring news'. We wondered whether we were going for a six months' spell to Paris or something. Then he brought out, 'We will all be in a serious action again in a few days'. You could hear going down the line 'You old bastard, etc.'. Birdwood must have heard it too, but he didn't bat an eyelid. He is and looks a splendid soldier and knows his AIF.

The 1st Division was still one-third under strength, with the infantry battalions most heavily affected. As the troops moved back into the line, there was a new wariness and a new suspicion; the veterans now knew what to expect. Even so, they were horrified to discover the extent of the desolation and the conditions of the trenches they were taking over. In the 4th Battalion's War Diary, Iven Mackay noted his troops discovered two abandoned Lewis guns and a number of wounded Australians. The 4th Battalion was on the extreme left of the Australian line. 'No British troops in trenches on our left for 500 yards. This is a very vulnerable point, and an enemy advance on a wide front could walk through unmolested to Pozières.' The future commander of the New Guinea Force and High Commissioner to India went in search of the British troops supposed to be on his left, discovered two subalterns of the 1/4th Oxford and Buckinghamshire Light Infantry and ordered them to carry a message to their commanding officer: the gap in the line was to be filled immediately.

Lieutenant Mathew Absom of the 6th Battalion moved up with his platoon on 17 August:

... trench blown to bits when I took over ... spent time in consolidating strongpoint. There was a so-called strongpoint out in front, but it wasn't too strong ... I tried to find the place during the day but the guide Private Griffiths couldn't find [it]. Shells were landing all around us ...

Walker had been given two tasks for his division: to complete the attack on Mouquet Farm and surround it; to strike eastwards and capture the new German trenches dug opposite the Windmill. But again, the same problems that had faced the 4th Division confronted Walker's troops. Time and time again, the perils of assaulting over distances greater than about 100 metres had been revealed; it was necessary for the Australians to complete a jumping off trench closer to Fabeck Graben. As well, Walker's attack also had to be timed to coincide with the assault on Guillemont by Rawlinson's Fourth Army on 18 August. The Australians also needed the support of the British II Corps on their left, and this formation had to move its line up to coincide with the Australian trenches. The gap which Mackay ordered closed when he took over had disappeared, but the British trench line still described a great dog-leg to the south, exposing the Australian flank.

The menial tasks confronting the Australians might have been implacably dull had it not been for the bombardment. By day, work was impossible; the slightest movement above ground brought instant artillery fire. If the Germans saw movement in the trenches, they judged — often rightly enough — that a relief was taking place and that too was met with another terrible barrage. The diaries and letters have a kind of terrible similarity as the soldiers grappled with the incomplete tools of their language to describe the experience.

In those terrible middle days of August, the Germans continued to counter-attack and attempted to regain the high ground of the Ridge: an exploratory nibble here, a strong patrol there, all the time probing for a gap in the lines, a weakness which might be exploited. The Reserve Army War Diary records one such attempt:

During the night 16/17th a small party of enemy left their trenches, ... and appeared to be about to attack the front of the I. A. & N.Z. A Corps, but were dispersed by our Lewis guns. Further attacks by the enemy continued throughout the night, none being successful. In one case the enemy attacked with seven lines of infantry, but were driven back with heavy losses. During the morning a hostile aeroplane fell in flames between Pozières and the Leipzig salient.

In his diary that day Lieutenant Absom noted he 'saw a German plane set on fire by one of our machine guns. The petrol caught fire the whole body of the machine was ablaze. The two airmen dropped down and I had a good view of the whole thing with my glasses . . .' However, Absom, who was in the forward trenches at this time, makes no mention of the strong German counter-attack.

It is not surprising. When the first Germans began to appear on the evening of 16 August, they were mistaken for an Australian work party. In fact, they were the first line of assault troops, filing into position for the attack. Just after dark, the German attack was launched. According to one Australian officer, the Germans rose from their hiding places, 'gave a feeble cheer' and charged the nearest Australian positions. Immediately, the Australians fired with Lewis guns and rifles: the attack faltered and stopped. Later the Germans recorded that someone had given the order to retire — *Zuruck! Kehrt Marsch!* — for which they blamed the Australian defenders. With some justification, too, for it was a common enough ploy by Australian patrols to escape capture in No Man's Land. All through that night, desultory assaults were launched against the Australians. Desultory because, given the sparseness of the troops on the ground, a concerted effort would almost certainly have pushed the Australians off the Ridge. Here, it was the Australians' reputation as soldiers, as much as their actual fighting skills, which brought about the apparent reluctance on the part of the Germans.

Yet the Germans intended this to be their major counter-attack. Not only did they have a clear idea of Gough's intentions from the captured document, but they had also interrogated a British officer captured by the *29th Regiment*. This officer, who has remained nameless, told the Germans that Gough would not attempt to attack Thiepval directly but would instead, direct the efforts of his army to cutting off the stronghold by breaking through at Mouquet Farm.

Unless the full weight of the counter-attack had fallen on Absom's platoon (which clearly it did not) there was probably no good reason why the young officer should have noted the event. More important to him — certainly more interesting to him — was the horrible sight of the German aircraft being shot down in flames and the two airmen falling from it. A platoon commander's war is necessarily restricted to what he can see and what he is told.

Reading through the letters and diaries of the soldier for this period, one is struck by the great resignation with which they faced their tasks. They had driven this great wedge in behind the German position; they had captured churned over fields and the devastated Ridge which others had failed to take. Yet now those successes were behind them. They were battering against the very strength of the German positions and with under-strength battalions, patched with reinforcements. The difficulties for officers and soldiers alike were horrendous: communications between the front trenches and the forward headquarters were poor, almost non-existent; the ground had been so blasted by artillery as to be unrecognisable. On 17 August, Smyth, commanding the 1st Brigade, was forced to go forward and confirm for himself the position of his front line, so conflicting were the reports from the troops.

Howell-Price, commanding the 3rd Battalion, also went forward into the muddy trenches of his front line, personally shooting compass bearings to determine his whereabouts. Howell-Price's view conflicted with Smyth's; both conflicted with the staff officers at the Divisional Headquarters who knew, with that glorious certainty born of map-reading at leisure, where the trenches were supposed to be. All this might seem amusing, a light-hearted variation on the theme of geographical embarrassment, except that this was the night the preparatory fire for the divisional attack was to begin. And it began, promptly at 6 p.m. Heavy shells fell into the front line of the 3rd Battalion. For nearly an hour it continued; Howell-Price sent two messages back, one with an artillery officer and one with 'a war correspondent' who could only have been Bean himself. As Bean notes: 'Both hurried back to advanced telephone stations and sent them, both were late'. Finally, at 6.45 p.m. Howell-Price's message got through. Under the circumstances, it is a masterpiece of politeness: 'Could this matter have attention, please? At present I am endeavouring by all means possible to stop our artillery from firing, and it is now 45 minutes since I sent my first message and one gun is still firing with disastrous effect'.

Howell-Price had been right, Smyth was out by about 200 metres and the divisional staff by about 300 to 400 metres. But establishing the accuracy of one's map-reading by artillery fire has its hazards.

It was hardly the most propitious beginning for an attack. Although the artillery fire was eventually lifted off the Australian trench, the damage had been done. All that night and the following day, the artillery continued to fire as preparation for attack along the ridge line back to Mouquet Farm. This attack, planned for 8 p.m. on 18 August, was timed to coincide with the attack of the 2nd Brigade eastward on to the new trenches opposite the Windmill.

'Order, Counter-Order, Disorder' is an old military cliché. It is true here. Again, the attack northwards was postponed, this time to coincide with the main British attack. To change the timing of an attack meant more than simply informing the troops waiting in their jumping off trenches; it also meant an adjustment to the artillery fire plan. In this attack, the Australians were to advance behind the new 'creeping barrage' which would be adjusted according to a pre-arranged timetable to fall about 100 to 150 metres in front of the advancing troops. The variation to the artillery fire plan was communicated to the batteries, but not to the waiting infantry — at least, not in sufficient time to brief troops and change attack plans.

At this distance in time, the events of that night are almost impossible to relate with any accuracy; even Bean's account is necessarily vague and confused. This much is known: of the brigade which attacked eastwards on to the new German trench positions, two battalions failed to reach anywhere near their objectives. That they failed is not surprising. They were not told about the change to the artillery plan, and, although some troops followed the barrage, they did so slowly and hesitantly, almost certainly because of lack of information. As one group of officers stood waiting in the communications trench for the amended details of the artillery plan, a shell exploded in their midst, severely wounding several, and half-burying Captain H. C. Anthony, a 26 year old timber merchant of East Malvern, Victoria. Anthony was ordered to take charge of the remnants of the battalion. He hurried along the line and ordered the troops to fix bayonets. Finally, 10 minutes after the British and Australian guns had begun to fire — 10 minutes after the proposed time of the assault — the amended order arrived by runner. Anthony quickly ordered his troops to attack, but already the Germans were replying with their artillery.

Just after the assault began, Anthony was wounded by the artillery fire. Still the assault went forward but one by one the officers and junior leaders fell. At some stage, a sergeant is alleged to have said, 'Come back, lads, it's no good', and the attackers retired, only to reform and try again.

The attack was virtually doomed to failure: doomed from the lack of preparation; from the late adjustment of the artillery plan; from the casualties to the leaders. Anthony wrote later that his company was at a disadvantage from the beginning, out of touch with the rest of the force. His men had to go 'two to three hundred yards east of our position'. As well, Anthony had to swing his attack around to link up with the flanking battalion, a manoeuvre perilously difficult at the best of times and almost impossible at night and under shell fire. Anthony had to cope with near-panic among his men. 'I think it was a case of shell-shock that gave the order to retire, but I'll never know. I gave the order to attack often enough.'

Even before he took command of the company, Anthony had been buried once. As he reached out to take the amended artillery orders, he was buried again, this time with the runner and the orders. Later, Anthony, who had the entire responsibility for a battalion attack as a young platoon commander, wrote that he didn't know what was in the orders. In the urgency of getting his men together and ready for the attack, he had no time to read the amended orders. He simply began the assault. Then, after he had gone about 10 metres, he was hit again, through the upper arm. 'It wasn't broken and I kept going. It bled profusely. I had some trouble in getting the men to keep to the left. I remember running up and down shell craters ... everything faded away and I don't remember anything.'

When Anthony awoke, he was on his back in a shell hole.

> My arm had bled freely, I was very weak and sick. Nobody was to be seen. The artillery had quietened down a lot but there was still machine gun and rifle fire. Having made several unsuccessful attempts to bandage my arm, I decided to crawl to my men or to the trench which I had left. I hadn't the least idea which way I was facing. Flares seemed to be going up all around me, flares and bullets coming from all directions. I looked for the telegraph post [a landmark used in the attack] but it wasn't there. There weren't any men about. I took my equipment off and started to crawl. I came to a road which I thought was the Pozières road, but it looked very different. However, I knew that if I struck back in a V shaped tangent I must find the trench which we had left. Well, with many rests I eventually came to a trench which was apparently unoccupied, although I could have sworn it was our hopping off trench. I just turned the first traverse when someone jumped up from a small funk-hole at the side, grabbed me by the throat and over I went on my back. I was in a German trench. I subsequently learned it was their support line. Was there strong enemy resistance? Yes there was. They were obviously expecting us to attack and turned everything they had, all their artillery and machine guns, on to us. I think our preparations had been observed. . . .

Anthony was right; the preparations for the attack had been watched all day. The Germans were expecting the Australian assault, not just from these observations, but also from the information obtained from the captured British prisoner and the II Corps documents. Anthony's shoulder straps were removed, probably to souvenir his badges of rank, his wounds were bound, he was given coffee, chocolate and later, two or three glasses of brandy. But his interrogation was desultory, almost half-hearted, as if the Germans already had the information they needed.

Smyth's brigade, ordered to attack north along the ridge line, faced similar difficulties from the artillery which was concentrated on their narrow salient. As well there was the immense difficulty locating the forward lines; difficulties which resulted in the Australian artillery falling on the Australian forward trenches. The confusion also caused other problems. Because Smyth's location was assumed to be right, the orders issued by all the formations — the Reserve Army, the Anzac Corps, the divisional headquarters — called for an assault of about 300 metres. Instead, the objective of Fabeck Graben was now more than 500 metres away. When this error was discovered, Walker ordered that jumping off trenches be dug closer to the enemy position. But this involved a preliminary operation, an advance over the intervening 200 to 300 metres, before these trenches could be dug.

The aerial photographs taken the previous day arrived in the 1st Division headquarters. They showed that the objective for Smyth's brigade was virtually on the Australian front line. Again, the orders were amended. This time the amended orders reached both the artillery and the infantry in time for the attack, but when the heavy artillery began to fire shells again fell on the Australians' forward positions. The bland words of the signal log in the brigade and divisional war diaries give no real sense of the urgency; the troops in the front lines could do little about the 9.2 inch shells that were exploding on top of their positions. The heavies, from both the Anzac and II Corps, had been firing throughout the morning with disastrous results for the Australians, particularly Howell-Price's 3rd Battalion.

The log of the 1st Division notes:

> General Napier [ANZAC Corps Commander Royal Artillery] rings up at 7.45 a.m. to say 'in answer to the statement that 9.2 shells had landed [in the 3rd Battalion position] — as am shelling trench little more than 100 yards forward of this point one must expect abnormal rounds to fall 100 yards short. They will just have to keep their heads down'.

Throughout the afternoon, the log records similar messages: requests from the brigades for the artillery to lengthen their ranges; replies from the artillery that the troops must expect a few 'drop-shorts'. Then, that evening, the artillery commanders adopted a different attitude: they were firing at Fabeck Graben '. . . after aeroplane registration. Most careful check has been made, and it appears that these must be enemy shells'. The Australians remained unconvinced. So far, the German artillery had not managed to register the troops in the forward trenches; the German fire was still falling heavily on the support lines.

Howell-Price moved his headquarters forward into an old artillery dugout on the right of his battalion line. At 8.35 p.m., he told Smyth that an increased barrage from the Australian heavy guns had been falling on his front lines now for half an hour. 'The front trench is almost demolished. I am doubtful whether we shall be able to carry out the stunt . . .' Despite message after message from Howell-Price pleading that the range of the artillery be increased, the Australian and British heavies continued to pound their own front line. And apart from one small gain, a strongpoint just in front of the Australian position, the 1st Brigade attack was a failure. It too, had to be withdrawn.

The 1st Brigade attack had failed to carry the strong German trench of Fabeck Graben. Now, Walker relieved that brigade and replaced it with the 3rd, although the 1st Battalion remained in the line, continuing to dig saps towards the German trenches. Like the 1st Brigade, the 3rd had been heavily depleted in the earlier fighting for the village. It had been pulled out of the line but the army still exacted its discipline, Bill Harney, a private in the 9th Battalion, recalled that rarely were the troops given any rest:

> Soon as we got behind the line, they'd start us back on the old drill parade and lick and polish and all this business. We'd have to form up and march in our respective companies to the battalion parade grounds and then we'd be dismissed and we'd go away to various jobs we had to do.

The 9th Battalion had been in the thick of the fighting on the right flank of the first attack. Its troops had been allowed to rest briefly but, as Harney pointed out, much of the time out of the line was spent either in parades or in marching to and from billet areas. For example, the 9th Battalion marched more than 60 kilometres to its billets at Bertaucourt where it rested briefly, paraded frequently, absorbed its reinforcements, reallocated its machine guns to the companies and then marched back to Pozières.

Vince Bowman noted in his diary that the 9th left Albert on 19 August for the front-line. Although the battalion's route took them through Pozières to the north — ground with which it was familiar — it still became lost north of Pozières. 'Got a severe shelling coming along past Pozières and through K trench. We had a number of casualties. Relieved the 4th Battalion.' From there on, Bowman's diary has a spare, almost cryptic quality. 'August 20. Rough night. Shell fire bad. To make matters worse, one of our batteries firing short. One killed and five wounded by our own shells.'

Bowman's dugout, near the quarry, provided scant shelter, merely enough to escape shrapnel from any artillery round bursting nearby. A direct hit on the dugout would have buried all its occupants. Even so, the Australians were required to post lookouts as a precaution against the frequent counter-attacks. 'It would be madness to man the trench heavily as it is being shelled frequently.' The landscape over which these sentries had to watch was desolate, churned over from the constant artillery fire, pitted and scarred with shell holes of all sizes from all calibres, littered with wire and posts and corpses, all the debris of war.

It was rarely quiet: even when the artillery paused, there would be the sharp crack of a sniper's rifle or the iron rattle of the machine guns or the muffled thuds of a work party, engaged in the never ending tasks of trench maintenance.

North of Pozières, the two trenches of Park Lane and Tom's Cut were constantly destroyed by the artillery, no matter how hard and long the work parties laboured. These trenches snaked over the high ground; movement along them was obvious to the Germans at Thiepval. Any movement by day brought sudden rounds from the artillery; any movement by night risked confusion in the absence of any landmarks. Small parties and larger groups alike floundered around, looking in vain for some sense of direction in this terrible corner. One battalion commander, Lt.-Col. Elliott of the 12th, personally checked the route his soldiers were to take through these battered trenches. His two companies moving up were largely reinforcements. Elliott decided to send them over the open ground rather than through the trenches 'to minimise the possibility of their being demoralised by the revolting sights they would necessarily pass in going up by the trenches'.

14

The Wedge Blows

As they neared Mouquet the resistance increased. Each of the last five blows has been stiffer to drive. On each occasion the wedge has been driven a little farther forward. This time the blow was heavier and the wedge went farther.
C. E. W. Bean, Letters from France, 7 September 1916.

Gough retained his dreams and grand visions of capturing Thiepval; Birdwood, ever the loyal subordinate, attempted to communicate some enthusiasm to his troops; Walker and White fretted and worried over the manner in which the dreams and the visions and the enthusiasms would be translated into objectives and trenches and military gains. During this bitter middle stage of August, the 1st Australian Division War Diary takes on a querulous, almost irritated tone, as the plans coming from Gough's headquarters were examined in minute detail by both the Anzac Corps and the Divisional Headquarters' staffs. It seems almost as if the planning staffs realised the impossibilities of the tasks being imposed upon the troops, numerically depleted by the fighting in July. On 19 August 1916, for example, White wrote Walker, a personal note expanding on an earlier formal instruction. 'My dear General, I hope our letter about your next operation is satisfactory to you. I confess that I do not like it, because it is rather a half-hearted measure.'

In both the official history, and in his later laudatory study of Brudenell White, Bean wrote that the latter realised the impossibility of Gough's tactics. According to Bean, had White prevailed on Birdwood to adopt a more independent stand against Gough, (the strong stand he adopted on several occasions later in the war), some of the more impractical operations would probably have been further modified or abandoned. The fact remains, however, that White failed to point out to Birdwood the immense folly of Gough's tactical plans. White later realised that he had been remiss in not doing so, and acknowledged as much to Bean in private correspondence. But, apart from taking a close interest in the planning carried out by the brigade and divisional staffs,

White remained silent as battalion after battalion was committed to narrow, shallow attacks against a hugely stronger enemy.

Certainly, White realised that the 1st Division, with its depleted battalions and its still exhausted troops, was capable of taking only limited objectives. Indeed, the narrowness of the Australian salient meant that from now on, a brigade was about the largest formation that could attack. The size of the Australian salient perturbed White; he looked at methods of capturing more ground, closer to the Fabeck Graben trench itself, so that the subsequent attacks could be carried out with larger forces; he looked at minor operations around and near Mouquet Farm that would not only conform with Gough's intentions but also be within the capability of the Australians to carry out. In his personal letter of 19 August to Walker, White wrote, almost despairingly: '. . . there does not seem to be any operation open to you except the minor one which our official letter has suggested'.

The 'minor one' suggested by Birdwood and White, and accepted without recorded comment or dissent by Walker, was a daylight assault on the Fabeck Graben trench east of Mouquet Farm. For the first time since they arrived at the Pozières battlefield, the Australians were to assault by day. It seems inconceivable that Birdwood, White, Walker or any other senior officer of the AIF would have committed troops to a daylight attack had it not been for the requirement to comply with British attacks elsewhere. No appreciation notes that might provide another explanation survive in the Australian records. Bean merely records that the attack took place in 'plain daylight' without offering either comment or explanation. Yet the entire experience of the Australians thus far in the major offensives from Fromelles a month earlier — not to mention the British experience on and after 1 July — had demonstrated the danger, almost the folly, of a daylight attack.

The timing for the attack was laid down by the Reserve Army; at 6 p.m., both the Anzac Corps (which meant this rather under-strength Australian division) and II Corps were to attack after an elaborate artillery preparation designed, so it was hoped, to confuse or deceive the Germans. The hopes proved futile. During the day, German observation aircraft were seen frequently over the Australian and British lines and their occupants were able to note the preparations for the coming attack at their leisure. As well, the Australians moving up for the attack had to cross the open, exposed ground on Pozières Ridge which was clearly in view of the Germans.

All through that afternoon, the German artillery fire fell on the Australian support and communication trenches. That night Vince Bowman noted in his diary: 'The 10th, 11th and 12th Battalions attacked today. Their objective was some trenches on the outskirts of

Mouquet Farm . . . Our only part [the 9th Battalion] was to swing our flank forward as they advanced, but we got all the backwash of Fritz's barrage. It was particularly severe'. Bowman added that 'Fritz must have seen the 12th Battalion assembling for the attack'. The Germans could hardly have missed doing so, for even to get into position required moving across open ground out of the trench system. Colonel Charlie Elliott, the commanding officer of the 12th, described how this was done:

> The whole line jumped the parapet and plunged headlong into the gully in extended order. This was dead ground and they were enabled to go slowly, but as soon as they came to the crest of the next ridge, where the firing line was situated, they had to do the fifty yards in double quick time, and fairly fell into the trench. This left them with about half an hour in which to organise the attack.

About half an hour before, German artillery had landed amid the waiting troops of the 10th Battalion, causing about 120 casualties. Now it began to fall among the 12th Battalion, which also suffered heavily. The third battalion in the attack, the 11th, was late arriving; its troops had been used in carrying parties for the attack and was some distance behind the line. Troops from this battalion had to pass through the barrage provoked by the movement of the 12th before they could get anywhere near the start line. Still, despite the terrible confusion, the attack began on time; the much depleted companies of the 10th and 12th rose and advanced behind a creeping barrage. Almost at once, they came under fire from German machine gunners firing through the barrage. Although the 10th Battalion lost all its officers except one, it pushed on to the Fabeck Graben Trench. It was hopeless. Enfiladed by a machine gun firing from their right, isolated from supporting troops, running low on ammunition, these few soldiers had no choice other than to abandon their attack and crawl to the relative safety of a nearby trench.

On their left, the 12th Battalion actually pushed through into the ruins of Mouquet Farm, but again their numbers were too small to hold on. Because of the very narrowness of the Ridge position, the Australians could not assemble sufficient troops so that gains won could be retained. Time and time again, the force of the German counter-attacks, launched by the local junior commanders, compelled the Australians to retire.

The following day, Vince Bowman recorded that the day's shell fire was as bad as any he had experienced at Pozières: 'All one can do is peep over the top from time to time'. On that afternoon, the 24th

Battalion tried to relieve the 9th. 'We could see them as they came over Pozières Ridge in K trench', Bowman wrote. 'Shortly after we saw them, Fritz also saw them, and put down an unearthly barrage on K Trench. We could see men scampering everywhere. Their losses must be enormous. They can't possibly reach our line to relieve us.' The 24th Battalion, from the 2nd Division, was now to try where the 9th had failed. The 3rd Brigade's losses were 840; the 1st Division's losses in this spell opposite Mouquet Farm were 92 officers and 2,558 men.

By now, these veterans were accepting death almost as an inevitable consequence of soldiering. A bank clerk, Sergeant D. G. J. Badger from South Australia, wrote to his parents before the 10th Battalion attack. 'When you see this, I'll be dead; don't worry . . . Try to think I did the only possible thing, as I tell you I would do it again if I had the chance. Send someone else in my place.' Badger was killed in the abortive attack on 21 August. On 24 August Lieutenant Bert Crowle of the same battalion wrote to his wife and son:

> Dearest Beat and Bill, Just a line you must be prepared for the worst to happen any day. It is no use trying to hide things. I am in terrible agony. Had I been brought in at once I had a hope. Not now gas gangrene has set in and it is so bad that the doctor could not save it by taking it off as it had gone too far and the only hope is that the salts they have put on may drain the gangrene out otherwise there is no hope.

Crowle had been wounded early in the attack. Stretcher bearers had carried him back, about 6½ kilometres, with the first part of the journey across the open ground in front of the German trenches. In front of this party, another stretcher bearer walked, waving a Red Cross flag. The Germans did not open fire. Crowle obviously rested before he finished his letter:

> . . . the pain is getting worse and worse. I am very sorry dear, but still you will be well provided for I am easy on that score. So cheer up dear I could write on a lot but I am nearly unconscious. Give my love to Dear Bill and yourself, do take care of yourself and him. Your loving husband Bert.

Crowle lost consciousness and died a few hours later.

Despite the inability of both the 4th and the 1st Australian Divisions to achieve any headway advance along the Pozières Ridge, Gough persisted with this approach. On 21 August, even as the attack on Fabeck Graben was failing, the Reserve Army headquarters issued others for the capture of Thiepval. This, Gough hoped, would be completed by 1 September; by 25 August, the I Anzac Corps would be holding a line 500 metres beyond Mouquet Farm. Given the pronounced failures along the Ridge since the Windmill position was captured, Gough's planning was based upon heroic assumptions. Neither Birdwood nor White challenged the Reserve Army commander; neither pointed out the futility of adopting such a predictable approach to the Thiepval strongpoint. Now the Australian gains were being measured — if there were any gains — in terms of tens of metres, not in the hundreds of metres so grandly won in the opening battle. Now too, the Australian front was lengthened around the salient, being held at any one time only by a depleted division. The peril of counter-attack was ever present.

Still Gough kept pushing the Australians on. Legge's 2nd Division returned to the line, charged initially with the responsibility of attacking Mouquet Farm from the western side. According to the staff of Gough's headquarters, an attack here would be relatively protected from the defenders in Fabeck Graben east of the farm; an objective seized here might provide an effective base for an attack to comply with their commander's optimistic objectives.

The responsibility for this attack fell to Gellibrand's brigade, the least affected of the 2nd Division from the previous tour of duty in the line. Once more the troops made the long and precarious route march through Albert, up the old Roman Road to Tara Hill and then through Sausage Valley. By now, of course, the sights and the sounds of battle were familiar; the sight of unburied corpses and shattered trenches unremarkable. And, as they neared the line, through the pulverised remains of the Pozières village, the sounds increased: now the booming artillery, intermittent and irregular; now the rattle of small arms. Through Pozières and into K Trench where they came under direct observation of the Germans. Vince Bowman noted how here the troops of the 24th Battalion scattered and ran before the artillery; that terrible passage was faced by every soldier of the relieving battalions.

In his letters home, Bean likened the assault on Mouquet Farm to splitting a log with a hammer and wedge. 'As they neared Mouquet the resistance increased. Each of the last five blows has been stiffer to drive. On each occasion the wedge has been driven a little farther forward.' Now, the log was proving to be tougher and the power of the splitter weaker. Although Gellibrand's brigade had suffered least in the earlier fighting, it was still considerably under strength: one of its battalions, the 21st, could muster 700 men; the 23rd and 24th each could muster about 600 and the 22nd could muster only 365. Because of this, Gellibrand decided to place the 21st east of the Farm, where the attack would probably be made, the weaker 23rd and 24th battalions on its left, and the 22nd, at less than half strength, was to be used for resupplying the troops in the front line.

Before moving his brigade forward, Gellibrand had taken the precaution of visiting the 1st Division headquarters and discussing the tactical position with Walker and Tom Blamey. On the basis of these discussions, Gellibrand decided to place his strongest battalion east of Mouquet Farm, in the right of the Australian line, because he and Blamey agreed that these trenches would need to be captured before any assault on the Farm itself would be successful. After the previous unsuccessful attacks west of the Farm, such an approach seemed eminently sensible both to Blamey and to Gellibrand.

Now the requirement for Gough to co-ordinate his attacks with those of Rawlinson's Fourth Army was beginning to affect the Australian planning. A week before, on 16 August, Haig told his army commanders that the new secret weapon, the tanks, would be arriving in France soon and would be available for the next great push, planned for mid-September. In the meantime, Rawlinson's army must capture both Guinchy and Guillemont, persistent and intractable obstacles on the right, while Gough's army must secure the Pozières-Thiepval high ground on the left.

Gough could not resist interfering in the latter task. The Reserve Army headquarters insisted that the next Australian attack be made on the west of Mouquet Farm, despite the failure of two previous attacks on this approach. Indeed, it was the failure of these attacks that had led both Blamey and Gellibrand to discard this approach and try from the east.

Enter Brudenell White. In a letter to the 2nd Division on 22 August, he suggested attacking west of Mouquet Farm but only after the gains to the east had been consolidated. White then planned to use both the 2nd Division and the 4th Division, which was moving up to take its place in the line once more, in a combined effort to reach the objectives laid down by Gough. The Reserve Army operation orders for this period reveal the extent to which a remote and superior headquarters involved itself in the detail of what was not much more than a brigade assault; it is one thing for the Reserve Army commander to identify the objectives to be taken, quite another to lay down methods by which his plans are to be carried out.

Paradoxically, Bean's eulogistic treatment of Brudenell White tends to obscure the difficulties faced by this capable staff officer. He was, after all, still only a brigadier-general and a relatively obscure officer on an ANZAC Corps headquarters. He possessed no authority of his own; he spoke and wrote and acted merely for his commander; he had to balance the competing demands of national identity and aspirations, of realistic tasks and of the optimistic objectives set by Gough's headquarters. In the official history, Bean attempts to be scrupulously fair to White but the question remains: what would have happened had White shown to Gough the same kind of independence of thought he had already shown to Haig?

As the brigade commander, Gellibrand was in an extremely difficult position. His precaution of discussing the proposed operations with Blamey seemed wise, particularly as the 1st Division headquarters and planning staff seemed to function more efficiently than their 2nd Division counterparts. The advantages of an assault east of the Farm were considerable, although it would have had to contend with an exposed right flank. But the main German strength was still concentrated upon Thiepval Ridge and it was the left flank in the successive assaults that had posed the problems. Moreover, the Australians still had only a sketchy idea of the strength of German defences in and around Mouquet Farm itself, for although small parties of troops had actually penetrated as far as the outskirts of the ruined buildings, they had not come under sustained and concentrated fire from the Farm itself. But Brudenell White's plan also had certain attractions. No doubt he realised the depleted strength of Gellibrand's brigade made it impossible to attack and capture the Farm in one operation. As well, merely to repeat the same plan of attack without variation was to invite a similar, certain failure like that which had greeted previous efforts.

Before Gellibrand could follow this amended plan, however, he had to move his forward battalions, bringing the stronger 21st from the right to the left of the line. Despite the immense risk of such unnecessary movement, this was achieved without the battalions suffering heavily.

Gellibrand was also hindered by poor knowledge of both the strength and the location of the German defences. Patrols had been pushed out, both by the 1st Division troops and now by Gellibrand, but the information with which they returned was puzzling and conflicting. Some reported that the Farm was heavily defended; others reported unoccupied dugouts and posts which, had the Germans been there in strength, would have certainly been occupied. As well, a known machine gun position in a dugout south of the Farm would make any assault precarious; it would need to be taken out.

Gellibrand moved his headquarters closer to the line. He held his conferences in a musty smoky dugout just north of the Pozières cemetery, attended by the battalion commanders and the officers commanding the other units of his brigade. At one such conference, this machine gun post was discussed. Would the 21st Battalion take it out before the main attack? (Gellibrand's gentle posing of the request in such a manner seems entirely typical of his approach to command.)

Impossible, replied the commanding officer of the 21st. With that, Gellibrand turned to the officer commanding the machine gun company and asked whether his men would like to try.

This officer clearly could not resist the challenge; the machine gunners would attempt what the infantry had turned down. The patrol went out, but failed to discover the machine gun post. Sadly, from that minor exchange, the soldiers of the 21st Battalion were saddled with a reputation for being unnecessarily cautious.

Gellibrand planned his attack to begin at dawn on 26 August, reasoning that to do so would give his troops the advantage of being able to assemble under the relative cover of darkness, to attack with sufficient light with which to see and to consolidate any gains in daylight. The only artillery Gellibrand planned to use were 26 heavy and medium howitzers, throwing a creeping barrage ahead of his troops as they advanced. If planning and preparation were any guides to success, Gellibrand's attack should have worked. Instead, it failed.

On the right, the troops of the 24th Battalion came under heavy fire from the machine gun of the Fabeck Graben trench, east of the Farm. As well, artillery from further east and from the Thiepval position fell among the assaulting troops. According to Arthur Whitear of the 24th Battalion:

> We were sighted by the enemy who immediately put down a very heavy barrage. We moved out behind our artillery formation, greatly reducing the target but finally we were forced to take cover. I scrambled into an old German gunpit which was very soon blown in on me. I was knocked unconscious and found myself at a CCS [Casualty Clearing Station] suffering from shell-shock.

In the centre, the assaulting troops actually swept around and past the Farm before they realised their mistake and tried to make their way back. These troops were mainly from the 21st Battalion, still smarting from the accusation that they were excessively cautious. Their enthusiasm to dispel this impression might well have made them unnecessarily anxious and careless.

Like so many previous attempts, this effort to take Mouquet Farm failed. The resistance in the centre of the attack was strong, and with good reason; the Germans had moved their *4th Guard Division* into the line in this section. They were élite troops and they were fresh. 'A fine stamp of men', one Australian described them, 'by far the finest Germans I have ever seen; the only troops I have ever seen taller even than our men.' By now the Australians were beginning to realise the extent of the defences at Mouquet Farm. Small parties of men who

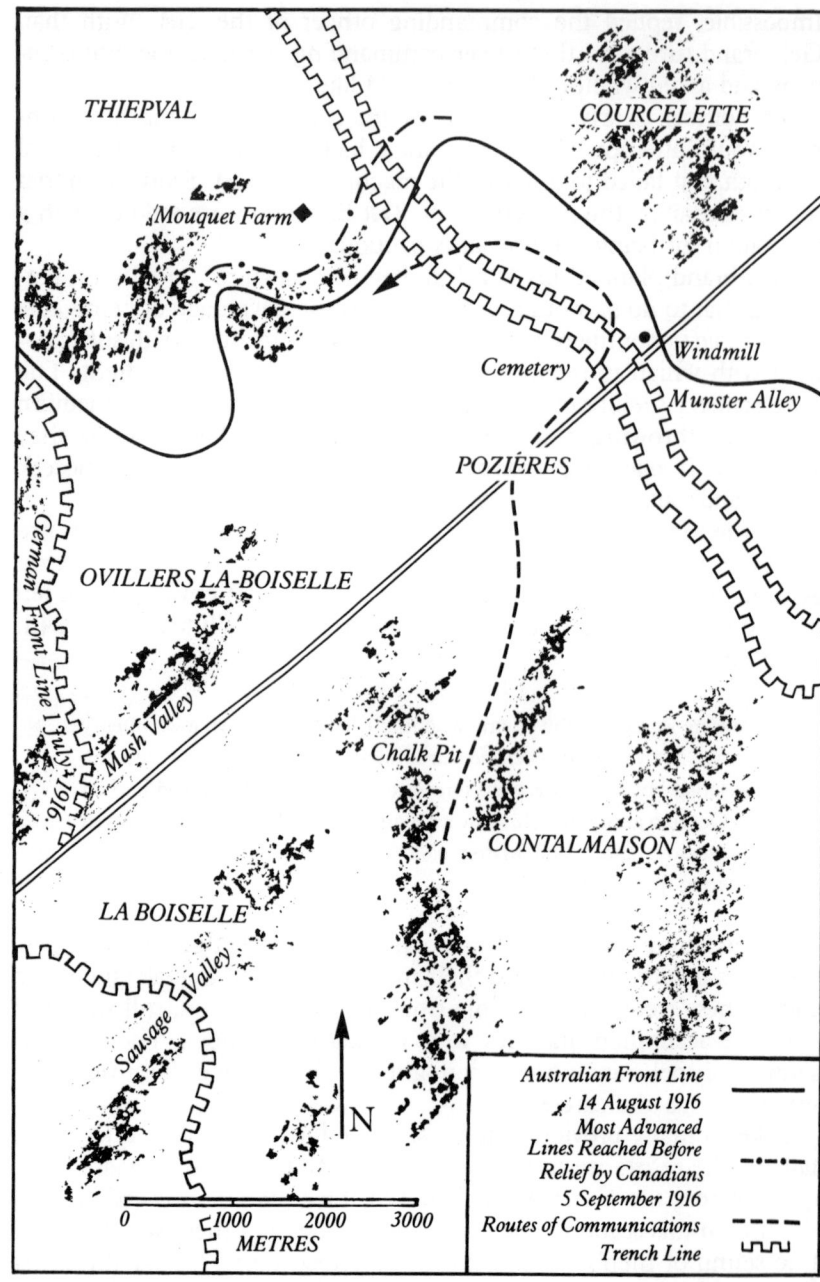

The Pozières-Mouquet Farm position, showing salient at its most advanced stage and result of attacks on Mouquet Farm, Aug/Sept 1916.

had taken part in the attack made their way back to the Australian line and told of being attacked from the rear by Germans who had appeared from hidden exits in and around the ruined buildings. Mouquet Farm itself was immensely strong; its deep cellars had been converted into safe dugouts; its connecting trench system made it virtually impregnable.

The 21st Battalion, relieved two days before the rest of the brigade, had lost 13 officers and 444 men. In the 24th, still in the line, Arthur Whitear had left the CCS and made his way back to his mates. In particular he wanted to find the soldier who had picked him out: 'My intention was to show my gratitude to my friend, but I had the horror of seeing him in the trench and before I could get near to him, he was blown to pieces'.

In four days, the 2nd Division had lost 1,268 men, of whom 896 were from Gellibrand's brigade; Mouquet Farm remained in German hands. On 28 August, the 2nd Division was relieved by the 4th Division. The hammer blows were becoming weaker; the backswing shorter; the wedge was not moving as far.

Still the battering ram tactics continued. The 4th Division was, like the 1st and the 2nd, barely rested and reinforced. E. J. Rule, in the 14th Battalion, recorded how much of the time was spent in training: bombing in small groups; attacking as battalions and as a brigade over clear, open fields. During one such exercise, Brig.-Gen. Brand rode up and down the line of troops, cursing and giving 'some of our officers a hot time'. One battalion commander who was slow to react attracted the attention of both Brand and the soldiers. '. . . in the opinion of some of us', Rule wrote, 'that officer could not have led in school children out of the rain.' Apparently Brand agreed, for soon afterwards this officer was returned to Australia.

The 14th Battalion had been resting for two weeks. According to Rule: 'Our nerves were still rattled, and the thoughts of another gruelling were not very welcome'. They marched back to the battlefield, although some of the new reinforcements threw themselves down on the ground and refused to go any further. 'Generally they crawled into our camp late, had to hunt around for a place to sleep in, and generally got the worst.' Just to add to their burdens, Rule's platoon of bombers were issued with suits of armour.

> We looked for all the world like a gang of Ned Kellys, and they were not by any means the lightest sort of article to carry around. After a good laugh we took a vote to see what should be done with them. Nearly all voted for dumping them, the view being that it was better to die by bombs than die from exhaustion carting these things about.

As the men of the 14th passed through Albert, it began to rain. In the dark and the wind and the rain, the Australians moved closer to the line, halting frequently while guides checked their positions. 'The trench we came into was the famous K Trench, the only communication trench leading from Pozières to the extreme left flank', wrote Rule. At daylight, Rule was surprised to find they were only a few hundred metres north of Pozières cemetery, about the same position that they had been in two weeks before. Soon, Rule was told that his bombing platoon would be attacking that night.

Legge, commanding the 2nd Division, still had responsibility for this sector of the front. The main concern was a series of numbered outposts of Mouquet Farm which needed to be taken before any attack on the Farm itself could be made. Now, Legge proposed using bombers to clear the strongpoints, then bringing infantry up to consolidate the position and prepare jumping off trenches for subsequent assaults. Brand had been told by the 2nd Division staff that his first task 'was the capture of Point 27 [near the south-west corner of the Farm] and the enemy machine guns in Mouquet Farm at a time to be selected by yourself. This evening is suggested'.

Not satisfied just with this task, Brand also suggested that his brigade attack another post, about 300 metres to the west. Where Gellibrand's brigade had attacked with nearly two battalions and failed, Brand was now proposing to attack with about one-eighth the strength. Curiously, both Legge and Bridges approved.

The heaviest responsibility for this attack would fall on the bombing platoon of the 14th Battalion, commanded by Lieutenant Archie Dean of Sydney. His platoon sergeant, Rule, wrote that Dean returned from receiving orders in:

> ... high spirits and very eager to put into practice the methods we had trained so hard to acquire. I myself could not rake up any enthusiasm over this new killing off. Somehow or other, I feared the worst, but, when I asked Lieutenant Dean a few questions about the show, he laughed, and said: 'As soon as they see you, they'll run'.

Rule went forward to look at the ground over which he was expected to attack that night. He had asked for directions and a runner from his headquarters but was refused. 'You can't miss it', were the only directions he received.

With two others, Rule made his way towards the Farm.

> Every now and then we came to places where the trench was blown in, and dead men were scattered all along the top; in many places also the

trench held mud knee-deep. The Hun was shelling it as we came along
so we did not wait to view any of the beauty spots . . .

Without a trench map or a compass, Rule had no idea of the direction
in which he was travelling.

All of us had grown disgusted at dodging and trying to follow the track
about, so we got on top and made off in the direction that we judged to
be the right one. Just on our right was a ridge, a few hundred yards away,
and the three of us came to the conclusion that our line must lie on the
top of it, and that we must be well behind our front. A little farther along
we noticed a heap of earth and timber, and decided to make for it.

Rule's party, unarmed because they had no intention of going anywhere
near the German position, made for this pile of 'earth and timber'.
They were within 20 metres when they heard a 'hiss and — "Hey" '.

The sound was so slight that we barely heard it. Glancing over my right
shoulder, I saw an Aussie crouching in a shell hole, peering at us from
behind a big clod of earth. Instantly I knew where we were, and that the
heap of earth was the famous Farm.

The Germans, watching from hidden positions amid the rubble, had
allowed Rule's party to approach, no doubt thinking they were a bold
reconnaissance patrol. The soldier in the shell hole seemed to sum it
up when he told Rule and his mates: 'Well, you're the luckiest b...s in
this world!'

That anecdote is worth relating because it indicates just how well
disguised the German positions were, and how the incessant bombardment had removed all traces of landmarks. Here was a large farm —
the surviving pre-war photographs show a fine courtyard and out buildings — pulverised and reduced to a 'heap of earth and timber'. On his
way back, Rule was spotted by a German machine gunner who fired
and missed. The sights that met them on the way back remained
through life. 'Our path was an old Hun trench, and by the looks of the
place, our guns must have caught them relieving, for the trenches
seemed to be carpeted with Huns.' Rule arrived back in his battalion
headquarters position, about 300 metres from the Farm and pointed
out the ground, as best he could, to Captain Stewart Hansen who would
be leading the attack.

The 14th Battalion was faced with a curious problem. It had to attack
the two strongpoints to the west of the Farm, Point 27 and Point 54.
Yet between these points, its own troops held Point 77, which earlier

had been captured by the 21st and retained. Capturing the three strong-points west of the Farm was certainly necessary before any attack could be launched on the Farm itself, but the presence of the party in Point 77 made it difficult. To add to the difficulties, the troops going into the attack were not given any plan but merely on outline of the barrage and supporting fire. It was to be left to the soldiers and their junior leaders to decide the best way of attacking these strongpoints.

Clearly the effect of the artillery fire on the German positions would be critical. At 3 p.m., Rule and his mates went up to watch the bombardment by the 'heavies' on the position they would be attacking. 'The hour arrived, and with it came one shell; a little while after, another one; and so on, until about six had come over — and not a blessed one hit the post. We went down into the dugout disgusted.' The perfunctory bombardment warned the Germans, however, and later that afternoon, the post was reinforced. Rule watched these troops move in, watched the flares rising from the German position after dark and became increasingly pessimistic about the attack.

Not only had the Germans reinforced the position but they were now bombarding the Australians, preventing parties moving up with extra bombs and ammunition for the attack.

> The shelling never let up at all, and I began to feel that the sooner it was all over the better, for I never expected to see the rise of the sun. I stayed in the trench for a long while watching the German post and noting where the flares were all coming from, until I felt sick of the whole thing and did not care if a shell blew me to pieces. I went down into the dugout and reported to Hansen [his company commander] what I'd seen, remarking that it was an impossible job for so few men. His reply was: 'It has got to go on'.

Rule lay down in a corner of the dugout and went to sleep. An hour later, he was woken by Hansen and told to get his men together. The attack was timed for midnight, after a five minute barrage. Under the cover of this barrage, Rule and his men crept closer to the German dugouts.

> We crept up until we could feel the force of the explosion, and then lay down. It was a wonder some of us were not hit, but we knew it was our only salvation to get up close and rush in before the German could get his head up. Watching the minute hand until it showed 12, we got up as the last shell burst in the post and the rest of the shells began to fly farther on to the back of the position.

Between them, Rule's bombers attacked three German strongpoints that midnight. At first, the attacks looked like succeeding; the Germans were stunned by the bombardment and the ferocity of the Australian assault. Gradually, however, the defenders' greater strength asserted itself; the Australian bombers fell wounded or dead. When the platoon commander leading the support troops arrived at Rule's position, the young sergeant asked him what he thought of the situation. 'No good', was the officer's understandable reply. 'Well,' thought Rule, 'if he's not going to take the risk, I've had enough.' Rule ordered the survivors in his party to pull back.

Archie Dean, commanding another group of bombers, had a similar experience to that of Rule. As Rule was going in, he saw flares rise from Dean's position:

> . . . I knew that it meant he had captured his ground. As I turned to leave Hansen's headquarters I noticed the number of wounded on the floor. The shelter was about the size of an ordinary kitchen and one could hardly walk about it for wounded men. Suddenly we heard Lieutenant Dean's voice outside: 'Here we are again, here we are again! and he staggered in, his face covered with blood. A bullet had lifted the top of his skull, . . . He was as game as any man could be, and refused attendance until the wounds of the others were dressed. He was one of the finest officers that I ever had anything to do with, and the men could not say enough in his praise.

Archie Dean died of his wounds, nearly four months later.

The 14th Battalion attack failed. Once again, the folly of assaulting strong, well defended positions with a mere handful of men was apparent; once again the Australian battalions were suffering from the persistent refusal of the Reserve Army commander to admit that this was not the way to Thiepval. The battalion history noted:

> There was not any doubt to anyone who had participated in the attack that the capture of Mouquet Farm and the adjacent strong points required an immensely strong force, backed up by artillery preparation and general surprise was excited in view of these facts by the information that the 4th was expected, in its present depleted state, to attack and capture the next evening the strong points that it had failed to capture on the previous night.

It was Stewart Hansen who convinced his commanding officer of the futility in these piecemeal attacks. Hansen, who had been in charge of the attack the previous night, realised that to commit forces of the same strength again would result in the same disaster. Dare, the battalion commander agreed, and told Brig.-Gen. Brand that the task his troops had been given was impossible. Here is probably the first example in France of an Australian unit commander protesting about the impossibility of orders from his superior commander. Brand ordered the 16th and the 13th Battalions to carry out the attack.

To describe the rest of the fighting by the Australians around Mouquet Farm from this point would be virtually to repeat earlier descriptions. Except that now it had begun to rain more heavily; every shell crater was a slimy, muddy pond, every trench was a slippery waterway. In this mud and slush, on the night of 28 August, the 13th and the 16th Battalions attacked; they failed to gain much headway against the now even stronger positions. Finally, the trenches to the east of Mouquet Farm were captured in early September and on 5 September the Australians were relieved by the Canadians. Still Thiepval had not been captured; Gough's optimistic planning, which had led to seven different offensives against the Mouquet Farm position, had counted for nothing. On 5 September, as the last of the Australians left the Pozières-Mouquet Farm sector of the Somme, Haig ordered Gough to stop attacking the Thiepval position. 'In front of General Gough's Army,' wrote the Commander-in-Chief, 'though the enemy suffered heavy losses in personnel; our gain in ground was slight.'

For their part in this slight gain of ground, the Australians suffered terribly. With the attack at Pozières, the I Anzac Corps lost 23,000 officers and men — 7,700 in the 1st Division, 8,100 in the 2nd, 7,100 in the 4th. At Fromelles, the 5th Division had lost 5,500 bringing total Australian casualties between 19 July and 5 September to more than 28,000.

The Australians had had enough. Despairing of the tactics forced on them by an over enthusiastic, largely incompetent Reserve Army headquarters, wary of the competence and courage of the Kitchener divisions on their flanks and distinctly unimpressed with the military qualities of the British Tommy, tired and terrified by their experiences in the line, the Australians wanted, in Rule's words, to get 'out of Hell'. Even Rule's 'little stunt' took a ghastly toll.

> I did not get over this experience for fully six months. During that time the thought of the front line sent me into shivers, and often at night I'd wake up, and in a dazed way live some of it over again. I know many to whom the same thing used to happen.

Rule was not exaggerating. In his letters home, Jack Bourke wrote of the terrible strain, made worse by the loss of his brother, Geoff

Bourke, killed in action in the 21st Battalion. In September he wrote to his parents, 'I suppose you have heard now about poor old Geoff . . .'

The diaries and the letters of this after-battle period are filled with a kind of stubborn despair, coloured with bitterness towards the high command — perhaps not quite as short-lived as Bean suggests — and an antipathy towards the British soldier. Before the battle Jack Bourke wondered 'How the British Tommy ever accomplished anything in history . . . A good heart and a wooden head must have carried him through'.

After the battle, Bourke wondered about the 'good heart'. In his last letter home, Alec Raws wrote that his friends had been 'murdered' through the 'incompetence, callousness and personal vanity of those high in authority'; Corporal A. G. Thomas of the 6th Battalion scribbled a note home under fire early in the fighting: 'For Christ's sake, write a book on the life of an infantryman and by doing so you will quickly prevent these shocking tragedies'.

Even writing within the constraints of an official historian, Bean was notably critical of the tactics adopted by Gough and, to a lesser extent, by Haig. Although it was the Commander-in-Chief's policy, Bean wrote: 'the actual steps by which that policy was carried Haig left . . . almost unconditionally in the hands of Gough. His own control barely went beyond the emission of few general maxims . . . The Australians learned to hate the reiteration of attacks on a narrow front and not unfairly attributed to [Gough] the responsibility, and their aversion to serving under him, which became pronounced the following year, dated from this time'. It was Gough's tactical approach which so dismayed the Australians. 'The prevailing tactics — repeated shallow advances on narrow fronts — were dreaded and detested . . . it is not surprising if the effect on some intelligent men was a bitter conviction they were being uselessly sacrificed.'

Apart from the disillusion with the high command — a feeling that extended to Birdwood — another, uglier consequence of Pozières soon made itself apparent. Some Australians decided that they would or could never again face such conditions and deserted. The actual number of desertions will never be known as some soldiers managed to avoid roll calls; many battalion diaries report the stark results of melancholy court martial proceedings. In the 4th Battalion just before Mouquet Farm, a young lance-corporal left his position and attempted to disguise his identity to avoid taking part in the attack. He was discovered, charged with desertion, court-martialled and found guilty. Iven Mackay promulgated the sentence: 'To suffer death by being shot. Sentence commuted to 15 years' penal servitude by General Haig. This sentence is now being undergone'. Haig was bound by a decision of the Australian Government; no Australian soldier would be shot for desertion.

Although Section 98 of the Australian Defence Act provided for a death sentence by a court martial, it added: 'no sentence of death passed by any court martial shall be carried into effect until confirmed by the Governor-General' which meant the Australian Government. From mid-1916, the British authorities, both military and civilian, attempted to pressure the Australian Government to change this stance. In May 1916, the sentence of death was passed on a sergeant from the 1st Pioneer Battalion, and forwarded by Birdwood to Second Army headquarters with the recommendation that the Australian Government remove the legal distinction between the British and Australian soldier. In response to Birdwood's request, the War Office asked the Australian Government to place its troops under the British Army Act without limitation, which would have allowed the death penalty to be carried out. The Australian Government refused to do so.

On 11 December 1916, when the strains of the Pozières campaign were still evident among the survivors, Birdwood again raised the subject. Writing to Rawlinson (the Anzac Corps was then serving in the Fourth Army), Birdwood said: 'I think that the discipline of the Australian troops is likely to suffer when the men realise that they are not on precisely the same footing in all respects as all other soldiers serving in France'. Rawlinson approved Birdwood's recommendation; during that bleak and bitter month, three death sentences were passed on soldiers in the I Anzac Corps; in each case, the subordinate formation commanders, brigade and divisional, had recommended the sentences be carried out. Of 182 offences for 'absent without leave' in Rawlinson's army, during that month, 130 had been committed by Australians. Rawlinson appealed to Haig: 'I cannot be responsible for the maintenance of discipline under my command unless the required alteration of the law is made forthwith'.

The concern for discipline expressed by Rawlinson is understandable, even if his proposed remedy is unattractive. Desertion among the Australian soldiers was a considerable problem: reinforcements arriving from England or wounded soldiers returning after convalescence took advantage of the relatively lax transport arrangements to disappear quietly into the French countryside. Haig had complained about this two weeks before Rawlinson's memorandum.

Part of the problem, however, was the general Australian attitude towards discipline. What might be regarded as an 'absent without leave' case in the British army — for example, a soldier leaving his billet for a couple of days in a nearby village *estaminet* — would provoke little concern in the Australian army, providing the offender returned and gave himself up. But there were other, more serious aspects. When the AIF was expanded in 1916, many commanding officers took the opportunity to post the 'no-hopers' out of their units hoping, not unreasonably, that they would become someone else's problem. After the casualties of July-August 1916 many of these individuals, who had been languishing in depots in Egypt or in England, found themselves on their way to units; Bean claims the 'persistent deserters were always men of this type — in some cases actual criminals who had enlisted without any intention of serving at the front, and ready to go to any length to avoid it'.

Without the death penalty, the extreme punishment which could be awarded to Australians was a substantial jail term or return to Australia in disgrace. After Pozières, return to Australia or a jail sentence was regarded as preferable by those who could not bear to face the rigours of the front again.

On 3 February 1917, the Secretary of State for the Colonies, Walter Hume Long, cabled the Australian Governor-General, Sir Ronald Crauford Munro Ferguson:

> My despatch 30th June [1916] Confidential Army Council regard matter as most urgent and ask that if legislation is necessary short Act to be in force during the war should at once be passed. Sir D. Haig has represented that in addition to the practice of deserting from drafts prevalence of absence from trenches is assuming alarming proportions amongst Australian troops. In December out of total 182 convictions for absence without permission 130 were from First Anzac Corps and Military Authorities regard it as essential that all troops should be placed on the same level as regards liability to the death penalty. The frequent infliction of this penalty is neither desired nor contemplated but at present immunity is relied on by absentees. Matter is of utmost gravity for discipline of whole army.

Three days later, Pearce noted: 'I recommend to Prime Minister that we not agree to this proposal'. On 22 February 1917, Hughes agreed with Pearce's recommendation; the Governor-General was requested to cable the Secretary of State for the Colonies that after 'careful consideration' the Government was unable to agree to the application of the death penalty.

In August 1917, Haig again sought the death penalty for Australians convicted of desertion. Long cabled Munro Ferguson on 23 August:

Sir Douglas Haig reports since date of his last representation as to the serious state of discipline of Australian Forces in France in relation to desertion and absence without permission condition of affairs has become much more serious and he considers that unless Commonwealth Government agree to place their troops under Army Act without any restrictions as regards death penalty fighting efficiency of these divisions will deteriorate to an extent which may gravely affect success of our arms. In respect of desertion in the British Expeditionary Force January to June 1917 5 Australian Divisions total convictions 171. 57 remaining divisions 506 . . . Your Ministers may be assured that power to inflict death penalty is very sparingly used only where offence is very deliberate and an example urgently required are such sentences confirmed. Sir D. Haig observes that he cannot think that when Commonwealth Government are aware of the situation they will continue to keep their troops in this privileged position bearing in mind that it may ultimately lead to state of affairs which may have far reaching results to the Empire. He adds that soldiers of all four Allied Armies on Western Front are liable to this maximum penalty for offence and so far as he is aware position is same in all other armies excepting Australian Imperial Force . . . In forwarding above representations Army Council express opinion that gravity of situation cannot be exaggerated and His Majesty's Government earnestly trust that your Ministers will give question of remedying this serious position their urgent attention.

The pressure on the Australian Government was growing. In May, 1916, Birdwood had recommended to the War Office that the Australian Government be approached and asked to remove the legal distinction between its soldiers and the British; a year later, he again suggested the imposition of the death penalty for desertion. And in August 1917, after the last request had been received, Munro Ferguson wrote privately to Long:

I much wish that it were possible to deal with the question of the death penalty for desertion. I have had very strong reports. Of course, I have not referred the private letters that I have had from Birdwood, because he would not wish this, and it would be improper to do so, but I know his views, and I know from many other sources that the fact is becoming known among other troops, with of course deplorable results.

From the beginning, 'Birdie', the soldiers' friend, was an ardent supporter of the death penalty for the troops under his command. Yet even this did not stop Haig grumbling to his wife about the control exercised by the AIF commander. On 28 February 1918, the Commander-in-Chief wrote to Lady Haig that the Australians were not nearly so efficient as the Canadians, who were;

> ... fine disciplined soldiers now and so smart and clean. I am sorry to say that the Australians are not nearly so efficient. I put this down to Birdwood who, instead of facing the problem, has gone in for the easier way of saying everything is perfect and making himself as popular as possible. We have had to separate the Australians into Convalescent Camps on their own because they were giving so much trouble when along with our men and put such revolutionary ideas into their heads.

A week later, after Godley had been attacked in the New Zealand Parliament and compared unfavourably with Birdwood, Haig noted in his diary that he had:

> ... sent a strong letter in reply supporting Godley and incidentally enclosed a graphic showing the numbers of men per thousand in prison because Birdwood was held up as an excellent disciplinarian. This table shows:
> 9 per thousand Australians in Prison
> 1.6 per thousand Canadians, NZ, South African
> 1 per thousand British (excluding above)
> That is to say, nearly one Australian in every hundred is in prison. This is greatly due to the fact that the Australian [Government?] refuses to allow capital punishment to be awarded to any Australian.

Indeed it did. In August, Munro Ferguson was forced to cable Long that the Australian Government could not agree to allow the death penalty to be inflicted on its soldiers convicted of desertion. The Government, said the Governor-General, fully recognised the gravity of the situation:

> ... but considers that to make the desired change at present would under existing domestic conditions be most unwise producing such an immediate and serious effect on recruiting as would in effect either compel the Government to submit the question of conscription again to the people under circumstances which would almost inevitably result in its rejection or alternatively make it impossible for Australia to maintain its present stream of reinforcements.

It was fear of the domestic political consequences that prevented the Australian Government yielding to the frequent and heavy pressure to permit the death penalty for its soldiers; considerations of humanity hardly seemed to apply. The pressures were persistent and constant, and came not only from the senior British officers but also from Australian commanders as well. In 1917 both Glasgow and Holmes urged Birdwood to press for the death penalty, as did Monash; in 1916 one Australian officer confided to his diary that it was regrettable 'that the foolish sentiment of a few old ladies in Melbourne won't let us shoot a few men who, through dishonorable cowardice, desert before an attack and then come back after their money runs out'. The enthusiasm for the death penalty was, however, confined to those officers who rarely had to face the risk of death from the enemy. Among the battalion officers, there was a general recognition that courage was a finite resource and that no two men had the same capacity for endurance. Significantly too, most of the complaints about the Australians' lack of discipline related to troops out of the line; their discipline in the line was rarely criticised. Moreover, the practice of reading to the Australian soldiers on parade reports of the death penalty inflicted on British soldiers merely served to widen the gap in attitudes between the Australian digger and the British Tommy. According to Bean, this 'ceremony . . . aroused in the Australians, officers and men, only a sullen sympathy and a fierce pride that their own people were strong enough to refuse this instrument to its rulers'.

Perhaps the Australian Government was, for whatever reasons, strong enough to refuse the demands for the death penalty; it was not strong enough, however, to resist other, similarly urgent demands for reinforcements after the shambles of Pozières and Mouquet Farm.

15

Other Casualties

I didn't raise my son to be a soldier,
I brought him up to be my pride and joy.
Who dares to put a musket to his shoulder,
To kill some other mother's darling boy.
Anti-conscription song, 1916.

Australia went to war in 1914 with a unanimity of national pride and imperial purpose, never seen again. In August 1914, at an election campaign in Colac, Victoria, the Liberal Prime Minister, Joseph Cook, urged voters to turn their eyes to Europe and 'give the kindest feelings towards the mother country at this time'. Cook prayed that a disastrous war might be averted. 'But,' warned the Prime Minister, 'should the worst happen after everything has been done that honour will permit, Australians will stand beside our own to help and defend her to our last man and our last shilling.' The reporter for *The Argus* noted that Cook's promise was greeted with 'Loud applause'. Cook's Liberals lost the subsequent election: not that it mattered, for the ardour with which the Australian Labor Party embraced the imperial cause almost surpassed that of their conservative opponents. Before the election, William Morris Hughes, the Welsh-born umbrella-mender-turned-politician-turned-barrister suggested the election be suspended to allow Cook and his Liberals to remain in office. For Hughes at least, the strength of imperial sentiment was greater than the loyalty of party membership.

Whether the people shared the unquestioning enthusiasm shown by their politicians is problematical. Perhaps they did not, although modern historians have been hard pressed to find much organised opposition, either to the war or to Australia's participation in it. Within the Labor movement, there were some mild murmurs of disagreement and the Roman Catholic Coadjutor of Melbourne, Daniel Mannix, proffered some disagreement from his pro-imperial archbishop.

This dissension was but a minor, misplayed note in an overwhelming chorus of approval. One year after the landing at Gallipoli, the newspapers at home were reflecting the domestic manifestations of the Anzac spirit.

Australia's oldest Roman Catholic newspaper, the *Free-man's Journal*, remarked unabashedly:

> No matter how the war may end — and it can only end one way — we are at last a nation, with one heart, one soul, and one thrilling aspiration. There is mourning in our homes and grief in our hearts, and the flower of our youth will not return to us; but there runs through the Commonwealth a lifting spirit such as it never knew before.

Within months that 'lifting spirit' had fallen flat. The unanimity of national pride and imperial purpose was lost; the divisions over the conduct of the war were yawning chasms.

Several separate yet related strains demolished this splendid unanimity: the British Government's extraordinarily inept handling of the Easter 1916 rising in Dublin soured thoughtful Australians, not all with Irish-Catholic antecedents, although the resulting sectarianism in Australian society imposed huge strains; the drain on the fledgling economy to fund the war increased prices and unemployment, both of which affected the working class greatly. And, from late 1915 onwards, there was the growing and bitter division of whether young Australian men should be conscripted for this imperial war.

Conscription was the most divisive issue of the war: at once social, economic, religious, political and military. It split the Labor Party, fanned the flames of religious bigotry and revealed the fragile nature of the nationalism-cum-imperialism taken for granted at the beginning of the war. For these reasons, conscription has attracted the attentions of historians to an almost compulsive extent and each account has had to assess the qualities, the intentions and the actions of Hughes, a politician who gave new dimensions to the adjectives 'devious' and 'complex'. Running through all the bitterness and the hatred, the tensions and the trials of the conscription debate in mid-1916 are the casualty figures from Fromelles, Pozières and Mouquet Farm. The casualty lists from those terrible battles began to appear in late July 1916, transmitted to Australia by telegram from AIF headquarters in Horseferry Road, London, accompanied by visits from sombre clergymen whose pastoral duties included ministering to their grieving and confused parishioners. In the newspapers, the casualty lists were published prominently, edged with bold black borders; the 'glorious dead' and 'our heroes of empire' were phrases that came easily to the pens of the headline writers. No newspaper expressed the terrible sentiment of Wilfred Owen:

My friend, you would not tell with such high zest
To children ardent for some desperate glory,
The old Lie: *Dulce et decorum est*
Pro patria mori.

With the names were, so often, the photographs: sad, innocent, boyish faces. Just in case some citizen had missed the grief in the street or the names in the newspaper, the lists were published and promulgated in public places: on ferry terminals and railway stations; in the notice cases at the local post office or police station; in clubs and factories and shops and offices. Such was the price of imperial loyalty.

That price was growing. We have already noted the results of the organised recruiting campaigns of 1915. Throughout that year, the Government and its conservative supporters applied a range of subtle and unsubtle pressures to young men in the fervent hope that they would enlist. In July 1915, the Australian Government followed the lead established by the British Government and introduced a national register of young men. Between 6 and 15 September 1915, a national census of men between 18 and 60 was taken: the Government wanted to know their names, addresses, ages, marital status, number of dependants, general health, current occupation, extent of any military training and place of birth. In December, it went once again to these young men with the four questions which provoked so much opposition:

Are you willing to enlist now? Reply 'Yes' or 'No'. If you reply 'Yes' you will be given a fortnight's notice before being called up. If not willing to enlist now, are you willing to enlist at a later date? Reply 'Yes' or 'No' and if willing, state when. If not willing to enlist, state the reason why, as explicitly as possible.

With the questions was a personal appeal from the Prime Minister: 'Not only victory but safety belongs to the big battalions' he said. Hughes' appeal produced results, but within three months, the enlistment figures began to decline again: 22,101 in January 1916; 18,508 in February; 15,597 in March; 9,876 in April; 10,659 in May; 6,582 in June; 6,170 in July. Not surprisingly either, for during those six months the debate over conscription was raging. Within the organised Labor movement, both industrial and political opposition to conscription was growing. It was seen as yet another manifestation of the militarism associated with capital. A meeting representing nearly half the trade unionists in the country in May 1916, with members voting according to the strength of their union's membership, overwhelmingly supported a motion expressing 'its undying hostility to conscription of life and labour.'

To the gruff protests of organised labour was added the shrill dissent of incipient feminist movements. Adela Pankhurst, daughter of the suffragette, popularised the ditty at the beginning of this chapter; in Victoria, Mannix's clerical fulminations found support in the Irish working class; Irish priests managed to weave the issues of conscription and Home Rule into their sermons with remarkable dexterity. On the other side of politics, newspapers supported the idea of conscripting their young male readers; the protestant and Anglican churches defined their interests in similar terms; conservatives in the community, from business leaders to senior army officers to academics in the great universities managed to reconcile notions of individual liberty with the greater good of imperial need. Increasingly clamorous and increasingly emotional, the debate was carried on while Hughes was out of the country, being entertained by the great and powerful of Britain, being awarded doctorates and honours and freedoms of cities whose only links with Australia were as a supplier of some of its people and a customer for some of its products: in short, while he was being 'duchessed'.

In Britain and France, Hughes was taken into the confidence of both Haig and Robertson; the Australian Prime Minister was pleased to reciprocate. As Haig noted: '[Hughes] said he had the most thorough confidence in me and would do all he could to help me in my difficult task'. As well, Hughes had seen the relative ease with which the British Government had introduced conscription, not only for single but for married men as well. In France, he had seen and admired the commitment of the French population, had watched the aged and the female peasants tilling the fields while their husbands and sons and brothers served as *poilus*. And, ever fearful of a resurgent, armed Japan, Hughes listened attentively to Foreign Office briefings about that country's aspirations in his corner of the Pacific.

In France and Belgium, Hughes was swept along by the feelings of nationalism inspired by the baggy khaki uniform and the big hat with the side turned up and the Rising Sun badge. During the great offensives on the Somme, the Prime Minister was returning to Australia in a troopship carrying sick and wounded soldiers, although some of his critics imputed less charitable motives for Hughes' journey under the protection of the Red Cross. This passage gave him opportunities to talk with the soldiers — even being massaged by one after complaining of insomnia — and his strong affection, admiration and respect for the Australian servicemen flourished in the salt air and relaxed atmosphere. That affection was returned, not just by the soldiers, but by cheering crowds in Fremantle — and in Melbourne where Hughes finally arrived by train on 8 August 1916. If he had been 'duchessed' in England, the Prime Minister was receiving similar, perhaps more open, approval at home. But he also arrived home to the casualty lists of the Somme.

As the voluntary enlistments were declining, the gap between the total of men required and those available was growing. For the Prime Minister, the appeals of Haig and Robertson were still strong; the logic of the former's attrition strategy still appealing; the demands on Australian manpower growing daily. To Hughes, it seemed clear that the pressure could be kept up by only one method: conscription.

A year before, Hughes had been opposed to conscription and said so in the uncompromising words that were to return and haunt him. Introducing the War Census Bill in the House of Representatives on 14 July 1915, Hughes said:

> The Bill does not contemplate conscription, nor is it a measure to legalise conscription necessary so far as service within Australia is concerned . . .
> I do not believe conscription is necessary. I do not say that the future may not hold within it possibilities which may shatter our present conceptions of what is necessary, for no man can say what this frightful war may yet involve. But this Bill has not been introduced with a view to conscription . . . It is to be regarded as a means for more effectively waging the present conflict upon the principle of voluntary service.

In November, just before he left for Britain, Hughes repeated this view, with a qualification. 'The Government,' Hughes told Parliament, 'had no intention of departing from the policy of voluntary enlistment, but it did propose to consider very carefully the position concerning the forces needed to bring the war to a satisfactory conclusion.'

When Hughes first arrived in Britain he still believed that conscription was neither militarily necessary nor politically possible. Gradually and perceptibly, however, he changed his mind. The factors which led to this change may be briefly listed; the weight to be given to each or any factor must remain a matter for speculation. Hughes was influenced by the reception he was given, carefully assisted by Keith Murdoch in his role as agent, factotum and general fixer; he was anxious that, when peace came, Australia should be heard and believed that its voice would be strengthened if it contributed more to the war effort; he was impressed by the ease with which conscription had been introduced in Britain. No ideological objections surfaced to give him pause or reason to rethink; as he often pointed out, both the union movement and the Labor Party derived much benefit from compulsion.

Two questions needed to be answered. Was conscription necessary to fill the manpower requirements of the military? Was it possible politically? The second question need not concern this narrative, for it has been examined and re-examined, almost to the point of exhaustion, in

Australian historical writing.* But the first question impinges directly upon this narrative and is directly influenced by the fighting of July-August 1916. To answer it satisfactorily, however, requires some background of the political events between Hughes' return to Australia and the first conscription referendum in October 1916.

When Hughes arrived in Fremantle, he was given a long letter from Pearce, the Defence Minister, outlining the problems faced in attracting sufficient volunteers for the AIF. 'The position at present is that during the month of June there were enlisted 6,582 while our requirements for reinforcements per month will be 11,862.' Pearce thought the flow of recruits, with those already in camp, sufficient to meet the demand for reinforcements up until October. But there remained the problem of how to meet the demand after November. One solution was to call up about 50,000 for home defence under the Defence Act. 'I am confident,' Pearce wrote, 'that a lot of these, after a period of training, will volunteer for active service abroad, but I am doubtful if by this means we can get sufficient numbers to meet requirements beyond, say, December.' Pearce noted that the outcry over conscription had diminished, 'but this might be due to the fact that we have made it quite clear that no action will be taken until your return'.

Hughes had returned to a parliamentary Labor Party now strongly opposed to conscription; Pearce, an enthusiastic supporter, was isolated from the mainstream of party opinion by his remoteness as a West Australian and as a Cabinet Minister. As well, Pearce's opinions were coloured by the perspectives of his ministerial office. During late July and August, Hughes stumped the country, praising the deeds of the heroic Anzacs, hinting at the need for conscription but not quite making the suggestion public. As a politician, he hoped to introduce the measures in such a manner that would not split his party. 'I shall endeavour,' he said often, 'to do my duty fearlessly, and I shall look to the people of Australia to support me.' This was a trying time for Hughes, as he wrestled with the competing demands upon his intentions, all the time being informed of the ghastly casualties being suffered by the Australians on the Somme.

On 15 August, in the midst of the grim deadlock around Mouquet Farm, Hughes wrote to Keith Murdoch in London. It had been good to hear from him, wrote the Prime Minister, but:

---

*See Sir Ernest Scott, *Official History of Australia in the War of 1914-18, Australia During the War*, Vol. 11, (Sydney, 1936); F. B. Smith, *The Conscription Plebiscites in Australia, 1916-17*, (Melbourne, 1971); L. L. Robson, *The First A.I.F. A Study of its Recruitment*, (Melbourne, 1982) and *Australia and the Great War*, (Melbourne, 1977).

It would be better still to have you by my side — for there are hot times ahead. Long before this reaches you the issue of 'Conscription' as they call it, will be reached in grim earnest. There is great feeling already — All or nearly all the Labour organisations — political as well as industrial — my own league included — have passed strong resolutions against compulsion. A large majority of our own party in the Parliament — are frightened out of their lives — many of course dare not call their souls their own. I'm not even sure of the *Cabinet*: God help the poor ... The Party meeting is fixed for the 24th. Parliament meeting on the 30th — There will be a tug of war. I am neither hopeful or hopeless — only resolved to go on. I may go down but I shall do what I think right. *One* thing of course would turn me from compulsion — I mean a really great victory. I doubt if this is in sight.

Hughes was a lonely man, with few friends and even fewer confidants, but Murdoch was one of the few in both categories. The Australian journalist had helped the Prime Minister's entry in British society by arranging dinner parties with the great and powerful; one party included Robertson, Lloyd George, Bonar Law, the Lords Milner and Northcliffe. This letter is as near to an expression of Hughes' personal opinion, not disguised by the need for political acceptance, that can be found in the surviving documents. In the last two sentences, Hughes reveals the importance of the fighting in France to the public debate in Australia. Of course, no such great victory was forthcoming.

The first reports of the Somme fighting spoke of victories but they were confused and misleading. There were no victories — at least, none worth trumpeting — and the casualty lists which were beginning to appear sat ill with public hopes of great advances and splendid victories. Amid this background of seemingly constant suburban grief, Hughes faced the prospect of convincing his own party that 'compulsion', as he called it, was really necessary. Now, the Prime Minister was also receiving urgent demands from the British War Office for reinforcements to fill the gaps left by the Australian dead and wounded on the Somme.

The first demand came on 16 August, in a cable from AIF headquarters in London to the Defence Department in Australia, drafted by Colonel Robert Murray McCheyne Anderson, who was both the commandant of the headquarters and Hughes' representative to the War Office. Despite his exalted rank and apparent responsibilites, Anderson's military career had been brief and peaceful. As a 21 year old bank clerk, he had been commissioned in the 2nd Infantry Regiment in December 1886, promoted to lieutenant in 1891 and captain in 1894. On the day after his promotion to captain, however, Anderson transferred to the reserve; his active militia service was over. Between 1897 and 1900 Anderson was city treasurer and then town clerk of Sydney. He became a partner in a timber and shipping company, served as a royal commissioner on the sugar industry between 1911-12 and by 1915, had attracted Pearce's attention sufficiently to become a frequent adviser to the government.

Anderson's expertise was mercantile. He helped reform the Paymaster General's Department, and examined the managements of both the Postmaster General's Department and the Department of Home Affairs. Anderson was 49 when war broke out in 1914; his age and his lack of military experience made him useless for any command or general staff position. In 1915, however, he returned to the army with the rank of colonel and the appointment of deputy quartermaster general of the AIF in Egypt. Here, his business training and acumen were invaluable; he quickly ended abuses in the canteen and supply systems, established a canteen organisation for the soldiers, rest camps in the Middle East and the Anzac Hostel in Cairo and instituted systems which prevented petty corruption in the ordnance and fodder accounting systems. In short, Anderson was a kind of grand business manager for the AIF.

Anderson moved to London with the AIF headquarters staff in May 1916. His arrival was greeted with pleasure by Hughes who immediately cabled Pearce: 'Anderson in London. I strongly recommend government appoint him our representative War Office. He can do great work for me. Of no use appointing a soldier as he cannot stand up against the War Office'. Although Pearce already had an Australian Officer specialising in munitions at the War Office, and another senior officer on the staff of the Australian High Commission, the Defence Minister agreed. Pearce merely asked to be informed 'as to what position and in what capacity Anderson would act'. Hughes replied that the representation at the War Office must be considered from two aspects:

> We want an expert and also representative looking after Commonwealth interests generally. For an expert will consult with Fisher [High Commissioner] re Leighton [munitions expert] and Buckley [staff officer at Commission]. For position representative Commonwealth Anderson is far the best man. Essential to his usefulness that he should not be subordinate to anyone but High Commissioner.

According to Hughes, Anderson's appointment was not greeted with approval by 'Wully' Robertson, the Chief of the Imperial General Staff.

Hughes told Robertson that the Australian Government needed a representative in the War Office who could keep them in touch confidentially with all that was going on. Robertson patiently heard Hughes out and then asked him whether he had someone in mind. Hughes replied that he had, and that he was a 'major of something in the Militia'. This, at least according to Hughes, was too much for 'Wully' Robertson. 'Militia, militia,' he shouted. 'We'll have no blasted militia here!' Hughes was unmoved. 'If that's the case, then, he can come as a civilian.' To Robertson, that was even worse. 'We'll have no blanky civilians in the War Office.' '... since a frontal attack was ruled out, a flank movement was indicated,' wrote Hughes. The Prime Minister then suggested that Robertson meet Anderson, and promised to make the Australian a 'general by 10 o'clock on Wednesday morning'. Anderson missed out on his promotion, if indeed it was ever offered, but he was soon in the War Office as Hughes' personal representative and intelligence source.

Anderson proved to be a thoroughly uninspired choice. Like so many civilians appointed to high military rank in war time, Anderson was accepted neither by the British professional officers at the War Office nor by the Australian militia officers holding so many high positions, in the AIF. Even Bean, the most charitable of men, thought Anderson's reign at AIF headquarters was:

> ... not altogether a happy one, since, though gifted with a keen sense of humour and quick intelligence, he lacked the facility of retaining the complete confidence of his colleagues. In a vast loyal service such as that of the AIF, efficiency hung on mutual trust and upon all official dealings being carried through with tact and restraint under the recognised forms and along the recognised channels. Of these Anderson was by nature impatient, and he was aggressive when thwarted.

It is difficult to imagine a position requiring more tact than the Australian Government's representative in the War Office during war time. It required not only tact, but experience, understanding and sound commonsense, not to mention a few useful contacts. In any such headquarters, as in diplomacy, it is the informal relationships — the ability to discuss a problem with a colleague of similar background over lunch or a quiet whisky — that is important. With his limited military experience, his businessman's approach and his civilian disdain for professional army officers. Anderson was politely but pointedly ignored by the War Office brass. Anderson might have had direct access to Hughes but this, too, was resented by the military establishment, both British and Australian.

In 1917, for example, the Australian Governor-General complained to Birdwood about 'the most extraordinary series of dispatches . . . that I have ever read in my life'. Before being transported to Australia as Governor-General, Munro Ferguson had been a Liberal M.P.; he had a fine appreciation of the roles and responsibilities of serving officers *vis-à-vis* their political masters. Birdwood replied that Anderson's letters to Australia were 'certainly of a most extraordinary nature, and when I last saw him I told him that, if they were written to me as Defence Minister I should have him out of his appointment within the next five minutes. His only reply was "Of course you would, but I feel I am here to write in the way I do".' But, Birdwood added, he had always had the greatest assistance from Anderson.

Birdwood was being polite. Anderson's enthusiasm for involving himself in areas in which he was unfitted by training or experience frequently caused significant problems for Birdwood. In the first week of August 1916, Anderson had taken part in discussions at the War Office about methods by which suitable reinforcements could be found for the depleted AIF divisions in France. Several possibilities existed: they could be drawn from 25,000 Australians in training camps and in the Light Horse division in Egypt; they could be found by drafts from the 3rd Division while retaining the basic divisional organisation; the division itself could be disbanded and its troops used as reinforcements elsewhere in the army.

Of these possible sources, drawing them from the 3rd, then in training was by far the worst. Monash, commanding the division, thought it was both stupid and unnecessary, particularly in view of the numbers in training camps. 'Men are being torn asunder who enlisted together, represent the same districts and home interests and hoped to work and fight side by side.' Birdwood shared Monash's views. As well, Birdwood looked forward to the day when the 3rd Division would take its place in France and the six divisions would be formed into an Australian army under his command. He argued that the 3rd should not be asked to provide reinforcements to the other divisions, much less be disbanded completely. On 15 August, Birdwood wrote to Maj.-Gen. Woodward, the Director of Organisation at the War Office:

> I feel confident the Australian Government would much dislike the idea of breaking up this division, on the formation of which they laid much stress . . . Rather than break up the 3rd Division, I feel confident that the Commonwealth Government would be quite willing to send a larger percentage of reinforcements so as to keep their five divisions going. I think therefore that . . . the Commonwealth Government [should] be informed as to the percentages thought necessary.'

It is not known when that letter arrived at the War Office but, unbeknown to Birdwood, the British now began to apply a little pressure on Anderson, of whom Hughes had expected such 'great work'.

On 15 August, Anderson was summoned to the Adjutant-General's office and told bluntly the Army Council had decided the necessary reinforcements would be met in one of two ways: either by disbanding the 3rd Division, or by borrowing from it sufficient men. On the basis of this briefing, Anderson cabled Pearce the following day:

> Insufficiency of reinforcements especially pressing owing to recent casualties causing War Office anxiety. As sufficient not immediately available from training centres War Office decided to borrow shortage from Third Division now training here. Alternative proposal discussed by War Council was to disband Third Division dividing members against for meanwhile anyway.

Anderson's cable is important for a number of reasons. First, although the War Council had authority to decide how reinforcements for the depleted divisions would be found, it certainly had no authority to order the 3rd Division be disbanded. In September 1914, when the Australian Government established the position of general officer commanding the Australian Imperial Force, it gave him the following powers, among others:

> The power within the authorised establishment to change, vary, or group units in such manner as he considers expedient from time to time; . . . the power to transfer officers and men when necessary from one corps or unit to another, and to detail them for any duty in any place which he considers expedient from time to time . . . the power to detail to units the *personnel* of first and other reinforcements in order to make good wastage due to any cause . . .

That decision looks straight forward enough; in practice, however, Haig retained control over reinforcements for the sick and wounded. In June when Hughes had discussed with Haig the prospect of forming an Australian army, the Commander-in-Chief agreed to Birdwood having full administrative command.

Later Hughes had written to Haig: 'The Australian Government desire that its troops in France should be placed directly under General Birdwood. And further we desire that he shall continue the work of

administration of *all* our troops outside Australia and Great Britain . . .
Haig's reply was, however, suitably qualified:

> . . . I cannot form an Australian army now, nor can I place all the
> Australian Forces in France under General Birdwood's command, in the
> full military sense of the term. I will bear the wishes of the Australian
> Government, in mind, however, and if at any future time I can see my
> way to employing all the Australian Forces together under his command
> for some special operation, I will gladly do so. I have discussed the whole
> problem with General Birdwood, who fully understands and agrees in
> the arrangements I propose to make, and I can assure you that I will give
> effect to the wishes of the Australian Government to the fullest extent
> that I can, with due regard to the primary object which they, in common
> with the rest of the Empire, have in view.

Haig had no intention of placing all the Australian divisions under
Birdwood's tactical control. As well,the Commander-in-Chief effectively
limited Birdwood's administrative control over the AIF, in the process
ignoring the decision of the Australian Government and the expressed
wishes of its Prime Minister.

Secondly, Anderson had no authority to send that cable other than
the informal power he possessed as Hughes' representative at the War
Office. Moreover, he lacked the military background and training necessary for dealing with such apparently impertinent treatment by the
War Council.

But as Hughes' man, Anderson did not question the War Council
attitude for another good reason. In a particularly unsubtle fashion, the
British Government was now applying pressure on the Australian Government to introduce conscription. Anderson realised the impact his
cable would have on the Australian Government in this sensitive stage
of the conscription debate. And as Hughes' man, Anderson worked
closely with Keith Murdoch who also had been told of the Army
Council's attitude by the Secretary of State for the Colonies, Bonar Law,
who added: 'I may tell you a piece of news which will help your
conscription campaign in Australia'. A note on a later cable from the
Governor-General leaves no doubt why the information was relayed to
Anderson: 'The military information referred to was given for a special
purpose — i.e. in connection with the conscription campaign'.

When Birdwood received a copy of Anderson's cable in France the
following day, he reacted quickly. He cabled the Defence Department
pointing out that Anderson had not referred the matter of reinforcements to him, that the matter was in hand and he hoped it would not
be necessary to interfere with the 3rd Division. On 22 August, Birdwood

cabled the Defence Department and suggested drawing the necessary reinforcements from Egypt. A copy of this cable was also sent to the War Office. But this suggestion, which would have preserved the integrity of the 3rd Division, was rejected by the British Commander-in-Chief in Egypt. The Australians, he said, were 'the keystone' of that country's defence. On 22 August, Anderson again cabled Hughes: 'Army Council at my request cabling you through Colonial Office estimated reinforcements required and exact position'. Two days later, that cable was sent:

> It is desired by Army Council that your Government be informed that it will be necessary to draw on 3rd Division for reinforcements owing to heavy casualties suffered by Australian Divisions in France. They therefore recommend that in addition to the normal monthly reinforcements a special draft of 20,000 infantry be sent as soon as possible to make good present deficit and so enable 3rd Division to be again brought up to strength. They recommend further that for three months following despatch of this special draft the monthly reinforcements of infantry sent should be calculated at 25 per cent of reinforcements, that is about 16,500 by month for five divisions. This is the only means of retaining 3rd Division for service in the field, though the Army Council are aware that the provision of this additional personnel may greatly inconvenience your Government in training and other arrangements.

Considering the social and political consequences of the resulting conscription debate in Australia, there is a splendidly unconscious irony in the last sentence of that cable.

Were the reinforcements really necessary? It has been suggested that the information about the need for reinforcements was deliberately inaccurate to help the Australian conscription campaign. That information was compiled by Birdwood and White, based on the casualties from the fighting at Pozières and Mouquet Farm, and on predictions of similar campaigns to come. Both Birdwood and Brudenell White favoured conscription; both urged the Australian Government be told of the need for reinforcements. Bean, whose assessment might well be influenced by his admiration for Brudenell White, wrote that both were strongly opposed to using this method of applying pressure to the Australian Government. 'Their estimate,' Bean added, 'was sincerely based on their estimate of the fighting ahead of the force, but it was a big mistake, pregnant with difficulty. They arrived at a staggering total, the War Office accepted it, and it was sent to the Australian Government as the recommendation of the Army Council: a special draft of

20,000 should be sent as soon as possible, and for the next three months, the monthly draft should be increased to 16,500!'

Bean's defence of his friend is understandable, and so, by extension is his treatment of Birdwood. But, as K. S. Inglis has noted: 'The years of the war were a great time for high-minded lies in defence of an imperilled civilisation'. Certainly Anderson and Murdoch in London had no qualms about using whatever influence they could bring to bear in support of conscription. In a sense, the attitude of the military commanders was irrelevant; conscription was ultimately a decision for the politicians, and in particular, for Hughes. During this time, the Prime Minister was not attempting to make up his mind one way or another about conscription. That decision had been made. For Hughes, now, it was merely a matter of finding the best methods of persuading his party, and then the country, to his view.

There is no need to follow the conscription campaign of 1916 through its various stages; it is sufficient merely to say that, armed with the demand for reinforcements and the threat to disband the 3rd Divison, Hughes managed to convince both the Labor Caucus and Cabinet to hold a referendum; he failed to convince the Labor movement of the need for conscription; he was expelled from the Australian Labor Party in September and the following month, the conscription referendum was lost. It is worthwhile, however, to examine how Hughes attempted to involve the military in what was fundamentally a political issue and how he hoped that a clear vote in favour of the conscription from the AIF might help swing public opinion.

The date set for the referendum was 28 October 1916.* 'Are you in favour', voters were to be asked, 'of the Government having, in this grave emergency, the same compulsory powers over citizens in regard to requiring their military service, for the term of this war, outside the Commonwealth, as it now has in regard to military service within the Commonwealth?' Sound administrative reasons existed for an earlier vote by the troops in France. Voting for the soldiers was set down for 16 October. The requirements of democracy were important, but they could not be allowed to interfere with the prosecution of the war; the Australians were returning to the Somme.

Anderson, as the AIF London headquarters commandant, was the returning officer; Murdoch, the Prime Minister's campaign director. The journalist had a canny perception of the feelings against conscription among the soldiers of the AIF — feelings which his efforts on

---

*Although Hughes could have introduced the necessary legislation to Parliament, he was far from certain of its success. The referendum was necessary in an attempt to pave the way for such legislation.

Hughes' behalf could not counter, On 7 October, Murdoch warned Hughes that possibly a majority of the soldiers were opposed to conscription but he was 'working hard and hopeful of substantial yes majority'. Three days before the soldiers were due to vote, Murdoch warned Hughes that a large number, possibly a majority, would vote 'No'.

Murdoch worked tirelessly for Hughes, organising the distribution to the soldiers of the Prime Minister's manifesto, newspapers and other campaign literature urging a 'Yes' vote. He also approached Haig, seeking the Commander-in-Chief's approval to have soldiers addressed by their officers on the need for conscription. Haig refused; Murdoch then changed his request. Instead of officers, could the soldiers be addressed by prominent civilians in favour of conscription? Haig agreed, on the condition that no officers be present. 'It was only by fighting his whole staff that I got him to agree to any meetings', Murdoch told Hughes. Murdoch also approached Birdwood to send a cable supporting conscription to the Australian people, but Birdwood refused, saying such an appeal might well be misconstrued as an order, but both Birdwood and Haig sent messages after the AIF had voted. Murdoch also managed to circumvent an instruction to Anderson from the Commonwealth Electoral Officer in Australia. No results of AIF voting, progressive or otherwise, were to be sent to Australia before the closing of the polls on 28 October. Murdoch, who would make certain he knew the results of the counting, promised to cable Hughes with progressive results. 'You can take steps, if desirable to secure publication either through me or locally', Murdoch said.

Murdoch's efforts were valuable to Hughes who realised that the conscription vote in Australia would be close. On 15 October, Hughes appealed to Murdoch by cable: 'Australians must hear the voices from the trenches calling to vote "yes" and send more troops'. This call, which the Prime Minister was certain would be easy to obtain, would have a powerful effect if cabled to Australia.

On the same day, Hughes also cabled Birdwood who was on leave in London. This appeal was more direct: Birdwood should put aside precedent and 'use his great influence with the troops . . . to induce them to carry conscription by a large majority, and thus give a lead to the people'.

The appeal perturbed Birdwood. To one friend, he wrote:

> I much disliked having to take this action, as I am so very much against soldiers mixing themselves up in any way in politics. Mr Hughes' appeal to me was, however, so urgent that I felt compelled to do for him what I would not have done for anyone else, though I quite realise one may easily get into trouble over it. I have, however, tried to avoid doing the

politician, and apparently issuing orders to the men as to how they should vote.

For an officer trying 'to avoid doing the politician' Birdwood's message to the troops was remarkably unambiguous. He began by saying that he knew it was not for him to influence the voting, but he knew 'all will vote as seems necessary in the best interests of Australia and the Great Empire to which we belong, whose freedom has been and still is in danger of being turned into slavery by Germany'. Then he turned to the need to keep 'these magnificent Australian Forces . . . whose fame is renowned throughout the Empire, up to their strength', something that was not possible under the present system.

> Every single man would, I am sure, bitterly resent and regret it if we had to reduce a single battalion, battery or company — every one of which has now made history, and established a tradition which, we all hope, will last as long as the British flag flies over the world-wide Empire.

The clarity of Birdwood's call for conscription is best expressed in his endorsement of Hughes' manifesto:

> In the magificent manifesto which our Prime Minister, Mr Hughes, has sent to us, he has shown what exemptions there will be when universal service is adopted. It will be seen from this that members of families, some of whom have already come forward, will be fully safeguarded, and no man need fear that there is danger of, we will say, the brother who has been left behind to look after the affairs of the family, being ordered to come out. The shirker, however, will be caught and made to do his share, instead of staying at home, as he has done up to now, not only evading his duties, but getting into soft jobs which we want to see kept for our boys here when they return, or for representatives of their families who have been left behind in Australia.

Finally, Birdwood urged the soldiers to act according to their conscience, for the good of King and country, the honour of the Australian people and the safety of their wives and children. That appeal was written late at night; later Birdwood confided to a friend that he had not thought out 'all the niceties' as they related to conscription and his position as their commander.

> On reading it over afterwards, I thought I would have been better advised to omit the paragraph referring to Mr Hughes' manifesto, as that of course deliberately appeals for conscription. However, it does not matter,

though I quite expect later on to hear a good deal of talking regarding it in some of the Australian papers, where I am afraid the whole question is still being fought very bitterly. The result of the referendum, as far as my men are concerned, was far better than I had anticipated for apparently my message to them at the last moment did some good . . .

Birdwood was deluding himself, as indeed, he attempted to mislead the readers of his autobiography, *Khaki and Gown*, which omits any mention of Hughes' request or the referendum itself.

As well as making the appeal to the troops, Birdwood postponed the referendum for three days, an action which he had no legal power to take. In some areas, however, voting had already begun before Birdwood's order was received; the early votes showed a 10 per cent majority against conscription. Now with voting stopped, there were three more days to campaign. In these days, Murdoch arranged for the troops to be addressed by the prominent civilians who happened to be in London. It was too late, and it seems likely that the troops, whose ideas of democracy and the freedom of the individual had not been smothered by military discipline, would have been more likely to vote 'No' as a result of being harangued. At least one appeal, by the South Australian Agent-General, F. W. Young, was remarkably inept.* Young told the soldiers of the 6th Brigade that Australia was first among the dominions in British eyes, but would lose that status if it did not adopt conscription. According to Bean, 'the attitude of the troops was quite clear':

> . . . they did not care whether Australia came first in the opinion of Great Britain or not — they desired that a sufficient number of Australians should be left after the war to develop their empty country . . . Australia, they held, was already 'doing enough'. Some were averse to the prospect of having in their regiments men who had avoided voluntary enlistment. Others feared that conscription would mean the introduction of the death penalty. Others again would vote as members of the Labor Party — The common argument that it would provide rest for their over-worked units did not impress them, for they well knew that replenished units were likely to be constantly sent into battle, and weaker ones rested. But beyond question the most general motive was one not without nobility. They themselves, when they enlisted, had not known the trials and horrors of war; and now that they did know, they would not, by their votes, force any other man into those trials against his will.

---

*Freed from the constraints of their officers, the troops gave Young a rowdy reception.

The vote was close, a small majority in favour of conscription, 72,399 against 58,894. How the soldiers voted in detail is one of those tantalising mysteries that will never be solved. The soldiers' votes were counted in with the total of votes from their States; according to Bean, 'it was the men on transports and in camp, rather than those actually at the front, who were responsible for the small excess of the "Yes" vote'. In the 3rd Division in England, Monash received Birdwood's order to stop the voting, along with his appeal, about midday on 16 October. By then, of course, voting was almost finished, with about 80 per cent of the soldiers under Monash's command having voted. Monash contacted Birdwood and was told to stop the voting. The 3rd Divisional commander refused to do so, and was supported by the returning officer. It is fascinating to speculate how the soldiers of the 3rd Division might have voted had they received Birdwood's message before they cast their votes.

Murdoch was ever keen to protect Hughes' interests. Before the soldiers' votes had been counted, but after the trend had become apparent, he cabled Hughes:

> Strongly urge you to prevent publication now or in the future of AIF voting. General Headquarters is very strong on this. It would be equal to a serious military defeat if partial army opposition to reinforcements was known, therefore you suggest without delay that Army Council prohibits publication men's voting — you can then submerge army's vote among the States.

Birdwood's appeal to the soldiers in the front line probably had the opposite effect to that intended by both the General and the Prime Minister. Bean clearly recognised the reasons why the soldiers at the front voted against conscription; Murdoch agreed with his more illustrious colleague.* In the field, the voting was 'three to one' against compulsion, Murdoch wrote later to Bonar Law; the 'Yes' majority was made up by the votes from Egypt 'where the Light Horse enjoys the fighting' and the new division (the 3rd) and the drafts on Salisbury Plain. 'It is a tragedy', Murdoch told Hughes in a letter, 'that our fine army should vote against their own reinforcements. Don't make any mistake about the feeling ... they are utterly sick of it and would welcome peace.'

---

*Bean and Murdoch were rivals for the post of Australian Official War Correspondent. Murdoch missed out but for both men, the First World War had profound and lasting effects on their subsequent careers. It is fascinating to speculate what might have happened had Murdoch been selected ahead of Bean.

The revulsion against the war quickly translated itself into feelings of distrust in their commanders. E. J. Rule, a careful and fair observer, noted that the leaders did not know their jobs; the same sentiment was expressed by 'Pompey' Elliott after Fromelles. Not naturally amenable to the more irksome forms of military discipline, suspicious of imposed authority, disdainful about the qualities of the British soldiers and derisive about the competence of the British commanders, the Australian soldiers now began to exhibit that national self-confidence so often mistaken, in Britain at least, for colonial arrogance. Gallipoli had re-revealed qualities which soldiers revere and which civilians suspect: mateship, courage, uncomplicated patriotism, unquestioning nationalism. Pozières produced all these qualities as well, but now there was a real bitterness.

The thoughtful soldiers resented Birdwood's interference; Monash, ever astute, thought the conscription campaign was lost because of the manner in which Hughes handle it. But for the soldiers who had endured the bombardments of Pozières, the issues were simply decided: they had joined of their own accord; they were not going to force some other blighter to share their experiences.

It is possible to make too much of the AIF vote in the first conscription referendum. But it was not the clear, decisive lead for which Hughes had hoped and Murdoch had worked. Indeed, so bad was the result that Hughes took Murdoch's advice and suppressed the AIF voting figures — as he did initially with the referendum figures as a whole, claiming it was at the request of the 'Imperial military authorities'. The War Council, however, knew nothing of the matter. Hughes lied.

The Prime Minister's machinations, on behalf of the Imperial cause and on behalf of his own substantial ambitions, continued to divide Australia. In 1917, another conscription referendum was lost, although again the AIF supported the proposal by a narrow margin. In a curious, yet unfanciful manner, Hughes was a casualty of Pozières — as indeed, was the Australian nation.

16

The Wearing-out Battle:
Afterwards

Here dead we lie because we did not choose
To live and shame the land from which we sprung.
Life, to be sure, is nothing much to lose;
But young men think it is, and we were young.
A. E. Housman, 'Here Dead We Lie'

In October, the Australians returned to the Somme again. This time, however, they lacked the enthusiasm and eagerness for battle that had so characterised their first journey up to the line. As they moved through the familiar villages and up the familiar roads, there was a heaviness in their step and a grimness in their faces. It was cold now, with bleak winds and driving rain. The month before, Haig had gambled on a breakthrough so that his armies could winter on the high ground of Bapaume. This offensive, using the tanks for the first time near the ruined village of Flers, was only partially successful; gradually the British secured Guillemont on 3 September, Guinchy on 17 September, and Thiepval on 26 September, only after it was assaulted by four divisions from Gough's army.

They were good successes, necessary for Haig's optimistic plans for penetrating the main German line and essential in any objective of wearing down the enemy. In the process of winning these victories, however, Haig was wearing down his own men. One British corps commander remarked acerbically, 'No one who has not visited the front can really know the state of exhaustion to which men are reduced'. The front was an unfamiliar place for Haig and his planners when the offensives were renewed in late October and early November. It was to these offensives that the Australians returned.

Never again did the morale of the First AIF fall so low as during these bitter winter months of 1916. The appalling climate, the continuing failures, the ignorance of the senior commanders, and the loss of so many good leaders in the earlier fighting, combined to affect the spirit of these enthusiastic volunteers. Bean watched one battalion coming out of the line and wrote: 'I was rather shocked with the look of the men. Not demoralised in any degree — but grey, drawn faces — and very very grim. It is the first time I ever passed an Australian battalion without seeing a single smile on any man's face'. There was little to smile about. These men had been the victims of Haig's 'wearing-down' policy, adopted after the wild gamble on a breakthrough had failed, so enthusiastically endorsed and followed by Gough.

Finally, on 13 November, the long-awaited breakthrough was achieved. Gough's Army, now named the Fifth, took advantage of a slight break in the wind and the rain to capture Beaumont-Hamel and Beaucourt-sur-Ancre, optimistic objectives nearly five months before. But Serre, on the left of the British attack, proved as intractable in November as in July. Now the offensive on the Somme could be brought to an honourable close. Gough's victory not only confirmed Haig's faith in the impetuous Irish cavalry general, it also strengthened the British hand at the coming conference in Chantilly. 'Nothing is as costly as a failure!' Haig wrote before the attack. 'But I am prepared to run reasonable risks.'

For the Australian divisions, those 'reasonable risks' involved the loss of some of its best officers and soldiers, its finest young leaders, and some of its willingness to submit to the rigours of battle. This is not to suggest that the Australians lost their collective courage, but from now an element of caution crept into the planning and their execution of operations. Pozières was, as many said, the standard by which subsequent fighting was measured, the yardstick by which artillery concentrations were judged. From now, all fighting was related to the experiences of those ghastly weeks of midsummer 1916.

The scars left by the fighting were visible for years, even among the men who survived the remaining two years of the war. So many of the veterans whose thoughts and writings appear in these pages never returned to Australia. The following year, Private Adkins was killed at Transloy; Captain Armitage died near Noreuil. Corporal Thomas, whose scribbled words under fire remain an inspiration to anyone attempting to tell the story of Pozières, survived until June 1918. That, in itself, was a remarkable effort for a volunteer of 1914.

Others returned to Australia weakened in mind and body. By the end of 1916, the military hospitals in Australia had started to receive the first of the shell-shock patients, men condemned to a life in the shadows of reality. Others had productive, full lives truncated by the effects of wounds and war service. Too often, the records reveal young men dying in the 1920s, men like the young Captain Anthony who was captured near Mouquet Farm and died in 1922 as a result of his wounds.

Bert Jacka, who should have won another VC on that day near the Windmill, returned home finally in 1920 after spending nearly two years in hospital recovering from a gas attack. Jacka married, established a firm of merchants and importers, became mayor of St Kilda and looked set for a comfortable and secure civilian life. Then came the depression. Jacka's business collapsed, partly because the old soldier was spending so much time helping his former comrades. In December 1931, Jacka's health gave out and a month later he died, not yet 40. 'I'm still fighting, Dad,' he whispered to his father just before his death.

'Pompey' Elliott was another upon whom the war left deep and lasting scars. In 1918, Elliott was aghast at being passed over for promotion to major-general by both Gellibrand and Glasgow. At least one of the divisions to be commanded by these officers belonged, Elliott believed, to himself. Elliott dashed off a letter to Birdwood complaining in terms that would hardly have helped his case and might well have raised doubts about his fitness to lead his brigade. Brudenell White, ever tactful and careful, gave Elliott the chance to withdraw the letter before it reached Birdwood. But Elliott continued to harbour a bitter, almost corrosive resentment; a feeling that was merely fuelled by the enormous respect in which he was held by his soldiers.

The corrosion continued into peace. In 1921, Elliott asked to be placed on the unattached list of the militia; he objected to serving under White, then Chief of the General Staff, and to the positions of his old rivals, Gellibrand and Glasgow, as militia divisional commanders. By then a Victorian senator, Elliott was using all his political and legal contacts to air his grievances, even pressing in the Senate for a judicial inquiry into his claims for promotion. Pearce, still the Defence Minister, rejected Elliott's call out of hand. This campaigning might have been dismissed as the bitterness of an ambitious man, had it not been for his work in the community and as a lawyer. Elliott was city solicitor for Melbourne, a director of a major trust company and largely responsible for drafting the constitution of the Returned Sailors' and Soldiers' Imperial League of Australia. In 1926, Elliott returned to the militia. Chauvel was now the CGS and a post was found for this fighting brigadier, but the bitterness still ate away. 'The injustice of the position as I conceive it has actually coloured all my post-war life,' Elliott once wrote to a friend.

Elliott also kept up his attack on the British command of the war, particularly Haking and his efforts at Fromelles. Again, the intemperate nature of Elliott's criticisms tended to obscure their fundamental good sense. Out of favour with the military hierarchy in the immediate postwar years, regarded as a good commander of fighting troops but limited where diplomacy and political astuteness were required, Elliott was something of an embarrassment to all but a few faithful supporters. In 1931, his health broke. He was admitted to hospital and treated for hypertension. Although soon discharged, Elliott did not return to the Senate and gave his legal practice only cursory attention. On 23 March 1931, Maj.-Gen. H.E. 'Pompey' Elliott died, a victim of a self-inflicted gunshot wound.

Of course, others survived both the war and the peace. Harry Murray went to Queensland and ran a huge sheep property until well into his seventies; Arthur Blackburn commanded a battalion of the AIF in the Second World War and spent nearly four years as a prisoner of the Japanese.

Spared the rigours of the trenches and the deprivations of the front line troops, most of the senior commanders survived the war. Haig died in 1928, a victim of 'the long strain of war', according to the sympathetic Duff Cooper. Gough, sacked in 1918 for his army's failures, died in 1963. Birdwood died quietly in 1951, perhaps still harbouring ambitions of becoming Australia's Governor-General. Brudenell White was killed in the aircraft crash near Canberra in 1940 which robbed the then Menzies Government of so many talented and wise advisers.

If one looks carefully, there are still reminders of the 1916 fighting on the Somme in Australia today. Most big cities have a Haig Road, or a Birdwood Street, although Gough is rarely remembered or commemorated. Pozières is a tiny hamlet on the Granite Belt of southern Queensland near the New South Wales border, where soldier-settlers battled agricultural ignorance and the fruit-fly in the 1920s and named their villages after the battles they remembered so well. In the 9th Battalion, The Royal Queensland Regiment, the name of Pozières is perpetuated in the Battle Honours and in the name of the soldiers' club. And occasionally, on Anzac Day, a veteran of the First AIF might appear in the club for a few moments, share a drink with today's young soldiers and ponder the name which has somehow missed its place in the Australian consciousness.

For Bean and the other legend makers of the First World War, Gallipoli and the landing on 25 April gave Australia a sense of nationhood. The legends have proved to be remarkably resilient and potent. Gallipoli, with all its optimism and hope, its classical setting and its poignant memories every 25 April, has indeed a special place in our national consciousness. Perhaps it suits us now to remember — indeed, to embroider — the legend in popular novels, films and television dramas; perhaps it suits us not to examine too closely the reality behind the legend for fear of what we might find. Gallipoli is somehow a place of light and hope; France and Flanders are places of darkness and despair; the associations are ones of mud and wire and men rasping up their lungs or blinded by gas.

If the Great War, with its bloodshed and its sacrifices and its casualty figures, gave this country a sense of nationhood then Pozières deserves a more important place in our memories. The members of the AIF at Pozières were good soldiers: not necessarily well-trained, as their experience of continental warfare against a powerful standing army all too quickly showed; not the bushmen-in-uniform of Bean's well-intentioned imagination; not the larrikin-turned-hero so vividly depicted by C. J. Dennis. Overwhelmingly they were a reflection of Australian society of the time, a society which had managed to reconcile nationalism and imperialism without much difficulty. Pozières began the real disillusion with the mother country. This disillusion had survived the dusty and exposed cliffs of Anzac Cove but flourished in the chalky earth of the Somme uplands, fed by the impossible demands of Haig and Gough and their willing subordinate, Birdwood.

The generals were not wicked or anxious to send younger men 'up the line to death'. They were ignorant and inadequate, limited by intellect, experience and training, incapable of understanding that warfare in 1916 required a different approach from the enthusiastic amateurism that so characterised the pre-war British officer. Haig, who understood better than most the problems posed by prosecuting a war of the industrial revolution, failed to come to terms with the command and control of his subordinates needed in a war of this scale. If Gough interfered too much, then Haig interfered too little. But these were niceties of military command that were not to worry the men of the AIF.

In the Australian Imperial Force — and the first two words of that title indicate the ease with which national and imperial interests were assumed to coincide — the senior Australian officers trusted and respected their British superiors until events proved otherwise. Even Brudenell White, arguably the most capable of Australian staff officers, hesitated to venture different opinions to anyone except his trusted confidant, Charles Bean; in mid-1916, military iconoclasts like 'Pompey' Elliott were singular oddities. Among the regimental officers and soldiers, however, the disillusion and the distrust was widespread. Alec Raws' feelings were echoed a year later by another officer who wrote that 'Everyone here is "fed-up" of the war, but not with the Hun. The British staff, British methods, and British bungling have sickened us. We are "military socialists" and all overseas troops have had enough of the English'.

In 1916, as today, the Australians were quick to detect any patronising by the British. Once the Gallipoli veterans reached England they reacted with surprise and disdain to the embarrassingly fulsome newspaper reports of their exploits; it was what Bean so euphemistically described as the harsh name which the Australian soldier gives to idle flattery. For flattery to be worthwhile, it needs to be given by people deserving of respect, whose opinions and judgements are respected. After Pozières, the opinions and judgements of British authority — whether clothed in the red badges of the staff or commanders, or in the cloying newspaper reports — were rarely respected.

The battles of Pozières and Mouquet Farm did not detract from the Australian soldier's huge self-respect, but they damaged forever the regard in which he held the British. If Australians wish to trace their modern suspicion and resentment of the British to a date and a place, then July-August 1916 and the ruined village of Pozières are useful points of departure. Australia was never the same again.

Notes and Sources

Introduction
page

ix — Sir Winston Churchill, *The World Crisis* (London, 1938), pp1091–2.

x — 'I was not convinced . . .': Churchill, *The Second World War* (London, 1950), Vol 5, p514. Ismay to Wavell, Letter, 7 Mar 44, Ismay's Papers, King's College, London. Inscription on Windmill site, author's note, made 1 August 1984.

xi — David Campbell's poem, 'The Somme' in Geoff Page (ed), *Shadows from Wire, Poems and Photographs of the Australians in the Great War* (Canberra, 1983), p92.

xii — 'Imagine a gigantic ash heap . . .': C.E.W. Bean, *Letters from France*, pp113–14. 'the key to the area': quoted in Bean, *The AIF in France, 1916*, p455 (hereafter Bean *III*).

Chapter 1 The Wearing-out Battle: Origins
page

2 — '. . . true viscerotonic . . .': Alistair Horne, *The Price of Glory*, pp20–1.

3 — 'The rare sally . . .': *ibid*, pp23–4. 'The best and largest portion . . .': Joffre, *Memoirs*, translated T. Bentley Mott (Paris, 1932), p123.

4 — '. . . it means an officer . . .': John Terraine, *Douglas Haig, The Educated Soldier*, title page.

5 — 'Talented, self-effacing, handsome, orthodox . . .': Anthony Farrar-Hockley, *The Somme*, p52. Charles Carrington, *Soldier From the Wars Returning* (London, 1965), p120. 'I have not got an army in France . . .': Robert Blake, *The Private Papers of Douglas Haig, 1914–1919* (London, 1952), p137 (hereafter Blake, *Haig*), 'Sunday, December 19 . . .': *ibid*, p119.

6 — 'I pointed out . . .': *ibid*, p122. Kitchener's instruction to French, Sir James Edmonds (ed), *Official History of the Great War, Military Operations, France and Belgium, 1916*, Vol I, Appendices, p40. Kitchener to Haig, 28 Dec 1915 'The defeat of the enemy . . .': Edmonds, *Official History, 1916*, Vol I, Appendix 5. Kitchener to French, 'every effort . . .': quoted in Terraine, *Haig*, p181. 'But I wish you distinctly to understand . . .': Kitchener to Haig, 28 Dec 1915.

7 — '. . . that the decision of the war . . .': quoted in Terraine, *Haig*, p182. See also, *Official History 1916*, Appendix 1. Kitchener, 'I don't know what is to be done . . .': quoted in J.F.C. Fuller, *The Decisive Battles of the Western World* (London, 1970), p347.

7–8 — 'Exasperated by these unprofitable assaults . . .': J.F.C. Fuller, *The Conduct of War 1789–1961* (London, 1961), p161.

8 — 'the strategy of evasion': *ibid*, pp160–5. Footnote: the description is from a personal account, Frank Richards, *Old Soldiers Never Die* (London,

9 1933), p36. Robertson to Haig, 'It is deplorable . . .': Blake, *Haig*, p122. Robertson to Haig, 'There is a fairly strong party . . .': *ibid*, p124.

Chapter 2 **'A Victory for Me'**

page

11 Haig, 'These attacks begin . . .': Blake, *Haig*, p125.

11–12 Possible courses of action. *ibid.*

12 Haig to Joffre, quoted in Terraine, *Haig*, p185.

12–13 'General Joffre began . . .': Blake, *Haig*, p129.

13–14 'I have directed . . .': Edmonds, *Official History 1916*, Vol I, pp26–7.

14 'more of a subsidiary nature . . .': Terraine, *Haig*, p187. Charteris, 'I am sure . . .': *ibid*. 'a war of attrition . . .': Edmonds, *Official History 1916*, Vol I, p33.

15 Edmonds, 'The decision of the French Commander-in-Chief . . .': *ibid*, p30. Farrar-Hockley, *The Somme*, p55.

16 For an appreciation of Falkenhayn's personality, see Alistair Horne, 'Field Marshal Erich von Falkenhayn' in Field Marshal Lord Carver (ed), *The War Lords: Military Commanders of the Twentieth Century* (London, 1976). Horne, *The Price of Glory*. Liddell Hart, *The History of the World War, 1914–18* (London, 1934). von Zwehl, *Erich von Falkenhayn* (Berlin, 1926). Horne, 'heart-breaking tragedy . . .': in Carver (ed), *The War Lords*, p113.

17 Horne, 'casualty lists moved him . . .': *ibid*, p112. Falkenhayn's appreciation, see Farrar-Hockley, *The Somme*, p38. 'Verdun: Falkenhayn's Strategy', *Army Quarterly* Vol XXIV, pp19–20.

18 von Tappen, 'the seizure of Verdun . . .': quoted in Horne, *The Price of Glory*, p390.

19 Haig to Robertson, 'I, of course, said . . .': Blake, *Haig*, pp130–1.

20 The most recent and probably the best discussion of the casualties of Verdun is by John Terraine, *The Smoke and the Fire* (London, 1980). See also Horne, *The Price of Glory*, pp327–8, Farrar-Hockley, *The Somme*, p51.

Chapter 3 **The 'Difficult Allies'**

page

22 Memorandum: 'Reasons for the Somme Offensive': Blake, *Haig*, p368. Haig's reasons. J.H. Boraston (ed), *Sir Douglas Haig's Despatches, December 1915–1919* (London, 1919), p20. Originally published as a supplement to the *London Gazette*, 29 December 1916 (hereafter Boraston (ed), *Despatches*).

23 Robertson to Haig, Blake, *Haig*, p135. See also for Joffre's demands and Haig's reactions.

24 Haig, 'The old man . . .': quoted in Terraine, *Haig*, p194. For an appreciation of Rawlinson, see Maurice, Maj-Gen Sir F. (ed), *Life of Lord Rawlinson of Trent* (London, 1928). Farrar-Hockley, *The Somme*. 'full of ambition . . .': Duff Cooper, *Haig*, (London, 1935) Vol 1, p307.

25–6 Haig's description of the Somme terrain, see Boraston (ed), *Despatches*, pp21–2.

26 'This is not a criticism . . .': Terraine, *Haig*, p202.

26–7 Rawlinson's plan, 3 April 1916. Edmonds, *Official History 1916*, Vol I, Appendix 8.

28   '. . . easy to understand . . .': Terraine, *Haig*, pp200–1.

29   'The first, and the most alluring one . . .': in Maurice (ed), *Rawlinson*, p155. 'It does not appear to me . . .': *Official History, 1916*, Vol I, Appendix 8. 'I studied Sir Henry Rawlinson's proposals . . .': quoted in Terraine, *Haig*, p200.

30   'Haig was known to favour . . .': Farrar-Hockley, *The Somme*, p65. Marshall-Cornwall, *Haig as Military Commander* (London, 1978), pp187–8.

31   GHQ to Rawlinson, *Official History 1916*, Vol I, Appendix 9. Rawlinson's concern about wire-cutting, *Official History 1916*, Vol I, Appendix 10. Haig to Rawlinson, 16 May 1916, *Official History 1916*, Vol I, Appendix 11, 'the Commander-in-Chief desires': *ibid*.

32   Criticism of Rawlinson: Farrar-Hockley, *The Somme*, p66. Martin Middlebrook, *The First Day on the Somme* (London, 1971), pp272–92. Rawlinson, 'I am quite clear . . .': quoted in Marshall-Cornwall, p188. Haig diary entry 24 May 1916. Blake, *Haig*, pp143–4.

33   Exchanges between Haig and Joffre. Blake, *Haig*, pp144–5.

33–4   *Ibid*, p145. See also Duff Cooper, *Haig*, Vol I, pp311–12.

35   Haig, 'Foch came in for a reprimand . . .': Blake, *Haig*, p146.

Chapter 4   **'All the Way to Pozières'**
page

37   'It believed in the reassurances . . .': J. Keegan, *The Face of the Battle*, (London, 1976) p215. 'The advance of isolated detachments . . .': Edmonds, *Official History 1916*, Vol I, p290. See also Appendices 17, 18.

38   'Nothing could exist . . .': Edmonds, *ibid*, p288.

39   'The assaulting columns . . .': *ibid*, p40.

40   Rawlinson, 'It must be remembered . . .': *Official History 1916*, Appendix 17.

41   Rawlinson's noteworthy facts: Maurice, pp160–1. Haig's doubts: Blake, *Haig*, p151. See also Farrar-Hockley, *The Somme*, p102. Rawlinson's objectives, *Official History 1916*, Appendix 13.

42   'The two assaulting divisions . . .': Edmonds, *Official History*, Vol I, p373.

43   'The 9/York & Lancaster', *ibid*, p46. 'There was no surprise . . .': *ibid*, pp388–9.

47   'The British soldier . . .': *ibid*, p392. 'Training of the infantry . . .': *ibid*, p393.

48   'For this disastrous loss . . .': *ibid*, p483. For an analysis of the casualties, see Terraine, *The Smoke and the Fire*, p45, Gordon, 'You Seem to Forget, Sir', 70th Brigade War Diary, CAB/45/188, PRO.

49   Haig's notes on casualties, see Blake, *Haig*, p154.

50   'We must remember . . .': *Official History 1916*, Appendix 18.

Chapter 5   **The Wearing-out Battle: Continued**
page

52   Haig's diary entries. See Blake, *Haig*, p153.

53   'mean comment . . .': Farrar-Hockley, *The Somme*, p167. 'They were to the effect . . .': Gough, quoted in Marshall-Cornwall, p193. '. . . prompt action taken . . .': Edmonds *Official History 1916*, Vol I, Appendix 15.

54   'The Army Commander . . .': Fourth Army Operation Order, 14 June

1916. Quoted in Farrar-Hockley, *The Somme*, p155.

55   'a butcher among generals': Anthony Farrar-Hockley, *Goughie, The Life of General Sir Hubert Gough* (London, 1975) pix. 'Now that Gough has become . . .': *ibid*, p183.

56   'The enemy has undoubtedly . . .': Blake, *Haig*, p154. Also Terraine, *Haig*, p208.

56-7   Details of the conference between Haig and Joffre, see Blake, *Haig*, pp154-5, Terraine, *Haig*, pp208-9.

58   von Below's order, quoted in Terraine, *Haig*, p208.

59   'These new orders . . .': quoted in Farrar-Hockley, *Goughie*, p185.

60   'any sense at all . . .': *ibid*, p186. 'the methods used . . .': Farrar-Hockley, *The Somme*, p179.

61   'After discussion with his corps commanders . . .': Edmonds, *Official History 1916*, Vol II, p62. 'which one cannot successfully do . . .': quoted in Terraine, *Haig*, p211. 'I gave him my opinion . . .': *ibid*. 'I considered that the experience of war . . .': *ibid*.

62   Edmonds, 'the whole sky . . .': *Official History 1916*, Vol II, p78. Exchange over Montgomery's hat: see Terraine, *Haig*, p213, Farrar-Hockley, *The Somme*, p189.

63   'The enemy has undoubtedly . . .': quoted in Terraine, *The Smoke and the Fire*, p120. 'The decision to attempt . . .': Boraston (ed), *Despatches*, pp28-9. 'West of Bazentin-le-Petit': *ibid*, p32.

Chapter 6   'Kings in Old Poems'

page

66   'They were a military body . . .': Bean, *Anzac to Amiens*, p183. 'instead of an idiotic cap . . .': Masefield in foreword to E.J. Rule, *Jacka's Mob*, pvii. 'from throwing Cairo . . .': *ibid.*, pviii. Hughes, 'The world has hailed you . . .': quoted in Horne, *In Search of Billy Hughes*, p65. See also Fitzhardinge, *The Little Digger*, p90. *London Opinion* report, 1 April 1916, quoted in McKernan, *The Australian People and the Great War*, p120. '. . . the doctors who passed them . . .': Scott, *Australia During the War*, p211. See also for Masefield, McKenzie descriptions.

68   'The shock was considerable . . .': Terraine, *The Smoke and the Fire*, p41. See also for the Gibbs quotation 'the dwarfed children . . .': 'skinny, sallow, shambling . . .': Carrington, *Soldier From the Wars Returning*, p256.

69   'the most magnificent reception': Ellsworth, letter 26 April 1916, DRL, Second Series, AWM. 'British staff here hate the Australians pretty badly . . .': Bean, quoted in McCarthy, *Gallipoli to the Somme*, p211. Bean's view of Murray, see *Two Men I Knew*, pp123-4. Also, Bean *III*, pp21, 56-7.

70   'Rarely can there have been a more brilliant example . . .': General Sir Frederick Morgan, *Peace and War, A Soldier's Life*, pp53-4. 'He bored the men and they bored him . . .': Robert Rhodes James, *Gallipoli*, p63.

71   'second to none in discipline, smartness and efficiency: Bean *III*, p57. 'we came here to fight for freedom . . .': quoted in Bill Gammage, *The Broken Years*, p121. 'I am in the best of health . . .': *ibid*, p150.

72   For recruiting figures, see Scott, Robson, *The First AIF*.

74   'some spirited and high-minded subordinate . . .': Bean *III*, p47. 'I felt as though . . .': *ibid*.

75   'There was no officer caste ...': Monash, *The Australian Victories in France*, p300.
76   'we find it necessary ...': Bean *III*, p62. 'Things at Verdun ...': *ibid.* 'He didn't see it served ...': Bean, quoted in McCarthy, p211. 'I have no wish ...': Bean *III*, p62.
77   'Two Australian divisions ...': Hughes to Pearce, AA CP 447/3. 'had had a bad morning with Hughes ...': Hankey, *The Supreme Command 1914–1918*, p61. 'Godley has done splendidly ...': Bean *III*, p153. 'It is essential ...': *ibid.*
77-8   'It was clear ...': *ibid*, p153. See also, Bean, *Two Men I Knew*, p126.
78   'if at any future time ...': Bean *III*, p156. 'It is probably true ...': *ibid*, p157. 'To the British staff ...': *ibid*, Derby to Haig, see Blake, *Haig*, p266.
79   'They are really fine disciplined ...': Blake, *Haig*, p290.

Chapter 7 'A Bloody Holocaust'
page
81   'like a plunge into Fairyland': Bean, *Anzac to Amiens*, p195. 'left an impression ...': Rule, *Jacka's Mob*, p40.
82   'as night fell ...': Bean, *Anzac to Amiens*, p196.
83   GHQ communique, quoted in Bean *III*, p200. See also for German version.
84   Birdwood to Plumer, *ibid*, p207.
85   'Godley always gave me a square deal ...': Geoffrey Serle, *John Monash, A Biography*, p258.
86-7   Details of the planning for Fromelles attack, see Bean *III*, p330 *et seq.* Edmonds, *Official History*, Vol II, p119 *et seq.*
88   Haking's orders, quoted in Bean *III*, p334. 'a tactical abortion ...': Elliott, 'The Battle of Fleurbaix', USI lecture, HQ XI Corps War Diary WO 95/881 PRO.
89-90 Background on Elliott, see Bean *III*, p52. Ellis, *The Story of the Australian Fifth Division*, p21. Bean, *The Story of Anzac*, Vol I, p133-4. Elliott's misgivings about the attack, see 'The Battle of Fleurbaix', *op. cit.*
92   Haig, 'Approved, except that ...': quoted in Bean *III*, p347. See also for subsequent correspondence on same subject. Original documents in XI Corps War Diary, 95/881 PRO.
94   'Suggested first as by Haking ...': Bean *III*, p350.
98   Haking, 'As you know ...': quoted in Ellis, *The Story of the Australian Fifth Division*, pp94-5.

Chapter 8 'Minor Offensive' or Raid?
page
99   d'Alpuget, Letter (15? July 1916) quoted in Gammage, *The Broken Years*, p157. 'The forward area was shrouded with smoke ...': H.R. Williams, 'All Through the Night', in Hammerton, Sir John, *The Great War, I was There* (London, 1939), p741. This is an extract from Williams, *The Gallant Company* (Sydney, 1933).
100   Elliott, 'Boys, you won't find ...': quoted in Bean *III*, p36. 'with little enemy retaliation ...': Ellis, *The Story of the Fifth Australian Division*, p95. 'Madame and her assistants ...': Williams, p741.
100-1 'In the village the church ...': Elliott, 'The Battle of Fleurbaix'. USI

	lecture, HQ XI Corps War Diary WO 95/881 PRO.
101-2	'We crept along . . .': Allsop, Diary 20 July 1916, quoted in Gammage, *The Broken Years*, p158.
102	Williams, p741.
102-3	'did not facilitate . . .': Edmonds, *Official History 1916*, Vol II, p127.
103	'They were really afraid . . .': Elliott, 'The Battle of Fleurbaix', *op. cit.*
103-4	Elliott to M'Cay, 'Every man who rises is being shot down . . .': quoted in Bean *III*.
104	'The records of the 16th Bavarian . . .': quoted in Bean *III*, p365. 'To halt in No Man's Land . . .': Ellis, *The Story of the Fifth Australian Division*, p96.
105	'. . . the bodies of the dead men . . .': Williams, p741. 'The enemy was caught in the act . . .': Ellis, *The Story of the Fifth Australian Division*, p97.
106	'The Australians strolled through the grass . . .': Bean, *Anzac to Amiens*, p229.
107	'under instructions from the corps commander . . .': 5th Australian Division War Diary, 19 July 1916, AWM.
108	'Had the several brigades . . .': Bean *III*, p394.
108-9	· 'We found the old No Man's Land . . .': Bean *III*, p395. 'The Australian' was almost certainly Bean.
109	'it became speedily apparent . . .': Elliott, 'The Battle of Fleurbaix'. 'Towards night . . .': Williams, 'All Through the Night', p742. Haking's orders come from the XI Corps War Diary, WO 95/881 PRO.
110	The account of Gibbin's death is drawn from Bean *III*, pp431-2. See also Gammage, *The Broken Years*, p223.
111	'we looked around us . . .': Williams, 'All Through the Night': p743. Capn. H.F.M. Maudsley's diaries, 20 July 1916, DRL, 3rd Series, AWM. Description of Tivey's reaction, Ellis, p105. Of Elliott's reaction, Bean, Diary 52, 20 July 1916, Bazley's description from the entry on Elliott in the *Australian Dictionary of Biography*. GHQ to Monro, OAD 78, GHQ War Diary, WO 95/5, PRO.
112	'Can the XI Corps . . .': Williams, quoted in P. Adam-Smith, *The Anzacs*, p189.
113	'We wanted . . .': Bean, Diary 52, 20 July 1916. 'In spite of . . .': Bean *III*, p443. Both Haking's reports are in XI Corps War Diary, WO 95/881 PRO.
114	Elliott's criticism came from his USI paper, 'The Battle of Fleurbaix', written after publication of Bean's volume. Edmonds' comments from *Official History 1916*, Vol II, p134.
115	'That the German riflemen . . .': Bean *III*, pp444-5. Edmonds–Bean correspondence, see OH Correspondence, AWM. Letter to Sturdee, about Elliott's lecture, XI Corps War Diary WO 95/881, PRO.
116	GHQ Communique, see Bean *III*, p446. See also Bean, Diary 52, 20 July 1916, AWM. Bean, *Two Men I Knew*, p133.

Chapter 9 A Powerful Accession of Strength

page

117	Mackay diary entry, quoted in Chapman, *Iven G. Mackay, Citizen and Soldier*, p72. 'Well, Billy . . .': Bean *III*, pp471-2. Caucus minutes, 14 September 16.

118   Hughes' hopes for Commonwealth divisions, see Farrar-Hockley, *Goughie*, p184. 'Though the commander-in-chief approved of ...': pp188–9. 'The men were looking splendid ...': quoted in Terraine, *Haig*, pp214–15. 'I told Gough to go ...': Blake, *Haig*, p55.

119   'West of Bazentin-le-Petit ...': Boraston (ed), *Despatches*, p32. 'that a mediocre plan ...': Bean *III*, p464.

120   'half the rate of loss ...': Terraine, *Haig*, p214.

121   'bloody slogging match ...': Farrar-Hockley, *The Somme*, p199. 'the painful inch gained here ...': Duff Cooper, *Haig*, p344. 'in thin low, driving black fog ...': Bean *III*, p466.

122   Operation Order for attack on Pozières, new line of demarcation GHQ General Staff War Diary WO 95/5 PRO. 'on our right ...': Boraston (ed), *Despatches*, p32.

123   'The right of the 48th Division ...': Edmonds, *Official History, 1916*, Vol II, p116.

124–5   'carry out methodical operations ...': see Edmonds, *ibid*, p114. Bean *III*, p468. Blamey's views on White: Bean, *Two Men I Knew*, p134. Gough's original orders to Walker: Edmonds, *Official History 1916*, Vol II, pp115–16.

126   'If he chose ...': Bean *III*, p468. Gough–Bean correspondence; Official History correspondence. Walker's opinion of Gough's command; Letter, Walker to Bean, 13 August 1928, OH Correspondence. Walker's After-action Report, 3 August 1916, Appendix 19, HQ 1 Aust Div General Staff War Diary, AWM.

127   'It was a fairly long march ...': Rule, *Jacka's Mob*, p58.

128   'We knew we were for it ...': Chapman, *Mackay*, p73. 'We are on the way to the Somme Valley ...': quoted in Bean *III*, p470. Gibbs reports, see *Daily Telegraph* and Gibbs, *The Battles of the Somme* (London, 1917), p17. 'the intermittent advances ...': Bean *III*, p470.

130   'Words cannot describe ...': Eric Moorhead, Diary, July 1916, DRL Second Series, AWM.

131   'in parts a filthy channel ...': Bean *III*, pp480–1. 'At company headquarters ...': Harris, quoted in Bean *III*, p480. 'Here in a quiet home ...': quoted in Hetherington, *Blamey, Controversial Soldier* (Canberra, 1973), p39. See also, McCarthy, *Gallipoli to the Somme*, pp103–4.

132   Details of the plan: HQ Q Aust Div General Staff War Diary, especially Appendix 19. 'As the distance ...': *ibid*. 'The roaring of our guns ...': Moorhead, Diary, July 16.

133   'Flashes like summer lightning ...': Bean *III*, p494. 'Most of these villages ...': Bean, *Letters from France*, pp103–4.

134   Private Preston's account: *Reveille*, 1 August 1935. Champion's account: Diary 23, July 1916, DRL Second Series, AWM.

135   'Their faults ...': Farrar-Hockley, *Goughie*, p189. Preston, *Reveille*, 1 August 1935. 'In the meantime ...': Champion, Diary 23 July 1916. 'no fear ...': Barwick, Diary, quoted in Gammage, *The Broken Years*.

136   'lots of [Germans] ...': quoted in Chapman, *Mackay*, p75.

137   'Counter attacks are the classic ...': quoted in John Ellis, *Cassino: The Hollow Victory* (London, 1985), p69.

138   'Probably they had made a great many more ...': Terraine, *The Smoke and the Fire*, pp121–2. 'Here's luck': Footnote, Bean *III*, p519. 'At 12.30 a.m. ...': War Diary, General Staff, HQ Reserve Army, WO 95/518

PRO. 'The 5th or Reserve Army . . .': Blake, *Haig*, p155.

139   Rawlinson, 'the Boche were very tired': quoted in Terry Norman, *The Hell They Called High Wood* (London, 1984), p157. *See also*, Edmonds, *Official History 1916*, Vol II, p47.

140   'long and careful preparation . . .': Boraston (ed.), *Despatches*, pp34–5.

141–2   Robertson-Haig correspondence. Blake, *Haig*, pp157–8.

Chapter 10   'Through . . . Hell Itself'

page

143   'These arrangements . . .': Appendix 19, HQ 1st Australian Division General Staff War Diary. 'I suppose the Higher Command . . .': Kinchington's account, *Reveille*, 1 August 1935.

144   'amid dozens of corpses and moaning wounded . . .': Mackay, Diary, quoted in Chapman, *Mackay*, p75. See also, Bean *III*, p537 fn.

145   Pte (Later Lt) J.V. Bourke, Diary 24 July 16, DRL Second Series, AWM (hereafter Bourke, Diary).

145–6   Laing's actions, Bean *III*, p541.

146–7   Bourke letter, DRL Second Series, AWM.

147   'At 1.10 p.m. . . .': Appendix 19, HQ 1st Australian Division General Staff War Diary.

148   German counter-attack orders, Bean *III*, p546. Preston's account, *Reveille*, 1 August 1935. L/Cpl R.E. Adkins, Letter, 1 August 1916, DRL Second Series, AWM.

149   'The ground . . .': Bean *III*, pp552–3.

150   'At the time of the bombardment . . .': Lord Moran, *The Anatomy of Courage* (London, 1945), p138.

150–1   'The guns . . .': Bourke, Diary.

151   For accounts of 2nd Bn, see Bean *III*, pp553–4, Chapman, *Mackay*, pp75–6. 'What is a barrage . . .': Bean, *Letters from France*, pp108–9.

153–4   Moorhead's account, Diary. Description of Lillie, Bean *III*, pp562–4. See also 5 Bn War Diary, AWM 24/25/26 July 1916.

156   'As the 1st Imperial . . .': Appendix 19, HQ 1st Australian Division General Staff War Diary. 'we burnt flares . . .': Moorhead, Diary. 'It was a most bloody . . .': Sir Arthur Conan Doyle, *The British Campaign in France and Flanders 1916* (London, 1918), pp192–3.

157   'The bombing fight on our left flank . . .': Moorhead, Diary.

158   4th Bn action, see War Diary, 4th Bn, 25/26 July, AWM, Chapman, *Mackay*, p76. Bean *III*, p572 *et seq.*

160   'July 25: considerable heavy shelling . . .': HQ Reserve Army General Staff War Diary WO 95/518 PRO. 'Again the enemy's artillery . . .': Bean, *Letters from France*, p109. 'All day long . . .': Barwick, Diary, 27 July 1916 quoted in Gammage, *The Broken Years*, p166. Bourke, Diary DRL, AWM. Preston, *Reveille*, 1 August 1932. Bowman, Diary, DRL Second Series, AWM.

161   Elliott's account, Bean *III*, p581, Moorhead, Diary, Reserve Army General Staff War Diary WO 95/518.

162   Absom, Diary, Diary DRL Third Series, AWM. Bennett, Jess accounts, Bean *III*, pp591–2.

163   'No attack followed . . .': Bean *III*, p591. 'losses now heavy . . .': quoted in Chapman, *Mackay*, p76.

164   'Although we knew it was still fighting . . .': Rule, *Jacka's Mob*, p61.

'were utterly different . . .': Bean *III*, p599.

165-6   'After your loving words . . .': Claridge, Letter, DRL Second Series, AWM.

166   'I tell you . . .': Angus, Letter, DRL Second Series, AWM. 'The situation here . . .': quoted in Terraine, *Haig*, p216. See also for details of Cunliffe Owen's sacking, Bean's sole reference is a footnote on p650 of Bean *III*. Edmonds does not mention the dismissal at all.

167   Birdwood to Walker, Letter 27 July 1916, HQ 1st Division General Staff War Diary AWM.

Chapter 11   'Conceited Colonials'

page

168   'it is one of the four best . . .': Slim, *Defeat into Victory* (London, 1954), p1. Background on Legge's appointment, see Bean *II*, pp418, 423–4, Bean *III*, pp602–3, A.J. Hill, *Chauvel of the Light Horse* (Melbourne, 1978), pp39, 53. Serle, *Monash*, p228. 'So it was hardly surprising . . .': Hill, *Chauvel*, p54.

170   'He was a leader . . .': Bean *III*, pp603–4. Holmes' background, Bean *III*, pp600–1.

171   Gellibrand's background, see *Australian Dictionary of Biography*, also Bean *III*, pp601–2, pp70–81. 'He was a direct speaker . . .': Bean *I*, p80.

172   Paton's background, see Bean *III*, p603. 'Once we allow him . . .': Farrar-Hockley, *Goughie*, p190. Orders from Reserve Army, Reserve Army War Diary, 28 July 1916 WO 95/518, Edmonds, *Official History 1916*, Vol II, p153. HQ 1st Anzac Corps General Staff War Diary, AWM.

174   'The 2nd Aust Division . . .': Legge's after action report, August 1916, HQ 2nd Australian Division General Staff War Diary (hereafter Legge's report).

174-5   '. . . his grave misgivings . . .': Bean, *Two Men I Knew*, p136, *III*, p606.

175   'Although anxious . . .': Edmonds, *Official History II*, p153. 'The front taken over . . .': Legge's report.

176   'The powdered debris . . .': Bean, *Anzac to Amiens*, p250. 'The enemy shelled Pozières . . .': Reserve Army War Diary, 27 July 1916, WO 95/518. PRO. 'Our guns . . .': Whitear, Letter, DRL Second Series, AWM. 'The 28th Battalion . . .': *Reveille*.

177   'Troops will be advanced . . .': Operation Order No 16, 1 ANZAC Corps General Staff War Diary, AWM.

178   Cohen's account, quoted in Gammage, *The Broken Years*, p166.

178-9   'The artillery programmes . . .': also 'Routes were reconnoitred . . .': Legge's report.

180   'The 20th Battalion . . .': Legge's report.

181   For account of use of tin plaques, 2nd Aust Division War Diary. 'While moving forward . . .': Legge's report.

182   'If you want the old battalion . . .': Popular World War I song. 'A man of mine . . .': Herbert Read, *My Company* both from Brian Gardner (ed), *Up the Line to Death, The War Poets 1914–18* (London, 1964).

183   Boys' letter, 2 August 1916, DRL Second Series, AWM. Brown's account, *Reveille*, 1 October 1932.

185   'At this stage . . .': Legge's report.

186   'Poor Vic Warry . . .': Boys letter, 2 August 1916.

187 'so complete . . .': Brown, *Reveille*. 'During the night . . .': Reserve Army War Diary 95/518 PRO. 'attack by the 2nd Australian Division . . .': Blake, *Haig*, p156.

188 'Birdwood never found favour . . .': Terraine, *Haig*, p215. 'You are not fighting Bashi-Bazouks now . . .': Blake, *Haig*, p156. See also Bean, *Two Men I Knew*, pp136-7, particularly for account of exchange between White and Haig.

189 'Troops must be able . . .': and 'Time is necessary . . .': Legge's report.

190 'In such a situation . . .': Legge's report. 'Like the 2nd Division Commander . . .': C.D. Coulthard-Clark, *A Heritage of Spirit, A Biography of Major-General Sir William Throsby Bridges* (Melbourne, 1979), p133. 'I understand . . .': quoted in Bean *III*, p645. 'The fine attack . . .': 2nd Australian Division War Diary, 30 July 1916.

191 White's reasons for the failure of the attack, Legge's report. See also Bean *III*, p649.

192 'It was a period . . .': Edmonds, *Official History 1916*, Vol II, p174. 'The present situation . . .': *Official History 1916*, II, Appendix 14, see also Bean *II*, p647 *et seq.*

193 For discussion of Haig's attitudes towards the tanks, see Terraine, *Haig*, pp218-28, also *White Heat, The New Warfare*, p238. 'To enable us . . .': Edmonds *Official History*, Vol II, pp174-5. 'For the present . . .': Bean *III*, p648.

194 Exchange between White and Bridges, Bean *III*, p665, *Two Men I Knew*, pp138-9, Haig's reaction, Blake, *Haig*, p157. 'Work was delayed . . .': Legge's report.

195 'Perhaps it is that the place . . .': Bean, *Letters from France*, pp114-15. '. . . dreadfully tired . . .': Bean, Diary 31 July 1916, see also Bean *III*, p616.

196-7 Raws' letters, DRL Second Series, AWM.

198 'The day was on the whole quiet . . .': Reserve Army War Diary. 'no one in rear . . .': Bean, *Two Men I Knew*, p138.

199 'The shelling at Pozières . . .': Bean *III*, p660. 'Strong men arrive from that experience . . .': Bean, *Letters from France*, p129. The 'boy' referred to was almost certainly Alec Raws. 'from the battlefields . . .': Raws' letters. See also p200.

202-3 Brown's account, 'The Old Windmill: Pozières' Tragic Landmark', *Reveille*, 1 October 1932.

204 'In an attack . . .': quoted in Ellis, *Cassino, The Hollow Victory*, p64.

205 'At 9.15 p.m. . . .': Reserve Army War Diary. Gough, Haig message, Bean *III*, p699, Farrar-Hockley, *Goughie*, p189.

206 'His over-riding inclination . . .': Terraine, *Haig*, pp217-18. Duff Cooper, *Haig*, p343.

207 von Below's order, Bean *III*, p699. Arnold Brown, *Reveille*, 1 October 1932. Whitear, Letter, DRL, AWM.

208 'There was nothing to report . . .': Reserve Army War Diary. 'Good God . . .': quoted in B.H. Liddell Hart, *The History of the First World War*, p336.

210 'Poor old Manning . . .': Bean, Diary 8 August 1916, quoted in McCarthy, *Gallipoli to the Somme*, p239.

210-11 Raws' letters, DRL, AWM.

Chapter 12   Counter-attack
page

212   'In the Australian force . . .': Bean, Diary 17, 26 September 1915, AWM.
214   'Have you seen him yet? . . .': Rule, *Jacka's Mob*, p5.
214–15   Background on Cox, see Rhodes James, *Gallipoli*, p148. Serle, *Monash*, p262. Bean *III*, pp706–7.
215–16   Background on Brand, Glasgow, Glasfurd, see Bean *III*, p707, 839–40.
217   'Army commander considers . . .': HQ 1 ANZAC Corps General Staff War Diary, 5 August 1916, AWM.
218   'There was nothing to report . . .': Reserve Army War Diary. 'accomplished with infinite difficulty . . .': Edmonds, *Official History 1916*, Vol II, p214. 'Ghastly sights . . . Scores of bodies . . .': Newton Wanliss, *A History of the 14th Battalion*, p135.
219   '. . . he came along, the picture of terror . . .': Rule, *Jacka's Mob*, pp63–4. Brown's account, *Reveille*, 1 October 1932.
220   '. . . the German artillery . . .': Wanliss, *A History of the 14th Battalion*, p138. '. . . this night stands out . . .': Rule, *Jacka's Mob*, pp68–9.
221–24   The account of Jacka's action is drawn from a number of sources, including Wanliss, pp139–41, Rule, pp70–3, Bean *III*, pp718–20, Anon, *Duckboard*, 1 February 1932.
225   'About 5 a.m. . . .': Reserve Army War Diary.

Chapter 13   'Mucky Farm'
page

227–8   '. . . when things would calm down a little . . .': Rule, *Jacka's Mob*, pp83–4.
229   '. . . the incessant drumfire . . .': Wanliss, *The History of the 14th Battalion*, p144. '. . . the brigade hopped the bags . . .': Rule, *Jacka's Mob*, p83.
231   'the staff of the *XIX Corps* . . .': quoted in Bean *II*, p762. 'During the evening of the 14th . . .': Edmonds, *Official History 1916*, Vol II, p219. 'We cannot move . . .': quoted in Bean *III*, p763.
232   Ross to Glasgow, Bean *III*, p763. See also 51st Battalion War Diary. 'worn out by six strenuous days . . .': T. Wells, 'First Stunt: Vivid Impressions', *Reveille*, 1 August 1932.
233   'At zero hour', Wells, *ibid*. 'The hottest fire . . .': H.W. Murray, 'His Hardest Battle. When Discipline Mastered Fear', *Reveille*, 1 December 1935.
234–6   Murray's account, *ibid*.
236–7   Armitage's account. Letter 17 August 16, DRL Third Series, AWM.
237–8   'During the night . . .': Reserve Army War Diary. Haig's instructions to Gough, see Edmonds, *Official History*, Vol II, p221. Farrar-Hockley, *Goughie*, p190, GHQ War Diary.
239   '. . . they had drubbed . . .': Bean *III*, p771, Mackay's opinion, Chapman, *Mackay*, p77. 'It was an awful bother . . .': Champion, Diary, DRL, AWM. 'No British troops . . .': 4th Battalion War Diary.
240   '. . . trench blown to bits . . .': M. Absom, Diary, DRL Third Series, AWM. 'During the night . . .': Reserve Army War Diary. 'saw a German plane set on fire . . .': Absom, Diary.
242   'Could this matter . . .': quoted in Bean *III*, p778.
243–4   Anthony's actions. See Bean *III*, p785, Account of his action and capture, DRL Third Series, AWM.

245   'General Napier ...': Signals Log, HQ 1st Australian Division War Diary, AWM. 'The front trench ...': quoted in Bean *III*, p789.

246   'Soon as we got behind the line ...': Bill Harney, *Bill Harney's War* (Melbourne, 1983), p34. 'Got a severe shelling ...': Vince Bowman, Diary, DRL Second Series, AWM. Elliott, quoted in Bean *III*, p792.

Chapter 14   The Wedge Blows

page

248   'My dear General ...': White to Walker, Letter, 19 August 1916, HQ 1st Australian Division War Diary. For White's opinions of Gough's tactics, see Bean *III*, p877, *Two Men I Knew*, p141.

249–50   'The 10th, 11th and 12th Battalions ...': Bowman, Diary.

250   'The whole line jumped the parapet ...': Elliott, quoted in Bean *III*, p795, 'All one can do ...': Bowman, Diary.

251   Bowman, Diary. 'When you see this ...': quoted in Bean *III*, p797. Crowle's letter, quoted in Gammage, *The Broken Years*, p167.

252   'As they neared Mouquet ...': Bean, *Letters From France*, p158.

255   'We were sighted by the enemy ...': Whitear, Letter, DRL, AWM. 'A fine stamp of men ...': quoted in Bean *III*, p822.

257–62   Whitear's account, Letter, DRL, AWM. 'some of our officers ...': Rule, *Jacka's Mob*, p88, Rule's account of his 'stunt', pp88–110.

263   'How the British Tommy ...': Bourke, Letter. Raws, Thomas, Letters, DRL. 'the actual steps ...': Bean *III*, pp871–2, 876.

264   Mackay's promulgation of the death sentence. 4th Battalion War Diary. Birdwood to Rawlinson, 'I think that the discipline ...': Rawlinson to Haig. 'cannot be responsible ...': quoted in Bean *IV*, p26.

265   'the persistent deserters ...': Bean *IV*, p27. Long to Munro Ferguson, 3rd February 1917. CAO Accession CP447/3 Item SC 15(11). See also for Hughes and Pearce.

266   Long to Munro Ferguson, 23 August 1917, *ibid*. Birdwood to War Office, May 1916, May 1917. Quoted in Bean *IV*, pp26, 29. Munro Ferguson to Long. Novar Papers, MS 696/1448, National Library of Australia.

267   '... fine disciplined soldiers ...': Blake, *Haig*, p290. '... sent a strong letter ...': *ibid*, p292. Munro Ferguson to Long, 31 August 1917, CAO Accession CP 78/31.

268   'the foolish sentiment ...': quoted in Chapman, *Mackay*, p79. See also Bean *IV*, pp26–31, Gammage, *The Broken Years*, pp236–7.

Chapter 15   Other Casualties

page

269   Cook's 'last man and last shilling' speech: *Argus*, Melbourne, 1 August 1914.

270   'No matter how the war ...': *Freeman's Journal*, Sydney, 27 April 1916.

271   The war census questions, quoted in L.L. Robson, *The First AIF, A Study of its Recruitment 1914–1918* (Melbourne, 1982), p63.

272   'Hughes said he had ...': quoted in Terraine, *Haig*, p215.

273   'The Bill does not contemplate ...': Commonwealth Parliamentary Debates, Vol LXVII, pp4833–4. 'The Government ...': CPD, Vol LXXIX, p7467.

274   'The position at present ...': Pearce to Hughes, 20 July 1916, Pearce

Collection, 3/3 AWM.

275 'It would be better still ...': Hughes to Murdoch, 16 August 1916, Murdoch Papers, NLA.

276 Hughes/Pearce cables on Anderson's appointment, 24 May 1916, 29 May 1916, 8 June 1916, Pearce Collection, AWM.

277 Hughes' account of Anderson's appointment, see W.M. Hughes, *Politics and Potentates* (Sydney, 1950), pp159-62. '... not altogether a happy one ...': Bean *III*, p175.

278 Ferguson to Birdwood, 5 February 1917, Birdwood to Ferguson, 4 April 1917. Munro Ferguson (Lord Novar) — Birdwood correspondence, AWM. Monash's views, Serle, *Monash*, p268, Birdwood to Woodward, quoted in Bean *III*, p864.

279 'Insufficiency of reinforcements ...': Anderson to Pearce, 15 August 1916, 'Referendum Cables 1916', Hughes Papers, NLA. Powers of the AIF commander, Order in Council, 17 September 1914, *Commonwealth of Australia Gazette*, 19 September 1914.

280 Hughes–Haig exchanges on formation of an Australian Army. *See* Bean *III*, pp148-53, Fitzhardinge, *The Little Digger, A Political Biography of William Morris Hughes*, pp114-15. 'I may tell you ...': quoted in Bean *III*, p866. 'The military information ...': Minute on dispatch 5 September 1916, PRO CO 418/145/7209.

281 Birdwood to Defence Department, War Office, 22 August 1916 'Referendum Cables, 1916', Hughes Papers, NLA. 'It is desired by Army Council ...': Secretary of State to Governor-General, 24 August 1916, 'Referendum Cables, 1916', Hughes Papers, NLA, See also Scott, p338, Bean *III*, p868. For attitude of Birdwood and Brudenell White, see Bean, *Two Men I Knew*, pp143-4.

282 'the years of the war ...': K.S. Inglis 'Conscription in Peace and War, 1911-1945' in R. Forward and R. Reece (eds) *Conscription in Australia* (Brisbane, 1968), p35.

283 Murdoch to Hughes, 7 October 1916, 13 October 1916. 'Referendum Cables, 1916', Hughes Papers, NLA. Murdoch's attempts to persuade Haig to allow the soldiers to be addressed on conscription, see Bean *III*, pp890-1. Hughes to Birdwood, see Bean *III*, pp890-1. Hughes cable was quoted in *Smith's Weekly*, 24 October 1936. 'I much disliked having to take ...': Birdwood to Rintoul, 16 October 1916, Birdwood Papers, IWM.

284 Birdwood's message to the troops is not quoted by Bean. A copy exists in Birdwood's Papers, Imperial War Museum and the full text also appears in L.C. Jauncey, *The Story of Conscription in Australia* (Melbourne, 1968).

285 '... they did not care ...': Bean *III*, pp891-2.

286 'Strongly urge you to prevent ...': Murdoch to Hughes, 21 October 1916, 'Referendum Cables, 1916', Hughes Papers, NLA. Murdoch to Bonar Law, quoted in Fitzhardinge, *The Little Digger*, p209.

Chapter 16   The Wearing-out Battle: Afterwards
page
289 'I was rather shocked ...': Bean *III*, p941. 'Nothing is as costly as a failure ...': Blake, *Haig*, p1976.

UNPUBLISHED SOURCES

AUSTRALIAN WAR MEMORIAL, CANBERRA
Unofficial records, manuscripts, etc.:
Donated records, including letters and diaries of members of the First AIF, indicated in the endnotes as DRL, --- Series, AWM.
Bean, C.E.W., Papers, particularly diaries and notebooks kept by the official correspondent during July–August 1916 and correspondence with Sir James Edmonds and others during the writing of the official histories. Indicated in endnotes by dates.
Birdwood, Field Marshal Lord, Papers. (See also IWM.)
Elliott, Major-General H.E., Papers.
Gellibrand, Major-General Sir John, Papers.
Official records:
Battalion, brigade, division and corps War Diaries (mostly G branch), including signal loss, orders, reports, maps and sketches. Most consulted were the I A&NZ G branch diaries for the 1st, 2nd, 4th and 5th Divisions.
Maps, including topographic maps of the Somme and trench maps of the Pozières–Mouquet Farm sector.

NATIONAL LIBRARY, CANBERRA
Hughes, W.M., Papers, particularly conscription.
Murdoch, Sir Keith, Papers.
Novar, Viscount, Papers.
White, Lieut.-General Sir Charles Brudenell, Papers.

IMPERIAL WAR MUSEUM, LONDON
War diaries and associated documents, Fourth Army. (Bound copies of the originals in the PRO.)
Birdwood Papers, particularly dealing with conscription debates.
Various manuscripts and donated records, marked in endnotes.

PUBLIC RECORDS OFFICE, KEW
War diaries and other documents of the Reserve Army headquarters, Fourth Army headquarters, various corps and division headquarters and GHQ for July-September 1916.

PUBLISHED SOURCES

Anon, 'Verdun: Falkenhayn's Strategy', *Army Quarterly*, Vol XXIV.
Anon, 'Jacka at Pozières', *Duckboard*, 1 February 1932.
Bean, C.E.W., *Anzac to Amiens*, (Canberra, 1946).
———, *Letters from France*, (London, 1917).
———, *The Official History of Australia in the War of 1914–1918. Volume I: The Story of Anzac*, (Sydney, 1921); *Volume II: The Story of Anzac, Vol II*, (Sydney, 1924); *Volume III: The Australian Imperial Force in France, 1916*, (Sydney, 1929); *Volume IV: The Australian Imperial Force in France, 1917*, (Sydney, 1933).
———, *Two Men I Knew, William Bridges and Brudenell White, Founders of the A.I.F.*, (Sydney, 1957).
———, 'The Reason for Fromelles', *Reveille*, 30 June 1931.
———, 'The Reason for Pozières', *Reveille*, 30 June 1931.

Beaufre, General André, 'Marshal Joseph Joffre' in Carver, Field Marshal Sir Michael (ed), *The War Lords: Military Commanders of the Twentieth Century,* (London, 1976).

Birdwood, William Riddell, 1st Baron Birdwood of Anzac, *Khaki and Gown,* (Sydney, 1941).

Blake, Robert (ed), *The Private Papers of Douglas Haig,* (London, 1952).

Boraston, J.H. (ed), *Sir Douglas Haig's Despatches,* (London, 1919).

Brown, Major Arnold, 'The Old Windmill: Pozières' Tragic Landmark', *Reveille,* 1 October 1932.

Buchan, John, *The Battle of the Somme, First Phase,* (London, 1916?).

Carrington, Charles (See also Edmonds, Charles), *Soldier from the Wars Returning,* (London, 1965).

Chapman, Ivan, *Iven G Mackay, Citizen and Soldier,* (Sydney, 1975).

Churchill, Sir Winston, *The Second World War,* Vol 5, (London, 1950).

———, *The World Crisis,* (London 1938).

Conan Doyle, Sir Arthur, *The British Campaign in France and Flanders, 1916,* (London, 1918).

Cooper, Duff, *Haig,* (London, 1935).

Coulthard-Clark, C.D., 'Duncan John Glasford', in *Australian Dictionary of Biography,* Vol 8, (Melbourne, 1981).

———, *A Heritage of Spirit, A Biography of Major-General Sir William Throsby Bridges,* (Melbourne, 1979).

Dixon, Norman F., *On the Psychology of Military Incompetence,* (London, 1976).

Edmonds, Brigadier-General Sir James, *Official History of the Great War, Military Operations, France and Belgium, 1916,* Vol I, (London, 1932). Vol II, compiled by Captain Wilfred Miles, (London, 1938).

Edmonds, Charles (Charles Edmond Carrington), *A Subaltern's War,* (London, 1984).

Ellis, Captain A.D., *The Story of the Fifth Australian Division,* (London, undated).

Ellis, John, *Cassino: The Hollow Victory,* (London, 1985).

Farrar-Hockley, Anthony, *Goughie, The Life of General Sir Hubert Gough,* (London, 1975).

———, *The Somme,* (London, 1983).

Fitzhardinge, L.F., *The Little Digger, A Political Biography of William Morris Hughes,* Vol II, (Sydney, 1979).

Fuller, J.F.C., *The Conduct of War 1789–1961,* (London, 1961).

———, *The Decisive Battles of the Western World,* (London, 1970).

Gammage, Bill, *The Broken Years,* (Canberra, 1974).

Gardner, Brian (ed), *Up the Line to Death: The War Poets 1914–18,* (London, 1964).

Gibbs, Philip, *The Battles of the Somme,* (London, 1917).

Greenwood, G. and Grimshaw, C., *Documents on Australian International Affairs, 1901–1918,* (Melbourne, 1977).

Hankey, Maurice P.A.H., 1st Baron, *The Supreme Command 1914–1918,* (London, 1932).

Harney, Bill, *Bill Harney's War,* (Melbourne, 1983).

Harry, Ralph, 'Sir Thomas William Glasgow' in *Australian Dictionary of Biography,* Vol 8, (Melbourne, 1981).

Hart, B.H. Liddell, *The History of the World War 1914–18,* (London, 1934).

———, *Through the Fog of War,* (London, 1938).

Hetherington, J.A., *Blamey, Controversial Soldier,* (Canberra, 1973).

Hill, A.J., *Chauvel of the Light Horse,* (Melbourne, 1978).

Horne, Alistair, *The Price of Glory,* (London, 1962).

———, 'Field Marshal Erich von Falkenhayn', in Carver (ed), *The War Lords: Military Commanders in the Twentieth Century*, (London, 1976).

Horne, Donald, *In Search of Billy Hughes*, (Melbourne, 1979).

Hughes, W.M., *Politics and Potentates*, (Sydney, 1950).

Inglis, K.S., 'Conscription in Peace and War, 1911–1945' in R. Forward and R. Reece (eds), *Conscription in Australia*, (Brisbane, 1968).

———, 'The Anzac Tradition', *Meanjin Quarterly*, 1/1965.

James, Robert Rhodes, *Gallipoli*, (London, 1984).

Jauncey, L.C., *The Story of Conscription in Australia*, (Sydney, 1968).

Keegan, J., *The Face of Battle*, (London, 1976).

Kinchington, P., 'Sidelights on Pozières', *Reveille*, 1 August 1935.

McCarthy, Dudley, *Gallipoli to the Somme, The Story of C.E.W. Bean*, (Sydney, 1983).

Macdonald, Lyn, *Somme*, (London, 1983).

McKernan, Michael, *The Australian People and the Great War*, (Melbourne, 1980).

Marshall-Cornwall, General Sir James, *Haig as Military Commander*, (London, 1978).

Maurice, Major-General Sir Frederick (ed), *Life of Lord Rawlinson of Trent*, (London, 1928).

Middlebrook, Martin, *The First Day on the Somme*, (London, 1971).

Miles, Captain Wilfred, *Official History of the Great War, Military Operations, France and Belgium, 1916* Vol II, (London 1938).

Monash, Sir John, *The Australian Victories in France*, (London, 1920).

Moran, Charles McMoran Wilson, 1st Baron, *The Anatomy of Courage*, (London, 1945).

Morgan, Sir Frederick, *Peace and War, A Soldier's Life*, (London, 1952).

Mott, Colonel T. Bentley, *The Memoirs of Marshal Joffre*, (London, 1932).

Murdoch, K. (ed), *'The Day' — And After, War Speeches of the Rt Hon W.M. Hughes*, (London, 1916).

Murray, H.W., 'His Hardest Battle, When Discipline Mastered Fear', *Reveille*, 1 December 1935.

Norman, Terry, *The Hell They Called High Wood*, (London, 1984).

Page, Geoff (ed), *Shadows from Wire, Poems and Photographs of the Australians in the Great War*, (Canberra, 1983).

Preston, H. 'Squatter', 'Sidelights on Pozières', *Reveille*, 1 August 1935.

Richards, Frank, *Old Soldiers Never Die*, (London, 1933).

Robinson, H. Perry, *The Turning Point*, (London, 1917).

Robson, L.L., *The First AIF, A Study of its Recruitment, 1914–1918*, (Melbourne, 1982).

Rule, E.J., *Jacka's Mob*, (Sydney, 1933).

Scott, Sir Ernest, *The Official History of Australia in the War of 1914–18, Australia During the War*, (Sydney, 1936).

Serle, Geoffrey, *John Monash, A Biography*, (Melbourne, 1982).

———, 'The Digger Tradition and Australian Nationalism', *Meanjin* 2/1965.

Slim, William Joseph, Viscount, *Defeat into Victory*, (London, 1954).

Sweeting, A.J., 'Charles Henry Brand' in *Australian Dictionary of Biography*, Vol 8, (Melbourne, 1981).

Terraine, John, *Douglas Haig, The Educated Soldier*, (London, 1963).

———, *The Smoke and the Fire, Myths and Anti-Myths of War, 1861–1945*, (London, 1980).

———, *White Heat, The New Warfare 1914–18*, (London, 1982).

———, *The First World War, 1914–18*, (London, 1983 re-issue).

Walsh, G.P., 'Sir Robert Murray McCheyne Anderson', *Australian Dictionary of Biography*, Vol 8, (Melbourne, 1981).

Wanliss, Newton, *A History of the 14th Battalion*, (Melbourne, 1929).
Wells, T., 'First Stunt': 'Vivid Impressions', *Reveille*, 1 August 1932.
Winter, Denis, *Death's Men, Soldiers of the Great War*, (London, 1978).
Williams, H.R., *The Gallant Company*, (Sydney, 1933).

Acknowledgements

With the recent re-issue of the *Official History of Australia in the War of 1914-18*, another book on the battles of Pozières and Mouquet Farm deserves some explanation. Surely, the interested browser is entitled to ask, has not Charles Bean covered it all? Bean's narrative of the battles which claimed 23,000 Australian casualties in just five weeks is both detailed and extensive. As Geoffrey Serle noted in the preface to his biography of John Monash, Bean remains the 'guide and inspiration' for anyone working in this field. But Bean was also the Australian official historian constrained, by his remarkable charity and his appointed responsibility, to be circumspect in his judgements of the senior British and Australian commanders. In Volume III of the Official History, Bean devotes the weight of effort to chronicling the efforts of the Australians; the efforts of the British soldiers around Pozières receive scant attention. As well, Bean made relatively little use of the diaries, letters and other accounts written by the soldiers who took part in the fighting.

In *Pozières 1916*, I have attempted to make judgements on the performances of the senior commanders; judgements which, for one reason or another, Bean largely avoided. I have also attempted to place the contributions of the Australian divisions, at Fromelles, Pozières and at Mouquet Farm, in the context of the mid-1916 fighting, of a coalition war in which those four divisions were an important, yet still relatively minor part.

Pozières was certainly a splendid Australian victory, but to treat it as solely an Australian victory is to ignore the very substantial British contribution in this sector of the Somme before 23 July 1916. For this reason, I have devoted several chapters to the British efforts, both on that terrible 1 July, and in the three weeks that followed. The extent of the fighting is chronicled at length in Edmonds' official histories, but it is probably little known to today's readers, both in Australia and in the United Kingdom.

I have also attempted to describe Pozières in light of the decisions which confronted the Allied commanders in 1916, both before and after Falkenhayn's assault on Verdun. The reason for the fighting around

Pozières, however competent tactically it might have been, can only be seen fully in the glare of the Allied plans.

In earlier books, I relied greatly upon the recorded recollections of the men who had taken part in the campaigns being described. The span of nearly seventy years suggested that this kind of approach might pose problems of verification. I have benefited greatly from discussions with some veterans, but in almost every case the descriptions of the fighting are from accounts written soon afterwards. The only exceptions are taken from the RSL's own magazines; I imagine that the unique comradeship of returned soldiers imposed its own disciplines over contributors. Other writers have used similar sources to tackle the task of describing life in the AIF in a general sense; I have attempted to depict what it was like to take part in this most terrible battle.

Many people have helped with this work: in Australia, the late Dr Denis Murphy first set me thinking seriously about Pozières and its effect on Australian society; at the Australian War Memorial Michael McKernan, Bill Fogarty, John Bullen and Bronwyn Self frequently responded to urgent telephone calls; at the Royal Military College, Duntroon, Captain Stephen Thornton helped in similar fashion. In England, I owe a debt of thanks to Leo Cooper for his support and to John Terraine, for the benefit of his wisdom and his knowledge. The staffs of the Imperial War Museum and the Public Records Office also made the task of a researcher on limited time much easier than I had expected. I would also like to thank my publishers, Susan Haynes and Ken Shearman of Methuen, for their support; Lee White for editing the manuscript; Margaret Evans, Joan Burnett and Cherie Powell for typing the manuscript; Michelle Hogan for drawing the maps and my wife Helen for compiling the index. She shared the battlefields and the research willingly and maintained the peace and quiet cheerfully. Mere thanks are not enough.

PETER CHARLTON
BRISBANE 1985

Index